West Germany

WORLD BIBLIOGRAPHICAL SERIES
General Editors:
Robert L. Collison (Editor-in-chief)
John J. Horton   Ian Wallace
Hans H. Wellisch   Ralph Lee Woodward, Jr.

Robert L. Collison (Editor-in-chief) is Professor emeritus, Library and Information Studies, University of California, Los Angeles, and was a President of the Society of Indexers. Following the war, he served as Reference Librarian for the City of Westminster and later became Librarian to the BBC. During his fifty years as a professional librarian in England and the USA, he has written more than twenty works on bibliography, librarianship, indexing and related subjects.

John J. Horton is Deputy Librarian of the University of Bradford and currently Chairman of its Academic Board of Studies in Social Sciences. He has maintained a longstanding interest in the discipline of area studies and its associated bibliographical problems, with special reference to European Studies. In particular he has published in the field of Icelandic and of Yugoslav studies, including the two relevant volumes in the World Bibliographical Series.

Ian Wallace is Professor of Modern Languages at Loughborough University of Technology. A graduate of Oxford in French and German, he also studied in Tübingen, Heidelberg and Lausanne before taking teaching posts at universities in the USA, Scotland and England. He specialises in East German affairs, especially literature and culture, on which he has published numerous articles and books. In 1979 he founded the journal *GDR Monitor*, which he continues to edit.

Hans H. Wellisch is Professor emeritus at the College of Library and Information Services, University of Maryland. He was President of the American Society of Indexers and was a member of the International Federation for Documentation. He is the author of numerous articles and several books on indexing and abstracting, and has published *The Conversion of Scripts* and *Indexing and Abstracting: an International Bibliography*. He also contributes frequently to *Journal of the American Society for Information Science, The Indexer* and other professional journals.

Ralph Lee Woodward, Jr. is Chairman of the Department of History at Tulane University, New Orleans, where he has been Professor of History since 1970. He is the author of *Central America, a Nation Divided*, 2nd ed. (1985), as well as several monographs and more than sixty scholarly articles on modern Latin America. He has also compiled volumes in the World Bibliographical Series on *Belize* (1980), *Nicaragua* (1983), and *El Salvador* (forthcoming). Dr. Woodward edited the Central American section of the *Research Guide to Central America and the Caribbean* (1985) and is currently editor of the Central American history section of the *Handbook of Latin American Studies*.

VOLUME 72

West Germany

The Federal Republic of Germany

Donald S. Detwiler
Ilse E. Detwiler

CLIO PRESS

OXFORD, ENGLAND · SANTA BARBARA, CALIFORNIA
DENVER, COLORADO

© Copyright 1987 by Clio Press Ltd.

British Library Cataloguing in Publication Data

Detwiler, D. S.
West Germany (World bibliographical series; 72).
1. Germany (West) – Bibliography
I. Title II. Detwiler, I. E. III. Series
016.943   Z2240.3

ISBN 1–85109–017–7

Clio Press Ltd.,
55 St. Thomas' Street,
Oxford OX1 1JG, England.

ABC-Clio Information Services,
Riviera Campus, 2040 Alameda Padre Serra,
Santa Barbara, CA 93103, USA.

Designed by Bernard Crossland
Typeset by Columns Design and Production Services, Reading, England
Printed and bound in Great Britain by
Billing and Sons Ltd., Worcester

THE WORLD BIBLIOGRAPHICAL SERIES

This series will eventually cover every country in the world, each in a separate volume comprising annotated entries on works dealing with its history geography, economy and politics: and with its people, their culture, customs, religion and social organization. Attention will also be paid to current living conditions – housing, education, newspapers, clothing, etc. – that are all too often ignored in standard bibliographies; and to those particular aspects relevant to individual countries. Each volume seeks to achieve, by use of careful selectivity and critical assessment of the literature, an expression of the country and an appreciation of its nature and national aspirations, to guide the reader towards an understanding of its importance. The keynote of the series is to provide, in a uniform format, an interpretation of each country that will express its culture, its place in the world, and the qualities and background that make it unique.

VOLUMES IN THE SERIES

For our son Henry

Contents

Contents

Contents

Introduction

The Federal Republic of Germany

Germany was divided as a consequence of the Second World War. Berlin, the capital, was placed (and still remains) under joint control of the four occupying powers, France, Great Britain, the Soviet Union, and the United States. Poland and Russia annexed much of eastern Germany. In 1949, two German states were established: The Soviet-occupied central part of the country was set up as the German Democratic Republic (GDR), commonly known as East Germany. In the western part of the country, under American, British, and French occupation, the Federal Republic of Germany (FRG), commonly known as West Germany, was organized.

Slightly over half the size of Germany in 1937, the Federal Republic, with an area of about 249,000 square kilometers (ca. 96,000 square miles), is somewhat larger than the United Kingdom or Illinois and Indiana combined. It is situated in the heart of Europe. The maximum extension from north to south is 876 kilometers (544 miles), from east to west 627 kilometers (389 miles).

With some 61,000,000 inhabitants in the mid-1980s, including over 4,000,000 foreigners, West Germany has a population density of 245 persons per square kilometer (635 per square mile), compared to 231 per square kilometer (598 per square mile) in the United Kingdom, and 25 (65) in the United States. The population in the Federal Republic is quite unevenly distributed; the most densely populated of the ten constituent states are the city states of Hamburg and Bremen, followed by North Rhine-Westphalia – which includes the highly industrialized Ruhr Valley – with 490 persons per square kilometer (1,270 per square mile).

West Berlin has been included in the statistics on the

population and area of West Germany. It is generally considered as part of (or together with) the Federal Republic, with which its democratically elected municipal administration maintains the closest possible ties, but being under foreign occupation and sovereignty it cannot become a full member of the West German federation.

The Federal Republic is a member of the Atlantic Alliance, into which its armed forces are integrated. It was a founding member of the European Community. In 1972, it concluded a 'Treaty on the Basis of Relations' with the German Democratic Republic, recognizing it as a separate German but not a foreign state. Since 1973, the Federal Republic has been a member of the United Nations.

Purpose and Structure of the Bibliography

The purpose of this volume is to provide the reader a guide to published materials on the Federal Republic, with consideration of Germany as a whole from the beginnings through the Second World War and the postwar occupation, and of West Germany and West Berlin since 1949. (On East Germany, see the companion volume in this series.)

Since the book was primarily written for the English-speaking reader, the majority of the well over 1,200 titles (a work and its translation are counted as one title) cited in the 534 numbered, annotated entries are in English. Some of the 534 numbered entries cite one work only; many include in addition secondary citations of one or more related titles. All of the titles, whether principal or secondary citations, are listed in the index.

In its organization, the work conforms with the standard outline of the World Bibliographical Series, utilizing standard topical headings even where relatively little is cited, and introducing nonstandard ones, such as 'West Berlin and Its Special Status,' only when unavoidable. Within this framework, the selection and annotation of the material included in the bibliography reflect to some extent the perspective, interests, and expertise of each of us as joint author.

Most of the works cited are available through the book trade or library channels. Many entries, however, include citations of government-sponsored publications issued by German offices from which – as indicated in the annotations – they may be solicited directly. The most important of these offices are:

German Information Center
950 Third Avenue
New York, NY 10022, U.S.A.

Federal Press and Information Office
Welckerstrasse 11
5300 Bonn 1, Federal Republic of Germany

Inter Nationes
Kennedyallee 91-103
5300 Bonn 2, Federal Republic of Germany

Bundeszentrale für politische Bildung
Beliner Freiheit 7
5300 Bonn 1, Federal Republic of Germany

Acknowledgements

We appreciate the cooperation and support we have received in preparing this volume. To Dr. Arnold H. Price we owe a special debt of gratitude for his encouragement and counsel from beginning to end. We thank Dr. Eric H. Boehm for inviting us to write the bibliography, and Dr. Robert G. Neville for his understanding in extending the deadline for submission of the manuscript. From the German offices noted above, especially from Miss Ingeborg Godenschweger at the German Information Center in New York, we received unfailing cooperation. We appreciate the research support our work on the bibliography has enjoyed at Southern Illinois University at Carbondale, particularly through Dean Michael R. Dingerson of the Graduate School. And we wish to acknowledge the indispensable bibliographical support provided by Morris Library at SIUC. Its extensive holdings, augmented by the statewide Library Computer System and an efficient inter-library loan service, enabled us to consider for citation far more titles than would otherwise have been possible.

Donald S. Detwiler
Ilse E. Detwiler
Carbondale, Illinois
January 1987

The Country and the People: Reference and General Works

1 **The Federal Republic of Germany at a glance.**
   Bonn: Press and Information Office of the Federal Republic of
   Germany, 1982. 14-page folder. 2 maps.

Attractive, informative introduction with well-reproduced postcard-style colour
illustrations in the 'Information' pamphlet series, which also includes titles on
'Territory and Population' (no. 1), 'Constitution and Structure' (no. 2),
'Transport' (no. 3), 'Environmental Protection, Nature Conservation' (no. 9),
'Berlin' (no. 20), and an unnumbered pamphlet on 'Germany and the USA.'
Copies are available, in limited quantities on a complimentary basis, in the United
States of America from the German Information Center, 950 Third Avenue, New
York, N.Y. 10022, elsewhere from West German embassies or directly from the
Federal Press and Information Office, Welckerstr. 11, 5300 Bonn 1, Federal
Republic of Germany.

2 **Facts about Germany: the Federal Republic of Germany.**
   Edited by Heinz Dieter Bulka and Susanne Lücking. Pictorial editor,
   Elisabeth Franke. English translation by Diet Simon.   Gütersloh:
   Bertelsmann Lexikothek Verlag for the Federal Press and
   Information Office, 1984. 4th, rev. ed. 415p. 18 maps. bibliog.
   (Published by Lexikon-Institut Bertelsmann).

Profusely illustrated with photos, graphs, and tables, this pocket-sized introduction, published for the government, provides brief but clear coverage of the
historical background; the political and legal system; the economy, society, and
culture; a detailed index; addresses in Germany from which further information
may be solicited; and a concise bibliography of works in English. *Tatsachen über
Deutschland. Die Bundesrepublik Deutschland* (4th ed., 1984), from which it was
translated, includes a German bibliography. It may be requested on a
complimentary basis from sources noted in the preceding entry.

1

3 **What's what in Germany 84. Führende Institutionen des öffentlichen Lebens in der Bundesrepublik Deutschland – Major institutions in the Federal Republic of Germany.** Edited by the Vereinigung Europäischer Journalisten Deutsche Gruppe – Association of European Journalists German Section. Bonn: Urheber Verlag, 1984. 436p.

This bilingual handbook, with German and English on facing pages, was initially prepared for foreign journalists, but should prove useful to anyone seeking detailed orientation on the institutional structure of West Germany. Brief essays on the Federal Republic and its capital are followed by concise introductions to each of 166 West German institutions and organizations. They are listed in five categories: *political*, including federal and state offices and agencies, political parties, and politically oriented foundations; *economic*, including financial and commercial associations, labour unions, and professional associations; *cultural, educational, and academic*, including learned societies, research institutes, and educational foundations; *religious and social*, including welfare, service, and religious organizations; and *media-related*, including associations of publishers and of journalists and the broadcasting and news services. Virtually uniform in length and format, the 166 articles describe the purpose, organization, membership, and public role of the institutions, name their leaders, and give their addresses, telephone and telex numbers, and the person or office to contact for further information. There are indexes of names, institutions, and abbreviations.

4 **BP Kursbuch Deutchland 85/86.** (BP guide to Germany 85/86.) Edited by Ulrich K. Dreikandt, Susanne Lücking, Herwart Stehr, and Ortwin Wabnik. Munich: Wilhelm Goldmann Verlag, 1985. 768p. maps. bibliog.

Prepared in consultation with a major European oil company at the Lexikon-Institut Bertelsmann, this is the initial edition of what is to be an annual publication. It is roughly comparable to *The World Almanac and Book of Facts* (New York: Newspaper Enterprise Association) published annually, but it deals exclusively with the Federal Republic and West Berlin. Divided into twelve major segments covering virtually every aspect of public affairs and of social, economic, and cultural life, the well-conceived and effectively produced volume includes detailed but readable articles generously illustrated with maps, graphs, and tables; bibliographies throughout, citing not only the standard literature (readily available in bookstores or libraries), but publications of government agencies and professional associations; numerous addresses (including sources for specialized publications); and a detailed index.

5 **Federal Republic of Germany: a country study.** Edited by Richard F. Nyrop, foreword by William Evans-Smith. Washington, D.C.: U.S. Government Printing Office, 1983. 2nd ed. 454p. 14 maps. statistical appendices (27 tables). bibliog. (Dept. of the Army Area Handbook Series: DA Pamphlet 550-173).

One of more than a hundred government-sponsored country studies, compiled at The American University in Washington, D.C., 'describing and analyzing [the countries'] economic, national security, political, and social systems and institutions . . . and the ways that they are shaped by cultural factors.' This volume supersedes the 1975 *Area Handbook for the Federal Republic of Germany*, principal coauthor Eugene K. Keefe, who also edited the volume on the German Democratic Republic published in the same series in 1982, *East Germany: A Country Study*, 2nd ed. (Dept. of the Army Pamphlet 550-155, 1982), which includes material on relations with West Germany.

6 Germany today: introductory studies.
Edited by J. P. Payne.   London: Methuen, 1971. 183p. bibliog.

Concise, well-informed essays on the reunification question; West German democracy; the West German press (with consideration of the problem of self-censorship); the structure of postwar society in East and West Germany; economic policies and problems in the two German economies; and the contemporary cultural and educational scene.

7 Germany: a companion to German studies.
Edited by Malcolm Pasley.   London: Methuen, 1972. 678p. 4 maps. bibliog. (Methuen's Companions to Modern Studies).

This collaborative handbook presenting sophisticated surveys of German history, music, language, philosophy, literature, and political, legal, and cultural institutions, supersedes the volume edited by Jethro Bithell in the same series. The editor notes in his preface that during the forty years since that volume first appeared, 'the assumptions brought by British scholars to German studies have changed a great deal, and that change is reflected here. It does not, I think, involve any lessening of the will for a sympathetic understanding of Germany and of her achievements, but it does mean a far greater hesitation in accepting Germany's interpretation of herself . . . .'

8 Contemporary Germany: politics and culture.
Edited by Charles Burdick, Hans-Adolf Jacobsen, and Winfried Kudszuz.   Boulder & London: Westview Press, 1984. 436p. bibliog.

A compendium, sponsored by German and American authorities, on Germany (primarily the Federal Republic) since 1945, with contributions generally reflecting a consensus on history, politics, economics, literature, and the arts.

9 Federal Republic of Germany: background notes.
Edited by Joanne Reppert Reams.   Washington, D.C.: U.S. Government Printing Office, 1983. 8p. map. (Dept. of State Publication 7834).

This politically oriented overview in loose-leaf format, addressed primarily to government employees, focusses on foreign relations and on Berlin, stating that 'although the city is not a part of the F.R.G. and continues not to be governed by it, strong ties have developed between the city and the F.R.G. over the years' (inset on p. 5).

3

The Country and the People: Reference and General Works

10 **Meet Germany.**
Edited by Irmgard Burmeister, preface by Walter Stahl.
Hamburg: Atlantik-Brücke, 1982. 18th ed. 140p.

Sixteen signed articles treating questions such as social security, relations between labour and management and between East and West Germany, and the current status of women. (See earlier editions, published under the same title by the same non-partisan private consortium, 'Atlantic Bridge,' Sanderskoppel 15, D-2000 Hamburg 65, for contributions supplanted by more current selections in later editions.)

11 **Federal Republic of Germany: post report.**
Foreign Affairs Information Management Center. Washington, D.C.: U.S. Government Printing Office, 1982. 48p. 7 maps. bibliog. (Dept. of State Publication 9266).

Designed for American officials and their families assigned to the Federal Republic, the report includes specialized information on Bonn, West Berlin, and the five major cities with consulates general. Potentially useful to others interested in a brief orientation.

12 **The Germans.**
Adolph Schalk. Englewood Cliffs, N.J.: Prentice-Hall, 1971. 521p. map. bibliog.

Chatty, heavily detailed introduction to the Federal Republic by an American journalist with several years of experience in writing on West Germany for Americans stationed there. The index makes the fact-crammed volume useful for reference.

13 **Germany reports.**
Press and Information Office of the Federal Government. (Edited by Helmut Arntz. Introduction by Ludwig Erhard.) Wiesbaden: Franz Steiner Verlag for the Press and Information Office of the Federal Government, 1966. 4th ed. 1,016p. 55 diagrams. 168 tables. folding map.

Dealing in the main with the development of Germany since 1945, this is an unabridged translation of the encyclopaedic government publication *Deutschland heute* ['Germany Today'], 7th ed., (Wiesbaden: Steiner Verlag for the Presse- und Informationsamt der Bundesregierung, 1965). It is meticulously compiled and tastefully produced. Updated extracts from this book are published separately by the government as sixteen monographs on the land and people; Germany past and present; foreign policy; the democratic state and its recent history; defence; agriculture, forestry, and fisheries; the economy and foreign trade; the building industry; public finances; transportation and communications; social conditions and social security; labour and management; youth affairs and sports; religious life; education and science; and cultural life.

14 **Germany.**
      Terence Prittie and the editors of *Life*.   New York: Time Inc.,
      1962. 176p. maps. bibliog. (Life World Library).
A handsomely illustrated, well-informed, clearly written introduction in historical
context to Germany as of 1961.

Geography

General

15 Germany: a general and regional geography.
Robert E. Dickinson. London: Methuen; New York: Dutton,
1961. 2nd ed. 716p. 121 maps. bibliog.
First published in 1953, this comprehensive standard work was reissued in a
revised second edition in 1961 with a supplement updating the extensive
bibliography (and cartography). The physical and cultural geography is illustrated
with a set of thirty-two (mostly aerial) photographs. A detailed table of contents,
giving pagination of sections within chapters, and an index facilitate use of the
book for reference.

16 West Germany: a geography of its people.
M. Trevor Wild. Folkestone, England: Dawson, 1979. 255p.
maps. bibliog.
An introduction to the geography of the Federal Republic oriented, as the author,
a University of Hull lecturer, puts it, 'towards the socio-geographic responses of
West Germany's postwar economic achievement.' Recent administrative boun-
dary changes are dealt with in a special section on *Neugliederung*.

17 Germany.
Thomas H. Elkins. London: Chatto and Windus, 1972. 334p.
maps. bibliog.
The revised edition of a standard textbook providing a solid introduction to the
geography of Germany (East and West) in historical and economic context.

18   **Germany: its geography and growth.**
     Karl A. Sinnhuber.   London: Murray, 1970. 2nd ed. 128p. maps.
     bibliog.

Generously illustrated with black-and-white photos, supplemented by sixteen pages of colour plates, this is a popular but by no means simplistic introduction to German geography, taking into account the Eastern territories annexed by the Soviet Union and Poland after World War II as well as Berlin and the two German republics.

19   **Divided Germany and Berlin.**
     Norman J. G. Pounds.   Princeton, N.J.: Van Nostrand, 1962.
     128p. 5 maps. bibliog. (Van Nostrand Searchlight Books, no. 1).

An introductory examination of the geographical division of Germany and of Berlin in historical and political context.

20   **Germany.**
     Great Britain, Naval Intelligence Division. London, Frome, and
     Edinburgh: for the Admiralty under the authority of H.M.
     Stationery Office, 1944-45. 4 vols. H. C. Darby, general editor.
     (Geographical Handbook Series).

Prepared, for official use only, during World War II in the Naval Intelligence Division of the Admiralty at its Cambridge sub-centre, this uniquely comprehensive, scholarly, yet readable Geographical Handbook on Germany was the product of wartime collaboration of leading British specialists. By no means confined to matters of naval or military interest, it was published in four volumes, made available to libraries after the war:
     Vol. I (B.R. 529), *Physical Geography*, by F. J. Monkhouse, A. F. A. Mutton, et al. (London: Keliher, Hudson & Kearns, under the authority of HMSO, 1944), 274p., 83 maps & diagrams, 1:2,000,000-scale pocketed map, 45 plates, bibliog., begins with the evolution of the German landscape, describes the river systems, and then provides detailed, illustrated accounts of the physical geography of the western, southern, central, northern, and coastal regions of Germany. The chapter on climate is augmented by tables on temperature, wind, humidity, various types of precipitation, etc. The last chapter, on vegetation, is followed by a chapter-length appendix on maps of Germany, an appendix on place-names, and seven conversion tables showing British and metric measures of length, area, yield per unit area, volume and capacity, weight, temperature, and pressure.
     Vol. II (B.R. 529A) *History and Administration*, by E. J. Passant et al. (London: Keliher, Hudson & Kearns, under the authority of HMSO, 1944), 547p., 63 maps & diagrams, bibliog., opens with a chapter on the German people, their language, and religion, with objective consideration of the racial composition of the Germans, of the fallacy of the popular conception of the 'pure race' in general and of the National Socialist 'Aryan-Nordic' dogma in particular, and of the use in Germany of racial theory as a political weapon. This is followed by a concise history of Germany from the Middle Ages to World War II and an essay on Anglo-German naval relations since 1894. In the final three chapters – on government, administration, and law; on education; and on public health – there are explanations of the system before Hitler's rule, the changes wrought under him, and the specific role of the National Socialist party

(the organization of which is also described in some detail). The appendix on 'Germany at War, 1939-43' reports on further changes, on German aims and strategy, and on Hitler's 'New Order.'

Vol. III (B.R. 529B), *Economic Geography*, by Elwyn Davies, W. O. Henderson, et al. (Edinburgh: Thomas Nelson and Sons, under the authority of HMSO, 1944), 710p., 111 maps & diagrams, 1:2,000,000-scale pocketed map, 96 plates, bibliog., provides a wealth of data with narrative explanation, illustrated by charts, photographs, etc. Whether your interest is in the transfer of German minorities from 1939 to 1941 or in the distribution of goats in 1931, you will find the answer here.

Vol. IV (B.R. 529C), *Ports and Communications*, by A. C. O'Dell, F. W. Morgan, et al. (Frome and London: Butler & Tanner, under the authority of HMSO, 1945), 672p., 148 maps & diagrams, 126 plates, bibliog., is a detailed description and evaluation of Germany's North Sea and Baltic ports, waterways, railways, and roads (right down to the planting of wild roses, with the hips as a valuable source of vitamin C, on central grass strips of the autobahn). There are appendices on civil aviation; the postal, telegraph, and telephone networks; shipping tonnage and measurement; and liner traffic. The use of the volume is facilitated by conversion tables and an index.

Regional

21 **The Moselle: river and canal from the Roman Empire to the European Economic Community.**
Jean Cermakian. Toronto & Buffalo: University of Toronto Press for the University of Toronto, 1975. 162p. 6 maps. bibliog.
(University of Toronto Department of Geography Research Publications, no. 14).

A scholarly monograph on the historical geography of the Moselle as an international waterway since the initiation of the first project to canalize it under Nero, in 58 A.D. Statistical appendix with sixteen tables. Abstracts in French and German.

22 **The Ruhr: a study in historical and economic geography.**
Norman J. G. Pounds. Bloomington: Indiana University Press, 1952; repr., New York: Greenwood Press, 1968. 283p. maps. bibliog.

A description of the Ruhr as an emerging industrial area in about 1800, 1850, and 1900, followed by an examination of the mid-20th-century industry, transportation, and social geography of the region and its leading place in the economy and politics of Europe.

23 **Your Swabian neighbors.**
Bob Larson, foreword by Lothar Späth. Stuttgart: Verlag
Schwaben International, 1981. 3rd ed. 220p. 2 maps.
This pocket-sized introduction to the southwest German state of Baden-Württemberg (with a foreword by its minister-president), addressed to American servicemen, provides information and insight on a region whose people the author considers as different from Bavarians or Prussians as Texans are from Yankees (to whom he compares the Swabians).

Economic

24 **Economic geography of West Germany.**
David Burtenshaw. London: Macmillan, 1974. 247p. maps.
bibliog.
Written with Britain's entry into the Common Market in mind to give teachers of geography and advanced students greater insight into the distribution and character of economic activity within the Federal Republic of Germany, this book provides an overall introduction, including treatment of transport, population, and the special situation of West Berlin.

Gazetteers

25 **Germany – Federal Republic and West Berlin: official standard
names approved by the U.S. Board on Geographic Names.**
U.S. Office of Geography, Department of the Interior.
Washington, D.C.: U.S. Government Printing Office, 1960. 2 vols.
(Gazetteer no. 47).
About 129,000 places and features in the Federal Republic of Germany and West Berlin are listed in alphabetical order (A-K, vol. 1: 778 pp.; L-Z, vol. 2: 780 pp.), and their locations are indicated by coordinates.

26 **Gazetteer Federal Republic of Germany: preliminary edition
Niedersachsen.** (Gazetteer Federal Republic of Germany:
preliminary edition Lower Saxony.)
Prepared by Ständiger Ausschuss für geographische Namen
(Standing Committee on Geographic Names) and Institut für
Angewandte Geodäsie (Institute for Applied Geodesy). Frankfurt
am Main: Institute for Applied Geodesy, 1977. 224p.
Preliminary edition of a segment of a *geographisches Namenbuch* (gazetteer) of the Federal Republic in the form of a 224-page computer-generated printout on

Lower Saxony, with introduction and page headings in English as well as German, presented on behalf of the government of the Federal Republic of Germany at the Third United Nations Conference on the Standardization of Geographical Names, Athens, 1977.

27 **Ortsbuch der Bundesrepublik Deutschland. Nach Unterlagen des Statistischen Bundesamtes unter besonderer Berücksichtigung der Standesamts- und Gerichtsbezirke.** (Directory of the communities of the Federal Republic of Germany on the basis of materials from the Federal Office for Statistics, with particular consideration of registrar and court districts.)
Edited by Willy Weber. Frankfurt am Main: Verlag für Standesamtswesen. 1978. 7th, fully rev. ed. Loose-leaf pp. xiv, A1-A379, B1-B553, & 23 subtitled interleaf dividers.

Towns, registrar and court districts, and other administrative units are listed systematically by location in Part A and alphabetically in Part B. See also *Müllers grosses deutsches Ortsbuch Bundesrepublik Deutschland. Vollständiges Gemeindelexikon* ['Müller's Large German Directory of the Federal Republic of Germany: Complete Community Lexicon'], 21st ed. (Wuppertal: Post- und Ortsbuchverlag Postmeister a. D. Friedrich Müller, 1982/83), an alphabetical listing, by name, with coded data, of over 109,000 cities, towns, and unincorporated communities.

28 **Unsere Ortsnamen im ABC erklärt nach Herkunft und Bedeutung.** (Our place names in alphabetical order, explained in terms of origin and meaning.)
Wilhelm Sturmfels and Heinz Bischof. Bonn: Ferd. Dümmlers Verlag, 1961. 3rd ed. 359p. bibliog.

Etymological and historical explanations are given for many place names in Germany, selected place names outside Germany, and the names of tribes and nations.

Maps and atlases

29 **Germany.**
Produced in the Cartographic Division, National Geographic Society, Richard K. Rogers, Assistant Chief Cartographer.
Washington, D.C.: National Geographic Society, 1978. 74 x 58 cm., scale 1:1,380,000 (21.8 miles per inch).

The coloured map shows relief by shading and by indication of high spots in feet of elevation above sea level; shows such features as boundaries (e.g., of the West German states and East German administrative districts), populated places, expressways (*Autobahnen*) and some major highways, railroads, canals, pipelines, and soundings in fathoms; and includes descriptive notes and an inset (5 miles per inch) of Berlin. (Available directly from the National Geographic Society, Washington, D.C. 20036.)

30 **Germany: interpretation of a map.**
Helmut Arntz. Wiesbaden: Wiesbadener Graphische Betriebe GmbH, n.d. 56p. maps.
A booklet providing a concise introduction, in historical context, to Germany within the borders of 1937. (Under the title 'Within the Frontiers of Germany,' a 40-page abridged edition was published for classroom distribution, with deletions that are indicated in the unabridged original.)

31 **Die Bundesrepublik Deutschland in Karten.** (The Federal Republic of Germany in maps.)
Prepared by Statistisches Bundesamt, Institut für Landeskunde, and Institut für Raumforschung. Mainz: W. Kohlhammer Verlag (for the Federal Ministry of Housing, Urban Construction, and Regional Regulation), 1965-69. 100 boxed sheets.
The official atlas of the Federal Republic, the most comprehensive cartographical work on Germany, was prepared as a collaborative project by federal offices and government-sponsored institutes concerned with geography, regional research, and statistics, utilizing census and survey data collected in 1960 and 1961. Far too large to be used as a bound volume by anyone but a weight-lifter, it is comprised of over 200 maps, mostly in colour, on 100 loose sheets (largely 83 x 111 cm., folded once) in a custom-built wooden mapcase (63 x 90 x 10.5 cm.). The scale of the principal maps is 1:1,000,000 or 1:2,000,000. As described in the table of contents in English, French, and German, the atlas is divided into five sections: (1) a general overview and administrative districts (showing, for example, the administrative divisions, as of 1964, of Germany within the 1937 boundaries, on a scale of 1:1,000,000, and the regional structure for the administration of justice and of finances on separate maps on a scale of 1:2,000,000); (2) physical geography (including geology and climate); (3) demography and social geography (including population density and distribution, internal migration, age structure, religious affiliation, distribution of refugees and expellees, the work force, housing, health services, the educational system, and recent national elections); (4) economic geography (including public utilities, agriculture, forestry, animal husbandry, mining, industry and crafts, commerce, tourism, transportation, and tax structure); and (5) regional planning and development (including nature reserves and regional planning units).

32 **Bundesrepublik Deutschland, einschliesslich Berlin: Verwaltungsgrenzen.** (Federal Republic of Germany, including Berlin: administrative boundaries.)
Frankfurt am Main: Institut für Angewandte Geodäsie (Institute for Applied Geodesy), 1978.
96 x 73 cm., with a scale of 1:1,000,000, this political map shows boundaries and seats of regional administrative units as of June 1978.

11

Geography. Maps and atlases

33 **Grosse JRO-Wandkarte Nord-, West- und Süd-Deutschland.** (Large
    JRO Wall Map of Northern, Western, and Southern Germany.)
    Produced under the direction of Dr. Ernst Kremling. Munich:
    JRO-Verlag, ca. 1975. (JRO Landkarte 3565).

Map, 186 x 136 cm., on two sheets, of 100 x 140 cm. each. With a scale of
1:500,000, this detailed map shows administrative boundaries in the Federal
Republic down to the local level, populated places (including villages), roads,
railways, and waterways. Spot heights are indicated in meters above sea level.

34 **Der Grosse Autoatlas Bundesrepublik Deutschland 1986.** (The
    Large Auto Atlas [for the] Federal Republic of Germany, 1986.)
    Hamburg: Falk-Verlag, n.d. 96p. with large folding map. (Falk
    Autoatlas 345).

81 x 176 cm., on a scale of 1:500,000, with insets of 1:250,000 for urban regions
and more detailed insets for cities, the Falk folding road map is the same scale as
the six-foot-high JRO wall map listed above, but is slit and creased so as to fold
neatly – together with an eighty-six-page index of cities and towns (with postal
codes) – into a seven-by-ten-inch (18 x 25 cm.) laminated paperback cover in such
a way that it can be readily opened to any spot without having to be unfolded.
The Falk Verlag. D-2000 Hamburg 1, Burchardstr. 8, with a record of seventy-five
million map sales, publishes (and distributes in the U.S.A. through Larousse &
Co., 572 Fifth Avenue, New York, N.Y. 10036) an extensive series of similarly
folded national, regional, and city maps generally updated every year or two,
e.g., *Berlin*, 47th ed., 1985/86, with a 64-page index (including consulates and
military missions); *Kassel*, 16th ed., 1985/86, 22-page index; *München*
['Munich'], 52nd ed., 1985, 64-page index; and *Wiesbaden/Mainz*, 17th ed.,
1984/85, 34-page index.

35 **Deutscher Generalatlas.** (General atlas of Germany.)
    Stuttgart: Mairs Geographischer Verlag, 1974. rev. ed. 302p.

Based on a map with a scale of 1:200,000, the Mairs Atlas provides meticulously
detailed cartographic coverage of both cultural and physical features of the
Federal Republic of Germany, together with an extensive index. The atlas also
has separate maps of individual cities and general maps of Germany and Europe
as a whole.

36 **Braunschweig 1976.** (Brunswick, 1976.)
    Brunswick: Bollmann-Bildkarten-Verlag, 1976.
    (Bollmann-Bildkarte [Pictorial Map] Nr. 159).

This 56-by-68 cm., folding pictorial map in colour (with a conventional map [scale
of 1:20,000] of Brunswick and its environs on the back) gives a bird's-eye-view of
the old central city, showing streets, parks, and buildings hand-drawn to a scale of
about 1:4,500. It is one of a recognized series, which began with the engraver
Hermann Bollmann's cartographic depiction of Brunswick in ruins in 1948 and
now includes pictorial maps of over fifty German and a dozen foreign cities
(including midtown Manhattan in New York, drawn on the basis of 67,000
photographs, almost a quarter taken from the air). Most of the pictorial maps fold
into attached booklets with a street index; all of them are available unfolded for

mounting. In 1968 the Bollmann-Bildkarten-Verlag, D-3300 Braunschweig, Lilienthalplatz 3, published a selection in bound form: *Städte-Bildatlas* ['Pictorial Atlas of Cities'], two 38.5 x 24 cm. volumes, each with twenty-five pictorial maps.

Tourist manuals

37 **Roman Germany: a guide to sites and museums.**
Joachim von Elbe. Drawings by Dorothea von Elbe. Mainz: Verlag Philipp von Zabern, 1975. 523p. folding map in pocket. bibliog.

More than a mere guidebook, this pocket-sized volume is also a companion to the study of Roman Germany, with well-written, authoritative descriptions and explanations of archaeological sites, museum holdings, and their historical significance, at 141 alphabetically listed locations.

38 **Happy days in Germany**
German National Tourist Board. Frankfurt am Main: Deutsche Zentrale für Tourismus (DZT), ca. 1983. 70p. 2 maps.

Available on a complimentary basis from German National Tourist Offices (747 Third Avenue, New York, N.Y. 10017, U.S.A.; 61 Conduit St., London W1R OEN, England; Beethovenstr. 69, D-6000 Frankfurt am Main, Federal Republic of Germany; and elsewhere), this magazine-format introduction to the Federal Republic and West Berlin, heavily illustrated with fine-quality colour photographs, provides information on tourist attractions, travel, accommodations, etc. in Germany, as well as addresses of sources of further information, including two dozen German tourist offices around the world.

39 **Baedeker's Germany.**
Text by Rosemarie Arnold, Rudolf Rautenstrauch, et al. Translated by James Hogarth. Edited by Baedeker Stuttgart. Englewood Cliffs, N.J.: Prentice-Hall, ca. 1984. 320p. maps.

One of a new series of Baedeker guides to Europe, this attractive, large pocket-format handbook, with a durable soft cover and easy-to-read print on high-quality paper, has a general introduction; fifty-four pages of practical information, including a series of maps showing casinos and golf courses, open-air museums, where one can go on old-fashioned steam locomotive excursions, etc.; descriptive treatment of places in Germany in alphabetical order from Aachen to Xanten, illustrated with 113 colour photographs and numerous town plans and maps in colour, as well as plans of such attractions as the zoo in Frankfurt and the German Museum in Munich; an index; and a folding road map from Mairs Geographischer Verlag attached to the inside of the rear cover. A smaller-format companion guide of the same style was published in 1984 by the Automobile Association in Great Britain, *Baedeker's Berlin*, 168p., together with a folding map; largely on West Berlin, it has coverage of 'East Berlin, A-Z' on pages 93-129.

40   **Tourist Guide Michelin. Germany: West Germany and Berlin.**
      London: Michelin Tyre Public Limited Co., 1982. 5th ed. 272p.
      maps. (Michelin Green Series).

This compact, small-print volume on Germany in the Michelin Green Series of touring guides provides information and commentary on towns, sights, and tourist regions listed in alphabetical order. The introduction includes a section, illustrated with drawings, on architectural styles. There are maps throughout the volume. It was produced as a complement to the Michelin Red Series guide to Germany cited below.

41   **1985 Michelin Deutschland.** (1985 Michelin [guide to] Germany.)
      Tourist Division, Michelin Tire Works, Karlsruhe, West
      Germany.   Karlsruhe: Michelin Reifenwerke KGaA, 1985. 855p.
      maps. (Michelin Red Series).

This annually revised, authoritative handbook provides graded ratings of hotels and restaurants. It has separate introductory tables of contents in German, French, English, and Italian, with a key, in each language, to the system of coded entries on establishments listed alphabetically by location, from Aach (p. 61) to [Bad] Zwischenahn (p. 838). There are city maps throughout the text, a map of the principal roads in segments on pp. 7-11, and a similarly segmented map on pp. 50-57 showing the location of places particularly noteworthy for their amenities, cuisine, or prices.

42   **Nagel's encyclopedia-guide Germany: Federal Republic.**
      Prepared by C. Harald Harlinghausen and Hartmuth Merleker.
      Geneva, Paris, Munich: Nagel Publishers; Lincolnwood, Ill.:
      National Textbook Co., 1981. 4th rev. & enl. ed. 944p.

A hardbound, pocket-sized guide, printed in small but clear type, produced as one of a series published in English, French, and German. It includes a general introduction with essays on art and architecture, music, the theatre, literature, philosophy, higher education and science, sports, food and drink, etc.; practical information; listings of regular hotels and of eighty-two castles converted into hotels; and some seven hundred pages of description and itineraries. The two largest cities, Hamburg and West Berlin, are treated in individual chapters; the remainder of the Federal Republic is dealt with on a regional basis ('The Rhine Valley,' 'Baden and the Black Forest,' etc.) in fifteen chapters. The guide is illustrated with seventy-five town plans, six of which fold out. The user of the 'fourth revised and enlarged edition,' published in 1981, will find that the revisions did not include updating 'current' information from the late 1960s or early 1970s in the introduction or showing expressways (*Autobahnen*) on the town plans of Berlin and Bremen.

43 **Germany: a Rand McNally pocket guide.**
Carole Chester. Chicago: Rand McNally, 1985. rev. ed. 96p.
maps.

This slim, well-produced volume, only slightly larger than a passport, has general information on the first twenty-four pages, followed by coverage of the five major tourist regions (northern Germany, Rheinland, Hesse, Baden-Württemberg, and Bavaria), illustrated, in colour, with maps of the regions, eighteen town plans, and photographs.

44 **Fodor's Germany, West & East, 1985.**
Edited by Thomas Cussans et al. New York: Fodor's Travel
Guides, 1985. 496p. 16 maps.

A general guide in a popular, well-established series, issued annually. Lists accommodations and restaurants. Treatment of the German Democratic Republic (East Germany) is limited to thirty pages. See also the 214-page *Fodor's Budget Germany '85*, ed. by Richard Moore, and the 106-page *Fodor's Munich 1985*, ed. by Andrea Dutton.

45 **Frommer's dollarwise guide to Germany.**
Darwin Porter. New York: Simon & Schuster, 1984. 1984-85 ed.
506p. 9 maps. (Sponsored by Lufthansa).

This volume, one of a regularly revised series for the cost-conscious, provides, as part of its coverage of the Federal Republic and West Berlin, numerous 'Readers' Selections' (signed letters with tips on food, lodging, and sightseeing). Suggestions are also given for a side trip to East Germany (pp. 460-502).

46 **Daytrips in Germany: 50 one day adventures by rail or car.**
Earl Steinbicker. New York: Hastings House, 1984. 272p. map.

Fifty practical itineraries, illustrated by the author with clearly drawn, full-page town plans and numerous black-and-white photos, for one-day excursions by car or rail, using Hamburg, Frankfurt, and Munich as bases. A well-conceived volume that does not attempt to cover all of West Germany, but usefully complements guides that do.

47 **Germany at its best.**
Robert S. Kane. Lincolnwood, Ill.: Passport Books, 1985. 356p.
maps.

A breezy travelogue, focussing on some forty cities from Aachen to Würzburg, by a popular American travel writer. More useful for tips and insight (if taken with a grain of salt) than as a basic guide.

48   **A pocket guide to Germany.**
      Washington, D.C.: U.S. Government Printing Office for the
      American Forces Information Service, 1981. 62p. map. (Dept. of
      Defense PG-3A).
An 'official Department of Defense publication for the use of personnel in the
military services' with practical information of general interest.

49   **Cities of Germany.**
      By the staff writers and photographers of *The Stars and Stripes*.
      Darmstadt: The Stars and Stripes, 1955. 197p. maps.
Originally carried in the newspaper of the American occupation forces in
Germany, each of the sixty-two essays describes one city's historical and cultural
background, modern development, and tourist attractions. The two-to-five-page
articles are arranged in alphabetical order – Aachen to Wuppertal – and
illustrated with many black-and-white photos.

50   **Literarischer Führer durch die Bundesrepublik Deutschland.**
      (Literary guide through the Federal Republic of Germany.)
      Edited by F. and G. Oberhauser. Foreword by Robert Minder.
      Frankfurt am Main: Insel Verlag, 1974. 658p. maps. bibliog.
This guide leads in eleven sections systematically (i.e., place names in
alphabetical order) through the ten states (*Länder*) of the Federal Republic –
starting with Bavaria in the south and ending with Schleswig-Holstein in the
north – and through Berlin. We find out what novelist, dramatist, philosopher,
historian, or theologian was born or died at a certain place, studied, worked or
vacationed there, met whom, wrote what there or about it, is remembered with a
monument, etc. Figures from history or legend are registered, as are convents and
cloisters, if they contributed to art and literature, and foreign visitors, such as
Mark Twain and Winston Churchill. The volume includes sixty-three photos. It
concludes with six suggested map-itineraries for seven writers; an extensive
bibliography of standard references to general and regional German literature; an
index of personal names; and an index of place names.

Picture books

51   **The Federal Republic of Germany today: insights into a country.**
      Edited by Bernd Schüth, text by Hans-Werner Klein, photography
      & design by Rainer Kiedrowski, translation by Diet Simon.
      Ratingen: Edition Rainer Kiedrowski, 1984. 3rd ed. 128p.
A collection of recent, quality colour plates with supporting text in English.

52 **The Federal Republic of Germany.**
   Otto Siegner, introduction by Arnold Schulz.   New York:
   Scribner's, copyright 1970. 271p. map.
A widely circulated picture book on West Germany, with close to two hundred
full-page photographs, half in colour, this volume has an extensive introduction
and captions in German, English, and French. A 239-page companion volume of
the same format, *Germany* (published, with an introduction by Adrian Mohr, by
Scribner's, and copyrighted, like its twin, by Verlag Ludwig Simon in 1970),
includes a number of the same photographs, but also gives coverage, mostly in
black and white, of the East.

53 **Germany: a panorama in color.**
   Introduction adapted from Rudolf Hagelstange, English translation
   by John Dornberg.   New York: Universe Books, 1969. 186p.
A collection of ninety colour plates with captions in English and French.

54 **Germany: countryside, cities, villages, and people.**
   Edited by Harald Busch and H. Breidenstein, introduction by
   Rudolf Hagelstange.   Frankfurt am Main: Umschau Verlag, 1956.
   224p.
242 full-page photographs, including sixteen colour plates, with captions in
German, French, and English, of scenes and works of art in the Federal Republic
of Germany, the German Democratic Republic, and areas in the East now part of
Poland and the Soviet Union.

55 **Bavaria: a German state in the heart of Europe.**
   Franz J. Baumgärtner, translated by Michael O'Donnell.   Munich:
   Bruckmann, 1970. 2nd ed. ca. 150p. map.
Translated from *Bayern*, this is an historically oriented introductory essay on the
art and tradition of this southern German state, illustrated with over a hundred
photographic plates, some in colour.

56 **Das Bild der Heimat Deutschland.** (The German homeland in
   pictures.)
   Edited by Theodor Müller-Alfeld, Peter Dreessen, and Willy
   Eggers.   Hamburg: Hoffman und Campe Verlag, 1953. 2nd ed.
   197p. map.
261 black-and-white pictures of Germany, with the location of the towns,
landscapes, and seascapes indicated on the endpaper maps. The introductory
notes before the depiction of each region are in German, English, and Spanish.

17

57 **Die schöne Heimat – Bilder aus Deutschland. Grosse Ausgabe des Blauen Buches.** (The beautiful homeland – pictures from Germany: large edition of the Blue Book.) Königstein: Langewiesche, 1961. 210p.

This fiftieth-anniversary edition of one of the most successful volumes in its genre is an expanded version of the 112-page original, *Die schöne Heimat – Bilder aus Deutschland.* The 'Blue Book' series also includes a volume of aerial photographs of Germany (*Deutsches Land in 111 Flugaufnahmen*), as well as individual volumes on cities, half-timber houses, cathedrals, castles, regional costumes, etc.

58 **Deutschland: Bilder seiner Landschaft und Kultur.** (Germany: pictures of its landscape and culture.) Introduction by Ricarda Huch. Zürich: Atlantis Verlag, 1964. 7th ed. 251p. map. (Orbis Terrarum series, ed. by Martin Hürlimann).

Over two hundred black-and-white photographs and eighteen colour plates picturing cities and landscapes in the East as well as in West Germany. The introduction at the beginning and the detailed annotations at the end of the book are in Germany only, but the brief captions of the individual pictures, often place names, are generally understandable without translation, and the quality of the photographs and their reproduction speaks for itself.

Flora and Fauna

General

59 **Der grosse ADAC-Führer durch Wald, Feld und Flur. Natur und
    Landschaft unserer Heimat.** (The large ADAC [Allgemeiner
    Deutscher Automobil-Club = General German Automobile Club]
    guide through forest, field, and meadow: nature and landscape of
    our homeland.)
    Stuttgart: Verlag Das Beste; in association with ADAC Verlag,
    Munich, 1981. rev. ed. 534p.

Published by the leading German automobile club, this is a fine, large-format,
one-volume encyclopaedia of nature in West Germany. It is richly illustrated with
photographs and drawings of the attractions of the countryside, and covers plant
and animal life in lucid entries that describe and often depict individual species,
and give their dimensions and Latin names.

Flora

60 **A guide to the vegetation of Britain and Europe.**
    Oleg Polunin and Martin Walters.   Oxford: Oxford University
    Press, 1985. 238p. followed by 48p. of colour plates. maps. bibliog.

Written for the layman and traveller, this guide to the vegetation of Europe, from
Britain to the Russian border, explains the most distinctive plant communities and
the most characteristic species in each community, showing their locations on
numerous maps, and illustrating them with drawings and 110 colour photographs.
The book, which seeks 'to bridge the gap between the scientific approach to

19

vegetation and that of the layman-naturalist,' includes an annotated listing of the National Parks and Nature Reserves of Europe (with their locations shown on maps); a glossary of terms; separate indexes in Latin and English of illustrated species; an index to plant communities of Europe; and a selected bibliography.

61 Flowers of Europe: a field guide.

Oleg Polunin. London: Oxford University Press, 1969. 662p. plus 192pp. with colour plates. bibliog.

Illustrated with fifty pages of line drawings and 192 pages of colour photographs, this field guide includes about 2,800 species – the majority of the more common flowers to be found in Europe. There is a table, alphabetized by Latin names, giving the English, French, German, and Italian names of flowers, and there are two separate indexes in English and in Latin. In addition to this large volume, see the pocket-sized *Wild Flowers of Europe: A Concise Guide in Colour* by Lorna F. Bowden, illustrated by Otto Ušák (London: Paul Hamlyn, 1969).

62 Trees and bushes of Britain and Europe.

Oleg Polunin. London: Oxford University Press, 1976; repr., Frogmore, St. Albans, Herts: 1977. 208p.

A guide to all the native trees and bushes that grow wild in Europe to over two metres, as well as commonly grown alien or naturalized trees and bushes, profusely illustrated with colour photographs and drawings. Locations of growth are noted in the individual descriptions. There is a nine-page table on 'Uses to man of selected trees and bushes,' and there is a single index of English and Latin names.

63 A field guide to the trees of Britain and northern Europe.

Alan Mitchell. Boston: Houghton Mifflin, 1974. 415p.

First American edition of a field guide with forty colour plates and 640 line drawings published in Great Britain by Collins. An introduction to trees and their identification is followed by coverage of all trees to be found in the countryside, parks, and gardens of Europe north of the Mediterranean littoral, except for some of great rarity confined to botanical gardens, specialist collections, and subtropical gardens. Natural distribution is indicated in individual entries, but not illustrated (the book includes no maps). The two indexes give the names of trees in English and in Latin.

64 German forestry.

Franz Heske. New Haven, Conn.: Yale University Press, 1938. 342p. maps. bibliog.

Prepared and published with the support of the Carl Schurz Memorial Foundation for the American reader, this dated though still useful introduction to German forestry and forest management – with consideration of the forest service, the state schools of forestry, and related matters nowadays referred to as environmental policy – is clearly written and well illustrated.

65 **Mein Garten in der Stadt: Haus- und Kleingärten, Balkone und Dachgärten ökologisch und biologisch richtig angelegt und gepflegt.**
(My garden in the city: house gardens and small gardens, balcony and roof gardens, ecologically and biologically properly planned and cultivated.)
Georg E. Siebeneicher. Munich: Südwest Verlag, 1981. 144p. bibliog.

Photographs and many varied sketches and plans show how to make use of smaller areas on, in, and around the house by planting trees, shrubs, vegetables, and flowers. Concrete suggestions on what to plant where, and how to care for it. Includes a chapter on the small garden plots commonly cultivated on the outskirts of many German towns.

66 **Guide to medicinal plants.**
Paul Schauenberg and Ferdinand Paris. From a translation by Maurice Pugh-Jones. Colour illustrations by Violette Niestle. Line illustrations by Paul Schauenberg. Guildford and London: Lutterworth Press, 1977. 349p. and 39 plates.

401 plants, from *aconitum napellus* (monkshood) to *zingiber officinale* (ginger), are described in this pocket-sized reference book, translated from the French (Neuchâtel and Paris: Delachaux & Niestle, 1974). There are forty-six black-and-white line drawings throughout the text and over two hundred thirty plants in colour in the plate section. The plants are grouped according to substances they contain, such as acids, alkaloids, antibiotics, bitter compounds, tannin, and vitamins. The individual entries give the name of the plant in Latin and English (both indexed), as well as French and German, its distribution, habitat, description, flowering season, active constituents, properties, and applications. The volume includes recipes, glossaries of botanical terms and therapeutic terms, and a list of maladies and treatments. The publisher 'strongly recommends' obtaining advice from a qualified herbalist, homeopath, biochemist or medical advisor in case of doubt, and disclaims all responsibility for 'use or application of any plants or preparations' mentioned in the guide. See also Erich F. Heeger, *Handbuch des Arznei- und Gewürzpflanzenbaues. Drogengewinnung* ['Handbook of Medicinal and Aromatic Plant Cultivation. Drug Extraction'] (Berlin: Deutscher Bauernverlag, 1956), and Heinrich Marzell, *Geschichte und Volkskunde der deutschen Heilpflanzen* ('History and Folklore of German Medicinal Plants'] (Darmstadt: Wissenschaftliche Buchgesellschaft, 1967).

67 **A colour atlas of poisonous plants: a handbook for pharmacists, doctors, toxicologists, and biologists.**
Dietrich Frohne and Hans Jürgen Pfänder. Translated by Norman Grainger Bisset. London: Wolfe Publishing, 1984. 291p. bibliog. (A Wolfe Science Book).

A well-documented volume with large colour photographs, translated from *Giftpflanzen. Ein Handbuch für Apotheker, Ärzte, Toxikologen und Biologen* (Stuttgart: Wissenschaftliche Verlagsgesellschaft, 1983), with a general introduction to plant poisoning, an extensive bibliography of books and articles in English

Flora and Fauna. Flora

and German, and illustrated coverage of the most important plants with alleged or actual toxic properties, their effects when touched or ingested, and the appropriate treatment. Included are such well-known sources of poison as hemlock and wolfsbane, but also tulip bulbs and a flowering meadow plant called cow parsnip or hogweed, contact with which may cause dermatitis. Poison ivy is one of several toxic sumach species that in Europe, it is noted, 'will only be encountered in botanical gardens,' and there they will usually be 'surrounded by a fence of some kind to prevent visitors coming into direct contact with them.'

68   **Illustrierte Flora. Deutschland und angrenzende Gebiete.**
     Gefässkryptogamen und Blütenpflanzen. (Illustrated flora of Germany
     and bordering areas: vascular cryptogams and phanerogams.)
     August Garcke. Edited by Konrad von Weihe.   Berlin and
     Hamburg: Verlag Paul Parey, 1972. 23rd, completely revised and
     newly illustrated ed. 1,607p. bibliog.

Published fifty years after the 22nd, the 23rd edition of Garcke's classic, compact handbook contains 3,704 individual black-and-white line drawings in 460 illustrations and five tables. The body of the text, including descriptions, is in German (with many technical terms and abbreviations), but the index includes Latin as well as German names. The introductory essay concludes with a short bibliography. For more extensive bibliographical coverage, largely in German, see *Bibliographie zur Flora von Mitteleuropa* ['Bibliography of the Flora of Central Europe'] by Ulrich Hamann and Gerhard Wagenitz (Munich: Hanser, 1970).

69   **Illustrierte Flora von Mittel-Europa. Mit besonderer**
     Berücksichtigung von Deutschland, Österreich und der Schweiz.
     Zum Gebrauche in den Schulen und zum Selbstunterricht.
     (Illustrated flora of Central Europe, with particular consideration of
     Germany, Austria, and Switzerland. For use in the schools and for
     self-instruction.)
     Gustav Hegi.   Munich: J. F. Lehmanns Verlag; Munich: Carl
     Hanser Verlag, 1909-1931 (being reprinted or revised as noted
     below). 7 vols. bibliog. maps.

The first edition of this encyclopaedia-format work of seven volumes (comprising thirteen books: vol. 4, consisting of 1,748 pages, was bound as three books; vol. 5, 2,630 pages, bound as four; vol. 6, 1,386 pages, bound as two) covers 150 families of flora comprehensively and 200 more in less detail. There are thousands of black-and-white illustrations (line drawings, photographs, and maps showing distribution), and scores of full-page colour engravings from beautifully executed paintings. World War II interrupted the second edition (vol. 1, 1936; vol. 2, 1939) of this definitive, standard work. It is now being cooperatively reissued in revised and greatly expanded form by Carl Hanser Verlag in Munich and Paul Parey Verlag in Berlin: *vol. 1*, 3rd ed., part 1, 1983, part 2, 1981, part 3, in prep.; *vol. 2*, 3rd ed., part 1, 1980, parts 2 & 3, in prep.; *vol. 3*, part 1, 3rd ed., 1981, part 2, 2nd ed., 1979, part 3, 2nd ed., 1974; *vol. 4*, 2nd ed., part 1, 1963, part 2a, 1966, part 2b, in prep., part 3, repr. of 1st ed.. with a supplement, 1964; *vol. 5*, 1st ed., 3 parts repr., with supplements, 1964 and 1966; and *vol. 6*, 2nd ed., part 1, 1974, part 2, in prep., part 3, 1966, part 4, in prep. In the new edition, some of the plates photographically reproducing the original edition's colour engravings are printed in black and white. Not yet in preparation is a new edition of the 562-page index volume, *vol. 7* (1st ed., 1931), which includes a 109-page illustrated glossary of botanical terms, indexes of German and Latin plant names, etc.

Fauna

70   **Collins guide to the sea fishes of Britain and North-Western Europe.**
Bent J. Muus. Illustrated by Preben Dahlstrom. Translated by
Gwynne Vevers.   London: Collins, 1974. 244p. maps.

Translated from the Danish (*Havfisk og Fiskeri*, G. E. C. Gads Forlag, 1964), this is a well-illustrated introduction to fishes and the fishing industry, particularly in the northeastern Atlantic and the Baltic. The body of the work consists of descriptions of 173 species, with colour illustrations of the fish (142 painted from freshly caught specimens), drawings of various kinds of boats, trawls, nets, traps, hooks, and spears (including illegal eel spears), and distribution maps. In addition, there are chapters on the biology of fishes, on fisheries biology, and on the fishing industry; identification keys highlighting conspicuous characteristics of the fishes; and indexes of the English and the scientific (Latin) names. Fresh-water fish and many aquarium fish are included in the 156-page *Fishes of the World*, by Hans Hvass (N.Y.: Dutton; London: Methuen, 1965), translated by Gwynne Vevers from the Danish (*Alverdens Fisk*, Politikens Forlag, 1964); the fishes, painted by Wilhelm Eignener, are swimming in the water and show great character. Of possible interest to older children. See also the hundred-page *Fische in Bach und Teich* ['Fishes in Brook and Pond'], by Heinz Geiler, with colour illustrations by Lieselotte Finke-Poser (Leipzig: Ernst Wunderlich, 1951) and Richard Gerlach's *Die Fische* ['The Fishes'] (Hamburg: Claassen Verlag, 1950), a well-written, general work of 468 pages, addressed to (but not 'down' to) the interested layman. The final chapter, on the history of ichthyology since antiquity, discusses the literature in the field (especially in the twentieth century) in English, German, French, etc.

71   **The reptiles of northern and central Europe.**
Donald Street.   London: B. T. Batsford Ltd., 1979. 268p. bibliog.

Covers all the species of reptiles (lizards, snakes, and tortoises) living in the British Isles, Scandinavia, and the northern and central parts of the European mainland, eastward from the Atlantic, through the Alps, up to and including the Carpathian region. (An eight-page appendix touches on 'The Reptiles of Southern Europe.') The account of each of the twenty-five species dealt with consists of a description of its physical appearance, habitat, behaviour, and distribution. The English and scientific (Latin) names of species are used in the entries and in the index, but local European names are listed in the languages of the countries where a given species occurs (e.g., in the case of the grass snake, in Czech, Danish, Dutch, Finnish, French, German, Hungarian, Italian, Norwegian, Polish, Romanian, Russian, Serbo-Croatian, Slovakian, and Swedish). The

23

Flora and Fauna. Fauna

volume is illustrated with eight colour photographs and forty-four black-and-white photographs and contains an eleven-page bibliography citing articles as well as books in English, German, and other languages.

72 **The encyclopedia of sea mammals.**
   David J. Coffey. London: Hart-Davis, MacGibbon, 1977. 223p. maps.

Copiously illustrated general introduction to three orders of sea mammals, the cetaceans (whales, dolphins, and porpoises), the pinnipeds (seals, sea lions, and walruses), and the sirenians (dugongs, sea cows, and manatees), with brief consideration of the sea otter, a marine carnivore. Whales and seals may be found in the waters off the German coast, but no sirenians inhabit the North Sea or the Baltic Sea, and sea otters are largely restricted to the northern Pacific along the coast of Alaska and Asia.

73 **A field guide to the mammals of Britain and Europe.**
   F. H. van den Brink. Transl. and edited by Hans Kruuk and H. N. Southern. Illustrated by Paul Barruel. Boston: Houghton Mifflin, 1968. 221p. maps. bibliog. (The Peterson Field Guide Series).

A guide covering all the mammals which occur in Britain and Europe (eastwards to 30°E), translated from the Dutch (*Zoogdierengids*, N. V. Uitgevers-maatschappij Elsevier, 1955). Nearly all – a total of 177 – are illustrated; all, except whales and some rare or introduced animals, are in colour; the range of all the species but the whales is shown on maps. The index gives the mammals' names in English and Latin. See also *Mammals in Colour*, by Leif Lyneborg, illustrations by Henning Anthon, translated and adapted by Gwynne Vevers & Winwood Reade (London: Blandford Press, 1971), with eighty pages of attractive, larger drawings in colour.

74 **The terrestrial mammals of Western Europe.**
   G. B. Corbet. Henley-on-Thames: G. T. Foulis; Philadelphia: Dufour Editions, 1966. 264p. bibliog.

A systematic review, by the Curator of Mammals, British Museum (Natural History), of all groups of mammals other than whales, seals, and bats in the whole of Europe to the west of Russia, illustrated with sixteen photographs and twenty-three figures. The volume includes a glossary and a single index giving both English and Latin names of animals. See also Jochen Niethammer and Franz Krapp, eds., *Handbuch der Säugetiere Europas* ['Handbook of the Mammals of Europe'], vol. 1 (476 pp.), *Nagetiere I* ['Rodents,' Part I], and vol. 2/I (649 pp.), *Nagetiere II* ['Rodents,' Part II] (Wiesbaden: Akademische Verlagsgesellschaft, 1978 and 1982, resp.); both books have extensive bibliographies (also in English). Vol. 2/II is to deal with hoofed animals.

75 **A field guide to the birds of Britain and Europe.**
Roger Tory Peterson, Guy Mountfort, and P. A. D. Hollom.
London: Collins; Boston: Houghton Mifflin, 1984. 4th, rev. ed.
384p.

Newly revised edition of a standard handbook that covers 'all the birds of Europe, including rare vagrants, from the tundra of northern Finland to the Mediterranean islands, westwards to Iceland, and eastwards to the Black Sea.' There are some 1,200 illustrations, largely in colour, of over 600 species. As in the other Roger Tory Peterson guides, birds are shown with pointers indicating their special, distinguishing features. Geographical range is shown on distribution maps. Names of birds are indexed in English and Latin, but the entries also give Dutch, French, German, and Swedish names. See also the *Hamlyn Guide to Birds of Britain and Europe*, by Bertel Bruun et al. (London: Hamlyn, 1970) and *The Birds of Britain and Europe with North Africa and the Middle East*, by Hermann Heinzel, Richard Fitter, and John Parslow (Philadelphia and N.Y.: Lippincott, 1972), with beautiful illustrations, all in colour.

76 **Die Brutvögel Mitteleuropas.** (The nesting birds of Central Europe.)
Walter Wüst. With 263 coloured pictures by Ludwig Binder.
Munich: Bayerischer Schulbuch-Verlag, 1970. 519p. bibliog.

A handsome book with fine illustrations, detailed discussion of the individual species, a listing of endangered birds, and an extensive bibliography. For treatment that would also interest children, see *Birds of Europe*, illustrations by John Gould, text by A. Rutgers (London: Methuen, 1966). Each of Gould's nineteenth-century paintings of a bird or a bird family is accompanied by readable, non-technical information on the facing page.

77 **A field guide to the nests, eggs, and nestlings of European birds, with North Africa and the Middle East.**
Colin Harrison. London: Collins, 1975. 432p. (Collins Pocket and Field Guides).

Intended as a supplement to guides used in identifying the birds of Britain and Europe, this volume provides information on the nesting of the various species, i.e., the habitat and nest-site, the appearance of nest, eggs and young, the breeding season, incubation, and care of the young in the early stages. It is illustrated with black-and-white drawings of nests and birds, sixteen colour plates showing from eight to fifteen nestlings each, and forty-eight colour plates showing eggs. There are separate indexes to the English and the scientific (Latin) names of the birds.

78 **Ten little housemates.**
Karl von Frisch. Illustrated by Richard Ehrlich. Translated by Margaret D. Senft. Oxford: Pergamon Press, 1960. 146p.

Translated from *Zehn kleine Hausgenossen*, 4th ed. (Munich: Ernst Heimeran, 1955), a short, readable, well-illustrated introduction to the lives and times of house flies, gnats or (in American parlance) mosquitoes, fleas, bed-bugs, lice, clothes moths, cockroaches, silver-fish, spiders, and ticks, and how to deal with them. For an account of the evolutionary development of insects, see Willi

Flora and Fauna. Fauna

Hennig's *Insect Phylogeny*, with notes by Dieter Schlee (Chichester and N.Y.: John Wiley & Sons, 1981), a 514-page volume with a forty-four page bibliography, translated (and edited) by Adrian C. Pont from *Die Stammes-geschichte der Insekten* ['The Genealogy of the Insects'] (Frankfurt am Main: Waldemar Kramer, 1969). See also Wolfgang Schwenke, ed., *Die Forstschädlinge Europas. Ein Handbuch in fünf Bänden* ['The Forest-Pests of Europe: A Handbook in Five Volumes'], vol. 1, *Würmer, Schnecken, Spinnentiere, Tausend-füssler und hemimetabole Insekten* ['Worms, Snails, Arachnids, Millepedes, and Hemimetabolous Insects']; vol. 2, *Käfer* ['Beetles']; vol. 3, *Schmetterlinge* ['Butterflies']; vol. 4, *Hautflügler und Zweiflügler* ['Hymenopterous and Dipterous Insects']; vol. 5, *Wirbeltiere* ['Vertebrates'] (Hamburg and Berlin: Paul Parey, 1972, 1974, 1978, 1982, and 1986, resp.). Each of these five volumes is illustrated with numerous, detailed black-and-white drawings and has very extensive, technical bibliographical references.

79   **Fauna von Deutschland. Ein Bestimmungsbuch unserer heimischen Tierwelt.** (Fauna of Germany: a classification [hand]book on the animal world of our homeland.)
      Paul Brohmer and Wolfgang Tischler.   Heidelberg: Quelle & Meyer, 1974. 12th ed. 580p. bibliog.

Copiously illustrated with clear line drawings, this pocket-sized manual gives a systematic overview of the German fauna from protozoa to mammalia. The text is in German, but names are given in Latin as well. There is a thirty-six page, three-column index.

Prehistory and Archaeology

80 **Die vorgeschichtliche Kunst Deutschlands.** (The prehistoric art of
Germany.)
Herbert Kühn. Berlin: Propyläen Verlag, 1935. 612p. 26 maps.
bibliog. (Die Propyläen-Kunstgeschichte, Ergänzungsband VIII [the
Propyläen history of art, supplemental vol. VIII]).
Encyclopaedia-format work on prehistoric art in Germany from the paleolithic
period to the age of the Germanic migrations and the Vikings, with a 193-page
monograph, some 300 pages of black-and-white photographs, and a score of
colour plates.

81 **Romans on the Rhine: archaeology in Germany.**
Paul MacKendrick. New York: Funk & Wagnalls, 1970. 269p.
9 maps. bibliog.
'An attempt to write cultural history from archaeological evidence,' as stated in
the foreword, this is an account of Germany and neighbouring areas in Roman
times, based on the interpretation of works of art and other artifacts, together
with the fragmentary historical record. The readable account is generously
illustrated with photographs, sketches, maps, and city plans, and includes an
extensive bibliography and a detailed index.

History

General

82 **Factors in German history.**
Geoffrey Barraclough.   Oxford: Basil Blackwell, 1946. 165p.
7 maps.

An interpretive overview of German history from the early third century to the
end of the Second World War, bringing out social, economic, and constitutional
factors underlying the more commonly stressed political, diplomatic, and military
course of events. On the interpretation of German history, see Georg G. Iggers,
*The German Conception of History: The National Tradition of Historical Thought
from Herder to the Present*, rev. ed. (Middletown, Conn.: Wesleyan Univ. Press,
1983) and Andreas Dorpalen, *German History in Marxist Perspective: The East
German Approach* (Detroit: Wayne State Univ. Press, 1985).

83 **Germany: a short history.**
Donald S. Detwiler.   Carbondale & Edwardsville: Southern Illinois
University Press; London & Amsterdam: Feffer & Simons, 1976.
273p. 12 maps. bibliog.

A concise narrative from Roman *Germania* to the mid-1970s supplemented by
twelve original maps with extended facing-page captions, a chronology, and a 29-
page bibliographical essay citing works in English only. (A revised and expanded
edition is in preparation.) The bibliography of William Harvey Maehl's 833-page
Germany in Western Civilization (University, Ala: Univ. of Alabama Press, 1979)
includes standard German references as well. Helmut M. Müller, *Schlaglichter der
deutschen Geschichte* ['Highlights of German History'] (Mannheim: Bibliographisches Institut, 1986) provides an illustrated overview with more recent
German bibliography. See also the *Lexikon der deutschen Geschichte* cited under
Directories and Encyclopaedias.

Antiquity

84   **The German policy of Augustus: an examination of the
      archaeological evidence.**
      C. M. Wells.   Oxford: At the Clarendon Press, 1972. 337p. maps.
      bibliog.

A detailed study, based on reexamination of ancient texts and modern
scholarship, and on evaluation of archaeological evidence (some of it relatively
recently discovered), of the imperial strategy of Augustus, the Roman advance
from the Rhine to the Elbe, and the background of the decision not to attempt
the reconquest of the province of *Germania* after the rebellion of Arminius and
his defeat of Varus in 9 A.D.

85   **The provinces of the Roman Empire from Caesar to Diocletian.**
      Theodor Mommsen, translated by W. P. Dickson, rev. & ed. by F.
      Haverfield.   London, 1909; repr., Chicago: Ares Publ., 1974, 2
      vols.

The first and fourth chapters of Mommsen's classic provide an account,
superseded in detail yet still well worth reading, of the clash between Rome and
the Germanic tribes early in the first century and their subsequent relations until
the third. The Haverfield edition takes into account Mommsen's final revisions of
the fifth volume of his Roman history, on the provinces from Caesar to
Diocletian, *Römische Geschichte*, vol. 5: *Die Provinzen von Caesar bis Diocletian*,
5th ed. (Berlin: Weidmannsche Buchhandlung, 1904). The 1974 reprint does not
include the maps prepared for Mommsen's original work and carried in the 1909
London edition.

86   **Tacitus on Britain and Germany: a translation of the 'Agricola' and
      the 'Germania.'**
      P. Cornelius Tacitus, translated with an introduction by H.
      Mattingly.   Baltimore & Harmondsworth: Penguin Books, 1948.
      175p. 2 maps. bibliog. (Penguin Classics).

Written at the end of the first century, the *Germania* is an essay on the Germanic
tribes, their character, customs, and homeland. Published in this volume with the
Roman senator Tacitus' biography of his father-in-law Agricola, famous governor
of Roman Britain, it was the first and, for centuries to come, only systematic
treatment of the subject. The translator's extended introduction explains the
historical background, the importance of Germany to the early Roman Empire,
and the perspective of Tacitus, a conservative who deplored the decadence of his
time and polemically contrasted the virtues of the unspoiled Germans with the
vices of the Romans.

The Middle Ages

87 **Medieval civilization in Germany: 800-1273.**
Franz H. Bäuml. New York: Praeger, 1969. 230p. 14 maps.
bibliog. (Ancient Peoples and Places, ed. by Glyn Daniel, vol. 67).
An illustrated survey of literature, architecture, painting, sculpture, etc., in
Germany during the Middle Ages.

88 **The origins of modern Germany.**
Geoffrey Barraclough. Oxford: Basil Blackwell, 1947, 2nd ed.;
paperback repr., New York and London: W. W. Norton, 1984.
481p. 9 maps. bibliog.
Indispensable for understanding the mediaeval background of modern German
history. Two-thirds of the work is devoted to the Middle Ages, on which Prof.
Barraclough issued translations of two important German works in his 'Studies in
Medieval History' series, published by Blackwell in Oxford and subsequently
reprinted in paperback: *Kingship and Law in the Middle Ages* by Fritz Kern and
Church, State and Christian Society at the Time of the Investiture Contest by Gerd
Tellenbach (both N.Y.: Harper Torchbooks, 1970). On the papacy, with which
the German monarchy was inextricably involved during the Middle Ages,
Barraclough wrote an introductory survey, *The Medieval Papacy* (N.Y.: Harcourt
Brace Jovanovich, 1968; paperback repr., N.Y.: Norton, 1979).

89 **Frederick the Second, 1194-1250.**
Ernst Kantorowicz. Translated by E. O. Lorimer. London:
Constable, 1931; republ., 1957. 724p. 7 maps. bibliog. (Makers of
the Middle Ages).
Authorized English version of the text volume of the evocative biography of the
controversial Hohenstaufen emperor, *Kaiser Friedrich der Zweite* (Berlin: Georg
Bondi, 1927). The second volume of the German original, published in 1931,
consists of documents and references to the sources on which the first volume was
based; it was not translated, but the author prepared, 'as a guide to the general
reader,' a 'Summary of Sources' (largely in German or Latin) for the English
edition (pp. xxv-xxvii). For an introduction to German scholarship on Emperor
Frederick II and the Holy Roman Empire during his time, and also for the impact
of Kantorowicz' remarkable work, see the 800-page collection *Stupor Mundi. Zur
Geschichte Friedrichs II. von Hohenstaufen* ['The Wonder of the World: On the
History of Frederick II of Hohenstaufen'], ed. by Gunther Wolf (Darmstadt:
Wissenschaftliche Buchgesellschaft, 1966).

90 **Old Europe: a study of continuity, 1000-1800.**
Dietrich Gerhard. New York and London: Academic Press, 1981.
147p. (Studies in Social Discontinuity).
Though not focussed exclusively on Germany, this essay illuminates one of the
least understood aspects of German history: how and why many of the institutions
and ideas of the Middle Ages persisted into the nineteenth century, and did so not

as moribund anachronisms, but as enduring, viable aspects of a society and culture whose continuity had been far less disrupted by the Renaissance and Reformation than by the French and industrial revolutions.

Modern Germany

91 **A history of modern Germany.**
Hajo Holborn. New York: Knopf, 1959, 1964, 1969. Vol. 1, *The Reformation*, 374p., 6 maps; vol. 2, *1648-1840*, 531p., 8 maps; vol. 3, *1840-1945*, 818p., 13 maps.
A standard survey of modern German history with clear maps. In his foreword to the final volume, the author refers the reader to the bibliography on Germany, Austria, and Switzerland that he compiled for *The American Historical Association's Guide to Historical Literature*, ed. by George F. Howe et al. (N.Y.: Macmillan, 1961, pp. 549-566), where he provided coverage of the standard literature (including periodicals) in German as well as English. For extensive excerpts from Holborn's more important studies dealing with modern German history (and aspects of German-American relations in his lifetime), together with a bibliography of his works, see *Hajo Holborn: Inter Nationes Prize 1969* (Bonn: Inter Nationes, 1969).

92 **Here I stand: a life of Martin Luther.**
Roland H. Bainton. London: Hodder & Stoughton; Nashville, Tenn.: Abingdon Press, 1950; paperback repr., Nashville: Apex Books. 422p. bibliog.
Authoritative yet most readable biography that evokes the spirit of the Reformation and of the man with whom it is most closely identified. Illustrated with contemporary prints. For selections from Luther's works, see *Martin Luther*, ed. by E. G. Rupp and Benjamin Drewery in the 'Documents of Modern History' series (N.Y.: St. Martin's Press, 1970).

93 **Wallenstein: his life narrated**
by Golo Mann. Translated by Charles Kessler. New York: Holt, Rinehart and Winston, 1976. 909p. maps. bibliog.
Translated from *Wallenstein. Sein Leben erzählt von Golo Mann* (Frankfurt am Main: S. Fischer Verlag, 1971), a 1,315-page bestselling biography by one of postwar Germany's most esteemed historians, this monumental historical biography, a work of widely recognized literary merit, brings to life an important and powerful leader during the Thirty Years' War in the first half of the seventeenth century.

94 **Frederick the Great: a historical profile.**
Gerhard Ritter. Translated, with an intro., by Peter Paret.
Berkeley: University of California Press, 1968. 207p.

This biographical essay by a leading German historian is well complemented by Prof. Paret's collection of a dozen articles, essays, and contemporary accounts (many previously not translated into English), with a bibliographical note, in *Frederick the Great: A Profile* (N.Y.: Hill and Wang, 1972).

95 **The sword and the scepter: the problem of militarism in Germany. Vol. 1: The Prussian tradition, 1740-1890; vol. 2: The European powers and the Wilhelminian Empire, 1890-1914; vol. 3: The tragedy of statesmanship – Bethmann Hollweg as war chancellor (1914-1917); vol. 4: The reign of German militarism and the disaster of 1918.**
Gerhard Ritter. Translated by Heinz Norden.   Coral Gables, Fla.:
University of Miami Press, 1969-1973. bibliog.

Translated from the 3rd, rev. ed. of vol. 1, the 2nd, rev. ed. of vol. 2, and the 1st ed. of vols. 3 & 4 of *Staatskunst und Kriegshandwerk. Das Problem des Militarismus in Deutschland* (Munich: R. Oldenbourg, 1964-68), this is an authoritative history of German militarism from the accession of Frederick the Great to the end of the First World War. John W. Wheeler-Bennett carries the story to the end of the Second World War in *The Nemesis of Power: The German Army in Politics, 1918-1945*, 2nd ed. (London: Macmillan; New York: St. Martin's, 1964). See also Martin Kitchen, *A Military History of Germany from the Eighteenth Century to the Present Day* (Bloomington: Indiana Univ. Press, 1975).

96 **The genesis of German conservatism.**
Klaus Epstein.   Princeton, N.J.: Princeton University Press, 1966.
733p. bibliog.

An account of the emergence of conservatism in Germany, from its origins as a response to the challenge of the Enlightenment in the latter half of the 18th century to its role in the reaction against the French Revolution and Napoleon.

97 **The German idea of freedom: history of a political tradition.**
Leonard Krieger.   Boston: Beacon Press, 1957. 540p. bibliog.

An account of the origins and assumptions of the liberal movement in Germany, and of its failure to achieve liberal democracy in the Western sense during the nineteenth century. On the unsuccessful attempt to institutionalize a liberal parliamentary monarchy in Germany in the mid-nineteenth century, see Frank Eyck, *The Frankfurt Parliament: 1848-1849* (N.Y.: St. Martin's, 1968) and the account by Friedrich Engels, originally published in the *New York Tribune* (in 1851-52), in *The German Revolutions*, ed. with an intro. by Leonard Krieger (Chicago: Univ. of Chicago Press, 1967).

98 **Germany 1866-1945.**
Gordon A. Craig. New York: Oxford University Press, 1978.
825p. bibliog. (Oxford History of Modern Europe).

A narrative synthesis of German institutional and cultural history from the period
of unification under Bismarck to the collapse of Hitler's Third Reich. Craig deals
with the postwar period in *The Germans* (N.Y.: Putnam, 1982).

99 **Bismarck: the white revolutionary.**
Lothar Gall. Translated by J. A. Underwood. London: Allen &
Unwin, 1986. 2 vols. bibliog.

In its synthesis of scholarship and humanistic insight into the complex personality
of one of the crucial figures of German history, this biography, translated from
Bismarck. Der weisse Revolutionär (Frankfurt am Main and Berlin: Propyläen,
1980), stands alone. For a concise introduction to Bismarck, his impact, and work
available on him in English as well as German, see George Kent, *Bismarck and
His Times* (Carbondale and Edwardsville: Southern Illinois Univ. Press, 1978)
and two volumes edited by Theodore S. Hamerow, *Otto von Bismarck: A
Historical Assessment*, 2nd ed. (Lexington, Mass.: D. C. Heath, 1972) and an
abridged translation of Bismarck's *Reflections and Reminiscences* (N.Y.: Harper
Torchbooks, 1968).

100 **The Kaiser and his times.**
Michael Balfour. Boston: Houghton Mifflin, 1964; paperback
repr., N.Y.: Norton, 1972. bibliog. 524p. (531p. in 1972 reprint,
which has an afterword beginning on p. 525.)

The life of Emperor William II overlapped the lives of Bismarck, whom he
discharged early in his reign, and Hitler, whom he congratulated from exile on his
triumphs early in World War II. Though basically unchanged, the picture of the
man is sharpened in *Kaiser Wilhelm II, New Interpretations: The Corfu Papers*,
ed. by John C. G. Röhl and Nicolaus Sombart (Cambridge and N.Y.: Cambridge
Univ. Press, 1982). See also three controversial works regarding Imperial
Germany's responsibility for the First World War by Fritz Fischer: *War of
Illusions: German Policies from 1911 to 1914*, foreword by Alan Bullock (N.Y.:
Norton, 1975), translated by Marian Jackson from an abridged revision of *Krieg
der Illusionen* (Düsseldorf: Droste, 1969); *Germany's Aims in the First World
War*, introductions by Hajo Holborn and James Joll (N.Y.: Norton, 1967),
translated (and abridged by the author) from *Griff nach der Weltmacht* ['Grasp
for World Power'] (Düsseldorf: Droste, 1961); and *World Power or Decline: The
Controversy over Germany's Aims in the First World War* (N.Y.: Norton, 1974),
translated by Lancelot L. Farrar et al., from *Weltmacht oder Niedergang* ['World
Power or Decline'] (Frankfurt am Main: Europäische Verlagsanstalt, 1965).

101 **Failure of a revolution: Germany 1918-19.**
Sebastian Haffner. Translated by Georg Rapp. London: André
Deutsch; New York: Library Press, 1972. 205p.

A translation of *Die verratene Revolution* ['The Betrayed Revolution'] (Munich:
Scherz Verlag, 1969), reprinted in 1979 by Kindler, also in Munich, as *Die
deutsche Revolution 1918/19* ['The German Revolution, 1918/1919'], this is a
scathing account of the revolution that ended the monarchy in Germany, but left
the social structure that had sustained it largely intact. Detailed treatment of the
background is given by Arthur Rosenberg in *Imperial Germany: The Birth of the
German Republic, 1871-1918*, transl. by Ian F. D. Morrow (N.Y.: Oxford Univ.
Press, 1931; paperback repr., Boston: Beacon, 1964).

102 **The path to dictatorship, 1918-1933: ten essays.**
Theodor Eschenburg et al. Transl. by John Conway. Intro. by Fritz
Stern. New York: Doubleday Anchor Books, 1966. 217p.

Translations of a series of ten radiocasts by prominent German scholars on
problems of the Weimar Republic. See also Henry Ashby Turner, Jr., *German
Big Business and the Rise of Hitler* (N.Y.: Oxford Univ. Press, 1985), and a
collection of ten essays edited by Hajo Holborn, *Republic to Reich: The Making
of the Nazi Revolution* (N.Y.: Pantheon Books, 1972) dealing not only with the
eclipse of the Weimar Republic, but the consolidation and culture of Hitler's
Third Reich. For more extensive treatment of the Weimar Republic, see Erich
Eyck, *A History of the Weimar Republic*, 2 vols. (Cambridge, Mass.: Harvard
Univ. Press, 1962 & 1963; paperback repr., N.Y.: Atheneum, 1970), translated
from *Geschichte der Weimarer Republik*, 2 vols. (Erlenbach-Zürich: Rentsch,
1956), by Harlan P. Hanson and Robert G. L. Waite, and S. William Halperin's
Germany Tried Democracy: A Political History of the Reich from 1918 to 1933
(N.Y.: Crowell, 1946; Ann Arbor, Mich.: University Microfilms International,
available [in reproduced form] on demand).

103 **Hitler: a study in tyranny.**
Alan Bullock. New York: Harper & Row, 1962. Rev. ed.
Paperback repr., N.Y.: Harper Torchbooks. 848p. bibliog.

This standard account, though superseded on some points, has not been
supplanted as a whole by later works, among the most competent of which are
Joachim C. Fest's full-length biography, *Hitler* (N.Y.: Harcourt Brace
Jovanovich, 1974), translated by Richard and Clara Winston from *Hitler. Eine
Biographie* (Frankfurt am Main and Berlin: Propyläen, 1973) and Norman Stone's
biographical essay, *Hitler* (London: Hodder and Stoughton, 1980).

104 **Hitler: the man and the military leader.**
Percy Ernst Schramm. Translated, edited, and with an introduction
by Donald S. Detwiler. Chicago: Quadrangle, 1971; London:
Allen Lane The Penguin Press, 1972; repr., N.Y.: Franklin Watts,
1978; Malabar, Fla.: Robert E. Krieger Publ. Co., 1986. 214p.

Analytical essays on Hitler's table conversations ('The Anatomy of a Dictator')
and the War Diary of the High Command of the German Armed Forces ('The
Military Leader'), by a German historian who was War Diary Officer in Hitler's

headquarters. See also the portrait of Hitler as he revealed himself to Otto
Wagener, chief of staff of his storm troopers during the years before he came to
power, *Hitler: Memoirs of a Confidant*, edited by Henry Ashby Turner, Jr. (New
Haven, Conn.: Yale Univ. Press, 1985), translated by Ruth Hain from *Hitler aus
nächster Nähe. Aufzeichnungen eines Vertrauten, 1929-1932*, ed. by H. A.
Turner, Jr. (Frankfurt am Main: Ullstein, 1978). Other perceptive interpretations
(also not biographies): Eberhard Jäckel, *Hitler's Weltanschauung: A Blueprint for
Power* (Middletown, Conn.: Wesleyan Univ. Press, 1972), transl. by Herbert
Arnold from *Hitlers Weltanschauung. Entwurf einer Herrschaft* (Tübingen: Rainer
Wunderlich, 1969); Sebastian Haffner, *The Meaning of Hitler* (N.Y.: Macmillan,
1979), transl. by Ewald Osers from *Anmerkungen zu Hitler* (Munich: Kindler
Verlag, 1978); and Rudolph Binion, *Hitler among the Germans* (N.Y., Oxford,
Amsterdam: Elsevier, 1976; repr., with a new preface, DeKalb, Ill.: Northern
Illinois Univ. Press, 1984).

105 **Inside the Third Reich: memoirs.**
Albert Speer. Translated by Richard & Clara Winston.
Introduction by Eugene Davidson. New York: Macmillan, 1970.
596p.; paperback repr., N.Y.: Avon, 1971. 734p. bibliog.

A best-selling, carefully crafted autobiographical memoir by a technocrat who
won Hitler's personal confidence and, in the course of the war, came to be one of
the most powerful of his lieutenants. Discrepancies between Speer's postwar
account and the historical record are documented by Matthias Schmidt in *Albert
Speer: The End of a Myth* (N.Y.: St. Martin's Press, 1984). The reader of the
German original, Speer's *Erinnerungen* (Berlin: Propyläen, 1969), may wish to
contrast Speer's postwar account of his role as Minister of Armaments with the
documentation in *Deutschlands Rüstung im Zweiten Weltkrieg: Hitlers Kon-
ferenzen mit Albert Speer 1942-1945*, ed. with an intro. by Willi A. Boelcke
(Frankfurt am Main: Akademische Verlagsgesellschaft Athenaion, 1969).

106 **The face of the Third Reich: portraits of the Nazi leadership.**
Joachim C. Fest. Translated by Michael Bullock. New York:
Pantheon, 1970. 402p. bibliog.

In addition to a sixty-five page study of Hitler, which served as a point of
departure for the author's subsequent full-length biography, this volume includes
biographical essays on Hermann Göring, Joseph Goebbels, Martin Bormann,
Rudolf Hess, Albert Speer, and others. The extensive backnotes of the original,
Das Gesicht des Dritten Reiches. Profile einer totalitären Herrschaft (Munich:
Piper, 1963) are translated, but without page references.

107 **We survived: fourteen histories of the hidden and hunted of Nazi
Germany.**
Eric H. Boehm. New Haven, Conn.: Yale University Press,
1949; repr., Santa Barbara, Calif.: ABC-Clio Information Services,
1985. 231p., including 1966 and 1985 epilogues. 2 maps.

Originally published under the title *We Survived: The Stories of Fourteen of the
Hidden and the Hunted of Nazi Germany*. Among the graphic personal accounts

are those of Rabbi Leo Baeck of Berlin, who survived imprisonment in a concentration camp, and a German Protestant churchman who became president of the lower house of the parliament of the Federal Republic of Germany.

108 **They thought they were free: the Germans, 1933-45.**
Milton Mayer. Chicago: University of Chicago Press, 1955;
Phoenix paperback repr., with a new foreword, 1966. 346p.

An account of the average citizen's life in Hitler's Germany, based on postwar interviews of a tailor, a baker, a teacher, and seven others in a town in the U.S. Zone of Occupation. See also Ernst von Salomon, *The Answers of Ernst von Salomon to the 131 Questions in the Allied Military Government 'Fragebogen'* (London: Putnam, 1954), translated by Constantine FitzGibbon from *Der Fragebogen* ['The Questionnaire'] (Hamburg: Rowohlt, 1951).

109 **The German dictatorship: the origins, structure, and effects of National Socialism.**
Karl Dietrich Bracher. Translated by Jean Steinberg. Introduction by Peter Gay. New York: Praeger, 1970. 553p. bibliog.

Originally published as *Die deutsche Diktatur. Entstehung, Struktur, Folgen des Nationalsozialismus* (Cologne and Berlin: Kiepenheuer & Witsch, 1969), this analytical account represents a mature synthesis of a quarter century of international scholarship, reflected in the extensive bibliography, on the background, development, and impact of the Third Reich as the institutionalization of Hitler's National Socialist racial ideology. Martin Broszat's *The Hitler State: The Foundation and Development of the Internal Structure of the Third Reich* (London and New York: Longman, 1981), translated by John W. Hiden from *Der Staat Hitlers* (Munich: Deutscher Taschenbuch Verlag, 1969), with a new foreword by the author for the English edition, focusses on the internal tensions in Hitler's Germany between the traditional authorities and those who challenged them. For a brief introduction, with bibliographical notes, see *Government, Party and People in Nazi Germany*, ed. by Jeremy Noakes, Exeter Studies in History, no. 2 (Exeter: Univ. of Exeter, 1980).

110 **The foreign policy of Hitler's Germany. vol. 1, Diplomatic revolution in Europe, 1933-36; vol. 2, Starting World War II, 1937-1939.**
Gerhard L. Weinberg. Chicago and London: University of Chicago Press, 1970 & 1980. 397p. & 728p. bibliog. in each vol.

Thorough, objective treatment through 1939 by an authority whose *World in the Balance: Behind the Scenes of World War II* (Hanover, N.H., and London: Univ. Press of New England, 1981), concludes with a bibliographical essay on the war. See also *Hitler's War Aims*, vol. 1, *Ideology, the Nazi State, and the Course of Expansion*, and vol. 2, *The Establishment of the New Order*, by Norman Rich (N.Y.: Norton, 1973 & 1974, resp.), a scholarly but readable narrative of Hitler's aggression in the context of German history and National Socialist ideology; extensive backnotes (explanatory as well as documentary), indices, glossaries of abbreviations, biographical sketches, and together over fifty pages of critical bibliography make the work useful also for reference.

History. Modern Germany

111 **The German opposition to Hitler: an assessment.**
Hans Rothfels. Translated by Lawrence Wilson. London: Wolff,
1961; paperback repr., 1970. 169p. bibliog. (German History
Series, no. 2).

Translated from the (subsequently revised) *Die deutsche Opposition gegen Hitler*
(Frankfurt am Main: Fischer-Bücherei, 1958), this is a classic introduction. For a
general treatment, see Peter Hoffmann's study, *The History of the German
Resistance, 1933-1945*, 3rd ed. (London: MacDonald & Jane's; Cambridge, Mass.:
MIT Press, 1977), translated by Richard Barry from *Widerstand, Staatsstreich,
Attentat*, 2nd ed. (Munich: Piper, 1970), with additional material by the author;
and for the particularly tenacious prewar opposition within the Army, see Harold
C. Deutsch's *Hitler and His Generals: The Hidden Crisis, January-June 1938*
(Minneapolis: Univ. of Minnesota Press, 1974).

112 **Holocaust.**
Jacob Robinson et al. Jerusalem: Keter Publishing House, 1974.
214p. 2 maps. bibliog. (Israel Pocket Library).

Compiled from material originally published in the *Encyclopaedia Judaica*, this
pocket-sized book includes a 57-page concise history of the Holocaust and articles
on the attitude of the Christian churches and on Jewish partisans.

113 **The Macmillan atlas of the Holocaust.**
Martin Gilbert. New York: Macmillan, 1982. 256p. 316 maps.
bibliog.

A comprehensive historical atlas with a concise narrative, black-and-white
photographs, a detailed index, and maps on not only German genocide during
World War II, but also the background of the Holocaust and related topics, e.g.,
anti-Jewish violence in Europe, 1918-1932; anti-Jewish riots in Poland, April-June
1938; German euthanasia centres, 1940; birthplaces of Jews executed in France
for resistance, 1941; Eastern escape route of Polish Jews, May 1940-May 1941;
the German conquest of Yugoslavia and Greece, April 1941; and deportations to
Auschwitz, 1942-1944. The sources on which the maps are based are cited in
detail, including personal testimony, e.g., a conversation in Jerusalem on 14 May
1979 with Leon Pommers on escape of Jews across the Trans-Siberian Railway.

114 **The destruction of the European Jews.**
Raul Hilberg. New York: Holmes & Meier, 1985. rev. ed. 3 vols.
maps. bibliog.

A comprehensive study based on original sources. For a brief selection of the
latter in translation, see *Documents of Destruction: Germany and Jewry, 1933-
1945*, edited with commentary by Raul Hilberg (Chicago: Quadrangle Books,
1971). For an extensive collection, see the contemporary records, compiled from
the Nürnberg Trial files and other records at the U.S. National Archives,
published in facsimile as *The Holocaust: Selected Documents* in 18 vols., edited by
John Mendelsohn (N.Y.: Garland, 1982), with individual volumes focussing on
topics such as the Crystal Night Pogrom (vol. 3), the medical experiments
(vol. 9), and the extermination camps (vol. 12, with an introduction by Henry
Friedlander).

115 **World War II policy and strategy: selected documents with commentary.**
Hans-Adolf Jacobsen and Arthur L. Smith, Jr.   Santa Barbara,
Calif.: Clio Books, 1979. 505p. maps.

Lucid, well-structured account of the war in the form of extensive documentation
interwoven with narrative commentary. See also *World War II German Military
Studies*, edited by Donald S. Detwiler with Charles B. Burdick and Jürgen
Rohwer, associate editors, 24 vols. (N.Y.: Garland, 1979), a collection of special
reports on the Second World War prepared under the aegis of the U.S. Army by
former officers of the *Wehrmacht* (Armed Forces) under the leadership of the
former chief of staff of the German Army, General Franz Halder. Vol. 1 is a
detailed introduction and guide not only to the 213 English manuscripts published
in facsimile, but to the entire series of over 2,500 studies on file in the U.S.
National Archives. In vols. 7-11 are drafts in English of the official German War
Diary of the High Command of the Armed Forces that were used in preparing the
German edition published in the 1960s.

116 **German foreign policy, 1918-1945: a guide to research and research
materials.**
Compiled and edited by Christoph M. Kimmich.   Wilmington,
Del.: Scholarly Resources, Inc., 1981. 293p. (Guides to European
Diplomatic History).

Basic bibliography, information about relevant archives, libraries, research
institutions, and reference resources, including major archival publications that
have made large bodies of German source materials widely available in English
translation: the joint Anglo-American edition of *Documents on German Foreign
Policy, 1918-1945*, Series C (1933-1937), 6 vols., and Series D (1937-1941),
13 vols. (Washington, D.C.: U.S. Govt. Printing Office; London: H.M.
Stationery Office, 1949-1983); the record of the proceedings of *The Trial of the
Major War Criminals before the International Military Tribunal, Nuremberg,
14 November 1945 – 1 October 1946*, 42 vols. (Nuremberg, 1947-1949), with
companion documentation issued by the Office of the U.S. Chief of Counsel as
Nazi Conspiracy and Aggression, 10 vols. (Washington, D.C.: U.S. Govt.
Printing Office, 1946-48); and records of the twelve U.S. Military Tribunal Trials,
issued by the Department of the Army, *Trials of War Criminals before the
Nuernberg Military Tribunals under Control Council Law No. 10, October
1946 – April 1949*, 15 vols. (Washington, D.C.: U.S. Govt. Printing Office, 1949-
1953).

Contemporary Germany (since 1945)

117 **West Germany: a contemporary history.**
Michael Balfour. London & Canberra: Croom Helm, 1982. 307p.
map. bibliog.
Extensively revised and updated version of the history of the Federal Republic of
Germany published in 1968 in Praeger's 'Nations of the Modern World' series,
with an annex on the West German voting system and a statistical appendix with
twenty tables of data.

118 **Americans as proconsuls: United States military government in
Germany and Japan, 1944-1952.**
Edited by Robert Wolfe. Carbondale and Edwardsville: Southern
Illinois University Press, 1984. 563p. bibliog. (Proceedings of a
conference in Washington, D.C., 20-21 May 1977).
Reflections on the occupation of Germany by Lucius Clay and John J. McCloy,
extensively annotated scholarly papers, and a record of the discussion by
conference participants, many of them also former occupation officials. The
volume includes a listing of relevant archival holdings at the U.S. National
Archives in Washington, D.C., and the Public Record Office in London.

119 **The death and life of Germany: an account of the American
occupation.**
Eugene Davidson. New York: Alfred A. Knopf, 1959. 422p.
bibliog.
A standard account, from wartime planning before 1945 to the restoration of
sovereignty in 1955, based on intimate knowledge of the subject, the records, and
interviews with many who were responsibly involved. For more detailed
treatment of the U.S. military occupation prior to the establishment of the
Federal Republic of Germany, see John Gimbel's *The American Occupation of
Germany: Politics and the Military, 1945-1949* (Stanford, Calif.: Stanford Univ.
Press, 1968). The occupation of Germany as a whole is covered in *Documents on
Germany under Occupation, 1945-1954*, selected and edited by Beate Ruhm von
Oppen, with a preface by Alan Bullock (London and N.Y.: Oxford Univ. Press,
1955). Issued under the auspices of the Royal Institute of International Affairs in
London, Ruhm von Oppen's 660-page volume includes extensive documentation
on Four-Power negotiations; agreements and disagreements on occupation policy;
Control Council laws and directives; landmark statements (such as the speech on
6 September 1946 in Stuttgart by Secretary of State Byrnes on U.S. policy toward
Germany); and agreements with the German authorities, culminating in the Paris
Accords of 23 October 1954, bringing about the end of the occupation of West
Germany by the three Western Powers. See also United States Department of
State, *Documents on Germany 1944-1985* (Washington, D.C.: U.S. Government

Printing Office, 1985), a 1,421-page compendium presenting an authoritative documentary record of U.S. foreign policy with respect to Germany from World War II to mid-1985.

120 **Winds of history: the German years of Lucius DuBignon Clay.**
John H. Backer. Foreword by John J. McCloy. New York: Van Nostrand Reinhold, 1983. 323p. bibliog.

Account of Clay's extraordinary contribution to improvisation as well as implementation of U.S. policy in postwar West Germany and Berlin, written by a former U.S. military government official during the occupation period, author also of *Priming the German Economy: American Occupational Policies, 1945-1948* and *The Decision to Divide Germany: American Foreign Policy in Transition* (Durham, N.C.: Duke Univ. Press, 1971 and 1978, resp.). As U.S. Commander in Chief in Europe and Military Governor of Germany, Clay played a decisive role in bringing about what at the time amounted to a drastic reversal of American policy toward Germany and in laying the foundations for the establishment of a democratic West German republic. What emerges from Backer's account far more clearly than from Clay's politic memoirs published soon after his retirement (*Decision in Germany*, Garden City, N.Y.: Doubleday, 1950) or from *The Papers of General Lucius D. Clay: Germany 1945-1949* (ed. J. E. Smith, 2 vols., Bloomington: Indiana Univ. Press, 1974), is that however difficult his relations may have been with the Russians and French, the greatest challenge he faced in Germany was the combination of opposition, inertia, and lack of understanding with which he was confronted in Washington – where his views prevailed less because of his will to impose them than because it was no secret that he would insist on his well-deserved and long-deferred retirement if called upon to implement policy that he could not in good faith support.

121 **The French in Germany, 1945-1949.**
F. Roy Willis. Stanford, Calif.: Stanford University Press, 1962. 308p. map. bibliog. (Stanford Studies in History, Economics, and Political Science, XXIII).

An extensively documented history of France's role in the occupation of postwar Germany in the context of French relations with the other occupying powers and the emerging West German state, showing how French policy fostered the two major aims of national security and economic exploitation without preventing achievement of the third, Franco-German *rapprochement*. See also F. Roy Willis, *France, Germany, and the New Europe, 1945-1967*, rev. & exp. ed. (Stanford, Calif.: Stanford Univ. Press; London: Oxford Univ. Press, 1968).

122 **The founding of the Federal Republic of Germany.**
John Ford Golay. Chicago & London: University of Chicago Press, 1958. 299p. bibliog.

Detailed account of the drafting in 1948-49 of the Basic Law of the Federal Republic (its constitution) by the former U.S. Secretary of the Allied High Commission in Bonn. For a more general treatment, see Peter H. Merkl, *The Origin of the West German Republic* (N.Y.: Oxford Univ. Press, 1963). Merkl describes the political setting and historical context; Golay focusses on the work of the Parliamentary Council that drafted the constitution under the frequently solicitous tutelage of the Western Powers. Both books include the Basic Law in translation.

123 Memoirs, 1945-53.
Konrad Adenauer. Translated by Beate Ruhm von Oppen.
Chicago: Henry Regnery Co., 1966. 478p.

The memoirs of the founding chancellor of the Federal Republic of Germany, covering the period from his release from Gestapo imprisonment late in 1944 to his first state visit to Washington in spring 1953, translated by Ruhm von Oppen from *Erinnerungen 1945-1953* (Stuttgart: Deutsche Verlags-Anstalt, 1965). The subsequent German volumes (*not* published in English translation, creative bibliographical citations notwithstanding) covered 1953-55 (Stuttgart, 1966), 1955-59 (Stuttgart, 1967), and, as uncompleted posthumous 'Fragments,' 1959-1963 (Stuttgart, 1968). Anneliese Poppinga, who had joined Adenauer's staff during his chancellorship and had stayed on with him, covered the retirement years, on which he had planned a final volume, in her own memoirs of Adenauer, *Meine Erinnerungen an Konrad Adenauer* (Stuttgart: Deutsche Verlags-Anstalt, 1970). For an introduction, with many photos, see the essays in *Konrad Adenauer* by Terence Prittie, Horst Osterheld, and François Seydoux (Stuttgart: Verlag Bonn Aktuell, 1983).

124 People and politics: the years 1960-1975.
Willy Brandt. Translated by J. Maxwell Brownjohn. Boston and Toronto: Little, Brown, 1976. 524p.

Brandt's memoirs, originally published as *Begegnungen und Einsichten* ['Encounters and Insights'] (Hamburg: Hoffmann & Campe Verlag, 1976), open with the building of the Berlin Wall in 1961, when he was mayor of the beleaguered city, and close with his assessment of the situation of Germany and the world in the mid-70s, following his resignation from the chancellorship after having set the course of West Germany's *Ostpolitik*. For a uniquely well-informed account of the origins and course of his chancellorship, see Arnulf Baring, in collaboration with Manfred Görtemaker, *Machtwechsel: die Ära Brandt-Scheel* ['Change of Power: The Brandt-Scheel Era'] (Stuttgart: Deutsche Verlags-Anstalt, 1982).

125 The velvet chancellors: a history of post-war Germany.
Terence Prittie. London: Frederick Muller Limited, 1979. 286p.
2 maps. bibliog.

Biographically-oriented survey by prominent British journalist, focussing on the first five chancellors of the Federal Republic (Konrad Adenauer, 1949-1963, Ludwig Erhard, 1963-66, Kurt Georg Kiesinger, 1966-69, Willy Brandt, 1969-74, and Helmut Schmidt, 1974-1982). See also Terence Prittie's biographies of *Adenauer* (London: Stacey, 1972) and *Willy Brandt* (N.Y.: Schocken, 1974) and Jonathan Carr's of *Helmut Schmidt* (N.Y.: St. Martin's Press, 1985).

126 **Erinnerungen.** (Memoirs.)
Carlo Schmid.   Berne and Munich: Scherz Verlag, 1979. 868p.
(Gesammelte Werke, Bd. 3).

A leading representative of the southwest German liberal democratic tradition, Carlo Schmid was chairman first of the West German Parliamentary Council committee that drafted the constitution and then, for many years, of the foreign affairs committee of the parliament in Bonn. His autobiography affords valuable insight into the West German political process.

Population

127   The decline of fertility in Germany, 1871-1939.
   John E. Knodel.   Princeton, N.J.: Princeton University Press,
   1974. 306p. maps. bibliog.

The second in a series of country studies on the decline of European fertility,
conducted by the Office of Population Research, Princeton University, with the
support of the National Institutes of Health, focusses on the decline of fertility in
Germany as an aspect of Germany's modernization – the transition in fertility
from high, pre-modern levels, to the lower levels characteristic of more developed
societies. It describes the decline in detail and analyzes its components within the
context of the social, economic, and demographic conditions prevailing in
Germany during this period. The monograph includes numerous clear maps,
tables, and figures, in addition to a bibliography citing official statistical sources,
books, and articles.

**128   The German exodus: a selective study on the post-World War II
   expulsion of German populations and its effects.**
   G. C. Paikert.   The Hague: Martinus Nijhoff, 1962. 97p. 2 maps.
   bibliog. (Publications of the Research Group for European
   Migration Problems, XII).

Introduction to the problem of the expulsion from the East and resettlement in
the Federal Republic of well over nine million. On the role of the United States
and the United Kingdom in the expulsion of Germans from Eastern and Central
Europe, see the extensively annotated study by Alfred M. de Zayas, *Nemesis at
Potsdam: The Anglo-Americans and the Expulsion of the Germans – Background,
Execution, Consequences*, with a foreword by Robert Murphy, 2nd ed. (London:
Routledge & Kegan Paul, 1979), published in Germany as *Die Anglo-Amerikaner
und die Vertreibung der Deutschen. Vorgeschichte, Verlauf, Folgen*, 3rd ed.
(Munich: Beck, 1978). See also the 264-page illustrated volume commemorating
the thirtieth anniversary of the beginning of the expulsion, at the end of the

Population

Second World War, issued by the expellees' organization in the prosperous southwest German state of Baden-Württemberg, Sepp Schwarz, ed., *Drei Jahrzehnte. Die Heimatvertriebenen in Baden-Württemberg. Berichte – Dokumente – Bilder* ['Three Decades – The Expellees in Baden-Württemberg: Reports, Documents, Pictures') (Stuttgart: Bund der Vertriebenen, 1975).

129 **Population change and social planning: social and economic implications of the recent decline in fertility in the United Kingdom and the Federal Republic of Germany.**
Edited by David Eversley and Wolfgang Köllmann, with contributions by Adelheid Gräfin zu Castell Rüdenhausen, John F. Ermisch, Peter Marschalck, and Elizabeth Overton. London: Edward Arnold (Publishers), 1982. 485p. bibliog.

Two teams, one working in the United Kingdom, the other in the Federal Republic, conducted the research for this book. The decline in fertility that was continuous from about 1964 turned out to have been halted in 1977. The volume includes two-part chapters (the first part on the United Kingdom, the second on the Federal Republic) on 'Demographic Changes and Housing and Infrastructure Investment,' on 'Regional Development and Changed Demographic Conditions,' and, in conclusion, on '. . . the Policy Implications of Demographic Changes.' There are many tables and graphs. The three-part bibliography separately lists English-language publications, British statistical sources, and German-language publications (including statistical sources).

Minorities

130 **Diaspora: an inquiry into the contemporary Jewish world.**
Howard M. Sachar.   New York: Harper & Row, 1985. 539p.
map. bibliog.

Study by an authority on modern Jewish and Israeli history of the approximately
four and a half million Jews who now live outside Israel and North America. The
Jewish community in Germany, treated in the first chapter, was 564,000 strong in
1925; it was reduced by emigration and the Holocaust to fewer than 20,000 by the
beginning of the 1950s. In the course of the next decade, the Jewish population of
the Federal Republic more than doubled due to an influx of Holocaust survivors
from Eastern Europe. This had an enduring impact on the character of Jewish
communal life, which once had been dominated by cultivated, old-line German-
Jewish families. By the 1980s, the leadership in many communities was in the
hands of the East Europeans. See also Norbert Muhlen, *The Survivors: A Report
on the Jews in Germany Today*, introduction by Hans Kohn (N.Y.: Crowell,
1962); Anson Rabinbach and Jack D. Zipes, editors, *Germans and Jews: A
Contemporary Reappraisal* (N.Y.: Holmes & Meier, 1985); and Peter Sichrovsky,
Strangers in Their Own Land: Young Jews in Germany and Austria Today (N.Y.:
Basic Books, 1986), translated by Jean Steinberg from *Wir wissen nicht was
morgen wird, wir wissen wohl was gestern war. Junge Juden in Deutschland und
Österreich* ['We Don't Know What Will Happen Tomorrow, But We Know What
Happened Yesterday: Young Jews in Germany and Austria'] (Cologne:
Kiepenheuer & Witsch, 1985). See also, on the Jewish tradition in Germany, the
last several entries in the section on philosophy and religion.

Minorities

131 **The destiny of Europe's Gypsies.**
Donald Kenrick and Grattan Puxon. New York: Basic Books,
1972. 256p. bibliog. (The Columbus Centre Series: Studies in the
Dynamics of Persecution and Extermination).

This monograph provides a brief review of the periodic persecutions of the
Gypsies from their arrival in Europe during the Middle Ages until 1933; a
documented history of their fate during the next twelve years, which saw the
extermination of some 220,000 (almost a quarter of their estimated population in
1939); and a concluding account of the discrimination they have continued to
suffer in postwar Europe, including the Federal Republic of Germany. They are
no longer threatened with genocide, but 'the subtler pressures of forced
assimilation and neglect . . . threaten them with extinction as a separate people.'
For more detailed coverage of the Gypsies in contemporary West Germany, see
Tilman Zülch, ed., *In Auschwitz vergast, bis heute verfolgt. Zur Situation der
Roma (Zigeuner) in Deutschland und Europa* ['Gassed in Auschwitz, Persecuted
until Today: On the Situation of the Romany (Gypsies) in Germany and Europe']
(Reinbek bei Hamburg: Rowohlt, 1979), as well as Zülch's article, 'Sinti und
Roma in Deutschland: Geschichte einer verfolgten Minderheit' ['The Sinti and
Romany (i.e., Gypsies) in Germany: History of a Persecuted Minority'], *Aus
Politik und Zeitgeschichte* (supplement to the Bonn weekly *Das Parlament*),
30 Oct. 1982, pp. 27-45.

132 **Ausländer.** (Foreigners.)
Helga Herrmann. Bonn: Bundeszentrale für politische Bildung,
1984. 32p. bibliog. (Informationen zur Politischen Bildung
[Information for Political Education], no. 201).

Well-written, illustrated monograph on foreign labour (*Gastarbeiter* or 'guest
workers') in the Federal Republic; in September 1983, 4.53 million foreigners
constituted ca. 7.2% of the population. Published in a bimonthly series of
magazine-size texts, in readable, three-column format, with well-captioned
illustrations and good bibliographies, for complimentary dissemination to German
schools, by the Federal Centre for Political Education, a non-partisan,
independent government agency. Free copies are available on request from the
Bundeszentrale für politische Bildung, Berliner Freiheit 7, 5300 Bonn. See also
Claudia Koch-Arzberger, 'Politische Orientierungen von Ausländern in der
Bundesrepublik Deutschland' ['Political Orientation of Foreigners in the Federal
Republic of Germany'] in *Aus Politik und Zeitgeschichte* ['From Politics and
Contemporary History'], (pp. 31-45), the supplement to the 31 August 1985 issue
of the Bonn weekly *Das Parlament*, also issued by the Federal Centre for Political
Education, and Wilfried Röhrich, ed., *Vom Gastarbeiter zum Bürger. Ausländer
in der Bundesrepublik Deutschland* ['From Guest Worker to Citizen: Foreigners
in the Federal Republic of Germany'], Beiträge zur Sozialforschung, vol. 2
(Berlin: Duncker & Humblot, 1982), a ninety-four-page collection of papers
(partly annotated with bibliographical citations) on foreign workers in Germany,
focussing on various social, educational, and legal questions.

Overseas Populations

General

133 **Deutschland und Übersee. Der deutsche Handel mit den anderen
Kontinenten, insbesondere Afrika, von Karl V. bis zu
Bismarck – ein Beitrag zur Geschichte der Rivalität im
Wirtschaftsleben.** (Germany and overseas: German trade with the
other continents, especially Africa, from Charles V to
Bismarck – a contribution to the history of competition in
economic life.)
Percy Ernst Schramm.   Brunswick: Westermann, 1950. 639p.
4 maps. bibliog.
A history of German involvement in overseas trade, particularly in Africa, from
the sixteenth through the nineteenth centuries, by a Hamburg-born historian. See
also his social history focussing on the nineteenth-century commerce of his native
city, *Hamburg, Deutschland und die Welt* ['Hamburg, Germany, and the World']
(Munich: Callwey, 1943).

134 **The Germanic people in America.**
Victor Wolfgang von Hagen.   Norman: University of Oklahoma
Press, 1976. 404p. 13 maps. bibliog.
The translation of a heavily illustrated introduction to the German contribution to
the Americas – Latin America as well as the United States – from the sixteenth
century to the twentieth. The tone of the work is suggested by the title of the
German original, *Der Ruf der neuen Welt: Deutsche bauen Amerika* ['The Call of
the New World: Germans Build America'] (Munich: Droemer Knaur, 1970).
There is a detailed index.

135 **Germans in Chile: immigration and colonization, 1849-1914.**
George F. W. Young. New York: Center for Migration Studies,
1974. 234p. maps. bibliog.

Based on a doctoral dissertation, this is an extensively documented account of
German immigration and settlement in Chile, with particular attention to the role
of Germans in opening up and developing the southern provinces.

United States of America

136 **Americans from Germany: a study in cultural diversity.**
Robert Henry Billigmeier. Belmont, Calif.: Wadsworth, 1974.
189p. bibliog. (Minorities in American Life Series).

A concise, readable monograph surveying with sympathetic objectivity the
German element in the United States of America from the beginnings to the past
decade, annotated with extensive bibliographical references. See also La Vern J.
Rippley, *The German-Americans* (Boston: Twayne Publ., 1976), and, for a more
extensive, popular treatment, Richard O'Connor, *The German-Americans: An
Informal History* (Boston: Little, Brown, 1968).

137 **Americans from Germany.**
Gerard Wilk. Intro. by Berndt von Staden. Foreword by Henry
Reuss. New York: German Information Center, 1976. 81p.

A collection of over forty biographical sketches (several illustrated) of prominent
German-Americans. See also *They Came from Germany: The Stories of Famous
German-Americans* by Dieter Cunz (New York: Dodd, Mead, 1966), a collection
of essays addressed to the younger reader.

138 **Roots in the Rhineland: America's German heritage in three
hundred years of immigration, 1683-1983.**
Christine M. Totten. New York: German Information Center,
1983. 80p. bibliog.

This clearly written overview, with a concise bibliography and index, starts with
the first thirty-three of some seven million German immigrants.

139 **The German element in the United States with special reference to
its political, moral, social, and educational influence.**
Albert Bernhardt Faust. New York: The Steuben Society of
America, 1927. 1,321p. 14 maps. bibliog.

The most comprehensive work on Germans in America, by a professor of
German at Cornell, was published in two volumes in 1909 and reissued, eighteen
years later, with a 123-page appendix, in one-volume format. The first part is a
history from the first German in America – Tyrker, in the eleventh century – to
permanent settlements, and the role of the Germans in American wars during the

eighteenth and nineteenth centuries; the second part is an account of the contributions of the German element (including German-American women) to various sectors of American life. For a recent, concise history of German migration to America, see *The German Dimension of American History* by Joseph Wandel (Chicago: Nelson-Hall, 1979). The first part deals with German immigration by period, region, and special areas of endeavour, such as music and publishing; the second part recounts the role of German-Americans in U.S. military history; the third part briefly surveys German-Americans in science and education.

140   **The tragedy of German-America: the Germans in the United States of America during the nineteenth century – and after.**
John A. Hawgood.   New York and London: G. P. Putnam's Sons, 1940. 334p. bibliog.

An annotated study, by a British scholar, of attempts during the nineteenth century to establish new German states in North America and the subsequent effort, sustained until U.S. entry into World War I, to resist assimilation and preserve German language and culture. For regionally focussed accounts of German immigrants and their descendants in America, see Clyde Browning, *Amish in Illinois: Over One Hundred Years of the 'Old Order' Sect of Central Illinois* (Decatur, Ill.: by the author, 1971); *The Amanas Today: Seven Historic Iowa Villages* and *The Amanas Yesterday: Seven Communal Villages in Iowa – Historic Photographs, 1900/1932*, collected by Joan Liffring Zug (Amana, Iowa: The Amana Society, 1974 & 1975); Dieter Cunz, *The Maryland Germans: A History* (Princeton, N.J.: Princeton Univ. Press, 1948); David W. Detjen, *The Germans in Missouri, 1900-1918: Prohibition, Neutrality, and Assimilation* (Columbia: Univ. of Missouri Press, 1985); Frederick C. Luebke, *Immigrants and Politics: The Germans of Nebraska, 1880-1900* (Lincoln: Univ. of Nebraska Press, 1969); John Fredrick Nau, *The German People of New Orleans, 1850-1900* (Leiden: E. J. Brill, 1958); G. D. Bernheim, *History of the German Settlements and of the Lutheran Church in North and South Carolina* (Philadelphia: Lutheran Book Store, 1872; repr., Spartanburg, S.C.: The Reprint Co., 1972); Ralph Wood, ed., *The Pennsylvania Germans* (Princeton, N.J.: Princeton Univ. Press, 1942) and Fredric Klees, *The Pennsylvania Dutch* (N.Y.: Macmillan, 1950); Terry G. Jordan, *German Seed in Texas Soil: Immigrant Farmers in Nineteenth-Century Texas* (Austin and London: Univ. of Texas Press, 1966) and a volume of contemporary documentation in translation, compiled and edited by Chester W. and Ethel H. Geue, *A New Land Beckoned: German Immigration to Texas, 1844-1847*, new and enl. ed. (Waco, Tex.: Texian Press, 1972); and Herrmann Schuricht, *History of the German Element in Virginia*, 2 vols. (Baltimore, Md., 1898 & 1900; repr. [in one vol.], Baltimore: Genealogical Publ. Co., 1977).

141   **Life in two worlds: a biography of William Sihler.**
Lewis W. Spitz.   St. Louis, Mo., and London: Concordia Publishing House, 1968. 199p. bibliog.

Biography of a conservative Prussian churchman who emigrated to America in the mid-1800s and played an important role in the development of Lutheranism in America.

Overseas Populations. United States of America

142 **Carl Schurz: revolutionary and statesman – his life in personal and official documents with illustrations; Carl Schurz: Revolutionär und Staatsmann – sein Leben in Selbstzeugnissen, Bildern und Dokumenten.**
Edited by Rüdiger Wersich. Translated from German to English by Louis Bloom. Munich: Heinz Moos Verlag, 1979. 172p. maps. bibliog.

Copiously illustrated bilingual edition, with German and English texts in parallel columns, of extensive excerpts from the memoirs of Carl Schurz. See also *The Reminiscences of Carl Schurz*: vol. 1, *1829-1852*; vol. 2, *1852-1863*; vol. 3, *1863-1869* (N.Y.: McClure, 1907-1908). Vol. 3 includes 'A Sketch of Carl Schurz's Political Career, 1869 to 1906' by Frederic Bancroft and William A. Dunning (pp. 311-455). For a general account of the mid-nineteenth-century revolutionary German immigrants to America, of whom Schurz became the most prominent, see Carl Wittke, *Refugees of Revolution: The German Forty-Eighters in America* (Philadelphia: Univ. of Pennsylvania Press, 1952; repr., Westport, Conn.: Greenwood Press, 1970).

143 **States of belonging: German-American intellectuals and the First World War.**
Phyllis Keller. Cambridge, Mass., and London: Harvard University Press, 1979. 324p. bibliog.

Portraits of Harvard psychology professor Hugo Münsterberg and the writers George Sylvester Viereck and Hermann Hagedorn, and the traumatic impact of World War I, which the USA entered against Germany in 1917, on them.

144 **The Deutschtum of Nazi Germany and the United States.**
Arthur L. Smith, Jr. The Hague: Martinus Nijhoff, 1965. 172p. bibliog. (International Scholars Forum, 15).

A heavily documented monograph on the work of the German Foreign Institute (Deutsches Ausland-Institut) in Stuttgart to further the cause of 'Germandom' in the United States during the 1930s – an endeavour that led to a certain amount of support for German-American studies, but did not provide an effective vehicle for the dissemination of National Socialism in America.

145 **The Intellectual migration: Europe and America, 1930-1960.**
Edited by Donald Fleming and Bernard Bailyn. Cambridge, Mass.: Harvard University Press, 1969. 748p.

An expansion of the second volume of *Perspectives in American History*, an annual publication of the Charles Warren Center for Studies in American History at Harvard University, this is a collection of fourteen substantial essays or memoirs on the intellectual implications of the migration from Hitler's Europe to the United States of leading scholars and scientists in biology, physics, mathematics, psychology, sociology, history, architecture, art history, literary criticism, and philosophy – but not, as noted in the introduction, economics, political thought, theology, or music. The opening essay, 'Weimar Culture: the Outsider as Insider' by Peter Gay, was subsequently expanded and revised for publication as a separate volume (cited under Literature). There is a list of '300 Notable Émigrés,' with concise biographical data, including bibliographical listings, which are also cited in the useful comprehensive index with which the volume concludes.

146 **The legacy of the German refugee intellectuals.**
Edited by Robert Boyers. New York: Schocken Books, 1972.
307p. bibliog.
A reprint of the special Fall 1969 and Winter 1970 issue of the quarterly *Salmagundi*, a journal of the humanities and the social sciences, with a memoir 'On Being an Exile,' by Henry Pachter, former Dean of the New School for Social Research, and seventeen articles, including 'The Heritage of Socialist Humanism,' by George L. Mosse, and contributions on Bertolt Brecht and on Thomas Mann in America.

147 **Project Paperclip: German scientists and the Cold War.**
Clarence G. Lasby. New York: Atheneum, 1971. 338p. bibliog.
A carefully documented account, based on archival research, of a unique chapter in the history of German immigration to America: the American government's postwar recruitment, in competition with a corresponding Soviet effort, of Germans who had been involved in scientific research and development in Hitler's Third Reich.

148 **Germany and America: essays on problems of international relations and immigration.**
Edited by Hans L. Trefousse. New York: Brooklyn College Press; distr. by Columbia University Press, 1980. 247p. bibliog.
(Brooklyn College Studies on Society in Change, no. 21).
Proceedings of a scholarly conference, with authoritative, annotated papers on German-Americans from the eighteenth century to the 1930s and 1940s and on German-American relations.

Language

General

149 **The German language today: its patterns and background.**
W. E. Collinson.   London: Hutchinson University Library, 1968.
3rd ed. 185p. bibliog.
A standard introduction in a widely recognized series.

150 **A history of the German language, with special reference to the
cultural and social forces that shaped the standard literary
language.**
John T. Waterman.   Seattle and London: University of
Washington Press, 1966. 266p. 4 maps. bibliog.
An introduction for the English-speaking student of the German language with
consideration of cultural history and comparative philology, with brief excerpts
from selected German texts and an extensive bibliography of relevant works,
especially in English. See also the concise, scholarly text by W. B. Lockwood, *An
Informal History of the German Language with Chapters on Dutch and Afrikaans,
Frisian and Yiddish* (Cambridge: W. Heffer and Sons, 1965) and R. E. Keller's
649-page volume in 'The Great Languages' series, *The German Language*
(London and Boston: Faber and Faber, 1978).

151 **The German language.**
R. Priebsch and W. E. Collinson.   London: Faber & Faber, 1966.
6th ed. 496p. map. bibliog. (The Great Languages).
A comprehensive introduction to German philology with systematic exposition of
the development of the modern language, taking into account dialects as well as
the standard language. The volume includes a chapter on the history of German

52

handwriting, a map of German dialects, and select bibliographies at the end of several chapters. See also Friedrich Stroh, *Handbuch der Germanischen Philologie* ['Handbook of Germanic Philology'] (Berlin: Walter de Gruyter, 1952, repr. 1985).

152 German: a linguistic history to 1945.
C. J. Wells. Oxford: At the Clarendon Press, 1985. 591p. bibliog.

Presupposing a fair acquaintance with modern German on the part of his English reader, Wells treats 'the formal historical grammar of German in conjunction with the social and historical developments in the speech-community,' from the origins of the language to the end of World War II. Included are extensive annotations, appendices on the High German consonant shift and on early German monastery dialects, and a fifty-four-page general bibliography. See also Joseph Wright, *Grammar of the Gothic Language*, 2nd ed. (Oxford: At the Clarendon Press, 1954); Joseph Wright, *A Middle High German Primer*, 5th ed. (Oxford: At the Clarendon Press, 1955); Joseph Wright, *Historical German Grammar*, vol. 1, *Phonology, Word-Formation and Accidence* (Oxford: At the Clarendon Press, 1907, repr. 1966); and W. B. Lockwood, *Historical German Syntax* (Oxford: At the Clarendon Press, 1968). On the discussion about reforming German grammar, see *Das Ringen um eine neue deutsche Grammatik. Aufsätze aus drei Jahrzehnten (1929-1959)* ['The Struggle for a New German Grammar: Articles from Three Decades (1919-1959)'], ed. by Hugo Moser, Wege der Forschung, vol. 25 (Darmstadt: Wissenschaftliche Buchgesellschaft, 1965).

153 Siebs, Deutsche Aussprache. (Siebs, German pronunciation.)
[Theodor Siebs.] Edited by Helmut de Boor, Hugo Moser, and Christian Winkler. Berlin: Walter de Gruyter, 1969. 19th, rev. ed. 494p. bibliog.

A 160-page monograph, with bibliographical references, followed by a 326-page, double-column alphabetical listing of German words and their correct pronunciation (using a phonetic alphabet with diacritical marks). See also *Der Grosse Duden*, vol. 6, *Aussprachewörterbuch* ['The Large Duden,' vol. 6, 'Pronunciation Dictionary,'] ed. by Max Mangold et al. (Mannheim: Bibliographisches Institut, 1962), with a 732-page listing of words; *The Pronunciation of German*, by Peter MacCarthy (London: Oxford Univ. Press, 1975); and *German Intonation: An Outline*, by Anthony Fox (Oxford: At the Clarendon Press, 1984).

154 Deutsche Fach- und Wissenschaftssprache.
Bestandsaufnahme – Theorie – Geschichte. (Technical and scientific German: current situation, theory, and history.)
L. Drozd and W. Seibicke. Wiesbaden: Oscar Brandstetter Verlag, 1973. 207p. bibliog.

An extensively annotated, in itself technical study of technical and scientific German as a 'subsystem' of the natural language, with consideration of the relationship between technical and ordinary language, of terminology theory, word-formation, etc. Summary in German and, translated by Dr. J. B. Sykes, in English. Bibliography 'designed for readers who, as users of language, terminologists, students, interpreters or translators, are interested in the phenomenon of technical and scientific German and the techniques needed for its investigation.' Turning from technological to ideological jargon, see *Aus dem Wörterbuch des Unmenschen* ['From the Dictionary of the Nonhuman'], by Dolf Sternberger, Gerhard Storz, and W. E. Süskind (Munich: Deutscher Taschenbuch Verlag, 1962) for essays on linguistic aberrations of the Hitler period. *Sprache in der verwalteten Welt* ['Language in the Administered World'], by Karl Korn (Olten and Freiburg im Breisgau: Walter-Verlag, 1959), is a collection of wider-ranging critical essays, with an index of the terms discussed and a select bibliography.

155 **dtv-Atlas zur deutschen Sprache. Tafeln und Texte. Mit Mundartkarten.** (dtv-atlas of the German language: figures and text; maps on dialects.)
Werner König. Graphics by Hans-Joachim Paul. Munich: Deutscher Taschenbuch Verlag, 1978. 247p. maps. bibliog.

History, linguistic structure, and regional distribution of German and German dialects, elucidated and illustrated by numerous graphs, charts, and maps (showing, in three cases, for example, the variations used in different parts of Germany for the terms *headache*, *stomachache*, and *small*). Bibliography of close to 400 entries. Indexes of subjects and of names.

156 **Deutsche Sprichwörterkunde.** (A basic study of German proverbs.)
Friedrich Seiler. Munich: C. H. Beck'sche Verlagsbuchhandlung, 1967. Reprint of the 1922 edition. 457p.

The author explains what proverbs, folk sayings, etc., are, and discusses them from earliest times to his own in a long but well-structured monograph, citing them by the hundred in a text where they are readily recognized, having been set in italics. There is a single alphabetical listing of names and subjects, but only the most noteworthy proverbs and sayings. For a thoroughly indexed reference volume, comparable in scope and convenience to John Bartlett's *Familiar Quotations*, edited by E. M. Beck et al., 15th, rev. & enl. ed. (Boston: Little, Brown and Co., 1980), which has extensive quotations in translation from German, see Georg Büchmann, *Geflügelte Worte*, 32nd ed., completely rev. by Gunther Haupt and Winfried Hofmann (Berlin: Haude & Spenersche Verlagsbuchhandlung, 1972).

157 **Deutsche Namenkunde.** (German names.)
Adolf Bach. Heidelberg: Carl Winter, Universitätsverlag, 1952-56. 3 vols. maps. bibliog.

Definitive study of German names, with a comprehensive index.
Bd. I, 1 und 2: *Die deutschen Personennamen* (vol. I, 1 and 2: 'German Proper Names'). Heidelberg: Carl Winter, Universitätsverlag, 1952. 2nd, exp. ed. 331p. & 295p. In the two-part first volume of his major work on German names, Bach deals with personal or proper names, explaining, with many examples, the origins, development, character, and meaning of both given (first) and family names. There is a wealth of bibliographical references throughout the two books. The second concludes with a subject index. For a quick and easy reference to German family names, consult the 185-page alphabetical listing in Albert Heintze,

Die deutschen Familiennamen – geschichtlich, geographisch, sprachlich ['German Family Names – Historically, Geographically, Linguistically'], 3rd, rev. & exp. ed. (Halle a. S.: Verlag der Buchhandlung des Waisenhauses, 1908). See also the two volumes of Josef Karlmann Brechenmacher's *Etymologisches Wörterbuch der Deutschen Familiennamen* ['Etymological Dictionary of German Family Names'], 2nd ed. (Limburg: C. A. Starke-Verlag, 1957).

Bd. II, 1 und 2: *Die deutschen Ortsnamen* (vol. II, 1 and 2: 'German Place Names'). Heidelberg: Carl Winter, Universitätsverlag, 1953. 451p. & 615p. 75 maps. The two-part second volume of Bach's work on German names explains and documents the origins, development, and meaning of place names, with a concluding section briefly considering the relevance of German place-name research to work in other fields. Bach cites and often comments on pertinent literature throughout the two books. The second concludes with a subject index.

Bd. III: *Registerband* (vol. III: 'Index Volume'). Prepared by Dieter Berger. Foreword by Adolf Bach. Heidelberg: Carl Winter, Universitätsverlag, 1956. 457p. The comprehensive index begins with a twenty-two-page subject index, comprised of the listings (with additions) at the end of each of the first two volumes. This is followed by listings of all citations of proper or personal names and of place names.

158 Modern German dialects.

C. A. M. Noble. New York: Peter Lang, 1983. 200p. bibliog. (American University Studies, series I: Germanic Languages and Literatures, vol. 15).

Introductory account of the nature, history, geography, and, to a lesser degree, the grammar of the dialects of the modern German language, with numerous maps, tables, and diagrams (pp. 110-153) as well as written dialect samples (pp. 157-191). See also R. E. Keller, *German Dialects: Phonology and Morphology with Selected Texts* (Manchester: Manchester Univ. Press, 1961) and Ernst Schwarz, *Die deutschen Mundarten* (Göttingen: Vandenhoeck & Ruprecht, 1950). For a field study with a bibliography of relevant literature, including articles in English, see Thomas L. Keller, *The City Dialect of Regensburg*, Hamburger phonetische Beiträge, vol. 19 (Hamburg: Buske Verlag, 1976). Wolfgang Bethge's and Gunther M. Bonnin's *Proben deutscher Mundarten* ['Samples of German Dialects'] (Tübingen: Max Niemeyer Verlag, 1969) provides thirty-two samples of the spoken dialect as recorded in the field, from Schleswig to the Bavarian Forest, with the phonetic transcription and its high German 'translation' printed on facing pages. On a new form of dialect that has emerged in West Germany, see the study that grew out of the Heidelberg Research Project on 'Pidgin-German,' directed by Wolfgang Klein, *Sprache und Kommunikation ausländischer Arbeiter. Analysen, Berichte, Materialien* ['Language and Communication of Foreign Workers: Analysis, Reports, Materials'] (Kronberg/Taunus: Scriptor Verlag, 1975).

159 **The German language in America: a symposium.**
Edited with an introduction by Glenn G. Gilbert. Austin and
London: University of Texas Press for the Department of
Germanic Languages of the University of Texas at Austin, 1971.
217p. 3 maps. bibliog.

Proceedings of a conference at the University of Texas at Austin in 1968, with
papers and discussions on topics including the dialectology of American Colonial
German, Pennsylvania German folklore research, German in Wisconsin and in
Virginia and West Virginia, and the sociolinguistic role of German in American
society. Nineteen-page bibliography.

160 **Studien zum Einfluss der englischen Sprache auf das Deutsche.**
(Studies on the influence of the English language on German.)
Edited by Wolfgang Viereck. Tübingen: Gunter Narr Verlag,
1980. 323p. bibliog. (Tübinger Beiträge zur Linguistik, 132).

A paper in English on 'American English post-1960 Neologisms in Contemporary
German,' and eight German papers on topics such as Anglicisms in radio
advertising, German pronunciation of Anglo-Americanisms, and understanding
and usage of Anglicisms. Some of the contributions have bibliographies.

Dictionaries

161 **Deutsches Wörterbuch. Mit einem 'Lexikon der deutschen
Sprachlehre.'** (German dictionary with a 'lexicon of German
grammar.')
Gerhard Wahrig et al. [n.p.] Mosaik Verlag; Lexikothek Verlag,
1980/1984. 2nd rev. ed. 4,358 columns. bibliog.

The second edition of a relatively comprehensive dictionary developed with the
use of a computerized data bank, comparable in scope to an American collegiate
dictionary or the *Concise Oxford Dictionary*, prefaced by a 93-page guide to
German grammar. For the pocket edition, see *dtv-Wörterbuch der deutschen
Sprache* ['dtv Dictionary of the German Language'], edited by Gerhard Wahrig et
al. (Munich: Deutscher Taschenbuch Verlag, 1978). See also *Der Sprach-
brockhaus. Deutsches Bildwörterbuch* ['The Language Brockhaus: Pictorial
German Dictionary'], 8th, rev. and exp. ed. (Wiesbaden: F. A. Brockhaus, 1979),
which is comparable in scope to the Wahrig dictionary, but has over 500 sets of
line drawings illustrating the use of some 15,000 terms, such as 'steering column'
and 'hub cap' or 'wheel cover' on interior and exterior sketches of a car. And
there is now a paperback edition of the monumental multi-volume dictionary
begun by the Brothers Grimm with the publication, in 1854, of their first volume,
from 'A' to 'Biermolke,' but not completed until long after the Second World
War: *Deutsches Wörterbuch* ['German Dictionary'] by Jacob and Wilhelm Grimm
et al., 33 vols. (Munich: Deutscher Taschenbuch Verlag, 1984).

56

162 **Langenscheidt's New College German Dictionary:**
German-English/English-German.
Heinz Messinger and Werner Rüdenberg. Berlin, Munich,
Vienna, and Zurich: Langenscheidt, 1978. 1,416p.

The German-English part is a 1973 revision of Langenscheidt's *Handwörterbuch*;
the English-German part, dated 1978, is based on the encyclopaedic Muret-
Sanders dictionary, with particular attention to modern terms and colloquial
usage. Both parts include tables of weights and measures and lists of
abbreviations and of proper names. See also the *Brockhaus Bildwörterbuch*
Englisch-Deutsch/Deutsch-Englisch ['The Brockhaus Pictorial Dictionary,
English-German/German-English'], edited by Will Heraucourt, Helmut Motekat,
et al., 7th ed. (Wiesbaden: F. A. Brockhaus, 1976), with hundreds of line
drawings illustrating the meanings of thousands of terms.

163 **The pocket Oxford German dictionary.**
German-English compiled by M. L. Barker and H. Homeyer;
English-German compiled by C. T. Carr. Oxford: At the
Clarendon Press, 1962. 2nd ed. 448 and 222p.

Current vocabulary of daily life, presented in 'a small but scholarly volume' that
can be recommended for precision and scope to the English-speaking reader of
German. Each part has a list of names as an appendix; the considerably longer
German-English part includes also a synopsis of German grammar, a list of strong
and irregular verbs, an appendix with German abbreviations, and an appendix on
German weights, measures, and money.

164 **Wörterbuch Musik: englisch-deutsch, deutsch-englisch – Dictionary**
of terms in music: English-German, German-English.
Edited by Horst Leuchtmann. Munich: K. G. Sauer Verlag,
1981. 3rd enlarged ed. 560p.

The 516-page dictionary section is followed by an appendix that includes diagrams
of musical instruments, examples of change-ringing methods, and an alphabetical
list of titles of musical works.

165 **The compact dictionary of exact science and technology: English-**
German – Compact Wörterbuch der exakten Naturwissenschaften
und der Technik: Englisch-Deutsch.
Antonín Kučera. Wiesbaden: Oscar Brandstetter, 1980. 571p.
bibliog.

Included are a detailed bibliography broken down by subject areas, two essays on
standards in the English-speaking Anglo-American countries, and a list of Nobel
Prize winners. (The companion volume is listed in the following entry.) See also
the *English-German Technical and Engineering Dictionary* by Louis De Vries and
Theo M. Herrmann, 2nd ed., completely rev. and enl. (N.Y.: McGraw-Hill;
Wiesbaden: Oscar Brandstetter, 1967).

166 **Compact Wörterbuch der exakten Naturwissenschaften und der Technik: Deutsch-Englisch – The compact dictionary of exact science and technology: German-English.**
Antonín Kučera. Wiesbaden: Oscar Brandstetter, 1982. 825p.

Printed on yellow paper, like its companion volume (cited in the foregoing entry), this more voluminous dictionary includes an essay in German on Patent and Trade Mark Law in the German-speaking countries and an essay in English on such law in the U.K. and the U.S.A. See also the *German-English Technical and Engineering Dictionary*, by Louis De Vries and Theo M. Herrmann, 2nd ed., completely rev. and enl. (N.Y.: McGraw-Hill; Wiesbaden: Oscar Brandstetter, 1966).

167 **The German businessmate.**
Compiled by LEXUS with Nicole Marin. Lincolnwood, Ill.: Passport Books, National Textbook Co., 1986. 175p.

A pocket book for the English-speaking business traveller in Germany, with potentially useful words and phrases, and their translations, in a single A-Z list. A supplement to a general dictionary rather than a substitute.

Philosophy and Religion

Surveys of philosophy in Germany

168 **The German tradition in philosophy.**
Claud Sutton. London: Weidenfeld and Nicolson; New York:
Crane, Russak & Company, 1974. 206p. bibliog.
Valedictory work of a British philosopher written to bridge (a) the gap between
university departments of philosophy and departments of language and literature,
(b) the gap between the specialized 'subjects' or fields of philosophy, such as
logic, theory of knowledge, ethics, political philosophy, etc. He sees philosophy,
in a broader sense, as needed to bring together our ways of thinking about
knowledge, including belief, with our ways of thinking about social action,
including communication. This broader conception of philosophy, he sets out to
show in his readable book, is 'a thread running through the German tradition,
from Kant to Habermas.' The bibliography lists English translations and
paraphrases as well as German philosophical works. For a classic survey, with
German philosophers treated in a general context, see Wilhelm Windelband, *A
History of Philosophy*, 2nd, rev. and enl. ed. (N.Y.: Macmillan, 1901; repr., 2
vols., N.Y.: Harper Torchbooks, 1958), transl. by James H. Tufts from
Geschichte der Philosophie, 2nd, rev. and enl. ed. (Tübingen and Leipzig: Mohr
[Siebeck], 1900). Windelband provides detailed treatment of German philosophy
to the mid-nineteenth century in *Die Geschichte der neueren Philosophie in ihrem
Zusammenhange mit der allgemeinen Kultur und den besonderen Wissenschaften*
['The History of Modern Philosophy in Connection with the General Culture and
the Particular Sciences'], vol. 1, *Von der Renaissance bis Kant* ['From the
Renaissance to Kant'], vol. 2, *Von Kant bis Hegel und Herbart – Die Blütezeit der
deutschen Philosophie* ['From Kant to Hegel and Herbart – The Flowering of
German Philosophy'], 5th, rev. ed. (Leipzig: Breitkopf & Härtel, 1911).

Philosophy and Religion. Surveys of philosophy in Germany

169 **West Germany and Austria.**
Hans M. Baumgartner. In: *Handbook of world philosophy:
contemporary developments since 1945.* Edited by John R. Burr.
Westport, Conn.: Greenwood Press, 1980, p. 191-214, incl.
bibliog.
Useful overview, translated by Lewis W. Tusken from Hans Michael
Baumgartner and Hans-Martin Sass, *Philosophie in Deutschland 1945-1975.
Standpunkte, Entwicklungen, Literatur* ['Philosophy in Germany 1945-1975:
Standpoints, Developments, Literature'] (Meisenheim: Verlag Anton Hain,
1978), though the fairly extensive bibliography does not note available English
translations of the German works cited. On West German philosophy since 1945
see also Jürgen Habermas, *Philosophical-Political Profiles* (Cambridge, Mass.:
MIT Press, 1983), translated, with an introductory essay, by Frederick G.
Lawrence, from *Philosophisch-politische Profile*, 3rd, exp. ed. (Frankfurt am
Main: Suhrkamp, 1981), with two essays, 'Does Philosophy Still Have a Purpose?'
(1971) and 'The German Idealism of the Jewish Philosophers' (1961), and profiles
of Karl Jaspers, Martin Heidegger, Ernst Bloch, Karl Löwith, Theodor Adorno,
Arnold Gehlen, Walter Benjamin, Herbert Marcuse, Hannah Arendt, Hans-
Georg Gadamer, and Gershom Scholem. The specialist may wish to consult the
much longer German original for Habermas' selections on the philosophical
anthropologists Alexander Mitscherlich and Helmuth Plessner, his incisive,
constructive review essay on Fritz K. Ringer's *The Decline of the German
Mandarins: The German Academic Community, 1890-1933* (Cambridge, Mass.:
Harvard Univ. Press, 1969), etc., but the English reader will be well served by the
well-crafted *Philosophical-Political Profiles* (with annotations citing translations),
which should be more useful to interested laymen and scholars working in other
fields than a complete translation would have been.

170 **Main currents in contemporary German, British, and American
philosophy.**
Wolfgang Stegmüller. Translated by Albert E. Blumberg.
Dordrecht, Holland: D. Reidel Publ. Co., 1969. 567p. bibliog.
Translated from *Hauptströmungen der Gegenwartsphilosophie. Eine kritische
Einführung* ['Main Currents in Contemporary Philosophy: A Critical Introduction'], 4th, exp. ed. (Stuttgart: Kröner, 1969), an introduction to the most
significant trends of the present century. In the bulk of the work, Stegmüller
presents in detail one outstanding representative of each major trend: Franz
Brentano (the philosophy of self-evidence); Edmund Husserl (methodological
phenomenology); Max Scheler (applied phenomenology); Martin Heidegger
(existential ontology); Karl Jaspers (the philosophy of existence); Nicolai
Hartmann (critical realism); and Rudolf Carnap and the Vienna Circle (modern
empiricism). He abandons this format in the last two chapters, 'Foundational
Studies and Contemporary Analytic Philosophy' and 'Ludwig Wittgenstein.'
They are followed by an eleven-page appendix on Noam Chomsky's theory of
language. Philosophies of language are treated extensively in the first chapter of
the (untranslated) continuation of Stegmüller's work, *Hauptströmungen der
Gegenwartsphilosophie. Eine kritische Einführung*, vol. 2 (Stuttgart: Kröner,
1975). Rüdiger Bubner's concise, scholarly *Modern German Philosophy*
(Cambridge: Cambridge Univ. Press, 1981) is a carefully structured series of

essays on the three main currents of twentieth-century German philosophy: phenomenology and hermeneutics; philosophy of language and theory of science; and dialectic and philosophy of practice. See also Ludwig Landgrebe's influential postwar *Philosophie der Gegenwart* ['Contemporary Philosophy'] (Bonn: Athenäum, 1952) and Herbert Albrecht's 427-page handbook, *Deutsche Philosophie heute. Probleme, Texte, Denker* ['German Philosophy Today: Problems, Texts, Thinkers'] (Bremen: Carl Schünemann Verlag, 1969), with over 200 pages of key excerpts from twentieth-century German philosophical works, a glossary of technical terms, and an alphabetical, bio-bibliographical listing of about a hundred philosophers.

171 **Philosophical understanding and religious truth.**
Erich Frank. New York: Oxford University Press, 1945. 209p.

In a series of lectures, a former Marburg professor builds a bridge between philosophy and theology. The text – on the nature of man, the existence of God, creation and time, truth and imagination, history and destiny, and letter and spirit – provides a generally understandable explanation of the rational limits of modern scientific thinking and philosophical understanding. The unusually extensive backnotes are both bibliographical and explanatory; they cite and discuss the literature, introducing and defining questions and problems that would have overburdened the lucid text. The basic text may therefore be recommended as an introduction to fundamental issues pursued in the notes and in the works cited there.

172 **Philosophie der Technik. Die geistige Entwicklung der Menschheit von den Anfängen bis zur Gegenwart.** (Philosophy and technology: the intellectual development of mankind from the beginnings to the present.)
Kurt Schilling. Herford: Maximilian-Verlag Kurt Schober, 1968. 244p. bibliog.

A systematic investigation, by a professor of philosophy at Munich University, of the increasing importance to mankind, from the Stone Age to the cybernetic revolution, of tools, techniques, and technology. Though not focussed on Germany, the essay is (readably) written from a German perspective, and the wide-ranging bibliography cites a wealth of literature dealing with various aspects of German science and technology, past and present.

Individual philosophers and movements

173 **Philosophical papers and letters: a selection**
Gottfried Wilhelm Leibniz. Translated and edited, with an
introducton by Leroy E. Loemker. Chicago: University of
Chicago Press, 1956. 2 vols. bibliog.

Extensive, annotated selections, in English translation, from the writings of
Leibniz (1636-1716), the first great German philosopher of the Enlightenment,
with a 107-page biographical introduction and a bibliography. See also *New
Essays on Human Understanding*, translated and edited by Peter Remnant and
Jonathan Bennett (Cambridge: Cambridge Univ. Press, 1981), and, for works on
Leibniz' political philosophy and a select, annotated bibliography, *The Political
Writings of Leibniz*, translated and edited, with an introduction and notes, by
Patrick Riley (Cambridge: At the University Press, 1972). In 'The Library of
Liberal Arts,' there is a convenient introduction to Leibniz: *Monadology and
Other Philosophical Essays*, transl. by Paul Schrecker and Anne Martin
Schrecker, with an introduction and notes by Paul Schrecker (Indianapolis:
Bobbs-Merrill, 1965). In German, see 'Leibniz und sein Zeitalter [Leibniz and
His Age]' in Wilhelm Dilthey, *Gesammelte Schriften* ['Collected Works'], vol. 3
(Stuttgart: B. G. Teubner; Göttingen: Vandenhoeck & Ruprecht, 1959).

174 **Kant's life and thought.**
Ernst Cassirer. Translated by James Haden. Introduction by
Stephan Körner. New Haven, Conn.: Yale University Press,
1981. 429p.

Translated from *Kants Leben und Lehre* ['Kant's Life and Teachings'] (Berlin:
Bruno Cassirer, 1918), originally published as the final volume of *Immanuel Kants
Werke* ['Immanuel Kant's Works'], ed. by Ernst Cassirer et al., 11 vols. (Berlin:
Bruno Cassirer, 1912-1922); the 'Note on the Translation' lists the English
translations of Kant's major works used for quotations in the text. William James
Booth, in *Interpreting the World: Kant's Philosophy of History and Politics*
(Toronto: Univ. of Toronto Press, 1986), seeks to explain the nature and relation
of Kant's two revolutions in thought: the first and negative one, which showed the
limits of reason; and the second, positive one, which grew out of the first and
showed the ability of reason to make sense of nature and to create moral law.
Immanuel Kant's Critique of Pure Reason, corrected ed. (London: Macmillan;
N.Y.: St. Martin's Press, 1933; repr., 1963), was translated by Norman Kemp
Smith from Immanuel Kant, *Kritik der reinen Vernunft*, 2nd, here and there [*sic*]
rev. ed. (Riga: Johann Friedrich Hartknoch, 1787). Immanuel Kant, *Critique of
Practical Reason and Other Writings in Moral Philosophy* (Chicago: Univ. of
Chicago Press, 1949; repr., N.Y.: Garland, 1976) was translated, and edited with
an introduction, by Lewis White Beck largely from the texts in Cassirer's edition
cited above; see also the separate publication of one of Kant's most influential
works (included in Beck's volume), *The Moral Law: Kant's 'Groundwork of the
Metaphysic of Morals'*, translated and analysed by H. J. Paton (London:
Hutchinson, 1948; N.Y.: Barnes & Noble, 1967). For a concise, copiously

Philosophy and Religion. Individual philosophers and movements

illustrated biography of Kant, with extracts from his writings, a chronology of his life, and an extensive bibliography, see Uwe Schultz, *Immanuel Kant in Selbstzeugnissen und Bilddokumenten* ['Immanuel Kant in His Testimony and Pictorial Documents'], Rowohlt's Monographs, no. 101 (Reinbek bei Hamburg: Rowohlt, 1965).

175 **The philosophy of Hegel.**
[G. W. F. Hegel.] Edited with an introduction and notes by Carl J. Friedrich. Translated by the editor and others. New York: Random House, Modern Library, 1953. 552p. bibliog.

A broad selection of the writings of Georg Wilhelm Friedrich Hegel, with a fifty-seven-page introductory essay on his life and works. See also Herbert Marcuse, *Reason and Revolution: Hegel and the Rise of Social Theory*, with a new preface, 'A Note on Dialectic,' by the author (Boston: Beacon Press, 1960), and Walter Kaufmann's *Hegel: Reinterpretation, Texts, and Commentary* (N.Y.: Doubleday, 1965), reprinted as two paperbacks: *Hegel: A Reinterpretation* (N.Y.: Anchor Books, 1966), with an extensive, partially annotated bibliography; and *Hegel: Texts and Commentary* (N.Y.: Anchor Books, 1966), with translated selections and commentary printed on facing pages. Hegel's *Reason in History: A General Introduction to the Philosophy of History* (Indianapolis: Bobbs-Merrill, 1953) was translated, with an introduction, by Robert S. Hartman. Franz Wiedmann, *Georg Wilhelm Friedrich Hegel in Selbstzeugnissen und Bilddokumenten* ['Georg Wilhelm Friedrich Hegel in His Testimony and Pictorial Documents'], Rowohlt's Monographs, no. 110 (Reinbek bei Hamburg: Rowohlt, 1965) provides a concise, copiously illustrated biography with extensive passages from Hegel's writings, a chronology of his life, and an extensive bibliography.

176 **From Hegel to Nietzsche: the revolution in nineteenth-century thought.**
Karl Löwith. Translated by David E. Green. New York: Holt, Rinehart and Winston, 1964; repr., N.Y.: Doubleday, Anchor Books, 1967. 468p. bibliog.

Translation of *Von Hegel zu Nietzsche. Der revolutionäre Bruch im Denken des neunzehnten Jahrhunderts. Marx und Kierkegaard* ['From Hegel to Nietzsche: The Revolutionary Break in the Thought of the Nineteenth Century. Marx and Kierkegaard.'], 3rd ed. (Stuttgart: Kohlhammer, 1953). A penetrating interpretation, taking as its point of departure Goethe's humane 'Christian paganism' and Hegel's synthetic 'philosophical Christianity.' Goethe and Hegel differed, but each was able to construct a world that was whole, one in which man could still live with himself. Löwith's book is an account of the collapse of this world in the nineteenth century, primarily in Germany. He focusses on the fragmentation of Hegel's philosophical system, as reflected especially in the works of Marx, Kierkegaard, and Nietzsche. See also Löwith's chapters on Burckhardt, Marx, and Hegel in his complementary study, *Meaning in History* (Chicago: Univ. of Chicago Press, 1949); the Marxist philosopher Georg Lukács' interpretation, extending to the mid-twentieth century, *The Destruction of Reason*, translated by Peter Palmer (London: Merlin, 1980), published in East Berlin under the title *Die Zerstörung der Vernunft. Der Weg des Irrationalismus von Schelling zu Hitler* ['The Destruction of Reason: The Path of Irrationalism from Schelling to Hitler']

Philosophy and Religion. Individual philosophers and movements

(Berlin: Aufbau-Verlag, 1955); and Hans Urs von Balthasar, *Prometheus. Studien zur Geschichte des deutschen Idealismus* ['Prometheus: Studies in the History of German Idealism'] (Heidelberg: F. J. Kerle, 1947), a new printing, unchanged except in title, of the Jesuit scholar's *Apokalypse der deutschen Seele* ['Apocalypse of the German Soul'], vol. 1 (Salzburg and Leipzig: Verlag Anton Pustet, 1937), with a detailed table of contents.

177 **Schopenhauer.**
Patrick Gardiner. Baltimore, Md., and Harmondsworth,
Middlesex: Penguin Books, 1963. 312p.

An Oxford authority's lucid account of the influential German philosopher's life (1788-1860) and thought. The preface includes a brief discussion of the German editions and English translations of Schopenhauer's works. There is an extensive bibliography of works in English in *Schopenhauer: His Philosophical Achievement*, edited by Michael Fox (Brighton, Sussex: Harvester Press; Totowa, N.J.: Barnes & Noble, 1980), which includes selections by Thomas Mann, Max Horkheimer, Georg Lukács, and fourteen others. For a translation of Schopenhauer's major systematic work, *Die Welt als Wille und Vorstellung*, 3rd ed. (Leipzig: Brockhaus, 1859), see *The World as Will and Idea*, translated by R. B. Haldane and J. Kemp, 3 vols. (London: Kegan Paul, Trench, Trübner, 1896; repr., N.Y.: AMS Press, 1977). *Parerga and Paralipomena: Short Philosophical Essays*, translated by E. F. J. Payne, 2 vols. (Oxford: Clarendon Press, 1974) is the large collection of writings on religion, ethics, politics, the university, women, suicide, etc., that Schopenhauer published toward the end of his life; for a selection, see *Essays and Aphorisms*, selected and translated, with an introduction, by R. J. Hollingdale (Baltimore and Harmondsworth: Penguin, 1970). For a concise, illustrated biography in German, with numerous passages from Schopenhauer's writings, a chronology of his life, and a bibliography, see Walter Abendroth, *Arthur Schopenhauer in Selbstzeugnissen und Bilddokumenten* ['Arthur Schopenhauer in His Testimony and Pictorial Documents'], Rowohlt's Monographs, no. 133 (Reinbek bei Hamburg: Rowohlt, 1967). See also the selection from his writings, with an introduction, by Reinhold Schneider, *Schopenhauer* (Frankfurt am Main: Fischer Bücherei, 1956), and the critical edition, Arthur Schopenhauer, *Sämtliche Werke* ['Complete Works'], edited by Arthur Hübscher, 3rd ed., 7 vols. (Wiesbaden: F. A. Brockhaus, 1972).

178 **Selected writings in sociology & social philosophy.**
[Karl Marx.] Translated by T. B. Bottomore. Edited, with an introduction and notes, by T. B. Bottomore and Maximilien Rubel. Foreword by Erich Fromm. London: C. A. Watts, 1956; repr. of corrected, 2nd impression of 1961, New York: McGraw-Hill, 1964). 268p. bibliog.

A forty-eight-page introductory essay, followed by selections in translation from the whole of Marx's writings, except correspondence, intended to present 'the main features of his method, and the main conclusions of his research.' The volume includes a large number of passages from the important early philosophical writings, including Marx's collaborative work on *The German Ideology*. Parts I and III of this work, an initial statement of what came to be called the philosophy of historical materialism, are available in English in Karl

Philosophy and Religion. Individual philosophers and movements

Marx and Frederick Engels, *The German Ideology*, edited, with an introduction, by R. Pascal (London: Lawrence & Wishart, 1938; N.Y.: International Publishers, 1947). Far more complete is Karl Marx, *Der historische Materialismus. Die Frühschriften* ['Historical Materialism: The Early Writings'], edited by S. Landshut and J. P. Mayer in collaboration with F. Salomon, 2 vols. (Leipzig: Kröner, 1932), a 1,052-page selection from Marx's early writings (including extensive excerpts from *Die deutsche Ideologie* ['The German Ideology']), with an introductory essay on their significance; many of the excerpts from *The German Ideology* were omitted from the one-volume postwar edition, *Die Frühschriften*, edited by S. Landshut (Stuttgart: Kröner, 1953). See also *Karl Marx 1818/1968)* (Bad Godesberg: Inter Nationes, 1968), an annotated 254-page compilation with selections on Marx by Golo Mann, Ernst Bloch, Karl Löwith, Georg Lukács, et al., eighty-nine pages of excerpts from his writings (with introductory headnotes), and a bibliography of works (including articles) in English. For a concise biography giving emphasis (with insight) to the development of Marx's political and social philosophy in historical context, see Isaiah Berlin, *Karl Marx: His Life and Environment*, rev. ed. (N.Y.: Oxford Univ. Press, 1963).

179 **The portable Nietzsche.**
[Friedrich Nietzsche.] Selected and translated, with an introduction, prefaces, and notes, by Walter Kaufmann. New York: Viking Press, 1954. 687p. bibliog.

The Twilight of the Idols ['Die Götzen-Dämmerung'], *The Antichrist, Nietzsche contra Wagner,* and *Thus Spoke Zarathustra* ['Also sprach Zarathustra'], in unabridged translation, with additional selections, to give as complete a picture of Nietzsche as possible in one small volume, from his other books, notes, and letters. There is an introductory essay with bibliography, and many selections have introductory headnotes. Walter Kaufmann's biography, *Nietzsche: Philosopher, Psychologist, Antichrist*, 4th ed. (Princeton, N.J.: Princeton Univ. Press, 1974), seeks to dispel the legends woven around Nietzsche by his sister (who misrepresented him, even to the point of forgery), the National Socialists, and others, and to analyze his philosophy, his psychology, and his critique of Christianity. Karl Jaspers' lecture, *Nietzsche and Christianity* (Chicago: Henry Regnery, 1961) was translated by E. B. Ashton from *Nietzsche und das Christentum* (Hamelin: Verlag der Bücherstube Fritz Seifert, n.d.). Friedrich Nietzsche, *Werke in drei Bänden* ['Works in Three Volumes'], edited by Karl Schlechta, 9th impression (Munich: Hanser, 1982), is a 4,033-page critical edition, in which the first two volumes contain the works Nietzsche finished during his lifetime; the third volume offers a selection of posthumously published essays, letters, and notes, as nearly as possible in the form in which Nietzsche left them, rather than as they were arranged by his sister.

Philosophy and Religion. Individual philosophers and movements

180 **Selected Writings.**
[W. Dilthey.] Edited, translated and introduced by H. P.
Rickman. Cambridge: Cambridge University Press, 1976. 270p.
bibliog.

A thirty-page introductory essay on the Berlin philosopher Wilhelm Dilthey
(1831-1911), who developed a philosophical rationale for the systematic study of
the *Geisteswissenschaften* as opposed to the *Naturwissenschaften*, i.e., cultural
sciences, human studies or humanities, as opposed to the natural sciences,
followed by selections from Dilthey's writings in translation, grouped under four
headings: 'Dilthey as a Historian of Ideas,' 'Dilthey's Approach to Psychology,'
'Dilthey's Philosophy of Life,' and Dilthey's 'Epistemology and Methodology.'
See Rickman's edition of Wilhelm Dilthey, *Pattern and Meaning in History:
Thoughts on History and Society* (N.Y.: Harper Torchbooks, 1962), initially
published as *Meaning in History* (London: Allen & Unwin, 1961) for more
extended exposition of Dilthey's philosophy of history; his application of it is
illustrated in his three studies on Leibniz and his age, on Frederick the Great and
the German Enlightenment, and on the eighteenth century in Wilhelm Dilthey,
Gesammelte Schriften ['Collected Writings'], vol. 3: *Studien zur Geschichte des
deutschen Geistes* ['Studies in the History of the German Spirit'], ed. by Paul
Ritter, 3rd ed. (Stuttgart: B. G. Teubner; Göttingen: Vandenhoeck & Ruprecht,
1959). For major works in poetics and aesthetics in translation, see Dilthey's
Selected Works, vol. 5: *Poetry and Experience*, edited by Rudolf A. Makkreel and
Frithjof Rodi, translated by Louis Agosta, R. A. Makkreel, et al. (Princeton,
N.J.: Princeton Univ. Press, 1985). H. A. Hodges, *Wilhelm Dilthey: An
Introduction* (N.Y.: Oxford Univ. Press, 1944; repr., N.Y.: Howard Fertig, 1969)
provides a systematic exposition of Dilthey's philosophy with translated extracts
from his writings, notes on special terminology, and a bibliography. 'Dilthey and
the Definition of the "Cultural Sciences",' in *Consciousness and Society: The
Reorientation of European Social Thought, 1890-1930*, by H. Stuart Hughes
(N.Y.: Knopf, 1958; repr., N.Y.: Vintage, 1961) is a perceptive, brief
introduction in the broader context of European intellectual history.

181 **The philosophy of Ernst Cassirer.**
Edited by Paul Arthur Schilpp. Evanston, Ill.: The Library of
Living Philosophers, 1949. 936p. bibliog. (The Library of Living
Philosophers, vol. 6).

One of a series in which each volume was planned to include expository and
critical essays on an individual philosopher's work; his response to them; his
intellectual autobiography; and a bibliography of his works. Because Ernst
Cassirer (1874-1945) unexpectedly died without having written his response and
autobiography for the volume in preparation, it was published with a biographical
essay by Dimitry Gawronsky, memorial tributes by Hajo Holborn and several
others, and, as a statement of Cassirer's philosophical position, a translation of his
article on ' "Spirit" and "Life" in Contemporary Philosophy.' The English
translation of Cassirer's intellectual biography of Kant is cited above. His last two
major works, both published in English, were *An Essay on Man: An Introduction
to a Philosophy of Human Culture* (New Haven, Conn.: Yale Univ. Press, 1944;
repr., N.Y.: Bantam, 1970) and *The Myth of the State* (New Haven, Conn.: Yale
Univ. Press, 1946).

182 **The philosophy of Martin Buber.**
Edited by Paul Arthur Schilpp and Maurice Friedman. La Salle,
Ill.: Open Court; London: Cambridge University Press, 1967.
811p. bibliog. (The Library of Living Philosophers, vol. 12).

Following the general pattern of the series, this volume includes expository and
critical essays on Buber's work; his response to them; autobiographical
reflections; and a bibliography of his writings. The majority of the thirty essays
contributed to the volume are on traditional aspects of Buber's philosophy – his
metaphysics, ethics, political philosophy, philosophy of history, etc. About a third
focus on one aspect or another of Buber's religious activities and concerns. The
Princeton philosopher Walter Kaufmann, in the final essay, 'Buber's Religious
Significance' (pp. 665-685), reviews Buber's *oeuvre* as a whole. He concludes that
'if we find the heart of existentialism in the protest against systems, concepts, and
abstractions, coupled with a resolve to remain faithful to concrete experience and
above all to the challenge of human existence . . . ,' then Martin Buber is a true
existentialist in a way that can hardly be said of Kierkegaard, Jaspers, Heidegger,
or Sartre. The English translation in this volume of Buber's 'Autobiographical
Fragments' and of his 'Replies to My Critics' was made by the joint editor,
Maurice Friedman, author of the three-volume biography of Buber cited below
with other titles on the Jewish tradition.

183 **The philosophy of Karl Jaspers.**
Edited by Paul Arthur Schilpp. La Salle, Ill.: Open Court,
augmented ed., 1981. 934 + 16p. bibliog. (The Library of Living
Philosophers, vol. 9).

Following the pattern of the series, this volume includes expository and critical
articles on the philosopher's work; his response to them; his intellectual
autobiography; and a bibliography of his works. This edition is augmented by
Jaspers' sixteen-page segment on Martin Heidegger, which was not to be
published during Heidegger's lifetime. Karl Jaspers, *Basic Philosophical Writings
– Selections*, edited, translated, with introductions by Edith Ehrlich, Leonard H.
Ehrlich, and George B. Pepper (Athens, Ohio: Ohio Univ. Press, 1986), a 556-
page volume, has extensive extracts from Jaspers' works, editorial commentary,
and a detailed bibliography. *Philosophy and the World: Selected Essays and
Lectures* (Chicago: Regnery, 1963), translated by E. B. Ashton from *Philosophie
und Welt. Reden und Aufsätze* (Munich: Piper, 1958), includes the autobiography
Jaspers wrote for 'The Library of Living Philosophers' volume cited above and
selections on the task of philosophy; the truth of religion; Kant's 'Perpetual
Peace'; and the idea of the physician and the relationship between doctor and
patient (Jaspers, a psychiatrist, taught medicine before becoming a philosophy
professor). *Man in the Modern Age* (London: Routledge & Kegan Paul, 1951)
was translated by Eden and Cedar Paul from *Die geistige Situation der Zeit* ['The
Intellectual Situation of the Time'], 5th, rev. ed. (Berlin: Walter de Gruyter,
1932; repr. 1955). *The Question of German Guilt* (N.Y.: Dial Press, 1947) was
translated by E. B. Ashton from *Die Schuldfrage. Ein Beitrag zur deutschen Frage*
['The Question of Guilt: A Contribution to the German Question'] (Zurich:
Artemis, 1946). *The Future of Germany*, with a foreword by Hannah Arendt
(Chicago: Univ. of Chicago Press, 1967), was translated by E. B. Ashton from

parts of *Wohin treibt die Bundesrepublik?* ['Whither Is the Federal Republic Drifting?'] (Munich: Piper, 1966) and *Antwort: Zur Kritik [. . .]* ['Reply: Concerning Criticism (. . .)' (of the 1966 book)] (Munich: Piper, 1967).

184 **Heidegger: the man and the thinker.**
Edited by Thomas Sheehan. Chicago: Precedent Publishing,
1981. 347p. bibliog.

A compilation providing insight into Heidegger and his philosophy: three selections from his own writings and some twenty from other sources, with bibliographies of his works in English translation and of the secondary literature (including articles) on him in English. The volume's emphasis is on philosophy, but two selections focus on Heidegger's controversial role as Rector of Freiburg University just after Hitler came to power: 'Heidegger and the Nazis,' by Karl A. Moehling, author of *Martin Heidegger and the Nazi Party: An Examination* (Ann Arbor, Mich.: University Microfilms International; DeKalb, Ill.: Northern Illinois Univ. Ph.D. dissertation, 1972); and Heidegger's posthumously published interview, ' "Only a God Can Save Us": The *Spiegel* Interview (1966),' translated by William J. Richardson, S.J., from *Der Spiegel*, 31 May 1976 (Nr. 23, Jg. 30). See also Christian Graf von Krockow, *Die Entscheidung. Eine Untersuchung über Ernst Jünger, Carl Schmitt, Martin Heidegger* ['The Decision: A Study of Ernst Jünger, Carl Schmitt, Martin Heidegger'] (Stuttgart: Ferdinand Enke, 1958), and *Martin Heidegger. Ein Philosoph und die Politik* ['Martin Heidegger: A Philosopher and Politics'], edited by Gottfried Schramm and Bernd Martin (Freiburg: Rombach, 1986). Heidegger's long introduction to his fundamental work, *Sein und Zeit* ['Being and Time'], 7th ed. (Tübingen: Max Niemeyer, 1976) – also available as vol. 2 of the *Gesamtausgabe* ['Collected Works'] (Frankfurt am Main: Klostermann, 1977) – is included, translated by Joan Stambaugh et al., in Martin Heidegger, *Basic Writings*, edited by David Farrell Krell (N.Y.: Harper & Row, 1977), which also includes 'On the Essence of Truth' and 'The End of Philosophy and the Task of Thinking.' The full text of *Sein und Zeit* was translated by John Macquarrie and Edward Robinson as *Being and Time* (Oxford: Blackwell, 1967). See Walter Biemel, *Martin Heidegger in Selbstzeugnissen und Bilddokumenten* ['Martin Heidegger in His Testimony and Pictorial Documents'], Rowohlt's Monographs, no. 200 (Reinbek bei Hamburg: Rowohlt, 1973), for a concise biography and German bibliography.

185 **The dialectical imagination: a history of the Frankfurt School and the Institute of Social Research, 1923-1950.**
Martin Jay. Boston: Little, Brown and Co., 1973. 382p. bibliog.

A major study of the work of the German social philosophers identified with the *Institut für Sozialforschung* [Institute of Social Research], founded in Frankfurt in 1923 and transplanted, after Hitler's accession ten years later, to New York City as the International Institute of Social Research at Columbia University. The well-annotated monograph concludes with an article-length epilogue on the reestablishment of the institute in Frankfurt in 1950 and the continuing influence of its work, particularly in critical theory, in postwar Germany. There is a detailed bibliography that includes publications, to the beginning of the 1970s, on the institute's history as well as studies that grew out of its work. H. Stuart Hughes provides a readable introduction, in the context of Western intellectual history, to Max Horkheimer, who became professor of social philosophy at Frankfurt

University and director of the Institute of Social Research in 1930, and Theodor W. Adorno (originally Theodor Wiesengrund), his associate since the late 1930s and successor as director of the (reestablished) institute in Frankfurt in 1958, in 'The Critique of Mass Society,' in *The Sea Change: The Migration of Social Thought, 1930-1965* (N.Y.: Harper & Row, 1975), the sequel to *Consciousness and Society*, cited in the entry on Dilthey above. See also Martin Jay, *Adorno* (Cambridge, Mass.: Harvard Univ. Press, 1984); George Friedman, *The Political Philosophy of the Frankfurt School* (Ithaca, N.Y.: Cornell Univ. Press, 1981); Zoltán Tar, *The Frankfurt School: The Critical Theories of Max Horkheimer and Theodor W. Adorno* (N.Y.: Wiley, 1977); and *Dialectic of Enlightenment* by Max Horkheimer and Theodor W. Adorno (N.Y.: Herder and Herder, 1972), translated by John Cumming from *Dialektik der Aufklärung. Philosophische Fragmente* ['Dialectic of Enlightenment: Philosophical Fragments'] (Amsterdam: Querido, 1947; reissued, Frankfurt am Main: S. Fischer, 1969).

Religion and the churches (general)

186 **The churches and politics in Germany.**
Frederic Spotts. Middletown, Conn.: Wesleyan University Press, 1973. 419p. maps. bibliog.

A well-informed, very readable account, in historical context, of the Roman Catholic and the Evangelical (or Protestant, i.e., Lutheran, Reformed, and United) churches in Germany since 1945. Spotts focusses on the Federal Republic, but also deals with the complex East-West ties within the churches and their political as well as ecclesiastical implications. He analyzes the ill-defined church-state relationship in the Federal Republic, anchored in the Basic Law's reaffirmation of the ambiguous provisions of the Weimar constitution on the subject. Spotts finds that the churches in the Federal Republic have maintained a relatively strong institutional position and corresponding political influence, particularly when one considers the great changes that have taken place in West German society since 1945. By 1970, secularization had gone so far that, in the words of the Jesuit theologian Karl Rahner, Germany had become a 'pagan land with a Christian past and vestiges of Christianity.' Nevertheless, as Spotts shows, the churches have continued to enjoy privileges that are 'extraordinary, in many respects unique in the world.' Heinrich Böll, for example, who in 1970 refused to pay the state-administered church tax, yet declined to leave the church, was sued by the archdiocese of Cologne, and in 1972, not long before being awarded the Nobel prize, was forced to pay his accumulated church tax. Spotts' extensively annotated book includes maps showing distribution of confessions in Germany in 1939 and in 1946; the provincial organization of the Evangelical (Protestant) church as of 1968; and the diocesan organization of the Catholic church as of 1971. There is a listing of archival sources, an extensive bibliography (citing a number of books and articles in English, particularly on the occupation period), and a detailed index.

Philosophy and Religion. Religion and the churches (general)

187 **Religious education in German schools: an historical approach.**
Ernst Christian Helmreich. Cambridge, Mass.: Harvard
University Press, 1959. 365p. bibliog.
A study of the place of religious education in the German school curriculum, both
as a concern of the churches and as a political and pedagogical problem. The
subject is treated in historical perspective, but with emphasis on the twentieth
century. The period from the Middle Ages and Reformation through the
revolution of 1918 is covered in the first hundred pages. There is more detailed
coverage of the Weimar Republic, the Hitler era, and the postwar period, with
individual chapters on the occupation, on each of the two German states, and on
developments in Berlin. Helmreich provides considerable information on and
insight into the German educational system. In addition to Catholic and
Protestant education in the schools, Jewish education is treated, from the time of
state recognition of Jewish schools in the nineteenth century (in the 1820s, for
example, in Württemberg). The volume is copiously annotated, has an extensive
bibliography, and a detailed index.

188 **The German churches under Hitler: background, struggle, and
epilogue.**
Ernst Christian Helmreich. Detroit: Wayne State University
Press, 1979. 616p. 3 maps. bibliog.
This comprehensive history of the Christian churches (including sects and free
churches) under Hitler begins with a hundred-page 'Background' segment that
reviews the development, since the Reformation, of the churches' status and role
in Germany up to 1933. The body of the book, the 'Struggle,' provides a well-
documented account of the years 1933-1945, in chapters focussing on individual
issues or episodes, such as the Concordat and the Confessing church. The
'Epilogue' has one chapter each on the postwar Protestant and Catholic churches,
and a final chapter, 'Survey and Evaluation,' with Helmreich's thoughtful
conclusions in historical perspective. The value of his fine work is enhanced by the
extensive bibliography and detailed index. *The German Church Struggle and the
Holocaust*, edited by Franklin H. Littell and Hubert G. Locke (Detroit: Wayne
State Univ. Press, 1974), includes useful contributions by leading specialists in
several disciplines and bibliographical citations in the annotations to their papers.
The Third Reich and the Christian Churches, edited by Peter Matheson
(Edinburgh: T. & T. Clark, 1981) is a hundred-page volume with sixty-eight
translated selections, many with explanatory headnotes, documenting relations
between the churches and the National Socialist régime, including substantial
segments of the Concordat of 20 July 1933, the declaration of 20 October 1934 of
the Confessing Church Synod at Berlin-Dahlem, and brief extracts from secret
police reports. For an extensive, well-annotated collection of such reports, see the
1,021-page *Berichte des SD und der Gestapo über Kirchen und Kirchenvolk in
Deutschland 1934-1944* ['Reports of the Security Service and the Secret State
Police on Churches and Church People in Germany, 1934-1944'], edited by Heinz
Boberach, 'Veröffentlichungen der Kommission für Zeitgeschichte bei der
Katholischen Akademie in Bayern [Publications of the Commission for
Contemporary History at the Catholic Academy in Bavaria],' series A, vol. 12
(Mainz: Matthias-Grünewald-Verlag, 1971).

189 **Christians and Jews in Germany: religion, politics, and ideology in the Second Reich, 1870-1914.**
Uriel Tal. Translated by Noah Jonathan Jacobs.   Ithaca, N.Y.: Cornell University Press, 1975. 359p. bibliog.

A carefully documented study, translated from the Hebrew (Jerusalem: The Magnes Press, The Hebrew Univ., 1969), of the relations between Christians and Jews in Germany from the time of German unification, when civil disabilities resulting from religious affiliation were removed, to the First World War. The volume includes an appendix with facsimiles of several contemporary documents, a bibliographical essay, and an index. Leo Baeck, *Judaism and Christianity*, translated with an introduction by Walter Kaufmann (Philadelphia: The Jewish Publication Society of America, 1958; repr., N.Y.: Harper Torchbooks, 1966), comprised of several essays by the most prominent German rabbi of the first half of the twentieth century, includes his critique of Christianity (with particular attention to Lutheranism), 'Romantic Religion.' See also Martin Buber's *Two Types of Faith: A Study of the Interpenetration of Judaism and Christianity* (N.Y.: Macmillan, 1951; repr., N.Y.: Harper Torchbooks, 1961) and the response by Hans Urs von Balthasar, *Martin Buber & Christianity: A Dialogue Between Israel and the Church* (London: Harvill Press, 1961), translated by Alexander Dru from *Einsame Zwiesprache. Martin Buber und das Christentum* ['Lonely Dialogue: Martin Buber and Christianity'] (Cologne: J. Hegner, 1958).

The Roman Catholic tradition

190 **The spirit of Catholicism.**
Karl Adam. Translated by Dom Justin McCann, O.S.B.   London: Sheed & Ward, 1929; New York: Macmillan, 1930; repr. (rev. ed.), Garden City, N.Y.: Image Books, 1954. 260p.

Based on a series of university lectures given in 1923 and subsequently published in a dozen languages, this classic statement of the fundamental tenets of the Roman Catholic church by a member of the Faculty of Catholic Theology at Tübingen was translated from *Das Wesen des Katholizismus* ['The Essence of Catholicism'], 4th ed. (Düsseldorf: Schwann, 1927). Another very widely read (and widely translated) work, representative of the Roman Catholic tradition in Germany in the first half of the twentieth century, addressing the laity no less than the clergy in intellectually sophisticated terms, is *The Lord* (Chicago: Regnery, 1954; repr., Cleveland: Meridian Books, 1969), translated by Elinor Castendyk Briefs from *Der Herr. Betrachtungen über die Person und das Leben Jesu Christi* ['The Lord: Reflections on the Person and the Life of Jesus Christ'] (Würzburg: Werkbund-Verlag, 1937), by Monsignor Romano Guardini, an Italian-born German youth movement leader in the 1920s, who was professor of religious philosophy and Catholic ideology in Berlin, until his chair was abolished by the National Socialist régime in 1939, and held a corresponding chair in the Faculty of Philosophy at Munich University after the war. For an account of the circumstances that led to the commissioning and publication of the English translation by Regnery, see *Memoirs of a Dissident Publisher* (N.Y.: Harcourt Brace Jovanovich, 1979), by Henry Regnery, who mentions that 'it became the most successful book in . . . [his] firm's history.'

191 **A Rahner reader.**
[Karl Rahner.] Edited by Gerald A. McCool. New York: Seabury Press, 1975. 381p. bibliog.

Selections, with introductory headnotes, from English translations of writings by Karl Rahner, S.J., who retired in 1971 as professor of dogmatic theology and the history of dogma in the Roman Catholic theological faculty at Münster University. The volume begins with the editor's sophisticated introductory essay on the philosophical theology of Rahner, a former student of Martin Heidegger and recognized leader of the German transcendental Thomists, and includes a bibliography citing Rahner's writings in translation, including his collected works (a continuing series with well over a dozen volumes by the early 1980s, both in the German original and in English translation): *Theological Investigations*, vol. 1- (London: Darton, Longman and Todd, 1961- ; N.Y.: Seabury, 1974-), translated from *Schriften zur Theologie* ['Writings on Theology'], vol. 1- (Einsiedeln: Benziger, 1954-). After retirement from Münster, Rahner published his systematic theology, *Foundations of Christian Faith: An Introduction to the Idea of Christianity* (N.Y.: Seabury, 1978), translated (as a 470-page volume) by William V. Dych from *Grundkurs des Glaubens. Einführung in den Begriff des Christentums* ['Basic Course of the Faith: Introduction to the Concept of Christianity'] (Freiburg im Breisgau: Herder, 1976), based on a course taught at Munich, where he had been Romano Guardini's successor, and at Münster. Robert Kress, *A Rahner Handbook* (Atlanta: John Knox Press, 1982), provides a brief introduction to the *oeuvre* of the prolific theologian whose response to the fundamental intellectual challenges of the contemporary world have led him to be regarded by many as a pillar of traditional Roman Catholic orthodoxy, notwithstanding the 'tangled inpenetrability' of his prose style (to cite Robert Nowell's apt characterization in *A Passion for Truth* listed below).

192 **The Catholic church and Nazi Germany.**
Guenter Lewy. New York: McGraw-Hill, 1964. 416p.

Among the topics discussed in this carefully documented, critical history of the relations of the Roman Catholic church with the National Socialists from before 1933 to 1945, are the Concordat between the Holy See and Germany, the church and Hitler's foreign policy, the conflict over German eugenic policies (including the effective public protest against euthanasia), the Jewish question (and the absence of effective public protest), and the problem of resistance. The concluding chapter deals with 'Catholic Political Ideology: The Unity of Theory and Practice.' The extensive backnotes include numerous bibliographical citations. Gordon C. Zahn, *German Catholics and Hitler's Wars: A Study in Social Control*, with a foreword by Daniel Berrigan, S.J. (N.Y.: Sheed & Ward, 1962; repr., N.Y.: Dutton, 1969), is addressed to the question of how and why German Catholics supported Hitler's war as they did. Members of the Catholic hierarchy assumed 'a significant role in marshaling the support of the Catholic population and bolstering the war morale of the Catholics in active service and on the home front.' There are explanatory footnotes, backnotes with German originals of passages cited in English translation in the text, and a bibliography.

193 **Hans Küng: his work and his way.**
Edited by Hermann Häring and Karl-Josef Kuschel. Translated by
Robert Nowell. London: Fount Paperbacks, 1979; New York:
Image Books, 1980. 254p. bibliog.

Translated from *Hans Küng – Weg und Werk* (Munich: Piper, 1978), a concise
introduction to the liberal theologian disavowed in 1979 by the Vatican as a
teacher, but not as a priest or as a director of doctoral and post-doctoral research
in the Roman Catholic faculty at Tübingen University, where he remains a
professor and directs the Institute for Ecumenical Theology. The volume includes
a complete bibliography through 1978 (listing articles and books in English
translation), an extended interview with Küng, and, among its selections, a letter
written by Karl Barth for publication with Küng's doctoral dissertation,
Justification: The Doctrine of Karl Barth and a Catholic Reflection (London: Burns
& Oates, 1966), translated by Thomas Collins et al. from *Rechtfertigung. Die
Lehre Karl Barths und eine katholische Besinnung*, 4th, exp. ed. (Einsiedeln:
Johannes-Verlag, 1957); an essay by Hans Urs von Balthasar on Küng's *The
Church* (London: Burns & Oates; N.Y.: Sheed & Ward, 1967), translated by Ray
and Rosaleen Ockenden from *Die Kirche* (Freiburg: Herder, 1967); and critical
reviews of Küng's *Infallible? An Inquiry* (Garden City, N.Y.: Doubleday,, 1971),
translated by Edward Quinn from *Unfehlbar? Eine Anfrage* (Zurich: Benziger,
1970) and *On Being a Christian* (Garden City, N.Y.: Doubleday, 1976),
translated by Edward Quinn from *Christ sein* (Munich: Piper, 1974). *Does God
Exist? An Answer for Today* (Garden City, N.Y.: Doubleday, 1980), was
translated by Edward Quinn from *Existiert Gott? Antwort auf die Gottesfrage der
Neuzeit* (Munich: Piper, 1978). See Robert Nowell, *A Passion for Truth – Hans
Küng: A Biography* (London: Collins, 1981) and, for documentation in
translation, *The Küng Dialogue* (Washington: U.S. Catholic Conference, 1980)
and Leonard Swidler's *Küng in Conflict* (Garden City, N.Y.: Doubleday, 1981).
The Vatican's perspective on many issues is reflected by a former colleague of
Küng in the Tübingen Catholic faculty in *The Ratzinger Report: An Exclusive
Interview on the State of the Church*, by Joseph Cardinal Ratzinger with Vittorio
Messori, translated by Salvator Attanasio and Graham Harrison (San Francisco:
Ignatius Press, 1985).

The Protestant tradition

194 **Luther's works, vol. 31: career of the reformer, I; and vol. 35:
word and sacrament, I.**
[Martin Luther.] Helmut T. Lehmann, general editor; Harold J.
Grimm, editor, vol. 31; E. Theodore Bachmann, editor, vol. 35.
Translated by E. Theodore Bachmann, Harold J. Grimm, et al.
Philadelphia: Muhlenberg Press, 1957 & 1960, respectively.
416 & 426 pp., respectively.

Documents of fundamental importance to the German Protestant tradition are
included in the American edition of Luther's works in readable English
translation with introductions to individual selections and explanatory footnotes

with bibliographical references. Luther's 'Ninety-five Theses *or* Disputation on the Power and Efficacy of Indulgences' of 1517 is in vol. 31, pp. 17-33. 'On Translating: An Open Letter' is in vol. 35 (pp. 175-202), as are his prefaces to all the books of the Bible (pp. 225-411). Luther's preface to the Epistle to the Romans ('really the chief part of the New Testament, and . . . truly the purest gospel'), pp. 365-380, is also available in booklet form as *Martin Luther's Preface to the Epistle of St. Paul to the Romans* (Nashville: Discipleship Resources, 1977), reprinted from another translation. On Luther himself, see, in addition to the classic biography by Roland H. Bainton cited in the history section of this bibliography, Erwin Iserloh, *The Theses Were Not Posted: Luther between Reform and Reformation*, introduction by Martin E. Marty (Boston: Beacon Press, 1968), translated by Jared Wicks, S.J., from *Luther zwischen Reform und Reformation. Der Thesenanschlag fand nicht statt*, 2nd ed. (Münster: Aschendorff, 1966), and Hanns Lilje's concise, well-illustrated biography of Luther, with numerous selections from his writings, *Martin Luther in Selbstzeugnissen und Bilddokumenten* ['Martin Luther in His Testimony and Pictorial Documents'], Rowohlt's Monographs, no. 98 (Reinbek bei Hamburg: Rowohlt, 1965).

195 **The Book of Concord: the confessions of the Evangelical Lutheran church.**
Translated and edited by Theodore G. Tappert in collaboration with Jaroslav Pelikan, Robert H. Fischer, and Arthur C. Piepkorn. Philadelphia: Fortress Press, 1959. 717p.

A new translation of *The Book of Concord*, a collection of basic documents originally published in 1580 as a standard compendium on the faith and practice of what came to be known as the Lutheran church. This edition is based on *Die Bekenntnisschriften der evangelisch-lutherischen Kirche* ['The Confessional Writings of the Evangelical-Lutheran Church'], ed. by Hans Lietzmann, Heinrich Bornkamm, Hans Volz, and Ernst Wolf, 2nd, rev. ed. (Göttingen: Vandenhoeck & Ruprecht, 1952). The volume includes the three traditional creeds (Apostles', Nicene, Athanasian); 'The Augsburg Confession' of 1530; the 'Apology of the Augsburg Confession,' a detailed commentary of 1531 by its principal author, Philipp Melanchthon; Martin Luther's short and long catechisms (1529) and his '[Smalcald] Articles of Christian Doctrine' [1537]; and the 'Formula of Concord' of 1577, an extended, collaborative work defining the Lutheran consensus. Each document is printed, with an introduction and annotations, in readable, modern English. The Augsburg Confession, having been prepared for presentation to Emperor Charles V in both German and Latin, has parallel translations into English. In most quotations from the Bible, the English of the Revised Standard Version has been used, but, where the context requires it, other versions or translations have been employed. The volume concludes with an index of biblical references and a detailed, general index.

196 **Harnack and Troeltsch: two historical theologians.**
Wilhelm Pauck. New York: Oxford University Press, 1968. 131p.

Lucid introduction to the lives and works of two scholar-churchmen influential in shaping the twentieth-century Protestant tradition, particularly in Germany: Adolf von Harnack (1851-1930), professor of church history in the theological faculty at Berlin (despite opposition by the state church, which deplored his

Philosophy and Religion. The Protestant tradition

liberalism); and Ernst Troeltsch (1865-1923), Heidelberg theology professor until 1915, then Berlin philosophy professor. Harnack's great best-seller was *Das Wesen des Christentums. Sechzehn Vorlesungen [. . .]* ['The Essence of Christianity: Sixteen Lectures (. . .)'] (Leipzig: Hinrichs, 1900; new ed., with an introduction by Rudolf Bultmann, Stuttgart: Klotz, 1950), translated by T. B. Saunders as *What Is Christianity?*, introduction by Rudolf Bultmann (N.Y.: Harper, 1957). His *Outlines of the History of Dogma* (N.Y.: Funk & Wagnalls, 1893; repr., with an introduction by Philip Rieff, Boston: Beacon Press, 1957) was translated by Edwin Knox Mitchell from *Grundriss der Dogmengeschichte* (Freiburg: Mohr [Siebeck], 1889-91), in which Harnack had summarized his *Lehrbuch der Dogmengeschichte*, 3 vols., 3rd, rev. ed. (Freiburg: Mohr, 1894-97), translated by J. Millar et al. as *History of Dogma*, 7 vols. (London: Williams & Norgate, 1896-99; repr., N.Y.: Russell & Russell, 1958). Troeltsch's great work that complemented Harnack's history of dogma was *Die Soziallehren der christlichen Kirchen und Gruppen*, vol. 1 of his *Gesammelte Schriften* ['Collected Works'] (Tübingen: Mohr [Siebeck], 1912), translated by Olive Wyon as *The Social Teaching of the Christian Churches*, 2 vols. (London: Allen & Unwin; N.Y.: Macmillan, 1931; repr., with an introduction by H. Richard Niebuhr, N.Y.: Harper Torchbooks, 1960). His *Christian Thought: Its History and Application*, lectures to have been delivered in England, appeared posthumously in a translation by Henry G. Atkins, Ernest Barker, et al., with an introduction by F. von Hügel (London: Univ. of London Press, 1923; repr., N.Y.: Meridian Books, 1957).

197 **The quest of the historical Jesus: a critical study of its progress from Reimarus to Wrede.**
Albert Schweitzer. Translated by W. Montgomery. Preface by F. C. Burkitt. London: Black, 1910; repr., New York: Macmillan, 1948. 413p.

This landmark study reviews the futile attempt of modern scholarship to reach an understanding of Jesus through historical research. 'Jesus as a concrete historical personality remains a stranger to our time,' concludes Schweitzer in his final chapter. 'It is not Jesus as historically known, but Jesus as arisen within men, who is significant for our time and can help it.' The English version is based on *Von Reimarus zu Wrede. Eine Geschichte der Leben-Jesu-Forschung* ['From Reimarus to Wrede: A History of Research on the Life of Jesus'] (Tübingen: Mohr, 1906) and therefore does not reflect revisions in the treatment of late Jewish eschatology (important for the spiritual climate of Jesus' time) in the second edition (entitled simply *Geschichte der Leben-Jesu-Forschung* [Tübingen: Mohr, 1913]), as Schweitzer notes with regret in his memoirs, *Aus meinem Leben und Denken* (Leipzig: Meiner, 1931; repr., Frankfurt am Main: Fischer Bücherei, 1952), translated by C. T. Campion as *Out of My Life and Thought: An Autobiography*, postscript by Everett Skillings (N.Y.: Holt, 1949), where he discusses his work on the study of Jesus. His study of Paul, *Geschichte der Paulinischen Forschung von der Reformation bis auf die Gegenwart* ['History of Pauline Research from the Reformation to the Present'] (Tübingen: Mohr, 1911), was translated by W. Montgomery as *Paul and His Interpreters* (London: Black; N.Y.: Macmillan, 1912; repr., N.Y.: Schocken, 1964). Schweitzer's medical dissertation, *Die psychiatrische Beurteilung Jesu* (Tübingen: Mohr, 1913), was translated by Charles R. Joy as *The Psychiatric Study of Jesus*, foreword by Winfred Overholser

Philosophy and Religion. The Protestant tradition

(Boston: Beacon Press, 1948). For a short introduction to the basic problem addressed by Schweitzer, taking his and subsequent work, particularly by German Protestant scholars, into account, see Joachim Jeremias, *The Problem of the Historical Jesus*, introduction by John Reumann (Philadelphia: Fortress Press, 1964), translated by Norman Perrin from *Das Problem des historischen Jesus* (Stuttgart: Calwer, 1960).

198 **The German phoenix: men and movements in the church in Germany.**
Franklin Hamlin Littell. Garden City, N.Y.: Doubleday & Company, 1960. 226p. map. bibliog.

A concise, sympathetic introduction to the contemporary German Protestant church in historical perspective, scholarly but quite readable, with references to relevant English and German literature in the annotations as well as the bibliography. The appendices include the 1934 Barmen Declaration (May 1934) of the Confessing church (a faction of the Protestant church opposing the National Socialists) and material on the postwar church. Arthur C. Cochrane's *The Church's Confession under Hitler*, 2nd ed. (Pittsburgh, Pa.: Pickwick Press, 1976) is a study, with documentation and bibliography, of this opposition Synod of Barmen. For further insight into the twentieth-century German Protestant church and its leadership, see James Bentley, *Martin Niemoeller* (Oxford: Oxford Univ. Press, 1984), a biography (based in part on extensive interviews) of the World War I submarine commander who became a prominent pastor in Berlin, a concentration camp inmate under Hitler, and a leader of the pacifist movement in postwar West Germany; Karl Barth, *The German Church in Conflict* (London: Lutterworth Press; Richmond, Va.: John Knox Press, 1965), a selection of writings from the 1930s on the contest with the Hitler régime, translated by P. T. A. Parker from *Karl Barth zum Kirchenkampf* ['Karl Barth on the Church Struggle'], edited by E. Wolf (Munich: Christian Kaiser Verlag, 1956); and Dietrich Bonhoeffer, *Prisoner for God: Letters and Papers from Prison*, edited by Eberhard Bethge (N.Y.: Macmillan, 1954; repr. [as *Letters and Papers from Prison*], 1962), translated by Reginald H. Fuller from *Widerstand und Ergebung. Briefe und Aufzeichnungen aus der Haft* ['Resistance and Submission: Letters and Notes from Prison'] (Munich: Kaiser, 1951). Inextricably linked with Barth's and Bonhoeffer's opposition to the National Socialist dictatorship (which cost the latter his life in 1945) was their work as theologians, noted in the next entry.

199 **The new theologian.**
Ved Mehta. New York: Harper & Row, 1966; repr., New York: Harper Colophon, 1968. 217p.

Originally serialized in *The New Yorker*, this is a readable introduction to several of the most important issues in modern Protestant thought. Taking as his point of departure John A. T. Robinson's *Honest to God* (London: SCM Press; Philadelphia: Westminster Press, 1963), an Anglican bishop's best-selling popularization of the work of a select group of German theologians, Mehta focusses in particular on Dietrich Bonhoeffer and includes an extended account of his interview with Bonhoeffer's biographer, Eberhard Bethge. In addition to *Prisoner for God*, cited in the previous entry, see *The Cost of Discipleship* by Dietrich Bonhoeffer, with a biographical sketch of him by Gerhard Leibholz, rev.

76

and unabr. ed. (N.Y.: Macmillan; London: SCM Press, 1959), translated by R. H. Fuller from *Nachfolge* (Munich: Kaiser, 1937); Eberhard Bethge, *Dietrich Bonhoeffer: Man of Vision, Man of Courage* (N.Y.: Harper & Row, 1970), translated by Eric Mosbacher et al. from the first (1967) edition of *Dietrich Bonhoeffer. Theologe. Christ. Zeitgenosse* ['Dietrich Bonhoeffer: Theologian, Christian, Contemporary'), 3rd, rev. ed. (Munich: Kaiser, 1970); and *The Place of Bonhoeffer: Problems and Possibilities in His Thought*, edited and introduced by Martin E. Marty (N.Y.: Association Press, 1962). On three other theologians whom Mehta interviewed, see 'What Am I? An Autobiographical Essay: Early Years,' by Paul Tillich, in *My Search for Absolutes* (N.Y.: Simon & Schuster, 1967; repr., 1984), pp. 23-54; the Jesuit theologian Hans Urs von Balthasar's sympathetic critique of *The Theology of Karl Barth* (N.Y.: Holt, Rinehart and Winston, 1971), translated by John Drury from *Karl Barth. Darstellung und Deutung seiner Theologie* ['Karl Barth: Presentation and Interpretation of His Theology'], 2nd ed. (Cologne: Hegner, 1962); and *Kerygma and Myth: A Theological Debate* by Rudolf Bultmann et al., edited by Hans Werner Bartsch, rev. ed. (N.Y.: Harper Torchbooks, 1961), translation, by R. H. Fuller, of selections from H. W. Bartsch, ed., *Kerygma und Mythos*, vol. 1- (Hamburg: Herbert Reich: 1948-), a multi-volume series with supplements.

The Jewish tradition

200 **The rise of modern Judaism: an intellectual history of German Jewry 1650-1942.**
Heinz Moshe Graupe. Translated by John Robinson.
Huntington, N.Y.: Robert E. Krieger Publ. Co., 1979. 329p.
bibliog.

A translation of *Die Entstehung des modernen Judentums*, 2nd, enl. & rev. ed. (Hamburg: Helmut Buske Verlag, 1977), based on lectures by the founding director of the Institute for the History of the German Jews, established at Hamburg in 1964, to students with little knowledge of the history or teachings of Judaism. For American readers possibly unfamiliar with German history as well, the author has introduced alterations and revisions in this translated edition. The opening chapters review the history of the Jews in Germany to the early modern period and provide an introduction to Jewish society and its traditional image on the eve of the seventeenth-century Enlightenment, the point of departure for the modernization not only of Germany as a whole, but also German Jewry. The balance of the work surveys their social and intellectual history from the seventeenth century through the first third of the twentieth, tracing the development of Jewish self-understanding and increasing participation in German cultural, social, and political life. The first of two select bibliographies cites scholarly sources in English, German, and Hebrew; the second lists English translations of works by the main thinkers and authors treated in the book. For an influential, pioneering work by a social and economic historian, see Werner Sombart's *The Jews and Modern Capitalism*, with an introduction by Bert F. Hoselitz (Glencoe, Ill.: Free Press, 1951; repr., N.Y.: Collier, 1962), translated by M. Epstein from *Die Juden und das Wirtschaftsleben* ['The Jews and Economic

Life'] (Leipzig: Duncker & Humblot, 1911). Although controversial and in some ways gravely flawed, Sombart's classic is recognized for having defined very important questions leading to new work in the field, as pointed out (with several citations) in Prof. Hoselitz' critical introductory essay and in the annotated 'Bibliographical Note' (which concludes with a section on 'Jewish History and Culture in its Relation to Modern Capitalism').

201 **The German Jew: a synthesis of Judaism and Western Civilization, 1730-1930.**
   H. I. Bach. Foreword by Albert H. Friedlander. Oxford: Oxford University Press, 1984. 255p. (The Littmann Library of Jewish Civilization).

A brilliant, beautifully written interpretation of German-Jewish cultural and religious history by the literary scholar Hans Bach (1902-1977), who fled to England in 1939. He sees the work during the early twentieth century of four eminent German-Jewish thinkers, Hermann Cohen (1842-1918), Leo Baeck (1873-1956), Martin Buber (1878-1965), and Franz Rosenzweig (1886-1929), as the culmination not merely of what has been described as the 'German-Jewish symbiosis,' but as something far more important and more enduring: a synthesis that has led to the maturity of modern Western Judaism – a legacy to mankind that assures the continuing viability of Judaism as a pillar, together with Christianity, of modern Western civilization. The German-Jewish symbiosis ended with the Holocaust, but it remains of enduring importance and interest because it provided the basis for the development of modern Western Judaism. For a description of the social and intellectual context in which Hermann Cohen worked, with particular insight into the challenges he faced in his distinguished professional career (he was the only Jewish professor of philosophy at a German university before 1919), see Peter Gay's 'Encounter with Modernism: German Jews in Wilhelminian Culture' in *Freud, Jews and Other Germans: Masters and Victims in Modernist Culture* (N.Y.: Oxford Univ. Press, 1978), pp. 93-168, esp. 114-120. As explained by Bach, Cohen's great legacy to Western Judaism is his posthumously published *Religion of Reason out of the Sources of Judaism*, with an introductory essay by Leo Strauss (N.Y.: Ungar, 1972), translated by Simon Kaplan from *Religion der Vernunft aus den Quellen des Judentums*, 2nd ed. (Frankfurt am Main: J. Kauffmann, 1929).

202 **Days of sorrow and pain: Leo Baeck and the Berlin Jews.**
   Leonard Baker. New York: Macmillan Publishing Co.; London: Collier Macmillan Publishers, 1978. 396p. bibliog.

A detailed, illustrated account, addressed to the general reader as well as the serious student, of Baeck's life and times, from his youth as the son of the rabbi of Lissa in the Prussian province of Posen to his last years as a naturalized British citizen spending several months each winter at Hebrew Union College in Cincinnati. The well-documented volume describes his leading role (discussed by H. I. Bach in a previously cited title) among the German Jews. The bibliography lists many of Baeck's writings, including a number of articles in English. Eric H. Boehm's *We Survived*, cited in the history section, includes (on pp. 284-298) Baeck's account of his experiences during the National Socialist dictatorship. See also Baeck's influential and widely disseminated work, *Das Wesen des Judentums*,

6th ed. (Cologne: Joseph Melzer, 1960), published, in Irving Howe's rendition of an earlier translation by Victor Grubenwieser and Leonard Pearl, as *The Essence of Judaism*, rev. ed. (N.Y.: Schocken, 1961), and the essays collected in *Judaism and Christianity*, cited in an earlier entry.

203 **Martin Buber's life and work: vol. 1, The early years, 1878-1923; vol. 2, The middle years, 1923-1945; vol. 3, The later years, 1945-1965.**
Maurice Friedman. New York: E. P. Dutton, 1981, 1983, &1983, resp. 455, 398, & 493 pp., resp.

Comprehensive biography by the joint editor, with Paul A. Schilpp, of the 'Library of Living Philosophers' volume on Buber cited above in the philosophy section. There are bibliographical citations in the 'Notes and Sources' at the end of each volume, but no general bibliography. There is a comprehensive bibliography of Buber's writings in the Friedman-Schilpp volume. See also Friedman's *Martin Buber: The Life of Dialogue*, 3rd, rev. ed. (Chicago: Univ. of Chicago Press, 1976), a sytematic one-volume study of Buber's thought, with an extensive bibliography and a detailed index. Buber's 1923 classic on the life of dialogue, *I and Thou*, 2nd ed., with a postscript (N.Y.: Scribner's, 1958; Edinburgh: T. & T. Clark, 1959), was translated by Ronald Gregor Smith from *Ich und Du*, with an afterword by the author (Heidelberg: Schneider, 1958). Buber's influential role in shaping modern Western Judaism, discussed in Bach's *The German Jew* (cited above), is reflected in 'The Early Addresses (1909-1918)', in Martin Buber, *On Judaism*, edited by Nahum N. Glatzer (N.Y.: Schocken, 1967), pp. 1-174, translated by Eva Jospe from corresponding selections in *Der Jude und sein Judentum. Gesammelte Aufsätze und Reden* ['The Jew and His Judaism: Collected Compositions and Speeches'], with an introduction by Robert Weltsch (Cologne: Melzer, 1963). See also Buber's *Two Types of Faith*, cited above near the beginning of the listings on religion, together with the response by Hans Urs von Balthasar; Hans Kohn's early study, with a supplement for 1930-1960 by Robert Weltsch, *Martin Buber, sein Werk und seine Zeit. Ein Beitrag zur Geistesgeschichte Mitteleuropas 1880-1930* ['Martin Buber, His Work, and His Times: A Contribution to the Intellectual History of Central Europe 1880-1930'], 2nd, enl. ed. (Cologne: J. Melzer, 1961); and, for a concise, illustrated biography with excerpts from Buber's writings, a chronology, and a bibliography, Gerhard Wehr, *Martin Buber in Selbtzeugnissen und Bilddokumenten* ['Martin Buber in His Testimony and Pictorial Documents'], 2nd ed., Rowohlt's Monographs, no. 147 (Reinbek bei Hamburg: Rowohlt, 1971).

204 **Franz Rosenzweig: his life and thought.**
Nahum N. Glatzer. German texts translated by Francis C. Golffing et al. New York: Schocken Books, 1961. 2nd, rev. ed. 404p. bibliog.

Compiled by a Brandeis University professor who was closely associated with Rosenzweig, this is a 176-page account of Rosenzweig's life (1886-1929), much of it told in his own words, in the form of extracts from letters to friends and family, followed by substantial selections from his writings. The volume includes a chronological outline of his life (noting major publications) and a select bibliography of works by and about him. His *magnum opus*, which Rosenzweig

Philosophy and Religion. The Jewish tradition

began while a soldier on the Macedonian front late in World War I and completed in Berlin a few months after the armistice, was a modern reformulation of the timeless faith of Judaism: God, world, and man are related by creation, revelation, and redemption – six cardinal points symbolized by the six-pointed Star of David, for which the book is named. *The Star of Redemption*, foreword by Nahum N. Glatzer (London: Routledge & Kegan Paul; N.Y.: Holt, Rinehart and Winston, 1971), was translated by William W. Hallo from *Der Stern der Erlösung*, 2nd ed. (Berlin: Schocken, 1930). In two of the essays reprinted in *Kleinere Schriften* ['Shorter Writings'] (Berlin: Schocken, 1937), translated by William Wolf as *On Jewish Learning*, edited and introduced by Nahum N. Glatzer (N.Y.: Schocken, 1955), Rosenzweig proposed the establishment of an Academy for the Science of Judaism, which was founded in Berlin in 1919, and of a modern Jewish adult education programme, which was developed at the *Freies Jüdisches Lehrhaus* (Free House of Jewish Studies) in Frankfurt am Main. Rosenzweig became director of the *Lehrhaus* in 1920. Among his closest associates there was Martin Buber, with whom he began a new German translation of the Hebrew Scriptures (the Old Testament), completed, after his death in 1929, by Buber alone: *Die Schrift* ['The Scriptures'], vols. 1-3 translated by Martin Buber and Franz Rosenzweig, vol. 4 by Martin Buber, rev. ed. (Heidelberg: Lambert Schneider, 1954-1962).

205 **Judaism: development and life.**
Leo Trepp. Belmont, Calif.: Dickenson Publishing Co., 1966.
216p. bibliog.

Until 1938 rabbi of Oldenburg in northwestern Germany, and after the war a rabbi and college professor in Napa, California, Trepp presents a lucid introduction to the history and religion of the Jewish people. A self-contained survey, relatively short, and not too involved, it is intended to give readers with genuine interest but little or no background a reasonably well-informed appreciation of the Jewish heritage. In the Federal Republic it was published, with a revised foreword by the author, in a widely circulated paperback series, translated by Karl-Heinz Laier, as *Das Judentum. Geschichte und lebendige Gegenwart* ['Judaism: History and Living Present'] (Reinbek bei Hamburg: Rowohlt, 1970). On the situation of Jewish Germans in postwar West Germany, see Howard Morley Sachar's *Diaspora* and related titles in the section on minorities.

Social Conditions

206 **The German family: essays on the social history of the family in nineteenth- and twentieth-century Germany.**
Edited by Richard J. Evans and W. R. Lee. Totowa, N.J.: Barnes & Noble Books; London: Croom Helm, 1981. 302p.

This collection of nine essays begins with 'The German Family: A Critical Survey of the Current State of Historical Research,' by Robert Lee, a thirty-two page introduction to the literature with 128 notes providing numerous bibliographical citations. Other contributions deal with role-division in the family in the nineteenth century, social structures in a German village between the world wars, and women garment workers in pre-World War I Berlin and Hamburg. All the papers are annotated, and there are numerous tables and figures. For a concise introduction to the family addressed primarily to German students in their mid to late teens, see *Die Familie in der Bundesrepublik Deutschland* ['The Family in the Federal Republic of Germany'], by Wolfgang W. Weiss, a thirty-six-page monograph published in magazine format as issue no. 206 of *Informationen zur politischen Bildung* [Information for Political Education] (Bonn: Bundeszentrale für politische Bildung, 1985). The monograph, which is available gratis on request from the Bundeszentrale (the Federal Centre for Political Education) at Berliner Freiheit 7, 5300 Bonn), includes a section on contemporary alternative life styles as well as an annotated bibliography.

207 **Germany's women go forward.**
Hugh Wiley Puckett. New York: AMS Press, Inc., 1967. 329p. bibliog.

A history of the 'Woman Question [*Frauenfrage*],' the feminist movement in Germany, from its beginnings, long before the French Revolution, to the late 1920s, when this work, originally published in 1930 (this is a reprint) was completed. The 169-item bibliography includes a number of titles in English. See also two wide-ranging collections of essays, Ruth-Ellen B. Joeres and Mary Jo

Social Conditions

Maynes, eds., *German Women in the Eighteenth and Nineteenth Centuries: A Social and Literary History* (Bloomington: Indiana Univ. Press, 1986) and John C. Fout, ed., *German Women in the Nineteenth Century: A Social History* (N.Y.: Holmes & Meier, 1984), with a bibliography to 1945, and the monograph by Renate Wiggershaus, *Frauen unterm Nationalsozialismus* ['Women under National Socialism'] (Wuppertal: Peter Hammer Verlag, 1984).

208 **Women in the two Germanies: a comparative study of a socialist and a non-socialist society.**

Harry G. Shaffer. New York: Pergamon Press, 1981. 235p. bibliog. (Pergamon Policy Studies on Social Issues).

On the basis of a systematic comparison of the status of women in the two German states, the conclusion is drawn in this monograph that 'complete de facto sex equality cannot be found in either the Federal Republic or the GDR,' but that West German women, living in a society 'steeped in the Judeo-Christian heritage of male dominance,' are far behind their East German counterparts. Apart from the status of women, considerable insight into the social structure of contemporary West Germany is offered by this extensively annotated study. For a collection of essays on several prominent German authors who are women, noting their roles in contemporary society, see Manfred Jurgensen, ed., *Frauenliteratur. Autorinnen – Perspektiven – Konzepte* ['Women's Literature: Authoresses, Perspectives, Conceptions'] (Berne: Peter Lang, 1983; repr., Munich: Deutscher Taschenbuch Verlag, 1985).

209 **Society and democracy in Germany.**

Ralf Dahrendorf. New York: Doubleday & Co., 1967; repr., N.Y.: Doubleday Anchor Books, 1969. 457p. bibliog.

Translated by the author, a German sociologist and former liberal member of the Bonn parliament (who in 1974 became director of the London School of Economics), from *Gesellschaft und Demokratie in Deutschland* (Munich: Piper, 1965), this is a systematic analysis of the society of the Federal Republic, comparable in intent, as the author notes in his foreword, to Tocqueville's *Democracy in America*. Wide-ranging and uncommonly well informed, it remains illuminating and, in its field, unexcelled. A useful collection of essays analyzing various aspects of West German society was edited by Hans Steffen, *Die Gesellschaft in der Bundesrepublik. Analysen* ['Society in the Federal Republic: Analyses'], 2 vols. (Göttingen: Vandenhoeck & Ruprecht, 1970 & 1971). See also the article in the supplement to the Bonn weekly *Das Parlament* by Wolfgang Glatzer and Wolfgang Zapf, 'Die Lebensqualität der Bundesbürger [The Quality of Life of the Citizens (of the Federal Republic)],' *Aus Politik und Zeitgeschichte* ['From Politics and Contemporary History'], B44/84 (3 November 1984), pp. 3-25.

Health and Welfare

210 **The emergence of the welfare state in Britain and Germany 1850-1950.**
Edited by W. J. Mommsen in collaboration with Wolfgang
Mock.   London: Croom Helm, 1981. 443p.

The outcome of an academic conference held in 1978 in Berlin and published
under the auspices of the German Historical Institute in London, this is a
collection of twenty contributions (many extensively annotated with numerous
bibliographical citations) focussing on the socio-political development of the
welfare state in Britain and Germany since the nineteenth century, including 'The
Origins of British National Insurance and the German Precedent 1880-1914,' by
Roy Hay (Deakin Univ., Australia); 'German Post-War Social Policies against
the Background of the Beveridge Plan. Some Observations Preparatory to a
Comparative Analysis,' by Hans Günther Hockerts (Bonn Univ.); and 'From the
National Welfare State to the International Welfare System,' by Karl W. Deutsch
(Harvard Univ.). Publications on social security are cited under Labour.

211 **The limits of professional power: national health care in the Federal
Republic of Germany.**
Deborah A. Stone.   Chicago and London: The University of
Chicago Press, 1980. 212p. bibliog.

Undertaken as a study of the professional power of the physicians of West
Germany, this is an analysis of the health care system in which they function and
the way in which it is controlled through a government-mandated peer review
process, complemented primarily by health insurance funds (*Krankenkassen*) and
the Federal Association of Insurance Doctors (*Kassenärztliche Berufsvereini-
gung*). The volume concludes with 'Lessons for the United States.' English- and
German-language publications are listed separately in the bibliography.

Politics

212 **Politics and government in the Federal Republic of Germany: basic documents.**
Edited by Carl-Christoph Schweitzer, Detlev Karsten, Robert Spencer, R. Taylor Cole, Donald Kommers, and Anthony Nicholls. Leamington Spa: Berg Publishers, 1984. 444p. bibliog.

Selected documentation in English translation, introduced and annotated, on the origins of the Federal Republic, 1944-49; parliamentary democracy; chancellor, cabinet, and federal president; the judiciary; basic rights and constitutional review; federalism; political parties and party structure; public opinion; economic and social policy; foreign policy; defence policy: Berlin; and the Federal Republic and the German Democratic Republic. The volume, with information to 1983, includes statistical tables with demographic, economic, political, and social data, graphs on defence expenditures, a glossary of technical terms and abbreviations, and a well-chosen bibliography. See also the 404-page collection of public documents, including constitutions, statutes, and court decisions, in English translation, edited by John C. Lane and James K. Pollock, *Source Materials on the Government and Politics of Germany* (Ann Arbor, Mich.: Wahrs Publishing Co., 1964). The one hundred selections pertain primarily to West Germany since 1945, but there are six on Berlin and eleven on the German Democratic Republic.

213 **West German politics.**
Geoffrey K. Roberts. New York: Taplinger, 1972. 206p. map. bibliog. (Studies in Comparative Politics).

A concise introduction to the political system of the Federal Republic of Germany, taking into account its historical background, relevant social, geographic, economic, and diplomatic factors, and the political culture and issues that had emerged by the early 1970s. See also H. G. Peter Wallach and George K. Romoser, *West German Politics in the Mid-Eighties: Crisis and Continuity* (N.Y.: Praeger, 1985), a collection of original essays, particularly Romoser's own

84

contribution, 'Germany and the Germans – A Report from the Eighties' (pp. 5-23), which, like the others, has bibliographical citations in the backnotes. An earlier collection that is still quite useful with reference to the Adenauer era is Walter Stahl, ed., *The Politics of Postwar Germany*, introduction by Norbert Muhlen (N.Y.: Praeger, 1963), which includes translations of a good selection of articles published in representative German publications. The current consensus on the West German political process is synopsized in the well-illustrated 187-page paperback, *A Mandate for Democracy: Three Decades of the Federal Republic of Germany*, (Bonn: Federal Press and Information Office, 1980), translated by Lawrence S. Leshnik from *Demokratie als Auftrag. Drei Jahrzehnte Bundesrepublik Deutschland* (Bonn: Presse- und Informationsamt der Bundesregierung, 1979), reissued in 1983 in an updated revision under the title *Demokratie. Unser Auftrag. Drei Jahrzehnte Bundesrepublik*.

214 **Policy and politics in the Federal Republic of Germany.**
Edited by Klaus von Beyme and Manfred G. Schmidt. Translated by Eileen Martin. Aldershot, Hants, England: Gower Publishing Company Limited, for the German Political Science Association, 1985. 257p. bibliog. (German Political Studies, 6).

A collection of studies, both empirical and theoretical, by West German and West Berlin political scientists, of the policy-making process in the Federal Republic of Germany, focussing on changes that have taken place in it from the early 1950s to the start of the 1980s, particularly with reference to the traditional functions of the state, such as defence and legal affairs, but also more recent areas of intervention, such as environmental protection and energy policy. Each of the ten contributions ends with a listing – in some cases extensive – of 'Documents and Official Sources' and other bibliographical references. For a monograph based on survey data on the beliefs, attitudes, interests, and behaviour of the German electorate, see Kendall L. Baker, Russell J. Dalton, and Kai Hildebrandt, *Germany Transformed: Political Culture and the New Politics* (Cambridge, Mass.: Harvard Univ. Press, 1981). Werner Weidenfeld, ed., *Nachdenken über Deutschland. Materialien zur politischen Kultur der Deutschen Frage* ['Reflections on Germany: Materials on the Political Culture of the German Question'] (Cologne: Verlag Wissenschaft und Politik, 1985) is a well-focussed symposium volume of 182 pages, with contributions on the political implications of national and, specifically, German identity; see especially Christian Graf von Krockow's ten lucid theses on 'Probleme kollektiver Identität in der modernen Industriegesellschaft [Problems of Collective Identity in Modern Industrial Society],' (pp. 83-88). See also Krockow's 'Grenzen der Politik [Limits of Politics],' in *Aus Politik und Zeitgeschichte*, B32-33/82 (14 August 1982), (pp. 3-14), the supplement to the Bonn weekly *Das Parlament*, and his essay *Nationalismus als deutsches Problem* ['Nationalism as a German Problem'] (Munich: Piper, 1970), with coverage of postwar Germany and a good bibliography.

215 **Parliament in the German political system.**
Gerhard Loewenberg. Ithaca, N.Y.: Cornell University Press,
1967. 463p.

Standard, detailed description, analysis, and evaluation of parliamentary government in the Federal Republic, considering the formation of the cabinet, and its
role, as well as that of the Bundesrat (the Federal Council, representing the
states) and the Bundestag (the diet, representing the people) in the legislative
process. The illustrated volume is well indexed, has over forty tables, and
includes numerous bibliographical citations in the footnotes. See also Karl H.
Cerny, ed., *Germany at the Polls: The Bundestag Election of 1976* (Washington,
D.C.: American Enterprise Institute for Public Policy Research, 1978), with
contributions by Gerhard Loewenberg, Kurt Sontheimer, and others; Gerard
Braunthal, *The West German Legislative Process: A Case Study of Two
Transportation Bills* (Ithaca, N.Y.: Cornell Univ. Press, 1972); and Hans
Trossmann, *The German Bundestag: Organization and Operation,* rev. ed.
(Darmstadt and Bad Homburg vor der Höhe: Neue Darmstädter Verlagsanstalt,
1966), largely a revised translation of material in *Kürschners Volkshandbuch,* the
manual cited in the next entry.

216 **Kürschner's popular guide to the German Bundestag – 10th
Parliament 1983.**
[Carl-Christian Kaiser.] Rheinbreitbach: NDV Neue
Darmstädter Verlagsanstalt, 1984. 32p.

This abridged English introduction to the Bundestag consists of a translation of a
twenty-page essay on the institution's internal organization and operating
procedures, together with statistical data on the members (age, education, family
status, and religion), and a listing of the Federal President and the members of
the Federal Government. The booklet is based on a recent edition of *Kürschners
Volkshandbuch Deutscher Bundestag: 10. Wahlperiode 1983,* ed. by Klaus-J.
Holzapfel, 43rd ed. (Rheinbreitbach: NDV Neue Darmstädter Verlagsanstalt,
1985), a 272-page paperback that includes, in addition to Kaiser's essay on
organization and procedures, a listing of the members by state or electoral
district, detailed electoral statistics, a listing of the German members of the
European Parliament, and an illustrated biographical sketch of each member of
the Bundestag. *Amtliches Handbuch des Deutschen Bundestages: 10. Wahlperiode
(Stand: 31. Mai 1985)* ['Official Handbook of the German Bundestag: Tenth
Electoral Period (Status as of 31 May 1985)'], edited by the Bundestag
administrative staff (Rheinbreitbach: NDV Neue Darmstädter Verlagsanstalt,
1985) includes the full text of the *Grundgesetz* [Basic Law], as amended, as well
as other laws and the procedural rules of the Bundestag; statistics on the election
of the Tenth Bundestag on 6 March 1983; a detailed breakdown of the
organization of the Bundestag and its committees; a directory of the Federal
Government and the Federal Presidency; an illustrated directory of the
membership of the Bundestag (a full page per member); and a listing of the
German members of the European Parliament. (A loose-leaf volume of some 875
pages originally issued in 1983, it was updated to May 1985 by the fourth set of
replacement pages.)

Politics

217 **Die Parteien der Bundesrepublik Deutschland.** (The parties of the
Federal Republic of Germany.)
Ossip K. Flechtheim, editor.   Hamburg: Hoffman und Campe
Verlag, 1973. 597p.

A reader with 124 selected essays and documents on the origins, development,
and problems of the political parties in West Germany; on their programmes;
their legal status; their structure, governance, and internal controversies; and on
party financing, pressure groups, and inter-party relations. On the individual
parties and their leaders and programmes, see the following: Arnold J.
Heidenheim, *Adenauer and the CDU: The Rise of the Leader and the Integration
of the Party* (The Hague: Nijhoff, 1960), and the late chancellor's memoirs, cited
under History; Lewis J. Edinger, *Kurt Schumacher: A Study in Personality and
Political Behavior* (Stanford, Calif.: Stanford Univ. Press, 1965), and the memoirs
of the Social Democratic party chairman and former chancellor, Willy Brandt,
cited under History; Alf Mintzel, *Die CSU. Anatomie einer konservativen Partei
1945-1972* ['The CSU: Anatomy of a Conservative Party'] (Opladen:
Westdeutscher Verlag, 1975); Karl-Hermann Flach, Werner Maihofer, and
Walter Scheel, *Die Freiburger Thesen der Liberalen* ['The Freiburg Theses of the
Liberals'] (Reinbek bei Hamburg: Rowohlt, 1972), the political programme of the
Free Democratic party, with statements by three of its leaders; Ulrich Probst, *The
Communist Parties in the Federal Republic of Germany*, translated by Angelika G.
Beck (Frankfurt am Main: Haag und Herchen, 1981); Kurt P. Tauber, *Beyond
Eagle and Swastika: German Nationalism since 1945*, 2 vols. (Middletown, Conn.:
Wesleyan Univ. Press, 1967), on right-wing political movements (the second
volume consists of notes, appendices, an eighty-six-page bibliography, and two
indexes); and Fridtjof Capra and Charlene Spretnak in collaboration with
Rüdiger Lutz, *Green Politics* (N.Y.: Dutton, 1984), a sympathetic account of the
emergence and politics of the environment- and peace-oriented movement of 'The
Greens [*Die Grünen*]' in West Germany, with a concluding evaluation of their
first four years, through 1983, during which they won seats in the federal
parliament and in several state parliaments.

218 **The West German peace movement and the national question.**
Kim R. Holmes.   Cambridge, Mass., & Washington, D.C.:
Institute for Foreign Policy Analysis, Inc., in association with the
Fletcher School of Law & Diplomacy, Tufts University, 1984. 76p.
bibliog. (Foreign Policy Report, March 1984).

This monograph by the co-author of *The Greens of West Germany* in the same
series deals with the national question, neutralism, and *Ostpolitik* in the context
of the problem of German national identity. See also Clay Clemens, 'The
Antinuclear Movement in West Germany: *Angst* and Isms, Old and New,' in
James E. Dougherty and Robert L. Pfaltzgraff, Jr., eds., *Shattering Europe's
Defense Consensus: The Antinuclear Protest Movement and the Future of NATO*
(Washington, D.C.: Pergamon-Brassey's International Defense Publishers, 1985),
pp. 62-96, with bibliographical references in eighty-three notes; the dated but still
useful RAND Corporation study by Hans Speier, *German Rearmament and
Atomic War: The Views of German Military and Political Leaders* (Evanston, Ill.:
Row, Peterson and Co., 1957); Lutz Köllner, 'Die Entwicklung bundesdeutscher
Militärausgaben in Vergangenheit und Zukunft [The Development of German

Politics

Federal Military Spending in Past and Future]' in *Aus Politik und Zeitgeschichte*, B22/84 (2 June 1984), pp. 27-39, with tables and notes; Siegfried Grimm, . . . *der Bundesrepublik treu zu dienen. Die geistige Rüstung der Bundeswehr* ['. . . to Serve the Federal Republic Faithfully: The Spiritual Armour of the Federal Armed Forces'], with a preface by Wolf Graf von Baudissin (Düsseldorf: Droste, 1970); and Peter Zimmermann's article on the colleges of the Bundeswehr cited under Education.

Constitution, Administration, and Legal System

The Basic Law and the federal system

219 **The Basic Law of the Federal Republic of Germany.**
Promulgated by the Parliamentary Council on 23 May 1949, as
amended up to and including 23 August 1976. Wiesbaden:
Wiesbadener Graphische Betriebe for the Press and Information
Office of the Federal Government, 1981. 170p.
Official translation of the text of the constitution of the Federal Republic of
Germany, with amendments, an appendix, and a 75-page index.

220 **Grundgesetz für die Bundesrepublik Deutschland: Kommentar an
Hand der Rechtsprechung des Bundesverfassungsgerichts.** (Basic
Law of the Federal Republic of Germany: commentary on the
basis of the verdicts and decisions of the Federal Constitutional
Court.)
G. Leibholz and H. J. Rinck, in collaboration with K. Helberg.
Cologne-Marienburg: Verlag Dr. Otto Schmidt, 1968. 3rd ed.
800p.
Authoritative commentary, by Justice Leibholz of the Constitutional Court and
two others, on the Basic Law, its amendments, and its interpretation by the
Federal Republic of Germany's highest court.

Constitution, Administration, and Legal System. The Basic Law and the federal system

221   **Electoral Law.**
Introduction by Walther Keim.   Bonn: Inter Nationes, 1980. 56p.
bibliog. (Documents on Politics and Society in the Federal
Republic of Germany).

A concise explanation of the complex system whereby the members of the lower
house of the legislature of the Federal Republic, the Bundestag, are elected;
English translation of federal legislation on Bundestag elections; and a listing, by
translated title and place of publication, of legislation governing state and local
elections throughout West Germany and West Berlin.

222   **Constitutionalism in Germany and the Federal Constitutional
Court.**
Edward McWhinney. Introduction by Gerhard Leibholz.
Leyden: A. W. Sythoff, 1962. 71p. bibliog.

An introduction to the Constitutional Court, with particular reference to
landmark cases.

223   **Judicial politics in West Germany: a study of the Federal
Constitutional Court.**
Donald P. Kommers.   Beverly Hills, Calif., and London: Sage
Publications, 1976. 312p. bibliog. (Sage Series on Politics and the
Legal Order, vol. 5).

An account of the position of the Federal Constitutional Court, with complete
administrative autonomy, as the supreme guardian of the Constitution, of the
process by which its members are selected, of its procedures, and of the impact
that it has by asserting and exercising its authority in a system with
constitutionally mandated separation of powers between legislature, executive,
and judiciary. See also *Federalism and Judicial Review in West Germany* by Philip
M. Blair (Oxford: Clarendon Press, 1981), and *Das Bundesverfassungsgericht*
['The Federal Constitutional Court'] (Karlsruhe: Verlag C. F. Müller for the
Federal Constitutional Court, 1963), published by the high court after its first
decade, particularly the article on 'Der Status des Bundesverfassungsgerichts'
['The Status of the Federal Constitutional Court'], pp. 61-86, by Gerhard
Leibholz, who had drafted the court's 1952 memorandum (with the force of an
advisory opinion) rejecting administrative oversight by any other organ of
government as unconstitutional; Leibholz defined the issues in two articles
addressed to the English-speaking reader, 'The Federal Constitutional Court in
the Constitutional System of the Federal Republic of Germany,' pp. 271-285, and
'Judicial Power and the Authority of the State in the Federal Republic of
Germany,' pp. 324-331, in *Politics and Law* (Leyden: A. W. Sythoff, 1965).

224 **Law on the Federal Constitutional Court.**
Introduction by Gotthard Wöhrmann. Bonn: Inter Nationes,
1982. 69p. (Documents on Politics and Society in the Federal
Republic of Germany).

A 23-page introductory essay on the constitution and courts of the Federal
Republic is followed by excerpts from the Basic Law mandating the establishment
of the Federal Constitutional Court, from the legislation implementing that
mandate, and from the rules of procedure of the court.

225 **Die Verfassungen der deutschen Bundesländer.** (The constitutions
of the German federal states.)
Edited by Dieter Kakies. Introduction by Otto Bezold. Munich:
Wilhelm Goldmann Verlag, 1966. 342p. map. (Goldmanns Gelbe
Taschenbücher).

Inexpensive paperback edition of the constitutions of Baden-Württemberg,
Bavaria, Berlin, Bremen, Hamburg, Hesse, Lower Saxony, North Rhine-
Westphalia, Rhineland-Palatinate, Saarland, and Schleswig-Holstein, with an
index.

226 **Federalism, bureaucracy, and party politics in Western Germany:
the role of the Bundesrat.**
Edward L. Pinney. Chapel Hill: University of North Carolina
Press, 1963. 268p. bibliog.

In the West German federal system, the Federal Council (*Bundesrat*) represents
the states (*Länder*) comprising the Federal Republic. The deliberations of the
Federal Council are conducted not by representatives of the people elected, like
United States senators, to the upper house of the national legislature, but
generally by civil servants delegated by the state governments – i.e., by
representatives of the state bureaucracy. This study reviews the origins and
structure of the Federal Council and, on a case-study basis, describes how it fills
its role as guarantor of the interests of the states, with consideration of the
interaction of the bureaucracy and the political parties.

227 **Studies in comparative federalism: West Germany.**
Advisory Commission on Intergovernmental Relations.
Washington, D.C.: U.S. Government Printing Office for the
ACIR, 1981. 89p. map. bibliog. (Information Report M-128 of the
ACIR).

A report on fiscal federalism prepared by Prof. H. Zimmermann of Marburg
University for a permanent advisory commission created by the U.S. Congress,
representing the executive and legislative branches of federal, state, and local
government and the public. The report provides a description (supported by 32
tables, a chart, and a schematic figure) of the political process whereby significant
disparities in economic and financial capacity among the West German
governmental units are balanced, providing more or less equivalent resources on a
nationwide basis. The annotations and bibliography include several publications
in English of the Commission of the European Communities (based in Brussels).

Constitution, Administration, and Legal System. The Basic Law and the federal system

228   **Staatskirchenrecht. Ein Leitfaden durch die Rechtsbeziehungen zwischen Staat und den Religionsgemeinschaften.** (State law on the churches: a guide to the legal relations between the state and the religious communities.)
Axel Freiherr von Campenhausen.   Munich: Wilhelm Goldmann Verlag, 1973. 295p. bibliog. (Das wissenschaftliche Taschenbuch: Abteilung Rechts- und Staatswissenschaften).

The churches in the Federal Republic have generally retained much of their privileged status, including direct funding through a state-administered church tax. This heavily annotated monograph concisely reviews the historical background of the legal relationship between church and state in Germany, defines the constitutional position of the churches in the Federal Republic, and describes their legal status and corporate rights under present law.

229   **The foundations of European Community law: an introduction to the constitutional and administrative law of the European Community.**
T. C. Hartley.   Oxford: At the Clarendon Press, 1981. 551p. bibliog. (Clarendon Law Series).

A systematic textbook on the body of law of the European Community, which is distinct from the national law of the member states on the one hand, and international law on the other. The Federal Republic of Germany, like the other members of the European Community, has limited its sovereignty in favour of the Community legal order. The law of the Community takes precedence over German law in certain cases and affects German legislation in many others. For a brief orientation, see Richard Plender, *A Practical Introduction to European Community Law* (London: Sweet & Maxwell, 1980), which includes a bibliography and tables of treaties, of legislation, and of cases brought to the Court of Justice of the European Communities.

230   **German constitutional documents since 1871: selected texts and commentary.**
Edited by Louise W. Holborn, Gwendolen M. Carter, and John H. Herz.   New York: Praeger Publishers, 1970, 243p.

A documentary introduction to the constitutional structure and governmental machinery of the two German states and West Berlin, based on selected and annotated excerpts from their constitutions and related documents now in force, as well as corresponding material from the constitution of 1871, the constitution of 1919, and, in the relatively few cases where applicable, the National Socialist period, to provide historical perspective on the functional structure of the present system. See also H. W. Koch, *A Constitutional History of Germany in the Nineteenth and Twentieth Centuries* (London: Longman, 1984).

The legal and administrative system

231 Legal theory.
W. Friedmann.   New York: Columbia University Press, 1967. 5th
ed. 607p. bibliog.

A classic survey of the origins, theories, and problems of law from Antiquity to
the present, by a distinguished German emigrant whose explanation of the
differences in theory and in practice between the Anglo-American and
Continental systems is particularly helpful in understanding the functioning of the
law in Germany. Two chapters deleted from the 5th edition for lack of space may
be found in the 4th ed. (London: Stevens & Sons, 1960): chapter 28, 'Fascist and
National Socialist Legal Theories' (pp. 347-355), and chapter 34, 'Nationalist
Interpretations of Legal and Political Philosophy,' covering, *inter alia*, Ernst
Troeltsch's critique of German romanticism (pp. 530-38). See also Carl J.
Friedrich, *The Philosophy of Law in Historical Perspective*, 2nd ed. (Chicago &
London: Univ. of Chicago Press, 1963).

232 Max Weber on law in economy and society.
Edited with introduction and annotations by Max Rheinstein,
translated by Edward Shils and Max Rheinstein.
Cambridge, Mass.: Harvard University Press, 1954; repr., New
York: Simon and Schuster, Clarion Books, 1967. 363p. bibliog.

Translation from *Wirtschaft und Gesellschaft* ['Economy and Society'], 2nd ed.
(Tübingen: J. C. B. Mohr [Paul Siebeck], 1925) of Weber's classic analysis of the
social and economic function of law in comparative perspective, with illuminating
contrasts between the legal systems of modern Germany, France, and Britain,
imperial China, mediaeval Europe, and the Roman Empire.

233 Guide to foreign legal materials – French, German, Swiss.
Charles Szladits.   New York: Oceana Publications for the Parker
School of Foreign and Comparative Law, Columbia University,
1959. 599p. bibliog.

The second part of this volume (pp. 118-330) is a guide for the Anglo-American
lawyer to the use of West German legal materials. A brief introduction to the
political organizaton and the sources of law (enacted law and judicial review,
customary law, case law, etc.) is followed by a detailed description of repositories
of the law (constitutions, codes, statutes, decrees, orders, tax laws, etc.) with
annotations citing sources, giving further references, and providing explanations
of procedures. The volume includes a summary on the German Democratic
Republic (pp. 296-301), a note on books in English on German law (pp. 301-303),
and a 26-page list of German legal abbreviations and their translations.

Constitution, Administration, and Legal System. The legal and administrative system

234 **Manual of German law, vol. 1: general introduction, civil law.**
E. J. Cohn assisted by W. Zdzieblo. London: British Institute of International and Comparative Law; Dobbs Ferry, N.Y.: Oceana Publications, 1968. 2nd ed. 324p. bibliog. (Comparative Law Series, no. 14).

Based in part on a 1950 publication of H.M. Stationery Office for the Foreign Office, this volume, after an extended introduction to the legal system of the Federal Republic of Germany in historical context, provides a detailed synopsis of the Civil Code. The individual provisions of its five parts (general principles and definitions, law of obligations, law of property, law of domestic relations, and law of succession) are summarized and explained, together with relevant German technical terms and concepts foreign to Anglo-American jurisprudence. The purpose of the manual is to provide English-speaking lawyers with information on elementary aspects of German law. Specific cases and explanatory examples are cited throughout. It includes a list of abbreviations, a glossary of German terms, systematic and alphabetical indices, and a concise bibliography. For the full text of the code, see the translation of *The German Civil Code* by Ian S. Forrester, Simon L. Goren, and Hans-Michael Ilgen (South Hackensack, N.J.: Fred B. Rothman & Co., 1975).

235 **Manual of German law, vol. 2: commercial law, civil procedure, conflict of laws, bankruptcy, law of nationality, East German family law.**
E. J. Cohn, O. C. Giles, M. Bohndorf, and J. Tomass. London: British Institute of International and Comparative Law; Dobbs Ferry, N.Y.: Oceana Publications, 1971. 2nd ed. 329p. bibliog. (Comparative Law Series, no. 15).

Continuation of vol. 1 (cited above), to which it includes a brief supplement; it likewise includes a glossary, a list of abbreviations, indices, and a bibliography. It provides a detailed summary and interpretation of the German Commercial Code in the Federal Republic of Germany; an introduction, citing codes and precedents, to West German practice in cases of conflict of laws; an introduction to the law of civil procedure, citing applicable provisions of the law on the organization of the courts and the Code of Civil Procedure; an introduction to the German law of bankruptcy; a brief outline of the complex German law of nationality as practised in the Federal Republic; and a chapter on the law of the German Democratic Republic regarding marriage, divorce, and the family. See also the translation of *The German Commercial Code* by Simon L. Goren and Ian S. Forrester (Littleton, Colo.: Fred B. Rothman & Co., 1979); *Germany: Practical Legal Guide on Costs & Fees, Court Proceedings and Commercial Law* by Ruediger W. Trott (Brunswick: Hoyers Verlags GmbH, 1977); and Rudolf Mueller et al., *Doing Business in Germany: A Legal Manual*, 6th, rev. ed. (Frankfurt am Main: Knapp, 1971).

236 **Modern German corporation law.**
Enno W. Ercklentz, Jr.   Dobbs Ferry, N.Y.: Oceana
Publications, 1979. 2 vols. bibliog.

A general guide to corporate law in the Federal Republic of Germany, written to aid the English-speaking lawyer who has clients with an interest in German enterprises.

237 **The German law of agency and distributorship agreements.**
Fritz Staubach.   London: Oyez Publishing, 1977. 267p. (European
Commercial Law Library Series, no. 7).

One of a series of handbooks designed to present to the English businessman and his professional advisers in as clear and simple language as possible the commercial laws of the European Community countries. The author explains, for example, that there is no concept in German law corresponding precisely to that of 'agency' in English law – and goes on to explain the nuances and implications of the most closely corresponding German term (which is not a translation and could lead to serious misunderstanding if taken as such).

238 **American-German private law relations cases 1945-1955.**
Martin Domke.   New York: Oceana Publications for the Parker
School of Foreign and Comparative Law, Columbia University,
1956. 144p. bibliog. (Bilateral Studies in Private International Law,
no. 4).

A concise survey of the handling of a large number of private law cases during the first postwar decade, involving issues such as the administration of estates, monetary questions (e.g., German dollar bonds going back to the 1920s), the effect of measures taken during the National Socialist régime, and questions of procedure and of conflict of laws. The volume lists German and American references, includes the text of the 1954 German-American Treaty of Friendship, Commerce and Navigation, lists the cases cited in the 546 footnotes, and concludes with an author-subject index. For an account of the legal effort on behalf of forced labourers to secure belated financial reimbursement for their labour (postwar German indemnification law provided about a dollar a day for false imprisonment, but no compensation for labour), see *Less Than Slaves: Jewish Forced Labor and the Quest for Compensation* by Benjamin B. Ferencz, with a foreword by Telford Taylor (Cambridge, Mass., and London: Harvard Univ. Press, 1979).

239 **Press law in the Federal Republic of Germany.**
Helmut Kohl.   In: *Press law in modern democracies: a
comparative survey*, ed. by Pnina Lahav. New York & London:
Longman, 1985, p. 185-228.

A concise introduction by a Frankfurt law professor, taking into account the constitutional guarantee of freedom of the press, the individual's right to privacy, the role of the government (with coverage of the *Spiegel* affair), and the self-

Constitution, Administration, and Legal System. The legal and administrative system

regulatory function of the nongovernmental West German Press Council (*Presserat*). The 187 notes include extensive extracts, in English translation, of state and federal press laws, as well as citations of cases, laws, and the relevant literature (almost exclusively in German).

240 **Taxation in the Federal Republic of Germany.**
Henry J. Gumpel and Carl Boettcher. Chicago: Commerce Clearing House, 1963. 932p. bibliog. (World Tax Series, Harvard Law School International Program in Taxation).

After an introductory description of the general political and legal framework of the West German tax system as a whole, the individual kinds of taxes are taken up in sequence – income taxes, valuation taxes, and trade and turnover taxes – with a detailed explanation, in each case, of the origin of the tax, on whom and for what it is imposed, how it is calculated, and how it is administered. There is an extensive, annotated bibliography of mostly German sources.

241 **Anti-terrorist legislation in the Federal Republic of Germany.**
Miklos K. Radvanyi. Washington, D.C.: Library of Congress Law Library, 1979. 143p. bibliog.

A report on anti-terrorist measures enacted in the Federal Republic in the 1970s, with English translation of relevant legislation, including controversial measures affecting the civil service. For a critique of the legislation and related administrative measures, see Sebastian Cobler, *Law, Order and Politics in West Germany* (Harmondsworth & New York: Penguin Books, 1978), transl. by Francis McDonagh from *Die Gefahr geht von den Menschen aus* (Berlin: Rotbuch Verlag, 1976); for a concise statement of the rationale for the anti-terrorist programme, with particular consideration of safeguards for individual human rights and academic freedom, see *Civil Liberties and the Defense of Democracy against Extremists and Terrorists: A Report on the West German Situation*, by Wilhelm G. Grewe and others (Hamburg: Atlantik-Brücke in cooperation with the American Council on Germany, New York, ca. 1980).

242 **The administration of justice in the Federal Republic of Germany.**
Wolfgang Heyde. Limburg an der Lahn: Limburger Vereinsdruckerei for the Press and Information Office of the Federal Government, 1971. 150p. bibliog.

A systematic exposition of the constitutional authority and institutional structure of the courts and other administrative organs concerned with the administration of justice, and of the role of the legal profession in the Federal Republic.

243 **Lawyers and their society: a comparative study of the legal
profession in Germany and in the United States.**
Dietrich Rueschemeyer. Cambridge, Mass.: Harvard University
Press, 1973. 254p. bibliog.
Extensively annotated sociological study of the legal profession in Germany and
the United States, primarily in private practice, comparing the bar in the context
of the two societies, noting similarities and contrasts in professional ethics, and
the differences in historical tradition. See also Niklas Luhmann, 'The Legal
Profession: Comments on the Situation in the Federal Republic of Germany'
(pp. 98-114) in *Lawyers in Their Social Setting: Wilson Memorial Lectures,
University of Edinburgh*, ed. by D. N. MacCormick (Edinburgh: W. Green &
Son, 1976).

244 **Reforming West German law.**
Almut Klempt. Preface by Gerhard Jahn. Bonn: Inter Nationes,
1970. 36p. (IN-Press Special Report).
A compilation of six articles in English, addressed to the concerned layman (and
released by the press service of Inter Nationes, a government information agency
in Bonn), on the need for reforms pertaining to divorce law, the rights of
illegitimate children, the penal code, the prison system, the sexual penal code
(beyond decriminalization of adultery in September 1969), and abortion. The
Federal Minister of Justice stated in his preface that the publication was not
intended to represent the position of the Brandt administration (in office since
1969), but to reflect the full breadth of the West German debate on legal reform.

West Berlin and Its Special Status

245 The siege of Berlin.
Mark Arnold-Forster. London: Collins, 1979. 172p. 2 maps.
bibliog.

A lucid, readable account, by the author of the BBC television series 'The World at War,' of the ordeal of Berlin from the end of the Second World War to the stabilization of its status under the Four-Power Agreement twenty-five years later. See also the popular, large-format, heavily illustrated 'coffee-table' book by Frederic V. Grunfeld et al., with photographs by Leonard Freed, *Berlin*, 'The Great Cities' series (Amsterdam: Time-Life Books, 1977), and the forty-page monograph, issued for distribution to schools by (and available on request from) the nonpartisan Federal Centre for Political Education, Berliner Freiheit 7, 5300 Bonn, by Udo Wetzlaugk, *Berlin*, 'Informationen zur politischen Bildung [Information for Political Education],' no. 181 (Bonn: Bundeszentrale für politische Bildung, September 1979), a well-illustrated overview (with tables, graphs, bibliography, and addresses for further information) of the postwar history of the city and its situation following the Quadripartite Agreement and related accords of the 1970s.

246 Documents on Berlin, 1943-1963.
Edited by Wolfgang Heidelmeyer and Günter Hindrichs.
Munich: Oldenbourg, 1963. 373p. maps. bibliog.
(Forschungsinstitut der Deutschen Gesellschaft für Auswärtige
Politik: Dokumente und Berichte, Band 22).

English edition of a volume published by the Research Institute of the German Society for Foreign Policy in Bonn with 211 documents (or excerpts) from late 1943 to mid-1963, appendices with statistical data, a selected bibliography, and a map of Germany divided into occupation zones and of Berlin, showing the four sectors and the Wall erected in 1961. See also the 68-page booklet *Berlin: Crisis and Challenge* (N.Y.: German Information Center, 1963) and the documentation on Berlin in the U.S. State Department's document volume on Germany, 1944-1985, cited under History.

247 **The defense of Berlin.**
Jean Edward Smith. Baltimore: Johns Hopkins Press, 1963.
431p. map. bibliog.

Annotated account from the wartime agreements regarding the occupation of Berlin to the aftermath of the building of the Berlin Wall in August 1961. On the crisis triggered by the building of the wall, see the 54-page essay by Howard Trivers, a U.S. diplomat serving there at the time, in *Three Crises in American Foreign Affairs and a Continuing Revolution* (Carbondale and Edwardsville: Southern Illinois Univ. Press, 1972) and the 509-page monograph by Robert M. Slusser, *The Berlin Crisis of 1961: Soviet-American Relations and the Struggle for Power in the Kremlin, June-November 1961* (Baltimore: Johns Hopkins Univ. Press, 1973). See also Avi Shlaim, *The United States and the Berlin Blockade, 1948-1949: A Study in Crisis Decision-Making* (Berkeley: Univ. of California Press, 1983).

248 **The Quadripartite Agreement on Berlin of September 3, 1971.**
Bonn: Press and Information Office of the Federal Government, 1971. 119p.

The English version of the September 1971 agreement on Berlin between France, the United Kingdom, the United States, and the Soviet Union, the annexes, and the Final Quadripartite Protocol (signed in June 1972, putting the accord into effect) are printed in this booklet, together with documentation on the relationship of West Berlin to the Federal Republic and an account of the historical background, the substance, and the significance of the agreement. The 190-page German edition, *Das Viermächte-Abkommen über Berlin vom 3. September 1971* (Bonn: Press and Information Office; Hamburg: Hoffmann und Campe, 1971), is annotated and also includes (on pp. 179-192) the text of the agreement, annexes, and protocol in English. (A German translation could not be agreed upon; only the English, French, and Russian texts are authoritative.)

249 **A balance sheet of the Quadripartite Agreement on Berlin: evaluation and documentation.**
Honoré M. Catudal, Jr. Foreword by Ambassador Kenneth Rush. Berlin: Berlin Verlag, 1978. 303p. bibliog. (Political Studies, no. 13).

This is a sequel to Catudal's *Diplomacy of the Quadripartite Agreement on Berlin* (Berlin: Berlin Verlag, 1978). The first half focusses on the political and economic situation of Berlin after the Quadripartite Agreement; the second half is made up of appendices, including an extensive chronology (1943-1978), documentation, and a detailed bibliography (with articles and often overlooked official publications). For a complementary study focussing on the legal and constitutional situation of Berlin, particularly the complex relationship of West Berlin to the Federal Republic, see Ernst R. Zivier's *The Legal Status of the Land Berlin:*

A Survey after the Quadripartite Agreement (Berlin: Berlin Verlag, 1980), translated by Paul S. Ulrich from the third edition of *Der Rechtsstatus des Landes Berlin. Eine Untersuchung nach dem Viermächte-Abkommen vom 3. September 1971* (Berlin: Berlin Verlag, 1977).

250   **Judgment in Berlin.**
Herbert J. Stern.   New York: Universe Books, 1984. 384p.
bibliog.

A U.S. federal judge's account of his unique assignment in Berlin, providing insight into the legal status of the still occupied city and the sovereign authority exercised there by American officials. In 1978, an East German couple had highjacked a Polish airliner, forcing it to land in West rather than East Berlin. To exercise criminal jurisdiction, the United States Court for Berlin, which had previously existed only on paper, was constituted in January 1979, with the author, on loan from the U.S. District Court for New Jersey, presiding. Flagrant violations of the constitutional rights of one defendant by U.S. military authorities led the court (with the prosecution's mortified consent) to dismiss her case. Despite strenuous objections by the occupation authorities, the other defendant was granted a trial before a jury of Berliners. Found guilty on only one of several charges, he was, in the end, sentenced to serve only the time he had already spent in detention – with the result that he left the court a free man. In addition to this criminal case, a civil case that could not be tried in a German court had been brought to the U.S. court: a group of Berliners contested the construction of a U.S. Army housing project in a public park. The State Department directed the federal judge not to exercise jurisdiction. When he refused to accept such direction, his Berlin appointment was immediately terminated, and, with it, the brief but memorable existence of the court.

251   **The future of Berlin.**
Edited by Martin J. Hillenbrand.   Montclair, N.J.: Allanheld,
Osmun Publ., 1980. 313p. maps. bibliog. (An Atlantic Institute for
International Affairs Research Volume).

Edited by the former U.S. ambassador to the Federal Republic of Germany, with Peter C. Ludz as principal consultant, this collaborative volume defines the situation of Berlin in historical context, its current status, and its prospects for the future. There is a detailed index. The work was also published in German: *Die Zukunft Berlins*, ed. by M. J. Hillenbrand (Frankfurt am Main: Ullstein, 1981).

Intra-German and Foreign Relations

General

252 **West Germany's foreign policy agenda.**
Roger Morgan. Preface by Ralf Dahrendorf. Beverly Hills,
Calif., and London: Sage Publications for the Center for Strategic
and International Studies, Georgetown University, Washington,
D.C., 1978. 80p. bibliog. (The Washington Papers, no. 54).

An assessment of the economic, security, and political interests of the Federal
Republic of Germany, focussing on the policy toward the East (*Ostpolitik*), the
Atlantic Alliance, and the European Community. See also Martin Sæter, *The
Federal Republic, Europe, and the World: Perspectives on West German Foreign
Policy*, Norwegian Foreign Policy Studies, no. 31 (Oslo: Universitetsforlaget,
1980), a 120-page essay originally written for the Research Institute of National
Defence in Stockholm, and the collection of essays edited by Viola Herms Drath,
Germany in World Politics (N.Y.: Cyrco Press, 1979), including 'Foreign Policy in
Germany: Ideological and Political Aspects of Intra-German Relations,' by Peter
C. Ludz (pp. 54-77), and 'Europe and America: A Reassessment,' by Ralf
Dahrendorf (pp. 116-126).

253 **West German foreign policy: the domestic setting.**
Gebhard Schweigler. Foreword by Walter Laqueur. New York:
Praeger Publ. for the Center for Strategic and International
Studies, Georgetown University, Washington, D.C., 1984. 124p.
bibliog. (The Washington Papers, no. 106).

A study of the internal constraints on West German policy, concluding that the
Federal Republic, by virtue of 'the internalization of values that provide for
political stability,' is firmly attached to the West (p. 86). See also, for studies of
political opinion in West Germany, Karl W. Deutsch and Lewis J. Edinger,

Intra-German and Foreign Relations. General

Germany Rejoins the Powers: Mass Opinion, Interest Groups, and Elites in Contemporary German Foreign Policy (Stanford, Calif.: Stanford Univ. Press, 1959), and Karl Deutsch, Lewis J. Edinger, Roy C. Macridis, and Richard L. Merritt, *France, Germany and the Western Alliance: A Study of Elite Attitudes on European Integration and World Politics* (N.Y.: Scribner's, 1967).

254 **West German foreign policy: 1949-1979.**
Edited by Wolfram F. Hanrieder.   Boulder, Colo.: Westview Press, 1980. 245p. bibliog. (Westview Special Studies in West European Politics and Society).

Sixteen papers by leading American and German authorities presented at a 1979 conference on the relations of the Federal Republic with France, the Soviet Union, the United States, and the Third World, on the role of the Federal Republic in NATO, and on other significant aspects of German foreign policy. See also Wolfram F. Hanrieder, *The Stable Crisis: Two Decades of German Foreign Policy* (N.Y.: Harper & Row, 1970). For a 105-page survey of West German foreign policy, followed by extensive documentation, a chronology, statistics, organizational charts, and maps, see the 990-page, illustrated volume issued by the West German Foreign Office, *Die Auswärtige Politik der Bundesrepublik Deutschland* ['The Foreign Policy of the Federal Republic of Germany'] (Cologne: Verlag Wissenschaft und Politik, 1972).

255 **The German path to Israel: a documentation.**
Edited by Rolf Vogel. Foreword by Konrad Adenauer.   London: Oswald Wolff; Chester Springs, Pa.: Dufour Editions, 1969, 325p.

A translation of *Deutschlands Weg nach Israel* (Stuttgart: Seewald, 1967), an illustrated documentary history of the relationship between the Federal Republic of Germany and Israel from the first contacts, early in the Adenauer chancellorship, to the development of full diplomatic and cultural relations. There are well over 100 documents, such as press reports, interviews, extracts of parliamentary proceedings, and texts of diplomatic protocols, including the West German agreement to provide several billion marks in restitution of material losses suffered under Hitler. On the restitution, see Nicholas Balabkins, *West German Reparations to Israel* (New Brunswick, N.J.: Rutgers Univ. Press, 1971). See also Lily Gardner Feldman, *The Special Relationship between West Germany and Israel* (Boston: Allen & Unwin, 1984).

256 **German foreign policies, West and East: on the threshold of a new European era.**
Peter H. Merkl.   Santa Barbara, Calif., and Oxford: ABC-Clio, 1974. 232p. bibliog. (Studies in Comparative Politics).

Introduction to a turning point in West German foreign policy: in the 1960s, the Federal Republic neither recognized the German Democratic Republic nor maintained diplomatic relations with any state, other than the Soviet Union, that did, but with the new policy toward the East (*Ostpolitik*) of Chancellor Willy Brandt (1969-1974), this changed. Relations were formally established between the two German states under the 'Treaty on the Basis of Relations' (known as the 'Basic Treaty' or *Grundvertrag*) of 1972; the two German states were simultaneously admitted to the United Nations; and Bonn no longer took exception to the recognition of East Berlin by other states. Prof. Merkl's study reviews the background of the transition in West German policy, shows the often controversial steps by which the change was brought about, and concludes with an assessment of German foreign policy in an era in which it is being conducted by two German states.

257 **The Ostpolitik of the Federal Republic of Germany.**
William E. Griffith.   Cambridge, Mass.: The MIT Press, 1978.
325p. (Studies in Communism, Revisionism, and Revolution, no. 25).

A study, in historical context, of the Federal Republic's policy toward the East, beginning with the Grand Coalition established in the middle 1960s, and reaching its culmination under Chancellor Brandt. The backnotes have numerous bibliographical references. *The Ostpolitik and Political Change in Germany*, edited with an introductory essay by Roger Tilford (Westmead, England: Saxon House; Lexington, Mass.: Lexington Books, 1975), has papers by W. E. Paterson, Geoffrey Pridham, David Childs, Geoffrey K. Roberts, and Roger Morgan, respectively, on the implications of the new *Ostpolitik* for régime stability in West Germany, for the opposition in West Germany, for domestic politics in East Germany, for relations between the two Germanies, and for West Germany's external relations. See also Wilhelm Wolfgang Schütz, *Rethinking German Policy: New Approaches to Reunification* (N.Y.: Praeger: 1967), a revised and updated edition of *Reform der Deutschlandpolitik* (Cologne: Kiepenheuer & Witsch, 1965); Schütz' memorandum, 'Was ist Deutschland? [What is Germany?],' together with his account of the controversy its publication in 1967 triggered, in Schütz, *Deutschland-Memorandum. Eine Denkschrift und ihre Folgen* ['Germany Memorandum: A Memorandum and Its Consequences'] (Frankfurt am Main: Fischer Bücherei, 1968); Ernst Majonica, *East-West Relations: A German View* (N.Y.: Praeger, 1969), an English version of *Deutsche Aussenpolitik* ['German Foreign Policy'] (Stuttgart: Kohlhammer, 1965); and the West German government's 606-page volume documenting the debate in 1972 concerning the treaties and their implications: Bundesminister für innerdeutsche Beziehungen [Federal Minister for Intra-German Relations], *Meinungen und Dokumente zur Deutschlandpolitik und zu den Ostverträgen* ['Opinions and Documents on German Policy and on the Eastern Treaties'] (Bonn: Gesamtdeutsches Institut, June 1972).

258 **West German foreign aid 1956-1966: its economic and political aspects.**
Karel Holbik and Henry Allen Myers.   Boston: Boston University Press, 1968. 158p. maps. bibliog.

An analysis of the first ten years of the West German foreign aid programme, when the Federal Republic ranked fourth and occasionally third as donor nation to underdeveloped countries. The bibliography includes official sources on as well as descriptions and evaluations of West German foreign aid. For a concise overview of development policy, with bibliographical citations, see Dieter Oberndörfer, 'Das Entwicklungsproblem aus heutiger Sicht [The Development Problem as Seen Today]', pp. 184-208 in Karl Kaiser and Hans-Peter Schwarz, eds., *Weltpolitik: Strukturen – Akteure – Perspektiven* ['World Politics: Structures, Actors, Perspectives'], Schriften des Forschungsinstituts der Deutschen Gesellschaft für Auswärtige Politik (Stuttgart: Klett-Cotta, 1985), a 742-page compendium of scholarly articles, with citations of current literature (in English as well as German and other languages), defining and assessing regional and global problems in the world today.

259   **The German problem reconsidered: Germany and the world order, 1870 to the present.**
David Calleo.   Cambridge: Cambridge University Press, 1978. 239p. bibliog.

A concise interpretation of the origins of contemporary Germany as a politically and ideologically divided nation, concluding with a bibliographical essay acknowledging the principal sources and analyses to which the author feels most indebted. See also: *The German Question,* edited by Walther Hubatsch (N.Y.: Herder Book Center, 1967), translated by Salvator Attanasio from *Die deutsche Frage,* 2nd ed. (Würzburg: Ploetz, 1964); J. K. Sowdon, *The German Question, 1945-1973: Continuity in Change* (London: Bradford Univ. Press in asso. with Crosby Lockwood Staples, 1975); Ferenc A. Váli, *The Quest for a United Germany* (Baltimore: The Johns Hopkins Press, 1967); Carl Landauer, *Germany: Illusions and Dilemmas* (N.Y.: Harcourt, Brace & World, 1969); and Karl Jaspers, *The Future of Germany,* cited in the section on philosophy and religion.

Intra-German relations

260   **Intra-German relations: development, problems, facts.**
Hansjürgen Schierbaum.   Munich: tuduv Verlagsgesellschaft, 1979. 68p. 8 maps. (Reihe Politologie/Soziologie, Band 8).

Written by a German authority to fill the need for a concise English-language introduction to the problem of relations between the two German states, this booklet first reviews the period from the end of World War II to the conclusion of the Basic Treaty between the Federal Republic of Germany and the German Democratic Republic in 1972; it then considers the German problem in international context, with particular reference to the East-West conflict; finally, it describes, in practical terms, the application of the intra-German agreements in matters such as the regulation of traffic, trade, and communications between the two German states, cultural and scientific relations, and facilitation of the reunification of families. See also Gerhard Wettig, *Das Freizügigkeitsproblem im geteilten Deutschland 1945-1986* ['The Problem of Freedom of Movement in Divided Germany 1945-1986'], Berichte des Bundesinstituts für ostwissenschaftliche und internationale Studien (BIOst), no. 31/1986 (Cologne: BIOst, 1986), a forty-page study, with bibliographical citations in the annotations and a two-page English summary, in a publication series issued by the autonomous, nonpartisan Federal Institute for Eastern and International Studies, Lindenbornstr. 22, 5000 Cologne 30.

261 **German unity: documentation and commentaries on the Basic Treaty.**
Edited by Frederick W. Hess. Kansas City, Mo. 64152: Governmental Research Bureau, Park College, 1974. 96p. bibliog. (East Europe Monographs, 4).

Published in a series edited by Prof. Jerzy Hauptmann of Park College and Prof. Gotthold Rhode of Mainz University, this booklet includes English translations of the Basic Treaty (*Grundvertrag*) of 1972 between the two German states, the 1973 Federal Constitutional Court decision on the treaty, and an explanation of the fundamental issues that were raised by the treaty, taken to the high court by the State of Bavaria, and resolved by the court's ruling: the Basic Treaty was not incompatible with the Basic Law and therefore not unconstitutional because, construed very narrowly (as spelled out in a unanimous opinion much longer than the treaty itself), it does not recognize the German Democratic Republic as a sovereign foreign state, sanction the division of Germany, or compromise the rights of German citizens. The German text of the *Grundvertrag* is included, together with previous intra-German agreements and documentation of negotiations leading to the Basic Treaty of 1972, in *Verträge Bundesrepublik Deutschland – DDR* ['Federal Republic of Germany – DDR Treaties'], ed. Rolf Ehlers (Berlin: Walter de Gruyter, 1973). For the official translation of the Basic Treaty and related documentation, see the sixty-nine-page booklet *Treaty on the Basis of Relations between the Federal Republic of Germany and the German Democratic Republic* (Bonn: Press and Information Office of the Federal Republic of Germany, 1973). It is also included, with the text of the West German treaties with the Soviet Union (1970), Poland (1970), and Czechoslovakia (1973), as well as the Four-Power Berlin Agreement (1971), and other documents, in the 296-page paperback *Documentation Relating to the Federal Government's Policy of Détente* (Bonn: Press and Information Office of the Federal Republic of Germany, 1978).

262 **Die Rechtslage Deutschlands nach dem Grundlagenvertrag vom 21. Dezember 1972.** (The legal situation of Germany after the Basic Treaty of 21 December 1972.)
Georg Ress. Berlin and New York: Springer-Verlag for the Max-Planck-Institut für ausländisches öffentliches Recht und Völkerrecht, 1978. 436p. bibliog. (Beiträge zum ausländischen öffentlichen Recht und Völkerrecht, Band 71).

Thoroughly documented monograph analyzing the status of the two German states and the legal problems of their bilateral relations in the light of the Basic Treaty of 1972 and of the 1973 ruling of the Federal Constitutional Court regarding its compatibility with the Basic Law. The detailed English summary (pp. 390-405) is footnoted with eighty-four cross-references to the foregoing German text. There is an appendix with the text of the Basic Treaty and related documentation, and an extensive bibliography.

263 **Two Germanys in one world.**
Peter Christian Ludz. Westmead, Farnborough, Hants, England:
Saxon House for the Atlantic Institute for International Affairs,
Paris, 1973. 64p. bibliog.

An assessment by a leading West German authority on East Germany of the
relationship between the two German states and their relations with Europe and
the world. For another analysis, see Karl E. Birnbaum, *East and West Germany:
A Modus Vivendi* (Westmead, England: Saxon House; Lexington, Mass.:
Lexington Books, 1973).

264 **Germany East and West: conflicts, collaboration, and
confrontation.**
Lawrence L. Whetten. New York and London: New York
University Press, 1980. 215p. bibliog.

An account of the development of intra-German relations to the end of the 1970s,
with tables on trade, travel, mail, etc., and an appendix listing the seventy-three
formal agreements between the two German states from 3 September 1949 to
29 November 1979 (the Basic Treaty of 1972 was the thirtieth). See also the same
author's *Germany's Ostpolitik: Relations between the Federal Republic and the
Warsaw Pact Countries* (London: Oxford Univ. Press for the Royal Institute of
International Affairs, 1971).

265 **Die DDR.** (The GDR.)
Hans-Georg Wehling and Rosemarie Wehling. Bonn:
Bundeszentrale für politische Bildung, 1984. 40p. map. bibliog.
(Informationen zur Politischen Bildung [Information for Political
Education], no. 205).

Published by (and available on request from) the autonomous, nonpartisan
Federal Centre for Political Education, Berliner Freiheit 7, 5300 Bonn, for
distribution to schools, this forty-page, large-format, illustrated monograph, with
a map, tables, graphs, and an annotated bibliography, provides a well-informed
introduction to the German Democratic Republic, and its relationship to the
Federal Republic, in historical context. The final section (pp. 38-40), addressed to
teachers, discusses the treatment of the subject in instruction and has a
supplementary bibliography of instructional materials. See also the three articles
on intra-German relations and the national question (annotated with current
bibliographical references) comprising the 21 December 1985 issue of *Aus Politik
und Zeitgeschichte* ['From Politics and Contemporary History'] (B 51-52), the
supplement to the government-sponsored Bonn weekly *Das Parlament*, including
a perceptive review of West German Eastern and intra-German policy from
Adenauer to Kohl by Christian Hacke, professor at the Bundeswehr University,
Hamburg.

Relations with the United States of America and NATO

266 Germany and the United States: A "special relationship?"
Hans W. Gatzke. Foreword by Edwin O. Reischauer.
Cambridge, Mass., and London: Harvard University Press, 1980.
314p. 5 maps. bibliog. (The American Foreign Policy Library).
German-American relations in historical perspective, as seen by a leading
authority, concluded with an extensive bibliographical essay. See also the full-
length study by Manfred Jonas, *The United States and Germany: A Diplomatic
History* (Ithaca, N.Y.: Cornell Univ. Press, 1984) and the booklet by Joachim H.
Schwelien, *Encounter and Encouragement: A Bicentennial Review of German-
American Relations* (Bonn: Bonner Universitäts-Buchdruckerei, 1976).

267 German-American relations.
W. R. Smyser. Preface by Richard Lowenthal.   Beverly Hills,
Calif., and London: Sage Publications for the Center for Strategic
and International Studies, Georgetown University, Washington,
D.C., 1980. 88p. bibliog. (The Washington Papers, no. 74).
A review of political, strategic, and economic issues in German-American
relations at the beginning of the 1980s. See also the papers that grew out of a
symposium at the Woodrow Wilson International Center for Scholars in 1983 on
'German-American Relations and the Future Role of the Federal Republic in
Europe and the World,' edited by James A. Cooney, Gordon A. Craig, Hans
Peter Schwarz, and Fritz Stern, *The Federal Republic of Germany and the United
States: Changing Political, Social, and Economic Relations* (Boulder, Colo.:
Westview Press, 1984), and *Common Values/Common Cause: German Statesmen
in the United States/American Statesmen in Germany, 1953-1983: Statements and
Speeches*, foreword by Peter Hermes (N.Y.: German Information Center, 1983).

**268 The United States and West Germany, 1945-1973: a study in
alliance politics.**
Roger Morgan.   London: Oxford University Press for the Royal
Institute of International Affairs and the Harvard Center for
International Affairs, 1974. 282p. bibliog.
The background and development of the alliance between West Germany and the
United States from the postwar occupation to the chancellorship of Willy Brandt.
See also the official history of one aspect of postwar German-American relations,
published as the third of a series of historical monographs on cultural relations
programmes by the U.S. State Department's Bureau of Educational and Cultural
Affairs, *Cultural Relations as an Instrument of U.S. Foreign Policy: The
Educational Exchange Program Between the United States and Germany 1945-
1954*, by Henry J. Kellermann (Washington, D.C.: U.S. Government Printing

Intra-German and Foreign Relations. Relations with the United States of America and NATO

Office, 1978), and the 1,421-page volume of documents on postwar U.S.-German relations published by the State Department in 1985 and cited in the section on history.

269   **Deutsches Vermögen in den Vereinigten Staaten. Die Auseinandersetzung um seine Rückführung als Aspekt der deutsch-amerikanischen Beziehungen, 1952-1962.** (German property in the United States: the controversy over its restitution as an aspect of German-American relations, 1952-1962.)
Hans-Dieter Kreikamp.   Stuttgart: Deutsche Verlags-Anstalt for the Institut für Zeitgeschichte, 1979. 315p. bibliog. (Studien zur Zeitgeschichte, Band 14; Beiträge zur Wirtschafts- und Sozialpolitik in Deutschland nach 1945, Band 2).

A publication in the Institute for Contemporary History monograph series on postwar economic and social policy in Germany, this is an extensively documented account of the West German government's unsuccessful attempt, from 1952 to 1962, to elicit from the United States government funds to provide compensation for private German assets in the United States confiscated as enemy alien property during World War II. Restitution would have required congressional approval, with the support of the President, for the authorization and appropriation of the hundreds of millions of dollars that would have been needed. The necessary legislation did come fairly close to being worked out toward the end of the Eisenhower administration, but was not passed and signed by the President. After Kennedy became President, negotiations collapsed.

270   **The German Army and NATO strategy.**
Stanley M. Kanarowski. Foreword by John S. Pustay.
Washington, D.C.: National Defense University Press, 1982. 94p. map. (National Security Affairs Monograph Series 82-2).

A monograph, based in part on declassified materials from the U.S. Joint Chiefs of Staff and the National Security Council, on the evolution of the NATO strategy and the development of the Army of the Federal Republic of Germany by Col. S. M. Kanarowski, a senior research fellow at the National Defense University at Fort McNair in Washington, D.C. There are appendices on U.S. defense policy guidelines since 1948 and early issues of nuclear strategy, as well as several tables on the development and structure of the Army of the Federal Republic.

271   **1776-1976: Zweihundert Jahre deutsch-amerikanische
Beziehungen – Two hundred years of German-American relations.
Eine Dokumentation – A documentary.**
Edited by Thomas Piltz. Transl. from German to English by
Louise Fontaine and Renata Lenart; transl. from English to
German by Uschi Gnade.   Munich: Heinz Moos Verlag, 1975.
188p. maps. bibliog.

This bilingual survey of German-American relations and German immigration to
the United States emphasizes cultural and social history. The volume concludes
with a listing of addresses, in both countries, of offices and organizations
concerned with German-American relations, and with a selective chronology
since 1456. The basic text in this profusely illustrated, large-format 'coffee-table
book' is published in a smaller paperback, with black-and-white illustrations,
under the title *Die Deutschen und die Amerikaner – The Americans and the
Germans*, ed. by Thomas Piltz (Munich: Heinz Moos Verlag, 1977).

Economics

272 **The German economy, 1870 to the present.**
Gustav Stolper, Karl Häuser, and Knut Borchardt. Translated by
Toni Stolper. New York: Harcourt, Brace & World, 1967. 353p.
bibliog.

A standard economic history, with chapters on the occupation period, the Federal
Republic, and the German Democratic Republic, translated from *Deutsche
Wirtschaft seit 1870*, 2nd ed. (Tübingen: J. C. B. Mohr [Paul Siebeck], 1966). On
the origins and development of the modern economic system, not only in
Germany, but in Europe and the Western world, see Max Weber's *General
Economic History*, translated by Frank H. Knight (N.Y.: Collier Books, 1961),
which is based on a lecture course entitled 'Outlines of Universal Social and
Economic History,' given by the great German political economist, one of the
founders of modern sociology, in the winter of 1919-1920, shortly before his
death. Weber's classic study of the relationship between religion and economics
was translated by Talcott Parsons as *The Protestant Ethic and the Spirit of
Capitalism*, with a foreword by R. H. Tawney (N.Y.: Scribner's, 1958). See also
Thorstein Veblen's uneven but illuminating study, originally published in 1915,
Imperial Germany and the Industrial Revolution, introduction by Joseph Dorfman
(Ann Arbor: Univ. of Michigan Press, Ann Arbor Paperbacks, 1966), and
Helmut Böhme's concise essay, *Prolegomena zu einer Sozial- und Wirtschafts-
geschichte Deutschlands im 19. und 20. Jahrhundert* ['Prolegomena to a Social and
Economic History of Germany in the 19th and 20th Century'] (Frankfurt am
Main: Suhrkamp, 1968), published as a 157-page paperback with a fifteen-page
bibliography citing a number of important works in English.

273 **The political economy of Germany in the twentieth century.**
Karl Hardach. Berkeley: University of California Press, 1980.
235p. 5 maps. bibliog.

Translated from *Wirtschaftsgeschichte Deutschlands im 20. Jahrhundert*
['Economic History of Germany in the Twentieth Century'] (Göttingen:
Vandenhoeck & Ruprecht, 1976), this is a scholarly overview of the German
economy and its political significance during the First World War, the Weimar
years, the Third Reich, the occupation period in the West, the post-occupation
period (to 1970) in the Federal Republic, and the postwar period as a whole in the
East. The bibliographies at the end of each chapter include periodical literature
and government publications in English and German. The following two books by
Pounds and Schnitzer also treat both East and West Germany. Norman J. G.
Pounds, *The Economic Pattern of Modern Germany* (London: John Murray,
1963) is a concise introduction to the economy of divided Germany, with
consideration of the agricultural regions, industrial development, and transportation and communications of the country as a whole. It is illustrated with twenty-
eight well-chosen photographs. Martin Schnitzer, *East and West Germany: A
Comparative Economic Analysis* (N.Y.: Praeger, 1972), is a more extensive
presentation, with numerous charts and tables, of the economic systems of the
two German states, including detailed treatment of industry and agriculture, the
fiscal system, money and banking, and labour, followed by comparative analyses
of productivity, income distribution, and living standards in East and West
Germany.

274 **The West German economy.**
Eric Owen Smith. London & Canberra: Croom Helm, 1983.
331p. map. bibliog.

A systematic presentation, with numerous charts, graphs, and figures, of the main
macro- and micro-economic trends of the period 1950-1980, by an economist at
Loughborough University, England. See also Graham Hallett, *The Social
Economy of West Germany* (N.Y.: St. Martin's Press, 1973), a 150-page survey
that includes chapters on agriculture, the media, social security, education, and
housing.

275 **Prosperity through competition.**
Ludwig Erhard. Translated by Edith Temple Roberts and John B.
Wood. London: Thames and Hudson, 1958. 263p.

Translated from *Wohlstand für Alle* ['Prosperity for All'] (Düsseldorf: Econ
Verlag, 1957), with a preface by the author, then Vice-Chancellor and Minister
for Economic Affairs of the Federal Republic, this is an account of the swift
postwar economic recovery of West Germany, which resoundingly vindicated his
concept of the 'social market economy,' i.e., a market-driven economy with a
minimum of state regulation, that he had advocated since serving during the
occupation (before the establishment of the Federal Republic) as Director for
Economic Administration for the Western zones. See also *The Economics of
Success* (London: Thames and Hudson, 1963), a translation, by J. A. Arengo-
Jones and D. J. S. Thomson, of some two-thirds of the collection of Erhard's
articles and speeches from late 1945 to early 1962, *Deutsche Wirtschaftspolitik*.

Economics

Der Weg der Sozialen Marktwirtschaft ['German Economic Policy: The Route of the Social Market Economy'] (Düsseldorf: Econ; Frankfurt am Main: Knapp, 1962).

276 **Germany's economic dilemma: inflation and the balance of payments.**
Patrick M. Boarman. New Haven, Conn.: Yale University Press, 1964. 344p. bibliog.

A study of the causes and consequences of the West German balance of payments surplus from 1950 to the beginning of the 1960s and of the related economic problem of chronic international disequilibrium. The extensive bibliography includes public documents, books, and articles in English as well as German. See also two addresses delivered in the 1950s by the influential West German banker Hermann J. Abs, 'The Struggle against Inflation' and 'The Safety of Capital,' in Abs, *Zeitfragen der Geld- und Wirtschaftspolitik. Aus Vorträgen und Aufsätzen* ['Current Question of Monetary and Economic Policy: From Speeches and Articles'], Schriftenreihe zur Geld- und Finanzpolitik, vol. 3 (Frankfurt am Main: Knapp, 1959), pp. 272-298.

277 **Europe's economy in crisis.**
Edited by Ralf Dahrendorf. Preface by Gaston Thorn. London: Weidenfeld and Nicolson, 1982. 274p.

Translated from *Trendwende* ['Change in Trend'] (Vienna: Verlag Fritz Molden, 1981), this is a collection of essays on the economic problems of several European countries and of the European Community as a whole, with a preface by the president of the Commission of the European Communities, and an introduction and conclusion by Ralf Dahrendorf, German sociologist and former member of the Bonn parliament who in 1974 became director of the London School of Economics. In his article on the Federal Republic, 'West Germany – Europe's Driving Force?' (pp. 21-45), Otmar Emminger (former president of the *Bundesbank*, the central state bank), reviews the West German economy from the early 1970s to the beginning of the 1980s and concludes that, although the Federal Republic's economic constitution is 'still eminently sound,' it is clear that 'the days when West Germany acted as a driving force for the European economy are, for some years to come, almost certainly over.' For a systematic analysis of the malaise of the European Community, heavily annotated with bibliographical references, see Hans Vorländer, 'Die Dauerkrise der Europäischen Gemeinschaft. Vor der Alternative von Integrationsverfall oder geänderter Integrationspolitik [The Long-term Crisis of the European Community – Faced with the Alternative of Eroding Integration or of a Different Integration Policy],' pp. 3-23 of the 18 July 1981 issue of *Aus Politik und Zeitgeschichte*, the supplement to the Bonn weekly *Das Parlament*.

Finance and Banking

278 International banking in the 19th and 20th centuries.
Karl Erich Born. Translated by Volker R. Berghahn. New York:
St. Martin's Press, 1983. 353p. bibliog.

This volume, translated from *Geld und Banken im 19. und 20. Jahrhundert*
['Money and Banks in the 19th and 20th Centuries'] (Stuttgart: Alfred Kröner
Verlag, 1977), reviews the development of currency, banking, capital export and
foreign policy, and the emergence of the banking systems of Germany and the
other major industrial and commercial countries before 1914. It provides fairly
detailed accounts of the financing of World War I and its consequences (with
particular attention to reparations and the German inflation), structural changes
after the war (with attention to banking in individual countries), the 'Great
Depression' (with a section on the German banking crisis of 1931 and the end of
reparations), and the financing of World War II; and concludes with a brief
review of currency and banking after the Second World War. The extensive
bibliography concentrates on English titles, omitting many works cited in the
German original. See also the chapter on 'Germany, 1815-1870,' by Richard Tilly
in *Banking in the Early Stages of Industrialization: A Study in Comparative
Economic History*, ed. by Rondo Cameron et al. (N.Y.: Oxford Univ. Press,
1967), pp. 151-182; Herbert Feis, *Europe, the World's Banker 1870-1914: An
Account of European Foreign Investment and the Connection of World Finance
with Diplomacy before the War* (New Haven, Conn.: Yale Univ. Press for the
Council on Foreign Relations, 1930), which has individual chapters on German
foreign investment and on finance and government in Germany; and Erich
Achterberg's illustrated *Frankfurter Bankherren* ['Frankfurt Bank Lords'], 2nd,
rev. and exp. ed. (Frankfurt am Main: Knapp, 1971).

Finance and Banking

279 **Germany's international monetary policy and the European monetary system.**
Hugo M. Kaufmann. New York: Brooklyn College Press, distributed by Columbia University Press, 1985. 152p. bibliog. (Brooklyn College Studies on Society in Change, no. 46).

Because the international monetary system, initially established in 1944 at the United Nations Monetary and Financial Conference at Bretton Woods, New Hampshire, and subsequently modified, could not prevent disruptive exchange rate fluctuations within the Common Market, its members established in 1979 the European Monetary System (EMS). This monograph focusses on the (initially reluctant) role played by the Federal Republic in the establishment of the EMS and on 'The Deutsche Mark-Dollar-EMS Triangle.' The appendix has eight tables, including 'Changes in the EMS exchange rates,' 'Major items of the balance of payments [of Germany],' and 'Indicators of convergence and divergence in the [European] Community economy, 1961-83.' See also the technical monograph by Wolfgang Filc, *Devisenmarkt und Geldpolitik* ['Foreign Exchange Market and Monetary Policy'], Veröffentlichungen des Instituts für Empirische Wirstschaftsforschung, vol. 20 (Berlin: Duncker & Humblot, 1981), and the collection of articles and addresses (1951-1966) by Otmar Emminger, *Währungspolitik im Wandel der Zeit* ['Monetary Policy in the Course of Time'], Schriftenreihe zur Geld- und Finanzpolitik, vol. 9 (Frankfurt am Main: Knapp, 1966).

280 **Capital formation in West Germany.**
Karl W. Roskamp. Detroit: Wayne State University Press, 1965. 287p. bibliog.

This study of the fiscal policies contributing to rapid capital formation in West Germany begins with a survey of economic conditions in 1948, reviews capital formation through 1960, describes the sources of savings for capital formation (e.g., tax incentives, such as tax exemptions on retained earnings), analyzes the important role of the government in capital formation, and notes that 'the all-out drive for economic growth has evidently led to large inequities in West Germany,' but that this has been partially offset by 'large scale public capital formation [that] favored lower income brackets especially' (through services rendered by government-owned and -operated enterprises such as the Federal Railway with its bus lines and the Post Office which also maintains the telephone network). Clearly written (notwithstanding the complexity of the subject), the text is supported by seventy-one tables.

281 **Financial integration in Western Europe.**
Etienne-Sadi Kirschen, with the collaboration of Henry Simon Bloch and William Bruce Bassett. New York: Columbia University Press, 1969. 144p.

This monograph on the financial integration of the Common Market deals with the difficulties faced by the European Economic Community, when it had only six members, in reconciling national policies, liberalizing the flow of capital, and restructuring (if not creating new) institutions in the fields of money, banking, and security exchanges. An English translation of 'The Main Articles of the Rome Treaty [of 1957] Concerning the Establishment of the Common Market' is appended. For a 167-page study addressed to the challenge of harmonizing at least credit policy throughout the Common Market, see Wolf-Dieter Klingelhöfer, *Grundlagen einer rationalen Kreditpolitik in der Europäischen Gemeinschaft* ['Foundations of a Rational Credit Policy in the European Community'], Veröffentlichungen des Instituts für Empirische Wirtschaftsforschung, vol. 17 (Berlin: Duncker & Humblot, 1978), with a bibliography that cites a number of European Community publications.

Industry

282 The arms of Krupp, 1587-1968.
William Manchester.   Boston: Little, Brown and Company, 1968.
976p. bibliog.

Best-selling, journalistic account of the leading German steel and munitions
concern and the family that owned it, with considerable emphasis on the role of
the Krupp family and firm in Hitler's Third Reich, and on the postwar
proceedings in which Alfried Krupp, who had managed the firm during World
War II, using slave labour, was sentenced to imprisonment as a war criminal in
1948, only to be pardoned three years later. The book is not fully documented,
but has a fairly extensive bibliography with relevant works in English. See also
Joseph Borkin, *The Crime and Punishment of I.G. Farben* (N.Y.: The Free Press,
1978), on the great German industrial cartel that during the Second World War
built and operated a large production complex at Auschwitz. For a brief
introduction to the role of Krupp and I.G. Farben under Hitler, see Telford
Taylor, *Sword and Swastika: Generals and Nazis in the Third Reich* (N.Y.: Simon
and Schuster, 1952; repr., Chicago: Quadrangle, 1969), particularly 'Krupp:
Weapons Forge of the Infant Wehrmacht' and 'I.G. Farben: Wizards of Ersatz'
(pp. 97-104).

283 Small wonder: the amazing story of the Volkswagen.
Walter Henry Nelson.   Boston: Little, Brown, 1967. rev. ed.
288p. bibliog.

Carefully researched and well-written account of a vehicle designed as a 'people's
car' under the Hitler régime, adapted for wartime use, and developed in postwar
Germany into one of the most successful industrial ventures in history.

284 **Managers and management in West Germany.**
Peter Lawrence. New York: St. Martin's Press, 1980. 202p.
bibliog.

This well-organized study of German industrial management by a British scholar
with historical and sociological training includes chapters on German economic
life, past and present; the structure of German firms; the background and the
character of German management; and the views of German managers on a range
of issues. The bibliography, which lists articles as well as books in both English
and German, includes 'a few works of fiction, evocative of the German mood or
experience.'

285 **Electrical engineering in West Germany: adjusting to imports from
less developed countries.**
Frank Dietmar Weiss. Tübingen: J. C. B. Mohr (Paul Siebeck),
1978. 115p. bibliog. (Kieler Studien, no. 155).

This study, prepared at the Kiel Institute of World Economics in a series on the
causes and consequences of structural change, is an investigation of the impact of
imports from less developed countries on one particular sector of the German
economy. During the world-wide recession of 1974-75, almost one million
manufacturing jobs were lost in the Federal Republic. Especially hard hit was the
West German electrical engineering industry, losing a significant share of the
German market to competition from less developed countries. Weiss analyzes in
some detail the causes for the decline in competitiveness of the German electrical
engineering industry. Cited in the bibliography are a large number of English-
language works, including U.N. and U.S. Government publications. On another
aspect of German industrial relations with less developed countries, see Peter
Müller, *Die Bedeutung der Industrialisierung unterentwickelter Länder für den
deutschen Industrieexport* ['The Significance of the Industrialization of Underdeveloped Countries for German Industrial Export'] (Hamburg: Deutsches
Übersee-Institut, 1968).

Agriculture

286 **German agricultural policy, 1918-1934: the development of a national philosophy toward agriculture in postwar Germany.**
John Bradshaw Holt. Chapel Hill: The University of North Carolina Press, 1936. 240p. maps. bibliog.

A study of the economic and political problems of German agriculture from the end of the First World War to the early years of the National Socialist régime. The historian Günther Franz' booklet *Politische Geschichte des Bauerntums* ['Political History of the Farmers'] (Hanover: Niedersächsische Landeszentrale für Heimatdienst, 1959) gives a brief overview from the Middle Ages to the first decade of the Federal Republic. Alexander Gerschenkron's *Bread and Democracy in Germany* (Berkeley: Univ. of California Press, 1943; repr., with a new preface, N.Y.: Fertig, 1966) focusses on the anti-democratic influence of the powerful grain growers in Eastern Germany during the early twentieth century. On agricultural policy under Hitler, including the effort to make Germany agriculturally more self-sufficient, see J. E. Farquharson's *The Plough and the Swastika: the NSDAP and Agriculture in Germany 1928-45* (London and Beverly Hills: Sage Publications, 1976).

287 **Die Landwirtschaft in der Industriegesellschaft.** (Agriculture in industrial society.)
Eduard Mändle. Bonn: Bundeszentrale für politische Bildung, 1974. 24p. bibliog. (Informationen zur Politischen Bildung [Information for Political Education], no. 158).

Clearly written, illustrated monograph on contemporary German agriculture and its place in the Common Market and the world economy, with select bibliography, in a bimonthly series of magazine-format texts for dissemination to schools and available on request from the Bundeszentrale für politische Bildung, Berliner Freiheit 7, 5300 Bonn. Ulrich Kluge's 'Vierzig Jahre Landwirtschaftspolitik der Bundesrepublik Deutschland 1945/49-1985: Möglichkeiten und Grenzen staatlicher Agrarintervention [Forty Years of Agricultural Policy in the Federal Republic of Germany, 1945/49-1985: The Possibilities and Limits of State Intervention],' in *Aus Politik und Zeitgeschichte*, no. 42/86 (18 October 1986), pp. 3-19, the supplement to the Bonn weekly *Das Parlament*, summarizes West German agricultural policy from Adenauer to Kohl. In the same supplement are three related articles dealing with agricultural problems in contemporary Germany and Europe (surplus production, environmental pollution, etc.), by Antonius John, Friedrich Golter, and Hermann Priebe. See also Karl-Heinz Kappelmann, *Der Agrarsektor als Wirtschaftsfaktor in der Bundesrepublik Deutschland* ['The Agricultural Sector as a Factor in the Economy of the Federal Republic of Germany'], European University Studies, vol. 440 (Frankfurt am Main: Peter Lang, 1983), a study of the relationship between the agricultural sector and the labour market in West Germany, and Kurt Nover, *Mit Raiffeisen fing as an* ['It Began with Raiffeisen'], Sonderdienst [Special Service] SO 1-86 (Bonn: Inter Nationes, 1986), a thirty-three page essay, issued as an IN-Press release, describing the rural cooperative credit movement, inaugurated in Germany by Friedrich Wilhelm Raiffeisen (1818-1888), the worldwide spread of the movement, and its structure and operations in the Federal Republic.

288 **Agricultural policy and the Common Market.**
    John Marsh and Christopher Ritson.   London: Chatham House: PEP [Political and Economic Planning], 1971. 199p. (European Series, no. 16).

West German agriculture does not exist in isolation. Since the establishment of the Common Market, it has increasingly been integrated with that of the other states of the European Community (EC), and is subject to the Common Agricultural Policy (CAP) of the Community. This monograph, one in a series, is an examination of the character and development of this policy within the EC, addressed primarily to the English reader concerned about the implications of membership in the Community. See also the earlier, fifty-seven page booklet in the same series, T. K. Warley, *Agriculture: The Cost of Joining The Common Market*, European Series, no. 3 (London: Chatham House, PEP, 1967). The perspective of West German agriculture is presented in Fritz Baade and Franz Fendt, *Die deutsche Landwirtschaft im Ringen um den Agrarmarkt Europas* ['German Agriculture in the Struggle for the European Agricultural Market'], Schriftenreihe Europäische Wirtschaft, vol. 43 (Baden-Baden: Nomos Verlagsgesellschaft, 1971). See also Andreas Leitolf, *Das Einwirken der Wirtschaftsverbände auf die Agrarmarktorganisation der EWG* ['The Influence of the Economic Interest Groups on the Organization of the Agricultural Market of the European Economic Community'], Schriftenreihe Europäische Wirtschaft, vol. 58 (Baden-Baden: Nomos Verlagsgesellschaft, 1971).

Agriculture

289 **Kulturpflanzen und Haustiere in ihrem Übergang aus Asien nach Griechenland und Italien sowie in das übrige Europa. Historisch-linguistische Studien.** (Cultivated plants and domestic animals in their transition from Asia to Greece and Italy as well as to the rest of Europe: historical-linguistic studies.)
Victor Hehn. Edited by Otto Schrader. With botanical contributions by Adolf Engler and Ferdinand Pax. Berlin: Gebrüder Borntraeger, 1911, 8th, rev. ed.; repr., Hildesheim: Georg Olms, 1963. 665p.

Fascinating, encyclopaedic work of cultural and agricultural history, tracing from the earliest times man's use of plants and animals, on the basis of references to them in texts since antiquity, showing how, in many cases, they were brought from the ancient Orient to Greece and Rome, and then to northern Europe. Among the plants discussed are the grape vine, the fig and the olive tree; rice, maize, and wheat; nuts and fruits; roses, violets, and tulips. Among the animals are horses and cattle, donkeys, rabbits, and cats. The large volume concludes with a twenty-eight-page three-column index.

290 **Fish aquaculture: technology and experiments.**
Christoph Meske. Edited and translated by Frederick Vogt. Oxford: Pergamon Press, 1985. 237p. bibliog.

Translated from *Aquakultur von Warmwasser-Nutzfischen. Biotechniken und Tierversuche* (Stuttgart: Eugen Ulmer, 1973), enlarged and updated for this edition by the author, this is a basic work on fish farming, an emerging industry potentially capable of making a significant contribution by providing protein for food and employment for those engaged in its production. Prof. Meske first notes problems in traditional fishing, such as declining yields due to overfishing, and danger of exposure to toxins because of increasing pollution. He goes on to describe the methods currently used for the production, by aquaculture, of warm-water table fish, and then discusses new methods and techniques by which production may be substantially increased.

Transport

291 **Transport and communications.**
Frank-Roland Schnell (Transport); Federal Ministry of Posts and
Telecommunications (Posts and Telecommunications).
Wiesbaden: Press and Information Office of the Government of
the Federal Republic of Germany, 1972. 4 maps. 48p.

This illustrated booklet provides a systematic introduction to transportation policy
in the Federal Republic; to the railway, highway, airway, and inland waterway
networks and their interaction; to overseas shipping and international cooperation; and (in the last seven pages) to the postal and telecommunications system of
the Federal Republic. More extensive, but also more dated coverage may be
found in the chapters on 'Transport and Traffic' and 'Communications' in
Germany Reports (1966), cited in the first section of this bibliography. See also
Nigel Despicht's eighty-five page booklet, *The Transport Policy of the European
Communities*, European Series, no. 12 (London: Chatham House: PEP [Political
and Economic Planning], 1969).

292 **Die Binnenschiffahrt im Gemeinsamen Markt.** (Inland navigation in
the Common Market.)
J. Heinz Müller, in collaboration with Volker Maushardt and
Michael Drude. Baden-Baden: Nomos Verlagsgesellschaft, 1967.
240p. (Schriftenreihe zum Handbuch für Europäische Wirtschaft,
vol. 28).

Systematic presentation of (1) the common (i.e., joint) traffic policy of the
European Economic Community, with particular consideration of navigation on
inland waterways; (2) the inland waterways network of each of the Common
Market countries and of Common Market projects pertaining to it; (3) the inland
waterways fleets of the individual countries; (4) freight traffic on the waterways of
each of the countries and on the Rhine; and (5) the regulation of waterway traffic

in each country and on the Rhine. The statistical appendix (pp. 167-240) includes well over fifty tables. See also, in the same series (but with a changed series title), Helmut Rittstieg, *Rheinschiffahrt im Gemeinsamen Markt. Eine Untersuchung zur Kollision zwischenstaatlicher Rechtsordnungen* ['Rhine Navigation in the Common Market: An Investigation of the Collision of Inter-state Legal Systems'], Schriftenreihe Europäische Wirtschaft, vol. 62 (Baden-Baden: Nomos Verlagsgesellschaft, 1971).

293 **100 Jahre Automobil – Geschichte, technisch-industrielle Entwicklung und Motorisierung in Deutschland.** (100 years of the automobile: history, technical-industrial development, and motorization in Germany.)
Karsten Schröder. Bonn: Inter Nationes, 1986. 37p. bibliog. (Sonderdienst SO 3-86).

An illustrated essay with a listing of automobile museums in Germany and a bibliography, issued as an IN-press release by the government agency (Kennedyallee 91-103, D-5300 Bonn 2). See also Erich H. Moneta, *Die europäische Automobilindustrie. Unternehmungen und Produktion* ['The European Automobile Industry: Enterprises and Production'], Schriftenreihe zum Handbuch für europäische Wirtschaft, vol. 27 (Baden-Baden: Verlag August Lutzeyer [Nomos Verlagsgesellschaft], 1963). On cost-benefit-analysis of urban motor traffic, see Friedhelm Plath's monograph, based in part on experience gained in collaboration with city planners and engineers of the city of Hanover and specialists at Hanover University, *Nutzen-Kosten-Analyse für Städtische Verkehrsprojekte* ['Cost-Benefit-Analysis for Urban Traffic Projects'], Schriften zur angewandten Wirtschaftsforschung [Writings in Applied Economics Research], no. 35 (Tübingen: J. C. B. Mohr [Paul Siebeck], 1977); the study is heavily annotated with citations of relevant British and American works.

294 **150 Jahre Deutsche Eisenbahnen – Geschichte, Gegenwart und Zukunft eines Verkehrsmittels.** (150 years of railroads: history, present, and future of a means of transportation.)
Rolf Eisenberg. Bonn: Inter Nationes, 1985. 17p. bibliog. (Sonderdienst SO 1-85).

Issued as an IN-press release by a federal agency (at Kennedyallee 91-103, D-5300 Bonn 2), this seventeen-page essay with a brief bibliography provides an overview of the history of railroads in Germany and of the Deutsche Bundesbahn (the government-owned federal railway system in West Germany), and briefly discusses railway development projects in which German consultants are involved in Algiers, Sri Lanka, and Turkey. See also three publications of the German Federal Railways: the large-format monthly journal *Die Bundesbahn* ['The Federal Railways'], published by Hestra-Verlag, D-6100 Darmstadt 1, Postfach 4244 (ISSN 0007-5876); the monthy newsletter *Kundenbrief* ['Client Letter'] (ISSN 0011-4758), issued by the Deutsche Bundesbahn Zentrale Verkaufsleitung, D-6500 Mainz, Rhabanusstr. 3; and the weekly *DB artikelservice* ['DB (Deutsche Bundesbahn=German Federal Railways) Article Service'], the illustrated press release series of the Pressedienst der Bundesbahn – Hauptverwaltung, D-6000 Frankfurt am Main 11, Postfach 110423, from which glossy masters of printed, numbered photographs may be requested.

295   **The history of Lufthansa.**
    Joachim Wachtel.   Cologne: Lufthansa German Airlines Public
    Relations, 1975. 103p.

In addition to this illustrated history of the leading German airline, initially
founded in 1925, and reestablished in the Federal Republic after the Second
World War, in 1953, see Peter Supf, *Das Buch der deutschen Fluggeschichte* ['The
Book of German Aviation History'], 2nd, rev. and exp. ed., 2 vols. (Stuttgart:
Drei Brunnen Verlag, 1956 and 1958), and Paul A. Jackson, *German Military
Aviation 1956-1976* (Hinckley: Midland Counties Publications, 1976).

Trade

296 **Federal Republic of Germany.**
Prepared by American Embassy Bonn. *Foreign Economic Trends and Their Implications for the United States*, April 1985 (FET 85-28). 14p. (International Marketing Series).

A concise, accurate overview of the German economy in the eighties, with particular emphasis on trade, in both industrial goods and agricultural products, within the Common Market and abroad (especially the United States). It is issued semi-annually by and available from the International Trade Administration (ITA), U.S. Department of Commerce, Washington, D.C. 20230, which also issued (in March 1985), as an 'Overseas Business Report [OBR]' in the International Marketing Series, a more comprehensive analysis of the German market: *Marketing in the Federal Republic of Germany* (OBR 84-14), prepared by ITA's Office of Western Europe in cooperation with the Foreign Commercial Service Staff of the U.S. Embassy in Bonn. This large-format, double-column forty-four-page monograph, addressed to those interested in trade with or investment in West Germany, provides introductory coverage of the foreign trade outlook, industrial policy and trade, the government role in the economy, transportation and utilities, labour, distribution and sales channels, advertising and market research, banking and credit, investment, taxation, business organization (including that of foreign firms), industrial property protection, trade regulations, and a summary market profile. There are also six tables on German exports and imports and sections providing 'Guidance for U.S. Business Travelers' and information sources (listing books and serial publications, both in English and German). See also the ITA's ninety-page *German Trade Fairs: A Handbook for American Exhibitors and Exporters* (1986) and the annual *United States-German Economic Survey*, with its extensive comparative statistical review of the American and German economies, effectively presented in clear graphs and tables, issued since 1975 by the German American Chamber of Commerce, 666 Fifth Avenue, New York, NY 10103.

297 **Der innerdeutsche Handel – ein Güteraustausch im Spannungsfeld von Politik und Wirtschaft.** (Intra-German trade – an exchange of goods in a field of political and economic tension.)
Horst Lambrecht. *Aus Politik und Zeitgeschichte* ['From Politics and Contemporary History'], B 40/82 (9 October 1982), pp. 3-17.

A brief, competent survey of trade between the Federal Republic of Germany and the German Democratic Republic, reviewing its legal basis, analysing it by category of goods from 1971 to 1981, and estimating its long-term economic and political significance, published in the supplement to the Bonn weekly *Das Parlament*, issued by the Bundeszentrale für politische Bildung [Federal Centre for Political Education], a non-partisan, autonomous agency of the Federal Government. See also two articles with annotations citing recent literature on trade between the two German states, Karl-Heinz Gross, 'Der innerdeutsche Handel aus internationaler Sicht [Intra-German Trade in International Perspective],' and Fritz Homann, 'Zur Zukunft des innerdeutschen Handels [On the Future of Intra-German Trade],' published in *Deutschland Archiv. Zeitschrift für Fragen der DDR und der Deutschlandpolitik*, 19. Jahrgang, Nr. 10 (October 1986), pp. 1075-1094.

298 **The European Community: from the summit conference at the Hague to the Europe of the ten.**
Federal Republic of Germany. Bonn: Government Press and Information Office, 1972. 136p.

Documentation in English translation on the accession of Denmark, Ireland, Norway, and the United Kingdom to the Common Market or European Economic Community (EEC). (Its members, linked also in the European Atomic Energy Community [EURATOM] and the European Coal and Steel Community [ECSC], constitute the European Community [EC]). The volume includes a summary of the more important agreements reached by 1972, a chronology, and statistics. The role of Germany in the Common Market and, in a broader sense, the European Community, is explained in two monographs by Gerhart Maier, Adalbert Rohloff, and Heinrich Schneider, *Die Europäische Gemeinschaft, 1: Probleme der europäischen Integration* ['The European Community, 1: Problems of European Integration'] and *Die Europäische Gemeinschaft, 2: Die Aussenbeziehungen der EG* ['The European Community, 2: The Foreign Relations of the EC'], 'Informationen zur politischen Bildung [Information for Political Education],' nos. 154 and 155, respectively (1973), repr. in 1979, in revised form, as a fifty-six-page double issue, *Die Europäische Gemeinschaft*, no. 154-155, by (and available on request from) the Bundeszentrale für politische Bildung [Federal Centre for Political Education], Berliner Freiheit 7, 5300 Bonn. See also Wolf J. Bell, *Die Europäische Gemeinschaft – Partner der Welt* ['The European Community: Partner of the World'], a thirty-one page essay published in 1978 as an IN-Press release in its *Sonderdienst* [Special Service] series (SO 2-78) by Inter Nationes, Kennedyallee 91-103, 5300 Bonn.

299 **Wirtschaftliche Verflechtung der Bundesrepublik Deutschland mit den Entwicklungsländern.** (Close economic involvement of the Federal Republic of Germany with the developing countries.) Siegfried Schultz, Dieter Schumacher, Herbert Wilkens.   Baden-Baden: Nomos Verlagsgesellschaft, 1980. 299p. (Wissenschaftliche Schriftenreihe des Bundesministeriums für wirtschaftliche Zusammenarbeit, vol. 36).

The purpose of this report, published in the research series sponsored by the Federal Ministry for Economic Cooperation, is to present a picture of the extent of West Germany's economic involvement, through the transfer of goods, services, capital, and labour. It includes numerous tables, based largely on statistics from the mid-1960s through 1977. The economic relations between the industrially developed and the less developed countries are also dealt with in the last part of a monograph on economics published by the Federal Centre for Political Education (Berliner Freiheit 7, 5300 Bonn) for distribution on request, Dietmar Krafft and Friedrich Wilke, *Wirtschaft, 5: Internationale Wirtschaftsbeziehungen* ['Economics, 5: International Economic Relations'], 'Informationen zur Politischen Bildung [Information for Political Education],' no. 183 (Bonn: Bundeszentrale für politische Bildung, 1980).

Labour

300 **Labour market and labour and management.**
Eduard Schlipf et al.   Wiesbaden: Steiner Verlag for the Press and
Information Office of the Federal Republic of Germany, 1969.
31p. (Germany Reports, ed. by Prof. H. Arntz).

The text of this booklet is a substantially revised and expanded version of pp. 765-
784 of *Germany Reports* (Wiesbaden: Steiner, 1966), cited above. It provides an
overview of the West German labour market, with data on the increasing
employment of foreign (i.e., non-German) workers, on government unemployment insurance and retraining programmes, and on the central (or umbrella)
organizations of employers and employees, and their constituent associations: on
the one hand, the Confederation of German Employers' Associations (*Bundes-
vereinigung der Deutschen Arbeitgeberverbände*, or *BDA*); and, on the other, the
three major employees' organizations, the Federation of German Trade Unions
(*Deutscher Gewerkschaftsbund*, or *DGB*), the German Employees' Union, a
professionally oriented white-collar organization (*Deutsche Angestellten Gewerk-
schaft*, or *DAG*), and the Federation of German Civil Servants (*Deutscher
Beamtenbund*, or *DBB*).

301 **Labour and social security.**
Compiled by Detlev Zöllner. Revised by Achim André, Federal
Ministry of Labour and Social Affairs.   Bonn: Asgard Verlag for
the Press and Information Office of the Federal Republic of
Germany, 1973. 57p.

Clearly written, illustrated description and rationale of the West German network
of social services coordinated by the Federal Ministry of Labour and Social
Affairs. These services include monitoring working conditions conducive to safety
and health, administering a government-sponsored old-age, health, and survivor's
insurance programme, and regulating a large body of non-German 'guest'
workers. But that is only part of the picture. The Basic Law provides that 'all

Germans shall have the right freely to choose their trade, occupation, or profession, their place of work and their place of training' (Article 12, Par. 1). In fulfilment of what is interpreted as a positive constitutional mandate, the government, as described here, has set up the machinery to do everything it can to assure citizens their employment of choice; to provide them – if temporarily denied their right to work – temporary unemployment compensation at an appropriate level (based on previous income); and, if necessary (because of structural unemployment, for example), to provide them subsidized retraining, enabling them to exercise their constitutional right to work in another field of their choice. The booklet also notes special programmes to meet the needs of war victims, expellees and refugees, the disabled, etc. For more detailed coverage, including description of individual programmes, references to relevant legislation, and tables with funding levels, see the 270-page book *Survey of Social Security in the Federal Republic of Germany*, by Dieter Schewe, Karlhugo Nordhorn, and Klaus Schenke, transl. by Frank Kenny (Bonn-Beuel: E. Seidl for the Federal Minister of Labour and Social Affairs, 1972).

302 **Actual aims and problems of German trade unions.**
German Trade Union Federation. Hanover:
Buchdruckwerkstätten Hannover, 1969. 25p. bibliog.

Issued in December 1969, at the beginning of the Brandt administration, this booklet briefly sets forth the goals of the German trade union movement with reference to co-determination, to assure a greater share in decision-making power, and capital formation, to assure a more equitable distribution of wealth. It includes a list of relevant publications in English. See also, from the same period, R. Colin Beever, *Trade Unions and Free Labour Movement in the EEC*, European Series, no. 10 (London: Chatham House: PEP, 1969), a fifty-page essay concluding with tables comparing wages, paid holidays, etc., in Common Market countries and in the United Kingdom (which had not yet become a member).

303 **Labor in the boardroom: the peaceful revolution.**
James C. Furlong. Princeton, N.J.: Dow Jones Books, 1977.
170p.

A clearly written essay, explaining what the West German Codetermination Act of 1976 represents for labour and for management, how it came about, and what its initial impact has been in Germany. Furlong also discusses the trend toward industrial democracy that it represents and its implications for the United States. A translation of the 1976 law is appended. The notes include bibliographical references. *German Codetermination Act of May 4, 1976 and Shop Constitution Law of January 15, 1972 (English Translation)*, with a foreword by Herbert R. Northrup, Multinational Industrial Relations Studies, no. 3 (Philadelphia: Industrial Research Unit, the Wharton School, Univ. of Pennsylvania, 1976), includes the text of the 1976 Codetermination Act, as well as an earlier law also providing for labour involvement in management, comments on codetermination by the Confederation of German Employers' Associations, and an annotated article by Alfred L. Thimm, 'Decision-Making at Volkswagen, 1972-1975,' originally published in the *Columbia Journal of World Business* (Spring 1976), on the experience of the Volkswagen Corporation with its board with strong union representation. See also Frank Deppe et al., *Kritik der Mitbestimmung. Partnerschaft oder Klassenkampf? Eine Studie* ['Critique of Codetermination: Partnership or Class Warfare? A Study'] (Frankfurt am Main: Suhrkamp, 1969).

304 **Wirtschaft, 2: Arbeitnehmer und Betrieb.** (Economics, 2: worker and workplace.)
Helmut Keim. Bonn: Bundeszentrale für politische Bildung, 1978. 32p. bibliog. (Informationen zur Politischen Bildung [Information for Political Education], no. 175).

This clearly written, well-illustrated monograph begins with a discussion of work and the workplace, of a person's relationship to his job, and of the choice of a vocation or profession, and then describes the role of the worker in the modern economy, labour-management relations, and state regulation of social security, occupational safety and health, etc. Prepared for complimentary distribution to schools, it is available on request from the Federal Centre for Political Education, Berliner Freiheit 7, 5300 Bonn. See also an article in the supplement to the Bonn weekly *Das Parlament*, Stefanie Wahl, 'Langfristige Trends auf dem Arbeitsmarkt [Long-term Trends in the Labour Market],' *Aus Politik und Zeitgeschichte*, B 42/85 (19 October 1985), pp. 3-17.

305 **Die Freizügigkeit der Arbeitnehmer in Europa. Eine vergleichende Darstellung der Rechtslage in den Europäischen Gemeinschaften und auf dem Gemeinsamen Nordischen Arbeitsmarkt.** (The free movement of workers in Europe: a comparative presentation of the legal situation in the European Communities and in the Common Nordic Labour Market.)
Joachim Nelhans. Baden-Baden: Nomos Verlagsgesellschaft, 1975. 238p. bibliog. (Schriftenreihe Europäische Wirtschaft, vol. 77).

A Swedish scholar's comparison of the two separate common markets for labour in Scandinavia and in the European Community, including comparative coverage of such issues as non-discrimination, social insurance, the language problem, and the status accorded foreign workers in Scandinavia from countries not a party to the Nordic labour market agreement and the status accorded foreign workers in Europe from countries outside the Common Market. The appendices include the agreement of 22 May 1954 on a common labour market between Denmark, Finland, Norway, and Sweden, relevant provisions of the Treaty of Rome of 25 March 1957, establishing the Common Market, as well as a clear and extensive overview of eligibility for old-age pensions, information on the allocation of funds for resettlement, etc. The bibliography includes citations in English and French as well as German and Swedish, including articles on the free movement of workers in Europe in the *Common Market Law Review*. See also Hermann Wellmanns et al., *Das Deutsche Handwerk im Gemeinsamen Markt* ['German Craftsmanship in the Common Market'], Schriftenreihe zum Handbuch für europäische Wirtschaft, vol. 8 (Baden-Baden: August Lutzeyer [Nomos Verlagsgesellschaft], 1960), a 214-page monograph with selected extracts from the Common Market Treaty, a statistical overview of crafts and trades in the Federal Republic in the 1950s, charts and graphs, and a bibliography.

Statistics

306 **Handbook of statistics for the Federal Republic of Germany, 1970.**
Preface by Patrick Schmidt.   Stuttgart and Mainz: W.
Kohlhammer for the Federal Statistical Office, Wiesbaden, 1970.
211p. map. bibliog.

Pocket-sized handbook with the more significant official statistics (English version of *Statistisches Taschenbuch*, published at three-year intervals). Titles of the publications of the Statistical Office are listed in English in the bibliography, together with the address of the publisher, W. Kohlhammer GmbH, 6500 Mainz 42, Siemensstr. 3, Postfach 120. An overview of West German postwar demographic and economic development is provided by *Statistical Compass: Federal Republic of Germany* (Wiesbaden: Federal Statistical Office, 1971), a 22-page booklet with selected figures from all spheres of official statistics for the years 1950, 1960, and 1970. See also the compact 335-page statistical handbook issued by the Federal Press and Information Office, *Gesellschaftliche Daten 1977* ['Social Data 1977'], foreword by Herbert Ehrenberg, 2nd. ed. (Bonn: Presse- und Informationsamt der Bundesregierung, 1978), with coverage of 125 topics, grouped under headings such as population, health, the physical environment, and public finances.

307 **Germany – facts and figures about the two German states: a comparative study.**
Foreword by Egon Franke, Federal Minister for Intra-German Relations.   Bonn: Press and Information Office of the Federal Government in conjunction with the Federal Ministry for Intra-German Relations, 1973. 48p. 2 maps. bibliog.

A collection of data, understandably presented in text, graphs, and tables, on population, elections, trade, finance, economics, etc., in the two German states and Berlin, as of the early 1970s. Information on the German Democratic Republic is stated to have been taken from official publications produced in the GDR.

308 **Statistisches Jahrbuch 1985 für die Bundesrepublik Deutschland.**
(Statistical Yearbook 1985 for the Federal Republic of Germany.)
Foreword by Egon Hölder.   Stuttgart and Mainz: W.
Kohlhammer for the Federal Bureau of Statistics, 1985. 776p.

The official statistical yearbook of the Federal Republic of Germany has twenty-six main segments on virtually every aspect of state, society, and the economy, such as geographical and meteorological data, population, elections, taxes, church affairs, education and culture, social services, trade and balance of payments, environment, economic organizations and professional associations; appendices on the German Democratic Republic and East Berlin (pp. 589-623) and on international data (pp. 625-736); an outline of the sources for the data, including offices or agencies and their publications (pp. 737-758); and an extensive, cross-referenced index (pp. 759-776, in three columns). The data are not presented as bare statistics, but with extensive prefatory notes, annotations, captions, headings, and explanatory as well as documentary footnotes. The prefatory note on church affairs (p. 94), for example, concisely explains the organization of the Protestant and Roman Catholic churches in the Federal Republic, their legal status, the church tax, etc. The statistics on the Jewish congregations show that, as of 1984, they had 27,561 members in 65 congregations, fourteen rabbis, fifty-three synagogues, and fifty-five congregational libraries (p. 96).

Environment

309 **Defense of the environment in Germany.**
New York: German Information Center, n.d. 32p.
Lucid, well-illustrated booklet from the early 1970s on the environmental programme in the Federal Republic, with sections on blue-sky laws (against air pollution), noise control, the clean-water programme, disposal of garbage and waste, limiting the use of pesticides and biocides, conservation of the land, and the commitment to protect the environment through a research programme for the development of new technologies. For a more recent overview, see the twenty-four page essay published as an IN-press release by Inter Nationes, an autonomous federal agency (at Kennydyallee 91-103, D-5300 Bonn 2), *Umwelt-schutz in der Bundesrepublik Deutschland* ['Environmental Protection in the Federal Republic of Germany'], by Eva Karnofsky, Sonderdienst SO 3-85 (Bonn: Inter Nationes, 1985).

310 **Waldsterben im Schnittpunkt von Ökologie, Ökonomie und Politik.**
(The dying forest at the intersection of ecology, economics, and politics.)
Walter Sauter. *Aus Politik und Zeitgeschichte* ['From Politics and Contemporary History'], B20/85 (18 May 1985), pp. 14-30.
Article on the affliction of the forests in the Federal Republic: the causes (principally air pollution); the consequences for the environment, the economy, and the health of human beings; and the necessary counter-measures. See also the articles in the same issue of the supplement to the Bonn weekly *Das Parlament* by Peter Cornelius Mayer-Tasch on the necessity for international environmental policy (p. 3-13) and by Volker Prittwitz on the use of the smog alarm, particularly in the Ruhr area and in West Berlin during the past decade (pp. 31-45). All three articles have annotations citing current literature.

311 **The atom besieged: extraparliamentary dissent in France and
Germany.**
Dorothy Nelkin and Michael Pollak. Cambridge, Mass.: The
MIT Press, 1981. 235p. maps.

A comparative study of the opposition movements in France and in West
Germany against the conversion to nuclear power, with consideration of the
political context, the cycle of opposition, the nuclear opposition as a social
movement, and the containment of the conflict. The backnotes contain
bibliographical citations of literature in English on the environmental dimension
of the issue. This dimension is also considered in extensive extracts from a speech
given in Bonn by Carl Friedrich von Weizsäcker, as reprinted (pp. 28-29) in the
illustrated, magazine-format monograph by Detlev Rudel, *Energie*, 'Informationen zur Politischen Bildung [Information for Political Education],' no. 188
(February 1981) (Bonn: Bundeszentrale für politische Bildung), which includes a
bibliography and is available on request from the Federal Centre for Political
Education, Berliner Freiheit 7, 5300 Bonn.

312 **The law and practice relating to pollution control in the Federal
Republic of Germany.**
Heinhard Steiger and Otto Kimminich for Environmental
Resources Ltd. London: Graham & Trotman Ltd. for the
Commission of the European Communities, 1976. 420p. bibliog.

One of a series of volumes commissioned by the Directorate-General for
Scientific and Technical Information and Information Management of the
European Communities (i.e., the European Economic Community, EEC, or
Common Market, the European Atomic Energy Community or EURATOM, and
the European Coal and Steel Community or ECSC) on pollution control in the
member states. The book is no mere compilation of environmental legislation in
translation, though it includes an eight-page listing of principal federal and state
pollution-control laws (with titles in English). The body of the work (by
professors of public law at two West German universities) begins with
consideration of the 'Fundamentals of Environmental Protection,' explaining the
legislative mandate and the machinery for its enforcement at federal, state, and
local level; the section on 'Fundamentals' also covers town, regional, and country-
wide planning, the roles of interest groups and of the individual (including his
right to initiate legal action), research and technological development, and
international treaties and agreements. The following eight sections deal with air,
inland waterways, coastal waters, seas, disposal of wastes on land, noise, nuclear
energy, and product control. The bibliography, which does not list all references
cited in the extensive annotations, is followed by a brief index.

313   **The law and practice relating to pollution control in the member
       states of the European communities: a comparative survey.**
       J. McLoughlin for Environmental Resources Ltd.   London:
       Graham & Trotman Ltd. for the Commission of the European
       Communities, Directorate-General Information Market and
       Innovation, Luxembourg, 1982. 2nd ed. 357p.

One of a series of ten volumes, in which the other nine deal individually with the
countries of the European Coal and Steel Community, the European Economic
Community, and the European Atomic Energy Community. The body of this
work is an overview of environmental legislation, updated to at least 30 June
1981, summarizing the detailed treatment given each country in the other nine
volumes, topic by topic, according to a common outline (adhered to also by the
volume on Germany described above). There is neither an index, as in the first
edition (1976), nor a bibliography. See also the chapter on West Germany
(pp. 79-89) and the section on the European Economic Community (pp. 149-155)
in *Acid Rain in Europe and North America: National Responses to an
International Problem*, by Gregory S. Wetstone and Armin Rosencranz
(Washington, D.C.: Environmental Law Institute, 1983).

Science and Technology

314 **Science in the Federal Republic of Germany: organization and promotion.**
Reinhold Geimer and Hildegard Geimer. Bonn: Deutscher Akademischer Austauschdienst [German Academic Exchange Service), 1974. 3rd rev. & enl. ed. 108p. bibliog.

Systematic account of the organization and support of science and higher learning in the Federal Republic, whereby (as explicitly noted both in the text and in the notes) 'the short term "science" has been used as a translation of the German "Wissenschaft" to cover research and teaching in the natural sciences and medicine as well as the social sciences and the humanities.' The book describes the roles of government, the universities, industry, foundations, scientific associations and learned societies, libraries and documentation centres, archives and museums, and internationally oriented agencies and organizations, giving precise mailing addresses. The text is complemented by charts, graphs, and tables, and a select bibliography. See also Claus Müller-Daehn, *Wissenschaft und Forschung in der Bundesrepublik Deutschland* ['Science and Research in the Federal Republic of Germany'] (Bad Godesberg: Inter Nationes, 1969), an eighty-five-page overview with a select bibliography, an address list of the most important institutions and agencies, and an index.

315 **Alexander von Humboldt 1769/1969.**
Adolf Meyer-Abich et al. Bonn/Bad Godesberg: Inter Nationes, 1969. 169p. bibliog.

Published on the bicentennial of the birth of the distinguished naturalist and explorer, this illustrated volume consists of a shortened version, in translation, of a biographical study by Adolf Meyer-Abich, an essay by Cedric Hentschel entitled 'Alexander von Humboldt's Synthesis of Literature and Science,' translated selections from Humboldt's letters from his travels, a chronology, a bibliography of English-language publications on or by him, and a note on the

135

Science and Technology

Alexander von Humboldt Foundation. For the full text of the biographical monograph abridged in translation for the Inter Nationes volume, see Meyer-Abich's *Alexander von Humboldt in Selbstzeugnissen und Bilddokumenten* ['Alexander von Humboldt in His Testimony and Pictorial Documents'], Rowohlt's Monographs, no. 131 (Reinbek bei Hamburg: Rowohlt, 1967), which includes an extensive bibliography. The beautifully produced, popular biography by Douglas Botting, *Wilhelm von Humboldt and the Cosmos* (N.Y.: Harper & Row, 1973), includes a host of illustrations, many in colour. Further insight into Alexander von Humboldt and his times is provided in the two-volume biography of his brother, the Prussian statesman and educational reformer Wilhelm von Humboldt, by Paul R. Sweet, cited in the section on education.

316　**Rudolf Virchow: doctor, statesman, anthropologist.**
Erwin H. Ackerknecht. Madison: The University of Wisconsin Press, 1953. 304p. bibliog.

Rudolf Virchow (1821-1902) was most widely known as the father of cellular pathology, but he was also politically active, serving for decades in the Prussian legislature; he played an important role in public health reforms (helping, for example, to design and monitor the Berlin sewage system); and he took a keen interest in the emerging study of anthropology, supporting scholarly congresses, museums, and publications. Some of the passages dealing with Virchow's scientific discoveries are necessarily technical, but the biography as a whole (written by the chairman of the department of the history of medicine at the Univ. of Wisconsin) is addressed to the layman and provides a clear picture of the man and his work – particularly in the closely related areas of medical science and public health. See also Henry E. Sigerist's classic, *The Great Doctors: A Biographical History of Medicine* (London: Allen & Unwin; N.Y.: Norton, 1933; repr., Freeport, N.Y.: Books for Libraries Press; N.Y.: Dover, 1971), translated by Eden and Cedar Paul from *Grosse Ärzte. Eine Geschichte der Heilkunde in Lebensbildern*, 2nd, exp. ed. (Munich: Lehmann, 1933), a wide-ranging survey from antiquity to the beginning of the twentieth century with readable biographical essays on Paracelsus, Virchow, Robert Koch, Paul Ehrlich, and many others. The reminiscences of the famous twentieth-century Berlin surgeon Ferdinand Sauerbruch (1875-1951), *A Surgeon's Life* (London: André Deutsch, 1953), somewhat lifelessly translated (and abridged) by Fernand G. Renier and Anne Cliff from *Das war mein Leben* ['That Was My Life'] (Bad Wörishofen: Kindler und Schiermeyer, 1951), afford insight into medicine and the milieu of his time.

317　**The new science**.
Max Planck. Preface by Albert Einstein. Translated by James Murphy and W. H. Johnston. Cleveland, Ohio: Greenwich Editions, Meridian Books, 1959. 328p.

A collection of non-technical articles by the distinguished German physicist Max Planck (1858-1947), including translations of *Physikalische Gesetzlichkeit im Lichte neuerer Forschung* ['The Laws of Physics in the Light of Recent Research'] (Leipzig: Barth, 1926), *Das Weltbild der neuen Physik* ['The View of the World of Modern Physics'] (Leipzig: Barth, 1929), and *Vom Wesen der Willensfreiheit* ['On the Essence of Freedom of the Will'], 2nd ed. (Leipzig: Barth, 1937). The articles were previously published in *Where Is Science Going?* (N.Y.: Norton, 1932), *The*

Philosophy of Physics (London: Allen & Unwin, 1936), and *The Universe in the Light of Modern Physics*, new, expanded ed. (London: Allen & Unwin, 1937). See also Planck's *Wissenschaftliche Selbstbiographie, mit . . . der von Max von Laue gehaltenen Traueransprache* (Leipzig: Barth, 1948), translated by Frank Gaynor as *Scientific Autobiography . . . with a Memorial Address on Max Planck by Max von Laue* (N.Y.: Philosophical Library, 1949; repr., Westport, Conn: Greenwood, 1968).

318 **Scientists under Hitler: politics and the physics community in the Third Reich.**
Alan D. Beyerchen. New Haven, Conn., and London: Yale University Press, 1977. 287p. bibliog.
Based in part on interviews and correspondence, this well-documented study focusses on the response of leading German physicists, particularly at the universities and in state-supported research institutions, to the political environment of the Third Reich. Primarily a nontechnical study of science and government, the work provides insight into the decline of German physics under the Hitler régime. The extensive bibliography cites unpublished archival materials as well as published articles and books. On American recruitment of German scientists at the end of the Second World War, see Clarence G. Lasby's *Project Paperclip*, cited above in the section on German overseas populations.

319 **My life and my views.**
Max Born. Introduction by I. Bernard Cohen. New York: Charles Scribner's Sons, 1968. 216p.
The autobiographical essays comprising the first part of this volume by the German-Jewish Nobel laureate in physics (1882-1970), whose emigration from Germany in 1933 and the reasons for it are described in the study cited in the previous entry, were first published as 'Recollections of Max Born' in the *Bulletin of Atomic Scientists* (Sept., Oct., & Nov. 1965); the essays in the second part, including 'Development and Essence of the Atomic Age' and 'Europe and Science,' were first published in book form under the title *Von der Verantwortung des Naturwissenschaftlers* ['On the Responsibility of the Natural Scientist'] (Munich: Nymphenburger Verlagsbuchandlung, 1965).

320 **Across the frontiers.**
Werner Heisenberg. Translated by Peter Heath. New York: Harper & Row, 1974. 229p. (World Perspectives, vol. 48).
Translated largely from *Schritte über Grenzen. Gesammelte Reden und Aufsätze* ['Steps Across Borders: Collected Addresses and Essays'] (Munich: Piper, 1970), these sixteen selections by the German Nobel laureate in physics (1901-1976) include papers on 'Science in the Contemporary University,' 'Current Tasks and Problems in the Promotion of Scientific Research in Germany,' 'Changes of Thought Pattern in the Progress of Science,' and 'Scientific and Religious Truth.'

321 **The world view of physics.**
Carl Friedrich von Weizsäcker. Translated by Marjorie
Greene. Chicago: University of Chicago Press, 1952. 219p.

Translated from *Zum Weltbild der Physik*, 4th, enlarged ed. (Stuttgart: Hirzel,
1949), this is a carefully structured exposition of the philosophical consequences
of modern physics, with consideration of the two 'naive' schools of realism and
empiricism, and the philosophy of the *a priori* in the form given to it by Kant. In
considering the changes, brought about by science, in man's conception of the
universe and his place in it, Weizsäcker deals with such fundamental ideas as
time, space, causality, and natural law. See also two more recent works of
Weizsäcker (1912-): *Die Einheit der Natur. Studien* ['The Unity of Nature:
Studies'], 4th ed. (Munich: Hanser, 1972), with sections on science, language, and
methodology, on the unity of physics, on the meaning of cybernetics, and on
classical philosophy; and *Wege in der Gefahr. Eine Studie über Wirtschaft,
Gesellschaft und Kriegsverhütung* ['Ways in Danger: A Study of Economics,
Society, and the Prevention of War'], 3rd ed. (Munich: Hanser, 1976), in which
Weizsäcker discusses approaches to dangers facing contemporary mankind,
including war and the destruction of the environment.

322 **A history of Western technology.**
Friedrich Klemm. Translated by Dorothea Waley Singer.
London: Allen and Unwin; New York: Charles Scribner's, 1959.
401p. bibliog.

Translated from *Technik. Eine Geschichte ihrer Probleme* ['Technology: A
History of Its Problems'] (Freiburg: Karl Alber, 1954), this is a survey based on a
series of lectures on the history of the exact sciences and technology. Addressed
primarily to the layman and well illustrated, largely with contemporary drawings.
Although not particularly focussed on German science and technology, the work
provides relatively full coverage of German contributions, reflecting the
perspective of the author as librarian of the German Museum in Munich. See also
Franz Maria Feldhaus, *Die Technik der Vorzeit, der geschichtlichen Zeit und der
Naturvölker* ['The Technology of Prehistorical Times, of Historical Times, and of
Aboriginal Peoples'], 2nd, enlarged ed. (Munich: Heinz Moos, 1965), a 700-page,
illustrated encyclopaedia of technology, originally published in 1914, and reissued
over fifty years later in facsimile, with additions and corrections.

Education

323 **The school system of the Federal Republic of Germany.**
Wolfgang Mönikes. Translated by Brangwyn Jones. *Bildung und
Wissenschaft* [Education and Science] (Bonn: Inter Nationes),
1984, no. 10/11, pp. 139-184. bibliog.
A recent, concise overview of the West German school system, with statistics for
the period since 1960, a selected bibliography, and a list of addresses of
educational authorities and centres, published as a special issue in the *Bildung
und Wissenschaft* ['Education and Science'] series (ISSN 0172-0171) of Inter
Nationes (D-5300 Bonn 2, Kennedyallee 91-103). For a singularly lucid and
authoritative introduction to the traditional German educational system as a
whole, see chapter 7, 'Germany' (pp. 175-224), in Robert Ulich, *The Education
of Nations: A Comparison in Historical Perspective*, rev. ed. (Cambridge, Mass.:
Harvard University Press, 1967). The author of this work (which deals with the
historical and cultural foundations of education and their application in England,
France, the United States of America, and Russia, as well as Germany) served
during the Weimar period as the senior official in the Ministry of Education in
Saxony responsible for higher education. After emigrating to America, he taught
at Harvard, where he became James Bryant Conant Professor of Education. His
Three Thousand Years of Educational Wisdom: Selections from Great Documents,
2nd ed. (Cambridge, Mass.: Harvard Univ. Press, 1954) includes selections
totalling one hundred pages from works on education by Martin Luther, Johann
Friedrich Herbart, and Friedrich Wilhelm Froebel. On religious education in
German schools, see the monograph by E. C. Helmreich cited under Philosophy
and Religion.

Education

324 **Wilhelm von Humboldt: a biography.**
Paul R. Sweet. Columbus: Ohio State University Press, 1978,
1980. 2 vols. bibliog.

Full-length, scholarly but readable biography of the Prussian statesman and
educational leader Wilhelm von Humboldt (1767-1835) who was responsible for
the founding of Berlin University and took a decisive part in shaping the character
of humanistic education in modern Germany. *Humanist Without Portfolio: An
Anthology of the Writings of Wilhelm von Humboldt*, translated, with an
introduction, by Marianne Cowan (Detroit: Wayne State Univ. Press, 1963),
includes (on pp. 132-140) an abridged translation of Humboldt's fundamental
memorandum on the organization of the institutions of higher learning in Berlin;
the full German text is reprinted (on pp. 375-386) in *Die Idee der deutschen
Universität. Die fünf Grundschriften aus der Zeit ihrer Neubegründung durch
klassischen Idealismus und romantischen Realismus* ['The Idea of the German
University: The Five Basic Writings from the Time of Its Reestablishment
through Classical Idealism and Romantic Realism'], foreword by Ernst Anrich
(Darmstadt: Wissenschaftliche Buchgesellschaft, 1956), which also includes
selections from F. W. J. Schelling, J. G. Fichte, Friedrich Schleiermacher, and
Heinrich Steffens. For a distinguished twentieth-century educational philosopher's
retrospective interpretation, reaffirming the validity of the traditional ideal, see
the 138-page essay, addressed to the general reader, by Theodor Litt, *Das
Bildungsideal der deutschen Klassik und die moderne Arbeitswelt* ['The Educational Ideal of German Classicism and the Modern Workaday World'], 4th ed.
(Bonn: Bundeszentrale für Heimatdienst, 1957). The publisher, an independent,
nonpartisan government agency, was subsequently renamed Bundeszentrale für
politische Bildung [Federal Centre for Political Education]; a booklet on this
agency is cited in the following entry.

325 **Education for democracy in West Germany:
achievements – shortcomings – prospects.**
Edited by Walter Stahl. Introduction by Norbert Muhlen. New
York: Frederick A. Praeger, Publisher, for Atlantik-Bruecke,
1961. 356p. bibliog.

Wide variety of articles and extracts on German education (particularly political
education) reprinted in English translation from various sources, published by
Atlantik-Bruecke [Atlantic Bridge], a non-partisan private German group working
to further understanding between the United States and the Federal Republic. In
addition to essays on the West German school system, on the universities and the
reform of higher education in Germany, and on the educational role of the
Bundeswehr [the Federal Armed Forces], there is a twenty-four-page annotated
bibliography on political education. On the work of the Bundeszentrale für
politische Bildung [Federal Centre for Political Education], an independent,
nonpartisan government agency in Bonn, see the forty-six page booklet,
Bundeszentrale für politische Bildung. Bilanz und Ausblick nach 25 Jahren
['Federal Centre for Political Education: Balance and Prospect after 25 Years']
(Bonn: Bundeszentrale für politische Bildung, 1978). On the West German
Armed Forces, see the three extensively annotated articles in the 24 April 1982
issue of *Aus Politik und Zeitgeschichte* ['From Politics and Contemporary

History'], the supplement to the Bonn weekly *Das Parlament:* Martin Kutz, 'Offizierausbildung in der Bundeswehr [Officer Training in the Federal Armed Forces],' pp. 3-15; Peter Zimmermann, 'Die Hochschulen der Bundeswehr [The Colleges of the Bundeswehr],' pp. 17-42; and Peter Barth, 'Jugend und Bundeswehr [The Youth and the Federal Armed Forces],' p. 43-53.

326 **Report of the Federal Government on education, 1970: the Federal Government's concept for educational policy.**
The Federal Minister for Education and Science. Foreword by Willy Brandt. Translated by Alan Richie and Gerard Finan.
Bonn-Beuel: Repro-Druck GmbH for the Federal Government, 1970. 227p. maps.

This is a detailed description and critical evaluation of West German education from Kindergarten through university. Augmented by numerous tables and graphs, it argues that the traditional, highly structured, and relatively inflexible multiple-track system denies equality of educational opportunity. It advocates cooperative planning by federal and state authorities for urgently needed educational reform. This report was followed by a *Bildungsgesamtplan* ['Comprehensive Plan for Education'], 2 vols. (Stuttgart: Klett, 1973), developed by a commission of representatives of the Federal Government (*Bund*) and of the West German states (*Länder*), summarized in the *General Plan for Education (Abridged Version)*, by the *Bund-Länder*-Commission for Educational Planning, translation by K.-D. Gottschalk (Stuttgart: Ernst Klett for the Bund-Länder-Komission für Bildungsplanung, n.d.). Among the more effective contributions to the public discussion preceding the 1970 federal report and the 1973 commission reform plan, was a series of widely discussed articles by Georg Picht initially published in the weekly newspaper *Christ und Welt*, and reprinted, with additional material by him, in Georg Picht, *Die deutsche Bildungskatastrophe* ['The German Educational Catastrophe'] (Munich: Deutscher Taschenbuch Verlag, 1965). See also Norbert Weber's *Privilegien durch Bildung. Über die Ungleichheit der Bildungschancen in der Bundesrepublik Deutschland* ['Privilege through Education: On the Inequality of Educational Opportunity in the Federal Republic of Germany'] (Frankfurt am Main: Suhrkamp, 1973) and, for insight and background, the well-documented account of an American endeavour to bring about educational reform during the postwar occupation, James F. Tent's *Mission on the Rhine: Reeducation and Denazification in American-Occupied Germany* (Chicago: Univ. of Chicago Press, 1982).

327   The educational system in the Federal Republic of Germany –
       governance, structures, courses: a study prepared by the
       Secretariat of the Standing Conference of Ministers of Education
       and Cultural Affairs of the Länder in collaboration with the
       Federal Ministry for Education and Science and the West
       German Rectors' Conference.
       Published by the Foreign Office of the Federal Republic of
       Germany. Translated and produced by the German Academic
       Exchange Service [Deutscher Akademischer Austauschdienst
       (DAAD)].   Bonn: Courir-Druck for the German Academic
       Exchange Service (DAAD), 1982. 147p.

Official, unabridged translation of authoritative guide to the German educational
system, prepared by the staff of the consortium of the governing or coordinating
bodies responsible for the numerous institutions and cooperative programmes
involved, *Das Bildungswesen in der Bundesrepublik Deutschland. Kompetenzen –
Strukturen – Bildungswege. Eine Veröffentlichung der Kultusministerkonferenz
unter Mitarbeit des Bundesministeriums für Bildung und Wissenschaft und der
Westdeutschen Rektorenkonferenz* (Neuwied: Luchterhand, 1977). The translation
provides an accurate English-language introduction to, and outline of, the very
complex institutional structure of the educational system in the Federal Republic;
describes the courses of study and examination systems; and lists the various
diplomas and licenses awarded. The appendices (comprising well over half the
volume) include a diagram of the German educational system's structure; a list of
occupations for which accredited vocational training is required, and further
training available; the federal government's 'Vocational Training Directive for the
Watchmaker's Trade,' of 9 April 1976 (as a sample of the genre); and a list of
over twenty different kinds of doctoral degrees conferred in Germany, from
Arzneimittelkunde [pharmacology, *Dr. pharm.*] to *Zahnheilkunde* [dentistry,
Dr. med. dent.]). See also the two paperback handbooks listed in the next entry,
and the works on the various segments of the German educational system, and on
educational reform, cited in the entries that follow.

328   **Education, culture, and politics in West Germany.**
      Arthur Hearnden.   Oxford: Pergamon Press, 1976. 164p. bibliog.
      (Society, Schools, and Progress Series; Pergamon International
      Library of Science, Technology, Engineering, and Social Studies).

A general examination of the educational system of the Federal Republic, in the
context of the social and cultural climate, with consideration of educational
reform as a serious partisan political issue. For a case study of a school in a rural
community, see Richard L. Warren, *Education in Rebhausen: A German Village*
(N.Y.: Holt, Rinehart and Winston, 1967), an account, based on the author's
yearlong residence in southwest Germany, in which 'school and village are seen
not as interdependent but separate entities, but as interrelated dimensions of a
distinctive way of life.' The 114-page monograph has a brief, annotated
bibliography. More extensive coverage, particularly of the standard German
literature, is given in the bibliographies of two German paperbacks addressed to
the general reader: *Das Bildungswesen in der Bundesrepublik Deutschland. Ein
Überblick für Eltern, Lehrer, Schüler* ['The Educational Establishment in the

Federal Republic of Germany: An Overview for Parents, Teachers, Pupils'] by a Working Group at the Max Planck Institute for Educational Research, Berlin (Reinbek bei Hamburg: Rowohlt, 1979), a 280-page handbook prepared at a leading West German educational research centre on the basis of manuscripts for a series of presentations for use abroad; and Joachim H. Knoll, *Bildung und Wissenschaft in der Bundesrepublik Deutschland. Bildungspolitik/Schulen/Hochschulen/Erwachsenenbildung/Bildungsforschung. Ein Handbuch.* ['Education and Higher Learning in the Federal Republic of Germany: Educational Policy, Schools, Colleges, Adult Education, Educational Research – A Handbook'] (Munich: Hanser Verlag, 1977).

329 **Germany.**
Paris: Organisation for Economic Co-operation and Development (OECD), 1972. 151p. (Reviews of National Policies for Education).

The first part of this book is a critical report on the educational system in the Federal Republic, prepared as part of a systematic review of national educational policies in OECD member states by a special committee of OECD examiners (including Alain Peyrefitte of the French National Assembly and Prof. Fritz Stern of Columbia University); the second part is a summary of a 'confrontation meeting' late in 1971, at which there was a candid discussion with German authorities on proposed educational reforms, such as the introduction of comprehensive schools as an alternative to the traditional German system, in which access to higher education was generally restricted to the minority whose parents had enrolled them at the age of ten in the relatively rigorous, academically oriented secondary school (the *Gymnasium*), graduation from which was the prerequisite for admission to the university. Hans Werner Kilz, ed., *Gesamtschule. Modell oder Reformruine?* ['Comprehensive School: Model or Reform in Ruins?'] (Reinbek bei Hamburg: Rowohlt, 1980), is a readable report on the controversial comprehensive school experiment in West Germany as of 1980, together with a directory of the 180 schools in operation at the time. They were very unevenly distributed: twenty-three such schools in Hamburg, attended by one student in five; in Hesse sixty-five; but only three in Rhineland-Palatinate and two each in Bavaria and the Saarland. On another institutional innovation, at the higher educational level, see Bernd Drescher, *Gesamthochschulen in der Bundesrepublik Deutschland* ['Comprehensive Schools of Higher Learning in the Federal Republic of Germany'], *Bildung und Wissenschaft* ['Education and Science'], *BW* 1981 (no. 1/2), 23 pp., a report (with bibliography) from Inter Nationes, Bonn, on the new polytechnical institutes established to meet anticipated increases in university-level enrollment in the Federal Republic.

330 **The state and the university: the West German system.**
Donald S. Detwiler. *Bulletin of the Committee on Science and Freedom*, no. 18 (March, 1961; Manchester), pp. 16-23.

Concise description and criticism, from the perspective of an American doctoral candidate at a German university, of the institutional structure of higher education in the Federal Republic, on the eve of a protracted period of disruptive protest and extensive reform. For an overview of higher learning in West Germany before the expansion that began in the 1960s, see *Scientific and Academic Life in the Federal Republic of Germany: A Handbook* [of 174 pages],

Education

edited by F. E. Nord, rev. ed. (Essen: Stifterverband für die Deutsche Wissenschaft, 1963), issued by the Donors Association for Promoting Arts and Sciences in Germany, a foundation supported by business and industry. Rolf Neuhaus, ed., *Dokumente zur Gründung neuer Hochschulen . . . 1960-1966* ['Documents on the Establishment of New Institutions of Higher Learning . . . 1960-1966'] (Wiesbaden: Steiner, 1968), is a 1,095-page documentation on the establishment or major restructuring of institutions at Bielefeld, Bochum, Bremen, Constance, Dortmund, Hanover, Lübeck, Regensburg, and Ulm, with a bibliography (pp. 888-915) citing archival material as well as periodical and book publications. Gerhard Hess, *Die Deutsche Universität 1930-1970* ['The German University 1930-1970'] (Bad Godesberg: Inter Nationes, 1968) is a 52-page introduction addressed to non-Germans. Three extensively annotated articles appeared in *Aus Politik und Zeitgeschichte*, the supplement to the Bonn weekly *Das Parlament* (pp. 3-35 of the 21 January 1984 issue): Gerd Roellecke, 'Entwicklungslinien deutscher Universitätsgeschichte [Lines of Development of German University History]' Claudia Schmid, 'Staatliche Hochschulpolitik in der Bundesrepublik [State Policy, in the Federal Republic, on Institutions of Higher Education]'; and George Turner, 'Hochschulreformpolitik. Versuch einer Bilanz [Policy on Reforming Institutions of Higher Education: Attempt at an Assessment].'

331 **The Fachhochschulen in the Federal Republic of Germany.**
Ludwig Gieseke. *Bildung und Wissenschaft* [Education and Science] (Bonn: Inter Nationes), 1980 (no. 11/12), pp. 133-141.

A report on the new West German professional schools, largely developed since 1969, that provide practical courses of study – normally not exceeding three to three-and-a-half years – leading to a degree or diploma in such fields as engineering, social work, economics, or business administration. For other aspects of German education, see, in the same series, *BW* 1984 (no. 1/2), the report by K. J. Maass and Eckart Rohlfs on musical education, described below in the final entry on music in the section on the arts; Gerhard Charles Rump, *Kunsterziehung in der Bundesrepublik Deutschland* ['Art Education in the Federal Republic of Germany'], *BW* 1985 (no. 7-8), 91 pp., with a bibliography and a directory of institutions; Hermann Meyn, *Journalistenausbildung in der Bundesrepublik Deutschland* ['The Training of Journalists in the Federal Republic of Germany'], *BW* 9-78, pp. 169-200; Michael Schlicht, *Lebenslanges Lernen. Entwicklung der Weiterbildung in Deutschland* ['Lifelong Learning: The Development of Continuing Education in Germany'], *BW* 1986 (no. 1-2), 28 pp., with a brief bibliography and a directory; Bruno Prändl, *Das Sonderschulwesen in der Bundesrepublik Deutschland* ['Schooling of the Handicapped in the Federal Republic of Germany'], *BW* 1985 (no. 9-10), 28 pp.; Norbert Petersen, *Berufsbildung in der Bundesrepublik Deutschland* ['Vocational Training in the Federal Republic of Germany'], *BW* 1981 (no. 9/10), pp. 130-156, explaining the traditional German system of combining on-the-job training in the workplace with classroom instruction; and Hans Pakleppa, *Training and Further Training in the Federal Republic of Germany*, a thirty-three-page Inter Nationes report (SO 4-84) on a wide range of specialized vocational programmes, particularly for trainees from developing countries, and a listing of addresses of foundations and agencies with information on opportunities in various fields.

Literature

Literary history and criticism

332 **The Oxford companion to German literature.**
Henry and Mary Garland. Oxford: At the Clarendon Press, 1976.
977p.

Cross-referenced entries, in alphabetical order, on German literature from about
800 to the early 1970s. They are set up in two columns per page and include, in
addition to the names of authors and titles of works, other names and terms
relevant to the cultural and historical background. Easy-to-read, crisp black print.
See also the 140-page introduction by H[enry] B. Garland, *A Concise Survey of
German Literature*, 2nd ed. (London: Macmillan, 1976).

333 **Deutsches Dichterlexikon. Biographisch-bibliographisches
Handwörterbuch zur deutschen Literaturgeschichte.** (Encyclopaedia
of German poets and writers: a biographical-bibliographical
handbook and dictionary on German literary history.)
Gero von Wilpert. Stuttgart: Alfred Kröner Verlag, 1976. 2nd,
exp. ed. 791p. (Kröners Taschenausgabe, Band 288).

A standard biographical-bibliographical reference work in a pocket-format,
quality-bound series in which a volume is also available on contemporary writers:
Franz Lennartz, *Deutsche Dichter und Schriftsteller unserer Zeit* ['German Poets
and Writers of Our Time'], 10th, exp. ed., Kröners Taschenausgabe, vol. 151
(Stuttgart: Kröner, 1969).

334 **German literature: an annotated reference guide.**
Uwe K. Faulhaber & Penrith B. Goff.   New York & London:
Garland Publ., Inc., 1979. 398p. (Garland Reference Library of
the Humanities, vol. 108).

An indexed listing of 2,046 items topically arranged by category. Periodicals are
included, as well as a checklist of standard references in related disciplines. See
also Larry L. Richardson's *Introduction to Library Research in German Studies:
Language, Literature, and Civilization* (Boulder, Colo.: Westview, 1984), which
provides a systematic introduction to bibliographical access systems (catalogues,
bibliographies, data bases, etc.), and Paul Raabe's *Einführung in die Bücher-
kunde zur deutschen Literaturwissenschaft* ['Introduction to the Bibliography of
German Literary Scholarship'], 2nd ed. (Stuttgart: J. B. Metzlersche Verlagsbuchhandlung, 1961).

335 **Medieval German literature: a survey.**
Maurice O'Connell Walshe.   Cambridge, Mass.: Harvard
University Press, 1962. 421p. map. bibliog.

An extended review of German literature from its beginning in the mid-eighth
century to the early sixteenth century, written to acquaint the general reader with
the mediaeval treasures and to provide the student with a supplement to the
German works on the subject. In discussion of passages from individual works,
excerpts are given in English translation as well as the original, and the extensive
bibliography also cites studies in and translations into English.

336 **History of the German novel.**
Hildegard Emmel. English-language edition prepared by Ellen
Summerfield.   Detroit: Wayne State University Press, 1984. 389p.
bibliog.

This is a translation of the author's scholarly three-volume *Geschichte des
deutschen Romans* (Berne and Munich: Francke Verlag, 1972, 1975, 1978,
respectively), abridged and adapted to the needs of the English-speaking reader.
The notes necessarily include citations of material in German, but the eleven-page
bibliography lists German novels in English translation. Hans Wagener, *The
German Baroque Novel*, in 'Twayne's World Authors Series' (N.Y.: Twayne,
1973), deals with the early novel, in the seventeenth century; on the most
important novelist of that period, Grimmelshausen, see the anthology of scholarly
German articles, *Der Simplicissimusdichter und sein Werk* ['The Writer of
"Simplicissimus" and His Work'], ed. by Günther Weydt (Darmstadt: Wissen-
schaftliche Buchgesellschaft, 1969). The novel as it developed at the end of the
eighteenth and early in the nineteenth century in Germany is examined by Eric
A. Blackall in *Goethe and the Novel* and in *The Novels of the German Romantics*
(Ithaca, N.Y.: Cornell Univ. Press, 1976 and 1983, respectively). See also Martin
Swales, *The German Bildungsroman from Wieland to Hesse* (Princeton, N.J.:
Princeton Univ. Press, 1978), a study of the German novel of personal
development.

337 **Geschichte des deutschen Verses. Zehn Vorlesungen für Hörer aller Fakultäten.** (History of German verse: ten lectures for auditors from all faculties.)
Wolfgang Kayser. Berne: A. Francke Verlag, 1960. 156p.

Based on the Göttingen professor's popular lecture course for the university community and the public at large, and therefore addressed not only to specialists but also to laymen interested in an historical overview since the Middle Ages. Two systematic studies of verse (in terms of diction, meter, etc.) are Kayser's *Kleine deutsche Versschule* ['Little German Verse School'], 9th ed. (Berne: Francke, 1962) and Henry Gibson Atkins, *A History of German Versification: Ten Centuries of Metrical Evolution* (London: Methuen, 1923). Kayser's text (a modern classic) on the study of literature as a humanistic science, *Das sprachliche Kunstwerk. Eine Einführung in die Literaturwissenschaft* ['The Linguistic Work of Art: An Introduction to the Science of Literature'], 6th ed. (Berne: Francke, 1960) provides comprehensive treatment of poetry together with the other literary forms (and has a forty-two-page bibliography). For selections of German verse, in chronological sequence, see E. L. Stahl, ed., *The Oxford Book of German Verse: From the 12th to the 20th Century*, 3rd ed. (Oxford: Clarendon Press, 1967), with the poetry in German, but preface, backnotes, etc., in English, and Robert M. Browning, *German Poetry: A Critical Anthology* (N.Y.: Appleton-Century-Crofts, 1962), in which the poems are also printed in German without translations, but are individually introduced and very helpfully annotated in English. See also Browning's studies, *German Baroque Poetry, 1618-1723* and *German Poetry in the Age of the Enlightenment: From Brockes to Klopstock* (University Park: Pennsylvania State Univ. Press, 1971 and 1978, respectively).

338 **Handbuch des deutschen Dramas.** (Handbook of the German drama.)
Edited by Walter Hinck. Düsseldorf: August Bagel Verlag, 1980. 610p. bibliog.

Comprehensive, systematically structured, collaborative work of thirty-eight chapters by thirty-nine contributors, with extensive annotations and bibliography, on the history and theory of German drama, with consideration of major epochs, individual dramatists, and special questions or problems, such as the adaptation of dramas for television. A very concise introduction to the history of German drama as literature, and of the relationship between German literary drama and the German theatre is provided by Martin Esslin in his introductory essay to *The Genius of the German Theater*, the volume of plays and essays cited below under English-language anthologies and readers; in this context, W. H. Bruford's work on the theatre in Goethe's Germany, cited under the Arts, is informative. Margaret Herzfeld-Sander, ed., *Essays on German Theater*, 'The German Library,' vol. 83 (N.Y.: Continuum, 1985), is comprised of selections, in English, from thirty-seven writers, from Lessing and Schiller to Hochhuth and Walser. See also the translation of Goethe's essay on Shakespeare in vol. 2 of *The German Classics: Masterpieces of German Literature*, 20 vols., ed. by Kuno Francke (N.Y.: German Publication Society, 1913-1914; repr., N.Y.: AMS Press, 1969); J. M. Ritchie's *German Expressionist Drama*, in 'Twayne's World Authors Series' (N.Y.: Twayne, 1976); Friedrich Dürrenmatt's essay, 'Problems of the Theater,' in the collection (in translation) of his *Plays and Essays*, ed. by Volkmar Sander,

Literature. Literary history and criticism

'The German Library,' vol. 89 (N.Y.: Continuum, 1982); Bertolt Brecht's *Schriften zum Theater. Über eine nicht-aristotelische Dramatik* ['Writings on the Theater. On non-Aristotelian Drama'], compiled by Siegfried Unseld (Berlin: Suhrkamp, 1957); Franz Norbert Mennemeier and Frithjof Trapp, *Deutsche Exildramatik 1933 bis 1950* ['German Exile Drama 1933-1950'] (Munich: Wilhelm Fink, 1980); and Denis Calandra, *New German Dramatists* (N.Y.: Grove, 1983).

339 **A history of the German *Novelle*.**
E. K. Bennett. Revised and continued by H. M. Waidson.
Cambridge: At the University Press, 1965. 2nd ed. 315p. bibliog.

A standard, scholarly but readable overview, from its origin at the end of the eighteenth century to the mid-twentieth century, of an important genre in German literature, the novella – a narrative in prose, usually shorter than a novel, dealing with one striking, fateful event. See also Benno von Wiese, *Die deutsche Novelle von Goethe bis Kafka. Interpretationen* ['The German Novella from Goethe to Kafka: Interpretations'] (Düsseldorf: August Bagel Verlag, 1960), and the introductory essays by Harry Steinhauer to his collection of German novellas, cited under English-language anthologies and readers, and by Hugo von Hofmannsthal to *Deutsche Erzähler* ['German Storytellers'], vol. 1 ed. by Hofmannsthal, vol. 2 ed. by Marie Luise Kaschnitz (Frankfurt am Main: Insel Verlag, 1912 and 1971, resp.; both vols. repr. in 1979).

340 **The house of Desdemona or the laurels and limitations of historical fiction.**
Lion Feuchtwanger. Translated with a foreword by Harold A.
Basilius. Detroit: Wayne State University Press, 1963. 236p.
bibliog.

Author of about twenty historical novels, the German-Jewish emigrant Feuchtwanger died in California in 1958 before he was able to complete this study of historical fiction, particularly the historical novel, in American, British, French, and German literature. It was published in Germany as *Das Haus der Desdemona oder die Grösse und Grenzen der historischen Dichtung* (Rudolstadt: Greifenverlag, 1961). The book includes Feuchtwanger's outlines for the study and a bibliography of his works in their original German and first American editions. For a full-length biography with consideration of this study and of Feuchtwanger's views on historical fiction, see Lothar Kahn's well-informed and well-written *Insight and Action: The Life and Work of Lion Feuchtwanger* (Rutherford, N.J.: Fairleigh Dickinson Univ. Press, 1975); for a concise introduction to the man and his works, see Ilse E. Detwiler, *The Historical Novelist Lion Feuchtwanger: German, Jew, Emigrant* (Ann Arbor, Mich.: Univ. Microfilms International; Carbondale: Southern Illinois Univ. M.A. thesis, 1972). Georg Lukács, the celebrated Marxist critic and sociologist of literature discusses historical novels of, among others, Feuchtwanger, Fontane, Heinrich and Thomas Mann, Stifter, and Arnold and Stefan Zweig in *The Historical Novel*, transl. by Hannah and Stanley Mitchell, with a preface by Irving Howe (Boston: Beacon Press, 1963). See also Bruce M. Broerman, *The German Historical Novel in Exile after 1933* (University Park: Pennsylvania State Univ. Press, 1986).

Literature. Literary history and criticism

341 **German aesthetic and literary criticism: Winckelmann, Lessing, Hamann, Herder, Schiller, Goethe.**
Edited and introduced by H. B. Nisbet.   Cambridge: Cambridge University Press, 1985. 317p. bibliog.

The first of a projected series of three anthologies of aesthetic theory and criticism by German thinkers from Winckelmann to Hegel, this volume includes an introductory essay, substantial selections in translation with prefatory notes and extensive annotations, and a bibliography. See also the compilation of critical writings on the impact of major writers, edited by Karl Robert Mandelkow, *Wirkung der Literatur. Deutsche Autoren im Urteil ihrer Kritiker* ['Impact of Literature: German Authors in the Judgment of Their Critics'] (Munich: Beck; or Frankfurt am Main: Athenäum, 1969-1980); vol. 1, *Lessing – ein unpoetischer Dichter* ['Lessing – an Unpoetic Poet'], ed. by Horst Steinmetz (Frankfurt, 1969); vol. 2, in two parts, *Schiller – Zeitgenosse aller Epochen* ['Schiller – Contemporary of All Epochs'], ed. by Norbert Oellers, pt. 1, 1782-1859 (Frankfurt, 1970), pt. 2, 1860-1966, (Munich, 1976); vol. 3, *Benn – Wirkung wider Willen* ['Benn – Impact against His Will'], ed. by Peter Uwe Hohendahl (Frankfurt, 1971); vol. 4, *Hofmannsthal im Urteil seiner Kritiker* ['Hofmannsthal in the Judgement of His Critics'], ed. by Gotthart Wunberg (Frankfurt, 1972); vol. 5, in four parts, *Goethe im Urteil seiner Kritiker* ['Goethe in the Judgement of His Critics'], ed. by Karl Robert Mandelkow, pt. 1, 1773-1832 (Munich, 1975), pt. 2, 1832-1870 (Munich, 1977), pt. 3, 1870-1918 (Munich, 1979), pt. 4, in prep.; and vol. 6, *Jean Paul im Urteil seiner Kritiker* ['Jean Paul in the Judgement of His Critics'], ed. by Peter Sprengel (Munich, 1980).

342 **Germany in the eighteenth century: the social background of the literary revival.**
W. H. Bruford.   Cambridge: At the University Press, 1935; paperback repr., 1965. 354p. bibliog.

Bruford paints a picture of life as it was lived in Germany at the courts, in the towns, and in the countryside, and discusses its influence on the literature of that time. See also his more specialized study of Weimar as the cultural setting for the work of Wieland, Goethe, Herder, Fichte, and Schiller, *Culture and Society in Classical Weimar, 1775-1806* (Cambridge: At the University Press, 1962). The development of German during the eighteenth century is the subject of a work dedicated to Bruford by Eric A. Blackall, *The Emergence of German as a Literary Language, 1700-1775*, 2nd ed., with a new bibliographical essay (Ithaca, N.Y.: Cornell Univ. Press, 1978). Victor Lange, *The Classical Age of German Literature, 1740-1815* (N.Y.: Holmes & Meier, 1982) includes a fifty-three page bibliographical guide to the historical and critical literature, with extensive coverage of articles in German and English (but excluding, with few exceptions, collected works or editions of individual texts). Mark O. Kistler's *Drama of the Storm and Stress*, in 'Twayne's World Authors Series' (N.Y.: Twayne, 1969) is a study of J. M. R. Lenz, H. L. Wagner, J. F. Müller ('Maler Müller'), F. M. Klinger, and J. A. Leisewitz. On Lessing, see the concise account of the man and his work by H. B. Garland, *Lessing: The Founder of Modern German Literature* (Cambridge: Bowes & Bowes, 1937; repr., 1949) and *Lessings Leben und Werk in Daten und Bildern* ['Lessing's Life and Work in Dates and Pictures'], ed. by Kurt Wölfel (Frankfurt am Main: Insel Verlag, 1967).

Literature. Literary history and criticism

343 **Aristocracy and the middle-classes in Germany: social types in German literature, 1830-1900.**
Ernest K. Bramsted. Foreword by G. P. Gooch. London: P. S. King & Son, 1937 [published under author's original name, Ernst Kohn-Bramstedt]; rev. ed., with a new introduction, Chicago & London: University of Chicago Press, 1964. 364p. bibliog.

Using as one of his main sources the ninetenth-century novel, Bramsted investigates the relationship between the aristocracy and the middle classes in northern Germany. The concluding chapters deal with the social situation of the writer from 1830 to 1900. An aspect of German literature during the second half of the nineteenth century is studied by Clifford Albrecht Bernd in *German Poetic Realism*, in 'Twayne's World Authors Series' (Boston: Twayne, 1981), which includes chapters on the novella, lyric poetry, and the novel of the period, as well as an annotated bibliography. Richard M. Meyer, *Die deutsche Litteratur* [sic] *des Neunzehnten Jahrhunderts* ['German Literature of the Nineteenth Century'], 2nd ed. (Berlin: Georg Bondi, 1900) is a 960-page history of nineteenth-century literature (abridged and revised in the *Volksausgabe* [popular edition] of 1912) cited not only because of its detailed coverage, but for its *lack* of perspective; the patriotic fervour with which it is written affords a critical reader more insight than many a monograph into the nationalism of the Wilhelminian period. See also Meyer's thirty-eight page 'General Introducton' in vol. 1 of *The German Classics: Masterpieces of German Literature*, 20 vols., ed. by Kuno Francke (N.Y.: German Publication Society, 1909-1913; repr., N.Y.: AMS Press, 1969).

344 **The tyranny of Greece over Germany: a study of the influence exercised by Greek art and poetry over the great German writers of the eighteenth, nineteenth and twentieth centuries.**
E. M. Butler. Cambridge: Cambridge University Press, 1935; paperback repr. with a new preface, Boston: Beacon Press, 1958. 351p. bibliog.

A study of German Hellenism including full chapters on Winckelmann, 'the discoverer,' Goethe, 'the creator,' and Heine, 'the rebel.' The importance of classical education in the nineteenth and early twentieth centuries is also brought out in W. H. Bruford, *The German Tradition of Self-Cultivation: 'Bildung' from Humboldt to Thomas Mann* (Cambridge: Cambridge Univ. Press, 1975). For a postwar view by a distinguished, humanistically oriented German educator, see Theodor Litt's monograph on the classical German educational ideal and the modern working world, cited under Education.

345 **German romanticism.**
Oskar Walzel. Transl. by Alma Elise Lussky. New York: G. P. Putnam's Sons, 1932; repr. N.Y.: Capricorn Books, 1966. 314p.

A study of the intellectual origins of romanticism in philosophy, religion, and aesthetics, with particular attention to the impact of Herder, Schlegel, and Schleiermacher; and of the creative literature of romanticisim, with discussion of works by, among others, Tieck, Kleist, and Heine.

346 The German tradition in literature 1871-1945.
Ronald Gray. Cambridge: At the University Press, 1965. 384p.
bibliog.

Part I, 'Writers and Politics,' is a broad survey of literature against the political
background, from unification in 1871 to defeat in 1945; Parts II and III are studies
of works of Thomas Mann and Rilke. Part IV, 'Reshaping the Tradition,'
concludes with a chapter on 'English Resistance to German Literature from
Coleridge to D. H. Lawrence.' The bibliography is topically arranged and
partially annotated. A brief introduction to German literature since the last
decade of the nineteenth century is *Modern German Literature: The Major
Figures in Context* by Henry Hatfield (New York: St. Martin's Press, 1967). See
also *The Disinherited Mind: Essays in Modern German Literature and Thought*,
by Erich Heller (N.Y.: Farrar, Straus and Cudahy, 1957; repr., Cleveland:
World, Meridian Books, 1959) for essays on Goethe, Burckhardt, Nietzsche,
Rilke, Kafka, and others. *On Four Modern Humanists*, ed. by Arthur R. Evans,
Jr. (Princeton, N.J.: Princeton Univ. Press, 1970) is a volume with short but well-
annotated intellectual biographies of Friedrich Gundolf by Lothar Helbing and C.
V. Bock, Ernst Robert Curtius by Arthur R. Evans, Jr., Ernst H. Kantorowicz by
Yakov Malkiel, and Hugo von Hofmannsthal by Egon Schwarz. The paperback
Deutsche Literatur in unserer Zeit ['German Literature in Our Time'] (Göttingen:
Vandenhoeck & Ruprecht, 1959) has lectures by Wolfgang Kayser on literary life,
Benno von Wiese on lyrical poetry, Wilhelm Emrich on twentieth-century
narrative prose, Fritz Martini on drama, Max Wehrli on literature in German-
speaking Switzerland, and Friedrich Heer on Austrian literature, with bibliographical references following each lecture (on the subject of the German book
trade, in the case of the first), and a single index of names for the volume as a
whole.

347 The German bestseller in the 20th century. A complete bibliography and analysis, 1915-1940.
Donald Ray Richards. Berne: Herbert Lang, 1968. 276p. bibliog.
(German Studies in America, no. 2).

A study of the reception of books in the marketplace, as opposed to their
reception by critics and literary historians, with an essay by Heinrich Meyer on
'Bestseller Research Problems.' The bulk of the volume is comprised of two long
tables: one, alphabetized by author, gives sales figures for over 2,000 titles by
some 590 authors; the other lists, in descending order of sales, over 850 titles with
at least 50,000 copies printed. The latter table is headed by Thomas Mann's
Buddenbrooks, followed, in turn, by Alfred Hein's *Kurts Maler. Ein Lieblings-
roman des deutschen Volkes* ['Kurts Maler (an allusion to the popular writer
Hedwig Courths-Mahler): A Favourite Novel of the German People'], Erich
Maria Remarque's *Im Westen nichts Neues* ['All Quiet on the Western Front'] and
a children's book. See also Rudolf Schenda, *Die Lesestoffe der Kleinen Leute.
Studien zur populären Literatur im 19. und 20. Jahrhundert* ['The Reading Matter
of the "Little Man": Studies on Popular Literature in the 19th and 20th Century']
(Munich: Beck, 1976), with extensive annotations and bibliography, and, on a
very popular twentieth-century German writer who has generally been neglected
in serious literary criticism, H. J. Schueler, *Hans Fallada: Humanist and Social
Critic*, 'Studies in German Literature,' vol. 18 (The Hague: Mouton, 1970).

Literature. Literary history and criticism

348   **The writer in extremis: Expressionism in twentieth-century German literature.**
Walter L. Sokel.   Stanford, Calif.: Stanford University Press, 1959; repr., N.Y.: McGraw-Hill, 1964. 251p. bibliog.

Expressionism is a term used to designate an aspect of the modern revolution in art and literature which gained particular importance in Germany between 1910 and 1925. This book, published in the Federal Republic as *Der literarische Expressionismus* ['Literary Expressionism'], transl. by Jutta and Theodor Knust (Munich: Langen/Müller, n.d.), is a study of some of the basic assumptions of the German writers identified with Expressionism. See also Prof. Sokel's introduction to the anthology of German Expressionist drama, cited under English-language anthologies and readers; Egbert Krispyn's *Style and Society in German Literary Expressionism*, Univ. of Florida Monographs: Humanities, no. 15 (Gainesville: Univ. of Florida Press, 1964); and Roy F. Allen's volume in 'Twayne's World Authors Series,' *German Expressionist Poetry* (Boston: Twayne, 1979).

349   **Die deutsche Literatur in der Weimarer Republik.** (German literature during the Weimar Republic.)
Edited by Wolfgang Rothe.   Stuttgart: Philipp Reclam jun., 1974. 486p. bibliog.

Collaborative work comprised of twenty essays compiled for this volume, focussed on a wide range of topics during the period 1918-1932, including the essay, the literary cabaret, *völkische* ['folkish'] literature, provincial literature, forms of historical narrative, political-revolutionary theatre, the evaluation of the 1920s as reflected in novels with a contemporary setting, and the literary policy of the Communist Party during the Weimar Republic. The contributions are individually provided either with backnotes or a bibliography; most have both, in some cases quite extensive. There is a single index of names for the whole volume. For an introduction to the political and cultural setting of the period from 1918 to 1933, see Peter Gay, *Weimar Culture: The Outsider as Insider* (N.Y.: Harper & Row, 1968; repr., Harper Torchbooks, 1970); on life in the capital during that period, Otto Friedrich, *Before the Deluge: A Portrait of Berlin in the 1920's* (N.Y.: Harper & Row, 1972); and on the circle of left-wing writers – including Erich Kästner, Heinrich Mann, and Carl von Ossietzky – who provided the most consistent opposition to the ultra-nationalists, Istvan Deak, *Weimar Germany's Left-Wing Intellectuals: A Political History of the 'Weltbühne' and Its Circle* (Berkeley: Univ. of California Press, 1968).

350   **German literature under National Socialism.**
J. M. Ritchie.   London: Croom Helm; Totowa, N.J.: Barnes & Noble, 1983. 325p. bibliog.

Attempting 'to understand what National Socialists thought they had to offer that was new and valuable,' Ritchie first investigates the tradition in the Weimar Republic on which the National Socialists were able to build. He then considers, in turn, the writers in Germany who after 1933 supported the National Socialists, those who did not (whether in the withdrawal of the 'inner emigration' or in the resistance), and those who left Germany in opposition (but whose works he does *not* treat as a separate body of 'exile literature,' to be considered as something quite different from the German literature of the time). The final chapter discusses the comparative neglect, in postwar Germany, of works written in exile. The annotations and bibliography cite several unpublished American, British, and German dissertations. *Die deutsche Literatur im Dritten Reich. Themen, Traditionen, Wirkungen* ['German Literature in the Third Reich: Themes, Traditions, Effects'], ed. by Horst Denkler and Karl Prümm (Stuttgart: Philipp Reclam jun., 1976) is a compilation of twenty-three articles on various aspects, including the inner emigration, the resistance, the historical novel, film comedy, song, and *Jugendliteratur* [youth literature].

351 **Children's literature in Hitler's Germany: the cultural policy of National Socialism.**
Christa Kamenetsky. Athens, Ohio: Ohio University Press, 1984.
359p. bibliog.

Kamenetsky shows how children's literature was shaped and adapted to serve as an instrument of National Socialist ideology, explaining the mechanisms of control over writers and publishers, school curricula, and school libraries. The book begins with a survey of what German children had been reading since the eighteenth century. It is well documented and has an extensive bibliography. See also Peter Aley, *Jugendliteratur im Dritten Reich. Dokumente und Kommentare* ['Youth Literature in the Third Reich: Documents and Commentary'], 'Schriften zur Buchmarkt-Forschung [Writings on Book-Market Research],' vol. 12 (Gütersloh: C. Bertelsmann Verlag, 1967).

352 **The German novel, 1939-1944.**
H. Boeschenstein. Toronto: University of Toronto Press, 1949.
189p. bibliog.

A study of novels published in Germany during the final, wartime years of Hitler's 'anti-intellectual interregnum,' when many authors, 'even those of considerable merit,' withdrew into traditional styles, e.g., the peasant novel, because of the safety factor; so long as a writer sang the praises of country life, the critics would have to credit him 'at least with a wholesome, biologically valuable philosophy.' For a perspective written ten years earlier, see *The German Novel of To-day: A Guide to Contemporary Fiction in Germany, to the Novels of the Emigrants, and to Those of German-speaking Swiss Writers*, by Albert W. Bettex, transl. by F. A. Reeve (1939; repr. ed., Freeport, N.Y.: Books for Libraries Press, 1969). Helmut F. Pfanner's *Hanns Johst. Vom Expressionismus zum Nationalsozialismus* ['Hanns Johst: From Expressionism to National Socialism'] (The Hague: Mouton, 1970) is a study of a prominent National Socialist novelist. A systematic introduction to the literature of the period is provided in Ernst Loewy's *Literatur unterm Hakenkreuz. Das Dritte Reich und seine Dichtung. Eine Dokumentation* ['Literature under the Swastika: Writing and Poetry in the Third Reich. A Documentation'] (Frankfurt am Main: Europäische Verlagsanstalt, 1966); the volume includes fifty-five biographical sketches (with selected bibliographical citations). See also the compilation by Joseph Wulf, *Literatur und Dichtung im Dritten Reich. Eine Dokumentation* ['Literature and Poetry (and Literary Prose) in the Third Reich: A Documentation']; (Gütersloh: Sigbert Mohn Verlag, 1963; paperback repr., Reinbek bei Hamburg: Rowohlt, 1966).

Literature. Literary history and criticism

353 **Anti-Nazi writers in exile.**
Egbert Krispyn. Athens, Ga.: The University of Georgia Press,
1978. 200p. bibliog.

Brilliant critical synopsis, with well-selected, partially annotated bibliography and detailed index. Tells the moving story of a literary opposition whose message found so little resonance that it might as well have been played – in one emigré's image – on a violin of stone. Krispyn provides context and contrast by focussing his account on key figures in Germany as well as in exile, including Benn, Brecht, Döblin, Feuchtwanger, Hauptmann, Ernst Jünger, Jochen Klepper, Ossietzky, Nelly Sachs, Toller, Franz Werfel, Zuckmayer, Stefan Zweig, and particularly Thomas Mann, explaining the significance of his role as a spokesman for the literary opposition in exile until the end of the war, and of the acrimonious controversy regarding the 'inner emigration' in which he became embroiled in 1945. Finally, Krispyn explains why, in the long run, the tone of postwar West German writing was set not by veterans of the literary opposition in exile or of the inner emigration, but by an informally organized group originating with German veterans released from prisoner-of-war camps, including Alfred Andersch and Hans Werner Richter, former editors of a liberal publication produced for distribution in POW camps in America, who in 1947 constituted themselves as 'Gruppe 47.' See also Charles W. Hoffmann, *Opposition Poetry in Nazi Germany* (Berkeley: Univ. of California Press, 1962); *Exile Literature 1933-1945* (Bad Godesberg: Inter Nationes, 1968), with addresses by Golo Mann and Hans Mayer, and a listing of works written in exile; Manfred Durzak, ed., *Die deutsche Exilliteratur 1933-1945* ['German Exile Literature 1933-1945'] (Stuttgart: Reclam, 1973), a 624-page volume with thirty-nine essays and biographical data on some 400 writers in exile, listing works and citing English translations; and Wilhelm Sternfeld and Eva Tiedemann, eds., *Deutsche Exil-Literatur 1933-1945. Eine Bio-Bibliographie* ['German Exile Literature 1933-1945: A Bio-Bibliography'] 2nd ed. (Heidelberg and Darmstadt: Lambert Schneider, 1970.)

354 **Postwar German literature: a critical introduction.**
Peter Demetz. New York: Pegasus, 1970. 264p. bibliog.

A well-structured work, with introductory chapters on social and intellectual changes since 1945 in German-speaking Europe; essays on trends in the theatre and on problems of poetry and of fiction; twenty-two critical portraits of important writers; and a bibliography citing articles as well as books in English. *Die Literatur der Bundesrepublik Deutschland* ['The Literature of the Federal Republic of Germany'], ed. by Dieter Lattmann (Munich: Kindler, 1973), is a well-written, -illustrated, -annotated, and -indexed 800-page handbook with a general overview by the editor, sections on prose by Heinrich Vormweg, lyrical poetry by Karl Krolow, and drama by Hellmuth Karasek, and sixty-six pages of biographical sketches of German authors. *Deutsche Gegenwartsliteratur. Ausgangspositionen und aktuelle Entwicklungen* ['German Literature of the Present: Points of Departure and Current Developments'], ed. by Manfred Durzak (Stuttgart: Reclam, 1981), includes twenty-eight essays on various aspects of contemporary German literature (with some coverage of East German literature). On the postwar novel, see H. M. Waidson, *The Modern German Novel 1945-1965*, 2nd ed. (London and N.Y.: Oxford Univ. Press, 1971), which includes a list of English translations of the works mentioned; *The Contemporary Novel in German: A Symposium*, ed. with an intro. by Robert R. Heitner (Austin: Univ.

of Texas Press, 1967), with a paper by Gerd Gaiser on 'The Present Quandary of German Novelists'; and *The Uncompleted Past: Postwar German Novels and the Third Reich*, by Judith Ryan (Detroit: Wayne State Univ. Press, 1983). See also Peter Bürger, 'Literary Criticism in Germany Today' in Jürgen Habermas, ed., *Observations on 'The Spiritual Situation of the Age': Contemporary German Perspectives* (Cambridge, Mass.: MIT Press, 1984), transl. and with an intro. by Andrew Buchwalter from *Stichworte zur 'Geistigen Situation der Zeit'* (Frankfurt: Suhrkamp, 1979) and F. and G. Oberhauser's informative literary guide to West Germany, with suggested itineraries, cited above among the travel guides under Geography.

355 **The intellectual tradition of modern Germany: a collection of writings from the eighteenth to the twentieth century.**
Compiled by Ronald Taylor. New York: Barnes & Noble, 1973.
2 vols. bibliog.

Selections from thirty-one major German authors, representing a spectrum of philosophical, aesthetic, historical, and social thought. Largely essays or lectures, complete in themselves, the well-selected German texts are each preceded by an introduction and followed by commentary, both in English. The first volume, focussing on philosophy, religion, and the arts, includes pieces by Lessing, Schiller, Nietzsche, and Jaspers; the second, on history and society, includes selections by Hesse, Brecht, and Jünger, as well as the German text of Thomas Mann's address on 'Germany and the Germans,' delivered in English at the Library of Congress at the end of World War II and available in English in *Thomas Mann's Addresses Delivered at the Library of Congress, 1942-1949*, foreword by L. Quincy Mumford (Washington, D.C.: Library of Congress, 1963), pp. 45-66. See also two illustrated collections – 'to make available to students of German, early in their study of the language, mature primary material of the highest quality and the greatest intrinsic interest' – compiled and edited by Reginald H. Phelps and Jack M. Stein: *The German Heritage*, 3rd ed. (N.Y.: Holt, Rinehart and Winston, 1970), with passages (in modified German, with English introductions and marginal notes, and vocabulary at the end of the book) from, among others, Luther, Goethe, Marx and Engels, Hesse, and Günther Grass; and the similarly structured companion volume, in collaboration with their Harvard colleague I. Bernard Cohen, *The German Scientific Heritage* (N.Y.: Holt, Rinehart and Winston, 1962), with selections, often from papers announcing discoveries, from, among others, Leibniz, Mendel, Koch, Röntgen, Einstein, and Carl Friedrich von Weizsäcker.

356 **Modern German literature: a library of literary criticism.**
Compiled and edited by Agnes Körner Domandi. N.Y.:
Frederick Ungar, 1972. Vol. 1, Ilse Aichinger to Friedrich Georg
Jünger, 421p.; vol. 2, Franz Kafka to Stefan Zweig, 413p. bibliog.

Very useful collection of critical excerpts (in English or English translation) on writings of over two hundred twentieth-century German writers. Major works of an author are taken up in reviews, followed by a selected bibliography of his works.

Major writers and present trends

357   German men of letters.
Edited by Alex Natan and Brian Keith-Smith.   London: Oswald
Wolff, 1961-1972. 6 vols. bibliog.
Six volumes of essays on seventy-one German writers and their works. Each essay
is followed by a bibliography. There are translations into English of passages and
poems in German. As noted below, each of the volumes edited by Natan alone
has twelve essays; the fourth, edited by Keith-Smith, has ten essays on individual
writers and a collective essay on East German literature; the sixth, co-edited by
Natan and Keith-Smith, has eleven essays on individual writers. The last volume
includes a list of authors treated in the six volumes and a tribute to Alex Natan,
who did not live to see the completion of the set.
   Vol. 1: *Twelve Literary Essays* (1961, 273p.), ed. by Alex Natan, on Herder,
Tieck, Eichendorff, Droste-Hülshoff, Grillparzer, Hebbel, Storm, Keller, C. F.
Meyer, Fontane, Hauptmann, and Hofmannsthal.
   Vol. 2: *Twelve Literary Essays* (1963, 298p.), ed. by Alex Natan, on Nietzsche,
Sudermann, Schnitzler, Morgenstern, Wedekind, Sternheim, Kaiser, Walser,
Heinrich Mann, Stefan Zweig, Hesse, and Gertrud von le Fort.
   Vol. 3: *Twelve Literary Essays* (1964, 343p.), ed. by Alex Natan, on the literary
work of the twentieth-century writers Kokoschka, Barlach, Toller, Werfel, Benn,
Unruh, Feuchtwanger, Zuckmayer, Musil, Borchert, Frisch, and Dürrenmatt.
   Vol. 4: *Essays on Contemporary German Literature* (1969, 280p.), ed. by Brian
Keith-Smith. While there is no central theme to this volume, the introduction
states that the eleven essays 'spotlight the essentially divided character of German
writing today.' Featured are Wilhelm Lehmann, Hermann Kasack, Hans Erich
Nossack, Günter Eich, Gerd Gaiser, Heinrich Böll, Paul Celan, Ingeborg
Bachmann, Günter Grass, and Hans Magnus Enzensberger. The eleventh essay is
on East German literature.
   Vol. 5: *Twelve Literary Essays* (1969, 319p.) ed. by Alex Natan, on nineteenth-
century poets and writers 'linked by a feeling of spiritual loneliness': Jean Paul,
Brentano, E. T. A. Hoffmann, Grabbe, Platen, Lenau, Stifter, Mörike, Gotthelf,
Raabe, Nestroy, and Spitteler.
   Vol. 6: *Literary Essays* (1972, 318p.), ed. by Alex Natan and Brian Keith-
Smith. Eleven essays on eighteenth-century writers: Leibniz, Gottsched, Kant,
Wieland, Hagedorn, Lichtenberg, Lenz, Klinger, Winckelmann, Pestalozzi, and
(in a single essay) the Anacreontic poets Gleim, Uz, and Götz. The volume
includes a list of authors treated in the six-volume set, noting that revised versions
of the essays on Dürrenmatt, Frisch, Gotthelf, Keller, C. F. Meyer, Spitteler, and
Walser have been published in *Swiss Men of Letters*, ed. by Alex Natan (London:
Wolff, 1970).

358 **Goethe: his life and times.**
Richard Friedenthal.   London: Weidenfeld and Nicolson;
Cleveland, Ohio, and New York: World Publishing Co., 1965.
561p. bibliog.

Readable, modern account, translated by the author, in collaboration with John Nowell, from *Goethe – sein Leben und seine Zeit* (Munich: Piper, 1963); not annotated, but includes a bibliographical essay. See also the classic English biography by George Henry Lewes, *The Life of Goethe*, 4th ed. (London: Smith, Elder, & Co., 1890; repr., London: Dent, and N.Y.: Dutton, 'Everyman's Library,' 1908; repr., with an introduction by Victor Lange, N.Y.: Ungar, 1965). In German, see the widely read and appreciated interpretation of Goethe's life and works by Friedrich Gundolf, *Goethe* (Berlin: Bondi, 1916), and Peter Boerner's profusely illustrated paperback *Johann Wolfgang von Goethe in Selbstzeugnissen und Bilddokumenten* ['Johann Wolfgang von Goethe in His Personal Testimony and Pictorial Documents'], Rowohlt's Monographs, no. 100 (Reinbek bei Hamburg: Rowohlt, 1964), which has a detailed chronology and an extensive bibliography. Ronald Gray's *Goethe: A Critical Introduction* (Cambridge: At the University Press, 1967) provides English readers with an introductory essay on Goethe and his works, followed by a sensitive, helpful discussion of the latter (with English translations, in footnotes, of German words or passages) and a partially annotated bibliography; in Gray's companion volume, *Poems of Goethe: A Selection with Introduction and Notes* (Cambridge: At the University Press, 1966), the verse is untranslated but introduced and annotated in English. A shorter introduction, with a brief bibliography, is available in a 114-page volume in the 'Past Masters' series: T. J. Reed, *Goethe* (Oxford and N.Y.: Oxford Univ. Press, 1984). 'Goethe and His Time,' the second chapter in Hans Kohn's *The Mind of Germany* (N.Y.: Scribner's, 1960; repr., Harper Torchbooks, 1965) discusses Goethe as 'the last great man of the German Enlightenment.' See also Thomas Mann's thirty-three-page introductory essay to *The Permanent Goethe*, cited below under English-language anthologies and readers; Victor Lange, ed., *Goethe: A Collection of Critical Essays* (Englewood Cliffs, N.J.: Prentice-Hall, 1968); T. S. Eliot, 'Goethe as the Sage' in *On Poetry and Poets* (London: Faber and Faber, 1957); George Santayana, 'Goethe's "Faust" ' in *Three Philosophical Poets: Lucretius, Dante, Goethe* (Cambridge, Mass.: Harvard Univ. Press, 1910; repr., Garden City, N.Y.: Doubleday, 1953); and Albert Schweitzer, *Goethe: Five Studies*, translated, with an introduction, by Charles R. Joy (Boston: Beacon, 1961). Contemporary West German work on Goethe is reflected in Heinz Ludwig Arnold, ed., *Johann Wolfgang von Goethe* (Munich: edition text + kritik, 1982), a compendium of twenty contributions with a bibliography, listing, among primary sources, the contents, by volume, of the recently reprinted complete collection of the works known as the 'Weimar edition': *Goethes Werke* ['Goethe's Works'], edited at the order of Grand Duchess Sophie of Saxony, 143 vols. (Weimar: Böhlau, 1887-1919; repr., Tübingen: Niemeyer, 1974-75).

Literature. Major writers and present trends

359 **Schiller.**
H. B. Garland. London: Harrap, 1949; New York: Medill McBride, 1950. 280p. map. bibliog.
Concise biography of the poet, dramatist, and historian Schiller, whose reputation throughout much of the nineteenth century overshadowed that of his older contemporary and friend Goethe. Passages cited in German in the text are translated in footnotes. Most of the titles in the select bibliography are in German. More extensive bibliographical coverage is provided, together with a chronology, in the monograph by John D. Simons, *Friedrich Schiller*, 'Twayne's World Authors Series' (Boston: Twayne, 1981). See also two essays by Georg Lukács in *Goethe and His Time*, translated by Robert Anchor (N.Y.: Howard Fertig, 1978), 'The Correspondence between Schiller and Goethe' and 'Schiller's Theory of Modern Literature.' Insight into Schiller is offered in selections from his writings (largely letters), edited by Hugo von Hofmannsthal: *Schillers Selbstcharakteristik* ['Schiller's Self-characterization'] (Frankfurt am Main: S. Fischer Verlag, 1955; repr., Fischer-Bücherei, 1959). See also the 866-page biography by Benno von Wiese, *Friedrich Schiller*, 4th ed. (Stuttgart: J. B. Metzlersche Verlagsbuchhandlung, 1978), and, on Schiller's work as a dramatist, two compilations: Klaus L. Berghahn and Reinhold Grimm, eds., *Schiller. Zur Theorie und Praxis der Dramen* ['Schiller: On the Theory and Practice of His Dramas'] (Darmstadt: Wissenschaftliche Buchgesellschaft, 1972), with scholarly articles largely from the 1950s and 1960s; and Fritz Heuer and Werner Keller, eds., *Schillers Wallenstein* ['Schiller's "Wallenstein" '] (Darmstadt: Wissenschaftliche Buchgesellschaft, 1977), on one of the great historical dramas, with relevant material from 1798 to 1974, including a selection from 1955 by Thomas Mann.

360 **Georg Büchner.**
William C. Reeve. New York: Frederick Ungar Publishing Co., 1979. 186p. bibliog. (World Dramatists).
Well-structured treatment of the man, his works, and their reception on the stage. See also Herbert Lindenberger, *Georg Büchner* (Carbondale: Southern Illinois Univ. Press, 1964) for a readable introduction to the remarkably precocious nineteenth-century scientist and dramatist whose works came to be appreciated only in the twentieth century. Drawn to Switzerland as a political refugee because of his revolutionary activity, particularly the publication of his inflamatory pamphlet of 1834, *Der hessische Landbote* ['The Hessian Courier'], denouncing – fourteen years before the *Communist Manifesto* – the exploitation of the poor, Büchner joined the faculty of Zurich University in 1836. A few months later, typhus broke out, he was stricken, and in February 1837, at twenty-three, died. He left behind, in addition to *The Hessian Courier* and German translations of plays by Victor Hugo, a psychological novella, *Lenz*, and three dramas: a comedy, *Leonce and Lena*, and two tragedies, *Danton's Death* and *Woyzeck* (on which Anton Berg based his opera *Wozzeck*, first performed in 1925). See also David G. Richards, *Georg Büchner and the Birth of the Modern Drama* (Albany: State Univ. of New York Press, 1977), which has a good bibliography and a number of backnotes that summarize (in English) some of the issues and problems discussed in the German critical literature; for a more extensive introduction to the latter, see the twenty-five contributions in Wolfgang Martens, ed., *Georg Büchner* (Darmstadt: Wissenschaftliche Buchgesellschaft, 1965).

361 **Heinrich Heine: a modern biography.**
Jeffrey L. Sammons. Princeton, N.J.: Princeton University Press, 1979. 425p. bibliog.

A leading authority's documented account of the life of one of the greatest German poets, addressed to the general reader as well as the scholar. The selected bibliography begins with a listing of the works of Heine in English. The book is primarily biographical rather than interpretive; for Sammons' interpretation of Heine's writings, see his earlier *Heinrich Heine: The Elusive Poet* (New Haven, Conn.: Yale Univ. Press, 1969). A concise introduction to the man and his works is provided by Hanna Spencer, *Heinrich Heine*, 'Twayne's World Authors Series' (Boston: Twayne, 1982), which also has a chronology of his life and a well-annotated bibliography. Laura Hofrichter, *Heinrich Heine* (Oxford: At the Clarendon Press, 1963), was translated by Barker Fairley from the manuscript of the subsequently published *Heinrich Heine. Biographie seiner Dichtung* ['Heinrich Heine: Biography of His Poetry'] (Göttingen: Vandenhoeck & Ruprecht, 1966). See Frederic Ewen's forty-eight-page introduction to his edition of Heine's poetry and prose cited below under English-language anthologies and readers, Ludwig Marcuse's introduction to Heine's *Religion and Philosophy in Germany: A Fragment*, translated by John Snodgrass (Boston: Beacon, 1959), as well as Marcuse's *Heinrich Heine in Selbstzeugnissen und Bilddokumenten* ['Heinrich Heine in His Personal Testimony and Pictorial Documents'], Rowohlt's Monographs, no. 41 (Reinbek bei Hamburg: Rowohlt, 1960), and his biography of Heine, initially published as *Heinrich Heine. Ein Leben zwischen Gestern und Morgen* ['Heinrich Heine: A Life Between Yesterday and Tomorrow'] (Berlin: Rowohlt, 1932), which appeared in English as *Heine: A Life Between Love and Hate*, transl. by Louise M. Sieveking and Ian F. D. Morrow (N.Y.: Farrar and Rinehart, 1933), was published in a second, revised edition by Rowohlt in 1951, and appeared in an expanded, third edition as *Heine. Melancholiker, Streiter in Marx, Epikureer* ['Heine: Melancholic, Contender with Marx, Epicurean'] (Rothenburg ob der Tauber: Verlag J. P. Peter, Gebr. Holstein, 1970).

362 **Rilke: a life.**
Wolfgang Leppmann. Translated from the German in collaboration with the author by Russell M. Stockman. Verse translations by Richard Exner. New York: Fromm International Publ. Corp., 1984. 421p. bibliog.

Translated from *Rilke – sein Leben, seine Welt, sein Werk* (Berne and Munich: Scherz Verlag, 1981), this is a comprehensive biography of one of the finest poets of his time and an introduction to his works. See also the more concise biography by J. F. Hendry, *The Sacred Threshold: A Life of Rainer Maria Rilke* (Manchester: Carcanet, 1983); the studies by Siegfried Mandel, *Rainer Maria Rilke: The Poetic Instinct* (Carbondale: Southern Illinois Univ. Press, 1965), and E. M. Butler, *Rainer Maria Rilke* (N. Y.: Macmillan; Cambridge: At the University Press, 1941); Romano Guardini's *Rilke's Duino Elegies: An Interpretation* (Chicago: Regnery, 1961), translated by K. G. Knight from *Rainer Maria Rilkes Deutung des Daseins. Eine Interpretation der Duineser Elegien* ['Rainer Maria Rilke's Understanding of Existence: An Interpretation of the Duino

Literature. Major writers and present trends

Elegies'] (Munich: Kosel, 1953); and Egon Schwarz's introduction to the volume of Rilke's poetry and prose published in 'The German Library,' cited below under English-language anthologies and readers.

363 **Heinrich Mann.**
Rolf N. Linn. New York: Twayne Publishers, 1967. 144p. bibliog. (Twayne's World Authors Series).

A critical introduction to Heinrich Mann, elder brother of Thomas Mann, with a brief account of his life and an appraisal of his works which, seen together, are found to represent 'an almost complete intellectual and political history of Germany in the first half of the twentieth century.' The bibliography of the well-annotated monograph includes a listing of Mann's writings published in English. Lorenz Winter's *Heinrich Mann and His Public: A Socioliterary Study of the Relationship between an Author and His Public* (Coral Gables, Fla.: Univ. of Miami Press, 1970), transl. by John Gorman from *Heinrich Mann und sein Publikum. Eine literatursoziologische Studie zum Verhältnis von Autor und Öffentlichkeit* (Cologne: Westdeutscher Verlag, 1965), includes an enumerated list of 'The Writings of Heinrich Mann,' with ninety-two main entries, and an extensive bibliography citing articles as well as books in English, French, and German. A pamphlet published on the centenary of the writer's birth, *Heinrich Mann 1871/1971* (Bonn-Bad Godesberg: Inter Nationes, 1971) includes essays by Alfred Kantorowicz and André Banuls, author of *Heinrich Mann* (Stuttgart: Kohlhammer, 1970), revised and abridged from *Heinrich Mann. Le poète et la politique* ['Heinrich Mann: The Poet and Politics'] (Paris: Klincksieck, 1966). See also the concise, illustrated biography (incorporating many excerpts from his writings) by Klaus Schröter, *Heinrich Mann in Selbstzeugnissen und Bilddokumenten* ['Heinrich Mann in His Personal Testimony and Pictorial Documents'], Rowohlt's Monographs, no. 125 (Reinbek bei Hamburg: Rowohlt, 1967); his memoirs, *Ein Zeitalter wird besichtigt* ['An Age Is Viewed'] (Düsseldorf: Claassen, 1974), with extensive commentary added; and the annotated articles in the scholarly compendium edited by Klaus Matthias, *Heinrich Mann 1871/1971* (Munich: Wilhelm Fink, 1973).

364 **The ironic German: a study of Thomas Mann.**
Erich Heller. Boston: Little, Brown; London: Secker & Warburg, 1958. 298p. bibliog.

An illuminating study in which the major works of the great novelist are considered in biographical and historical context (with citations in translation). The bibliography includes a listing of Mann's works in English translation. Heller rewrote his work in German, revising and expanding it for publication as *Thomas Mann. Der ironische Deutsche* (Frankfurt am Main: Suhrkamp, 1959). See also Thomas Mann, *Diaries 1918-1939*, selection and foreword by Hermann Kesten, translated by Richard and Clara Winston (N.Y.: Harry N. Abrams, 1982), abridged from his *Tagebücher, 1918-1921, 1933-34, 1935-36, 1937-39* (Frankfurt am Main: S. Fischer, 1977-1980); *Letters of Thomas Mann, 1889-1955*, selected and translated by Richard and Clara Winston (N.Y.: Knopf, 1971), with twenty-four photographs and a thirty-four-page introductory biographical essay by Richard Winston; and the account of Mann's formative years by Richard Winston, *Thomas Mann: The Making of an Artist, 1875–1911*, with an afterword by Clara Winston (N.Y.: Knopf, 1981). On Mann's works, see Henry Hatfield's

Literature. Major writers and present trends

Thomas Mann: An Introduction to His Fiction (London: Peter Owen, 1952); *Thomas Mann: A Collection of Critical Essays*, ed. by Henry Hatfield (Englewood Cliffs, N.J.: Prentice-Hall, 1964); Georg Lukács, *Essays on Thomas Mann*, translated by Stanley Mitchell (N.Y.: Grosset & Dunlap, 1965); and the collection of critical studies in German by Helmut Koopmann, *Thomas Mann* (Darmstadt: Wissenschaftliche Buchgesellschaft, 1975). For a concise, profusely illustrated biography in German, incorporating numerous passages from Mann's own writings, see Klaus Schröter's *Thomas Mann in Selbstzeugnissen und Bilddokumenten* ['Thomas Mann in His Personal Testimony and Pictorial Documents'], Rowohlt's Monographs, no. 93 (Reinbek bei Hamburg: Rowohlt, 1964). On Thomas Mann's relationship with his elder brother Heinrich, see Nigel Hamilton's dual biography of the brothers Mann, as well as the other titles cited in the following entry.

365 **The Brothers Mann: the lives of Heinrich and Thomas Mann, 1871-1950 and 1875-1955.**
Nigel Hamilton. London: Secker & Warburg, 1978; New Haven, Conn.: Yale University Press, 1979. 422p. bibliog.

Well-written dual biography, especially interesting because it incorporates bits and pieces of correspondence and whole letters. Extensive passages, in translation, from the brothers' own pens enable the English reader to follow their intellectual development and to perceive contrasting and at times bitterly antagonistic philosophical values and political opinions which led to the famous breach between them during World War I. Their relationship is also dealt with by Alfred Kantorowicz in *Heinrich und Thomas Mann. Die persönlichen, literarischen und weltanschaulichen Beziehungen der Brüder* ['Heinrich and Thomas Mann: The Personal, Literary, and Ideological Relations of the Brothers'] (Berlin: Aufbau-Verlag, 1956). Heinrich Mann's collection of essays from 1905 to 1931, *Geist und Tat* ['Spirit and Deed'] (Berlin: Kiepenheuer, 1931; repr., Munich: Deutscher Taschenbuch Verlag, 1963), includes the piece – provoked by Thomas Mann's essay 'Gedanken im Kriege' ['Thoughts in Time of War'] – on Zola that he first published in 1915, to which his brother responded with *Reflections of a Nonpolitical Man* (N.Y.: Ungar, 1983), translated by Walter D. Morris from *Betrachtungen eines Unpolitischen* (Berlin: S. Fischer, 1918). On the conflict between the brothers and on Thomas Mann's revealing *Reflections*, see the second and third chapters of Kurt Sontheimer, *Thomas Mann und die Deutschen* ['Thomas Mann and the Germans'] (Munich: Nymphenburger Verlagshandlung, 1961; repr., Frankfurt am Main: Fischer Bücherei, 1965).

366 **Hermann Hesse: pilgrim of crisis. A biography.**
Ralph Freedman. New York: Random House, Pantheon Books, 1978. 432p.

A biographical interpretation of Hermann Hesse, 'a poet of crisis who achieved his identity as a pilgrim into the inner life.' This well-documented, illustrated study has no bibliography, but extensive discussion of the literature in backnotes. It also has a detailed index. Two shorter introductions, both with bibliography, are George Wallis Field, *Hermann Hesse*, 'Twayne's World Authors Series' (N.Y.: Twayne, 1970), and Walter Sorell, *Hermann Hesse: The Man Who Sought and Found Himself*, 'Modern German Authors' (London: Wolff, 1974). An

161

illustrated account in German, incorporating many passages from Hesse's own writings, is Bernhard Zeller's *Hermann Hesse in Selbstzeugnissen und Bilddokumenten* ['Hermann Hesse in His Testimony and Pictorial Documents'], Rowohlt's Monographs, no. 85 (Reinbek bei Hamburg: Rowohlt, 1963); see also Zeller's *Portrait of Hesse: An Illustrated Biography*, translated by Mark Hollebone (N.Y.: Herder and Herder, 1971). Anna Otten, ed., *Hesse Companion* (Frankfurt am Main: Suhrkamp, 1970; repr., with deletions and changes, Albuquerque: Univ. of New Mexico Press, 1977), was published, for English readers, the same year as Hesse's *Gesammelte Werke* ['Collected Works'], 12 vols. (Frankfurt am Main: Suhrkamp, 1970); it includes, in addition to essays in English on various aspects of Hesse's works, a selected bibliography (with articles in periodicals), a glossary, and vocabulary. See also Theodore Ziolkowski, *The Novels of Hermann Hesse: A Study in Theme and Structure* (Princeton, N.J.: Princeton Univ. Press, 1965), and a 955-page edition of political writings not included in the 1970 collection of literary works: Hermann Hesse, *Politik des Gewissens. Die politischen Schriften* ['The Politics of Conscience: The Political Writings'], vol. 1, *1914-1932*, vol. 2, *1932-1964*, foreword by Robert Jungk, ed., with an afterword, by Volker Michels (Frankfurt am Main: Suhrkamp, 1977).

367　**Franz Kafka.**
　　Meno Spann.　Boston: Twayne, 1976. 205p. bibliog. (Twayne's
　　World Authors Series).

Kafka (1883-1924) came from an old, established, German-speaking middle-class community in Prague. Spann gives a lucid overview of his life, times, and works, concisely explaining his social and cultural background and introducing the reader to his principal writings. The extensively annotated monograph concludes with a chapter entitled 'Kafka's Apotheosis,' on the reception of his works (published largely after his death). The bibliography includes journal articles in English as well as German and lists Kafka's works in English (several of which are included with the short novels and stories listed under English-language anthologies and readers). Two other concise introductions to Kafka and his works are Erich Heller's short volume in the 'Modern Masters' series, *Franz Kafka* (N.Y.: Viking, 1974), and *Franz Kafka* (Cambridge: At the University Press, 1973) by Ronald Gray, who edited *Kafka: A Collection of Critical Essays* (N.Y.: Prentice-Hall, 1962). For a full-length biography of Dr. Franz Kafka, legal counselor at the state Workmen's Accident Insurance Institute in Prague and, at the same time, a 'sleepwalker chasing dreams out of time, and driven to writing as others are to murder, ecstasy or drink,' see Ernst Pawel, *The Nightmare of Reason: A Life of Franz Kafka* (N.Y.: Farrar, Straus, Giroux, 1984). See also the account by Kafka's close friend, Max Brod, *Franz Kafka: A Biography*, 2nd, enl. ed., translated by Humphrey G. Roberts and Richard Winston (N.Y.: Schocken, 1960). For a cross-section in German, see *Franz Kafka*, 2nd ed. (Darmstadt: Wissenschaftliche Buchgesellschaft, 1980), a compendium of over a score of selections, edited by Heinz Politzer, author of *Franz Kafka: Parable and Paradox* (N.Y.: Cornell Univ. Press, 1962), a study of the style of Kafka as a 'narrator who told remarkably illuminating stories while searching for a way through the shadows which extended from his age to ours.'

Literature. Major writers and present trends

368 **Brecht: a choice of evils – a critical study of the man, his work, and his opinions.**
Martin Esslin. London: Methuen, 1984. 4th, rev. ed. 315p. bibliog. (Modern Theatre Profiles).

Revised biography of Bertolt Brecht (1898-1956), one of the most influential, innovative, controversial German writers of the first half of the twentieth century, using previously unavailable sources. In this new edition, for example, Esslin accounts for his judgement that 'Brecht was a polygamist' in some detail, and explains its relevance to Brecht's artistic personality. The final part of the volume, entitled 'For Reference,' consists of a chronology of Brecht's life, a descriptive list of his works (including previously unavailable letters), and a bibliography of his works (with a section on translations into English) and of works about him. For a full-length biography, see Frederic Ewen's 573-page *Bertolt Brecht: His Life, His Art and His Times* (N.Y.: Citadel, 1967), an illustrated, annotated account with extensive bibliography. See also Klaus Völker, *Brecht: A Biography* (N.Y.: Seabury, Continuum, 1978), translated by John Nowell from *Bertolt Brecht. Eine Biographie* (Munich: Hanser, 1976). On Brecht as dramatist, see Karl H. Schoeps, *Bertolt Brecht*, 'World Dramatists' (N.Y.: Ungar, 1977) and Ronald Gray, *Brecht the Dramatist* (Cambridge: Cambridge Univ. Press, 1976), and as poet, Peter Whitaker, *Brecht's Poetry: A Critical Study* (Oxford: Clarendon Press, 1985). See also Peter Demetz, ed., *Brecht: A Collection of Critical Essays* (Englewood Cliffs, N.J.: Prentice-Hall, 1962) and Marianne Kesting's *Bertolt Brecht in Selbstzeugnissen und Bilddokumenten* ['Bertolt Brecht in Personal Testimony and Pictorial Documents'], Rowohlt's Monographs, no. 37 (Reinbek bei Hamburg: Rowohlt, 1959).

369 **Group 47: the reflected intellect.**
Siegfried Mandel. Preface by Harry T. Moore. Carbondale and Edwardsville: Southern Illinois University Press, 1973. 232p. bibliog. (Crosscurrents/Modern Critiques).

Study of the works and influence of *Gruppe 47*, a circle of postwar German writers informally organized as a reading forum in 1947. After describing the origins of the group (its original leaders had edited a liberal newspaper for Germans in American POW camps), Mandel discusses their prose fiction, their poetry, and their works in three dramatic genres: the radio play, the documentary, and the traditional drama on stage. In an appendix, he lists the thirty meetings of Group 47, from 1947 to 1972, by place and month, and provides an alphabetical list of the authors who have read at Group 47 meetings, noting the ten among them who also received the group's prize: Ilse Aichinger, Ingeborg Bachmann, Jürgen Becker, Peter Bichsel, Johannes Bobrowski, Heinrich Böll, Günter Eich, Günter Grass, Adriaan Morriën, and Martin Walser. The political concern of many members of Group 47, noted by Mandel in his book, was reflected, late in Adenauer's chancellorship, by a volume containing the responses of twenty to the question posed in its title: *Die Alternative* oder *Brauchen wir eine neue Regierung?* ['The Alternative' or 'Do We Need a New Government?'], compiled, with an introduction, by Martin Walser (Reinbek bei Hamburg: Rowohlt, 1961). See also the illustrated volume on the group, with selections from readings at the meetings, edited by Hans Werner Richter in collaboration with Walter Mannzen, *Almanach der Gruppe 47, 1947-1962*

Literature. Major writers and present trends

['Almanac of Group 47, 1947-1962'] (Reinbek bei Hamburg: Rowohlt, 1962), and the monographs in 'Twayne's World Authors Series,' each with a chronology and a selected bibliography, on three of the most prominent members of Group 47: Robert C. Conard, *Heinrich Böll* (Boston: Twayne, 1981); W. Gordon Cunliffe, *Günter Grass* (N.Y.: Twayne, 1969); and Margaret E. Ward, *Rolf Hochhuth* (Boston: Twayne, 1977).

370 **Paul Celan.**
Jerry Glenn. New York: Twayne Publ., 1973. 174p. bibliog.
(Twayne's World Authors Series).

This first monograph in English on the lyric poet Celan (1920-1970) focusses on his works and includes an analysis of his most famous poem, 'Todesfuge [Fuge of Death],' a haunting evocation of the concentration camp. The book is well annotated; the bibliography cites both German and American dissertations. For Celan's personal background, largely on the basis of correspondence and interviews with surviving relatives and acquaintances, see the Jerusalem scholar Israel Chalfen's illustrated *Paul Celan. Eine Biographie seiner Jugend* ['Paul Celan: A Biography of His Youth'] (Frankfurt am Main: Insel Verlag, 1979). Celan's lyrical *oeuvre*, prose and speeches (including his address on receiving the Georg Büchner Prize in Darmstadt in 1960), as well as translations into German from seven foreign languages, with the original texts, are brought together in his *Gesammelte Werke* ['Collected Works'], 5 vols., ed. by Beda Allemann and Stefan Reichert in collaboration with Rudolf Bücher (Frankfurt am Main: Suhrkamp, 1983). Vol. 1 starts with *Mohn and Gedächtnis* ['Poppy and Memory'], the title of his first collection of poems published in Germany (Stuttgart: Deutsche Verlags-Anstalt, 1952). A volume of his verse in German, with English on the facing pages, is cited below under English-language anthologies and readers.

371 **The German novel and the affluent society.**
R. Hinton Thomas and Wilfried van der Will. Manchester: Manchester University Press, 1968. 167p. bibliog.

A study of the response to German society on the part of six leading postwar novelists (Gerd Gaiser, Wolfgang Koeppen, Heinrich Böll, Günter Grass, Martin Walser, and Uwe Johnson), based primarily on examination of their novels, but also taking into account published interviews, letters, and articles. Similar in scope and style is a more recent monograph by R. Hinton Thomas and Keith Bullivant, *Literature in Upheaval: West German Writers and the Challenge of the 1960s* (Manchester: Manchester Univ. Press, 1974). In this volume, there are also six chapters, but rather than being focussed on individual writers, they deal with literature and six themes: identity, politicization, 'the end of literature,' the documentary, the industrial world, and sub-culture. Each of the two volumes is annotated and has a bibliography and an index of names. A wide range of problems in society and literature is dealt with in the following two volumes of essays: Hans Magnus Enzensberger, *Critical Essays*, 'The German Library,' vol. 98, translated by Michael Roloff and others (N.Y.: Continuum, 1982); and Günter Grass, *On Writing and Politics, 1967-1983*, translated by Ralph Manheim (San Diego: Harcourt Brace Jovanovich, 1985).

372   **Das Amerika-Bild in der deutschen Gegenwartsliteratur.**
      Historische Voraussetzungen und aktuelle Beispiele. (The image of
      America in contemporary German literature: historical
      preconditions and present examples.)
      Manfred Durzak.   Stuttgart: Kohlhammer, 1979. 236p. (Sprache
      und Literatur, no. 105).

Scholarly monograph on America in German literature, including chapters
focussing on German travellers' accounts of America since the nineteenth century
and on the image of America in the recent German novel. Durzak's study has no
bibliography, but numerous citations in the extensive backnotes. See also
Amerika in der deutschen Literatur. Neue Welt – Nordamerika – USA ['America
in German Literature: The New World, North America, USA'], edited by Sigrid
Bauschinger, Horst Denkler, and Wilfried Malsch (Stuttgart: Reclam, 1975), a
collection of twenty-five individually annotated contributions on America as
reflected in German literature since the seventeenth century. Discussed are, for
example, the image of the American Indian, America in Heine's works, the view
in East Germany of the U.S. as 'an imperialist terror state,' and the fascination
exerted by Manhattan.

English-language anthologies and readers

373   **German literature in English translation: a select bibliography.**
      Patrick O'Neill.   Toronto, Buffalo, and London: University of
      Toronto Press, 1981. 242p.

An enumerated listing, with indices of authors and of translators, of some 1,900
works. Covering publications through the end of the 1970s, the entries are divided
into general collections; translations of works written before 1700; the eighteenth
century; the nineteenth century; and the twentieth century. Quality was a
criterion for selection in this compilation, but it is unannotated and eschews the
kind of individual critical evaluation to be found in Bayard Quincy Morgan's *A
Critical Bibliography of German Literature in English Translation, 1481-1927*,
2nd, rev. & augmented edition (N.Y.: Scarecrow Press, 1965, 690p.); Morgan
prepared a *Supplement Embracing the Years 1928-1955* (N.Y.: Scarecrow Press,
1965, 601p.) and Murray F. Smith a second supplement, *A Selected Bibliography
of German Literature in English Translation, 1956-1960* (Metuchen, N.J.:
Scarecrow Press, 1972, 398p.).

374 **The German library.**
Volkmar Sander, General Editor. New York: Continuum,
1982- .

Projected collection of 100 volumes in translation, with forewords by internationally known writers and introductions by prominent scholars. Published
(simultaneously in cloth and affordable paperback, initially at a rate of eight
volumes per year) to provide the English-speaking reader access to standard
works representing the German intellectual tradition since the Middle Ages. For
an informed discussion of the inception of the collection, see Gloria Flaherty's
review essay, 'The German Library' in *The German Quarterly*, vol. 59, no. 3
(Summer 1986). Among the earlier volumes printed are the following three
anthologies and selections from Schiller, Kleist, Schnitzler, and Rilke (with
volume numbers reflecting not the sequence of publication, but the structure of
the 100-vol. set as a whole):

Vol. 4, *German Medieval Tales* (1983), ed. by Francis G. Gentry, a collection
comprised of the anonymous '*Historia* & Tale of Doctor Johannes Faustus,'
translated and adapted from the oldest surviving manuscript of the mediaeval
Faust legend, written down about 1580, and five tales from the twelfth and
thirteenth centuries, including 'The Unfortunate Lord Henry [Der arme
Heinrich]' by Hartmann von Aue;

Vol. 6, *German Humanism and Reformation* (1982), ed. by Reinhard P.
Becker, has among its selections six chapters from 'The Ship of Fools,' Erasmus'
'Praise of Folly,' Luther's 'To the Christian Nobility of the German Nation,'
Thomas Müntzer's 'Sermon to the Princes,' and the 'Twelve Articles of Peasantry'
by Sebastian Lotzer.

Vol. 30, *German Literary Fairy Tales* (1983), ed. by Frank G. Ryder and
Robert M. Browning, with sixteen literary (as opposed to folk) fairy tales by
Goethe, Tieck, Wackenroder, Novalis, E. T. A. Hoffmann, Eichendorff,
Brentano, Hauff, Mörike, Storm, Hofmannsthal, and Kafka.

Vol. 15, *Plays* by Friedrich Schiller (1983), ed. by Walter Hinderer: 'Intrigue
and Love' and 'Don Carlos', together with letters by Schiller on 'Don Carlos.'
(Vol. 16 is to include 'Wallenstein' and 'William Tell,' vol. 17, 'Maria Stuart' and
Schiller's main aesthetic writings.)

Vol. 25, *Plays* by Heinrich von Kleist (1982), ed. by Walter Hinderer: 'The
Broken Pitcher: A Comedy'; 'Amphitryon: A Comedy after Molière';
'Penthesilea: A Tragedy'; and 'Prince Frederick of Homburg: A Play.'

Vol. 55, *Plays and Stories* by Arthur Schnitzler (1982), ed. by Egon Schwarz:
the plays 'Flirtations,' 'La Ronde,' and 'Countess Mitzi *or* The Family Reunion',
and the stories 'Casanova's Homecoming' and 'Lieutenant Gustl.'

Vol. 70, *Prose and Poetry* by Rainer Maria Rilke (1984), ed. by Egon Schwarz,
with selections from 'The Book of Hours,' 'The Sonnets to Orpheus,' 'Duino
Elegies,' and 'New Poems,' with German and English on facing pages, and 'The
Notebooks of Malte Laurids Brigge.'

375 **Anthology of German poetry through the 19th century in English translations with the German originals.**
Edited by Alexander Gode and Frederick Ungar. New York: Frederick Ungar Publishing Co., 1972. 2nd, rev. ed. 270p.

This volume of mostly new translations of verse by thirty-seven poets from Walther von der Vogelweide (ca. 1170-1228) to Detlev von Liliencron (1844-1909) was prepared with the editorial collaboration of the American Translators Association. For the twentieth century, see *Modern German Poetry 1910-1960*, edited and with an introduction by Michael Hamburger and Christopher Middleton, translated by Hamburger, Middleton, and others (London: MacGibbon & Kee; N.Y.: Grove Press, 1962), an anthology in German, with English verse translations on facing pages. Ronald Gray's *An Introduction to German Poetry* (Cambridge: At the University Press, 1965) discusses, in English, selections of poetry in German from the sixteenth to the middle of the twentieth century; it deals with the difficulties of translation, the poetic treatments of the same theme, and the interpretation of poems, evaluates differing English translations of the same German original, differing German versions of the same poem, etc. See also A. T. Hatto's prose translation, with a glossary of names and a bibliography, of the mediaeval epic poem by Wolfram von Eschenbach, *Parzival* (Harmondsworth: Penguin Classics, 1980); and the translations by George MacDonald, revised by Ulrich S. Leupold, of thirty-seven hymns of Martin Luther, with single-voice musical settings (the melody line), included in *Liturgy and Hymns* (vol. 53 of *Luther's Works*), ed. by Ulrich S. Leupold, gen. ed., Helmut T. Lehmann (Philadelphia: Fortress Press, 1965). In Stefan George, *Poems*, with a twenty-eight-page introduction by Ernst Morwitz (N.Y.: Pantheon, 1943; repr., N.Y.: Schocken Paperbacks, 1967), the translated poems, as 'rendered into English by Carol North Valhope and Ernst Morwitz,' are printed on the page opposite the German original. In *Primal Vision: Selected Writings of Gottfried Benn*, ed., with introduction, by E. B. Ashton, translated by E. B. Ashton and others (N.Y.: New Directions, 1960; repr., ND Paperbook, 1971), the verse is printed in the German original with the English translation on facing pages, the prose in translation only. Nelly Sachs, *'O the Chimneys': Selected Poems, Including the Verse Play 'Eli'*, translated by Michael Hamburger and others (N.Y.: Farrar, Straus and Giroux, 1967), has a brief introductory essay by Hans Magnus Enzensberger on the 1966 Nobel laureate in literature; the German originals are included except for the play. Paul Celan, *'Speech-Grille' and Selected Poems* (in German, with) translations by Joachim Neugroschel (N.Y.: Dutton: 1971), includes verse from *Mohn und Gedächtnis* ['Poppy and Memory'] in 1952 to *Atemwende* ['Breath-Turning'] in 1967; see also Paul Celan, *Poems: A Bilingual Edition*, selected, translated, and introduced by Michael Hamburger (New York: Persea Books, 1980). Hans Magnus Enzensberger, *poems for people who don't read poems* (N.Y.: Atheneum, 1968), is a collection of his verse with translations by him, Michael Hamburger, and Jerome Rothenberg.

376 **German writing today.**
Edited by Christopher Middleton. Baltimore and
Harmondsworth: Penguin Books, 1967. 238p. bibliog.

Selected poetry, prose, and drama, by forty-one authors, in translation, with
notes on the authors and their works available in English, as well as a listing of
translations from German since 1950 of novels and plays by writers not
represented in this volume. The book includes verse by Ingeborg Bachmann and
Nelly Sachs, a piece on 'Berlin, Border of the Divided World,' written by Uwe
Johnson before the building of the Berlin Wall in August 1961, and 'The Salt
Lake Line,' a radio play by Günter Grass. For an untranslated collection of works
in this genre (mostly by members of 'Group 47,' like Günter Grass) see *Hörspiele*
['Radio Plays'], with an afterword by Ernst Schnabel (Frankfurt am Main: Fischer
Bücherei, 1961). Well over a third of *Postwar German Culture: An Anthology*,
edited by Charles E. McClelland and Steven P. Scher (N.Y.: Dutton, 1974) is
devoted to translations of literary prose, poetry, and criticism. It includes poems
by Benn, Brecht, and Biermann; 'On the Unity of German Literature,' by Hans
Mayer; and 'Where I Live,' the title story of Ilse Aichinger's collection, *Wo ich
wohne. Erzählungen, Gedichte, Dialoge* ['Where I Live: Stories, Poems,
Dialogues'] (Frankfurt am Main: S. Fischer Verlag, 1954). See also *The German
Mind of the Nineteenth Century: A Literary & Historical Anthology*, edited by
Hermann Glaser, with a foreword by Christoph Wecker (N.Y.: Continuum,
1981), a carefully structured volume with ninety-nine well-introduced selections in
translation from 'poets, philosophers, publicists, historians, natural scientists, and
artists,' published in German as *Soviel Anfang war nie. Deutscher Geist im 19.
Jahrhundert. Ein Lesebuch* ['Never Was There So Much of a Beginning. The
German Mind in the 19th Century: A Reader'] (Munich: Carl Hanser, 1981).

377 **Great German short novels and stories.**
Edited, with an introduction, by Victor Lange. New York:
Random House, Modern Library, 1952. 486p.

Seventeen novellas, from Goethe's 'The Sorrows of Young Werther' to Kafka's
'A Country Doctor,' with an introductory essay by a leading authority. In *German
Short Stories – Deutsche Kurzgeschichten*, ed. by Richard Newnham (Baltimore:
Penguin Books, 1964), *German Stories/Deutsche Novellen: A Bantam Dual-
Language Book*, ed. by Harry Steinhauer (N.Y.: Bantam Books, 1961), and
Steinhauer's larger collection (containing many of the stories in the Bantam
paperback, others in addition, and introductions to the authors), *Deutsche
Erzählungen – German Stories: A Bilingual Anthology* (Berkeley: Univ. of
California Press, 1984), the selections are printed with the German original and
the English translation on facing pages. See also *Great German Short Stories*, ed.
and introduced by Stephen Spender (N.Y.: Dell, 1960); the collection (with
introductions to the authors) of *Twelve German Novellas*, ed. and translated by
Harry Steinhauer (Berkeley: Univ. of California Press, 1977); vol. 34 in 'The
German Library,' Heinrich von Kleist and Jean Paul, *German Romantic Novellas*,
ed. by Frank G. Ryder and Robert M. Browning (N.Y.: Continuum, 1985); F. J.
Lamport, ed., *The Penguin Book of German Stories* (Harmondsworth: Penguin,
1974), with George Büchner's 'Lenz' among its thirteen selections; *Selected Short
Stories of Franz Kafka*, translated by Willa and Edwin Muir, introduction by
Philip Rahv (N.Y.: Random House, Modern Library, 1952), particularly his most
famous novella, 'The Metamorphosis' (in none of the anthologies cited above);

Literature. English-language anthologies and readers

'The Recollections of Ludolf Ursleu the Younger,' by Ricarda Huch, translated by Muriel Almon, in vol. 18, of *The German Classics: Masterpieces of German Literature*, 20 vols., ed. by Kuno Francke (N.Y.: German Publication Society, 1913-1914; repr., N.Y.: AMS Press, 1969); and *German Women Writers of the Twentieth Century*, ed. by Elizabeth Rütschi Herrmann and Edna Huttenmaier Spitz (Oxford and N.Y.: Pergamon Press, 1978), with individually prefaced selections from Ricarda Huch, Gertrud von le Fort, Marie Luise Kaschnitz, Christa Wolf, and twelve others.

378 **The genius of the German theater.**
Edited and with introductions by Martin Esslin. New York: New
American Library, Mentor Books, 1968. 640p. bibliog.

A leading authority's one-volume, pocket-format introduction to German drama, with a lead-in essay, 'German Theater – Its Development and Character'; seven individually introduced plays in translation (some with revisions): Lessing's 'Emilia Galotti' (1772), Goethe's 'Faust – A Tragedy,' Part I (1808), Schiller's 'The Death of Wallenstein – A Tragedy' (1799), Kleist's 'Prince Frederick of Homburg – A Play' (1809), Büchner's 'Leonce and Lena – A Comedy' (1836), Wedekind's 'King Nicolo *or*, Such Is Life – A Play' (1901), Brecht's 'The Caucasian Chalk Circle' (1944-1945); and twenty-five pages of essays or extracts on the theatre by Lessing, Schiller, Goethe, Hebbel, and Esslin (his own treatment of Brecht's theory of the epic theatre). The volume concludes with a bibliography of fifty references, mostly in English. It is not intended to be comprehensive, but includes many works that 'can be used to start a bibliographical chain reaction.' See also *Three German Plays*, with an introduction by Martin Esslin (Harmondsworth: Penguin Books, 1963): 'Woyzeck,' by Georg Büchner, translated by John Holmstrom; 'Before Dawn [Vor Sonnenaufgang],' by Gerhart Hauptmann, translated by Richard Newnham; and 'The Threepenny Opera [Die Dreigroschenoper],' by Bertolt Brecht, translated by Desmond I. Vesey, verses by Eric Bertley. *Classical German Drama*, translated by Theodore H. Lustig, with an introduction and prefaces by Victor Lange (N.Y.: Bantam, 1963), has an essay on 'The German Classical Theatre' by John Gassner, a selected bibliography, and Lessing's 'Nathan the Wise,' Goethe's 'Egmont,' Schiller's 'Mary Stuart,' Kleist's 'The Prince of Homburg,' and Büchner's 'Danton's Death.' In a different vein, from the end of the eighteenth century, is Ludwig Tieck's 'Puss in Boots' ('a fairy tale for children in three acts, with interludes, a prologue and an epilogue'), translated by Lillie Winter, in vol. 4 of *The German Classics: Masterpieces of German Literature*, 20 vols., ed. by Kuno Francke (N.Y.: German Publication Society, 1913-1914; repr., N.Y.: AMS Press, 1969). Turning to a more recent period, *An Anthology of German Expressionist Drama: A Prelude to the Absurd*, edited, with an introduction by Walter H. Sokel (Garden City, N.Y.: Doubleday, Anchor Books, 1963), includes plays by Bertolt Brecht, Yvan Goll, Walter Hasenclever, Georg Kaiser, Oskar Kokoschka, Rolf Lauckner, Reinhard Sorge, and Carl Sternheim. See also *Three Plays by Ernst Barlach*, translated by Alex Page (Minneapolis: Univ. of Minnesota Press, 1964), and, in the 'German Expressionist Drama' series, edited by J. M. Ritchie, *Seven Expressionist Plays: Kokoschka to Barlach*, translated by J. M. Ritchie and H. F. Garten, and *Vision and Aftermath: Four Expressionist War Plays*, translated by J. M. Ritchie and J. D. Stowell (London: Calder and Boyars, 1968 and 1969, resp.) Translations of a total of seventeen German plays are included in a companion set on the period since world War I: George E. Wellwarth, ed., *German Drama between the Wars: An Anthology of Plays* [by Hermann Broch, Ernst Toller, Carl Zuckmayer, and others] and, edited and translated by Michael Benedikt and George E. Wellwarth, *Postwar German Theatre: An Anthology of Plays* [by Wolfgang Borchert, Friedrich Dürrenmatt, Max Frisch, Wolfgang Hildesheimer, Carl Laszlo, Peter Weiss, and others] (N.Y.: Dutton, 1972 and 1967, resp.).

379 **The Grimms' German folk tales.**
Jacob Grimm and Wilhelm Grimm. Translated by Francis P. Magoun, Jr., and Alexander H. Krappe. Carbondale and Edwardsville: Southern Illinois University Press, 1960; repr., SIU Press Arcturus Books, 1969. 674p.

Translation into modern, colloquial English of the famous collection of 210 German folk tales gathered by the brothers Grimm in part from oral tradition, in part from earlier printed sources. The translation is based on the 1912 edition by Reinhold Steig; it does not have any notes. For the extensive annotations of the original, in German, see the third volume of Jacob and Wilhelm Grimm, *Kinder- und Hausmärchen* ['Fairy Tales for Children and for the Home'], ed. by Heinz Rölleke: vol. 1, *Märchen Nr. 1-86* ['Fairy Tales No. 1-86']; vol. 2, *Märchen Nr. 87-200. Kinderlegenden Nr. 1-10* ['Fairy Tales No. 87-200; Children's Legends No. 1-10']; vol. 3, *Originalanmerkungen, Herkunftsnachweise, Nachwort.* ['Original Annotations; Documentation of Origins; Postscript'] (Stuttgart: Reclams Universal-Bibliothek, 1980). Vol. 29 of 'The German Library,' *German Fairy Tales*, by Jacob and Wilhelm Grimm and others, ed. by Helmut Brackert and Volkmar Sander, foreword by Bruno Bettelheim, illustrations by Otto Ubbelodhe (N.Y.: Continuum, 1985) has fifty-seven of the fairy tales in the translation of Margaret Hunt (initially published in London in 1884) and six additional tales translated by Margaret Humphreys: 'Puss-in-Boots,' included in the Grimms' 1812 edition of the fairy tales, but not in the revised edition of 1857; 'The Pied Piper of Hamelin,' from the Grimms' *Deutsche Sagen* ['German Sagas'], 2 vols. (Berlin: Nicolai, 1816/1818); three fairy tales from a collection published by Ludwig Bechstein in the 1850s, and a recent 'anti-fairy tale' by Iring Fetscher, 'The Goat and the Seven Small Wolves,' from *Wer hat Dornröschen wachgeküsst? Das Märchen-Verwirrbuch* ['Who Awakened Sleeping Beauty with a Kiss? The Fairy Tale Confusion Book'] (Hamburg: Claassen Verlag, 1972; repr., Frankfurt am Main: Fischer Taschenbuch Verlag).

380 **Simplicius Simplicissimus.**
Hans Jakob Christoffel von Grimmelshausen. Translated by George Schulz-Behrend. Indianapolis: Bobbs-Merrill, 1965. 353p. (The Library of Liberal Arts).

Grimmelshausen's entertaining, realistic novel about a soldier in the Thirty Years' War appeared first in 1668. Schulz-Behrend has summarized or omitted possibly boring passages, adapted archaisms, etc., to come up with a modern English version; he has prefaced his translation with a seventeen-page introduction. The novel is written in the form of an autobiography, as is its counterpart, Grimmelshausen's story of a woman's life during the same period, *The Runagate Courage*, translated by Robert L. Hiller and John C. Osborne (Lincoln: Univ. of Nebraska Press, 1965), which was a source for Bertolt Brecht's play, 'Mother Courage.'

381 **The permanent Goethe.**
[J. W. v. Goethe.] Edited, selected, and with an introduction by
Thomas Mann. Translated by Norbert Guterman, Isidor
Schneider, Stephen Spender, et al.   New York: Dial Press, 1948.
655p.

Selected translations of Goethe's poetry, dramas, essays, fiction, letters, travel
sketches, and autobiographical writings, compiled by Thomas Mann, whose
thirty-three page essay is an introduction not only to the volume, but to the life
and works of Goethe. A short anthology, *Great Writings of Goethe* (N.Y.: New
American Library, 1958) was edited, with an introduction, by Stephen Spender.
Both anthologies include 'Faust' (Part I) in translation; *Goethe's 'Faust'*,
translated and with an introduction by Walter Kaufmann (Garden City, N.Y.:
Doubleday, 1961), includes Part I and sections of Part II in translation, with the
German original on facing pages. Both parts of the work are given in full in 'The
World's Classics' series: *Faust: A Tragedy in Two Parts*, translated in the original
metres by Bayard Taylor, with an introduction by Marshall Montgomery and
notes [over fifty pages] by Douglas Yates (London: Oxford Univ. Press, 1932).

382 **The poetry and prose of Heinrich Heine.**
[Heinrich Heine.] Selected and edited, with an introduction, by
Frederick Ewen; translated by Frederic Ewen, Aaron Kramer,
Emma Lazarus, Louis Untermeyer, et al.   New York: Citadel
Press, 1948. 874p. bibliog.

A comprehensive anthology in translation, reflecting Heine's work as a poet,
thinker, story-teller, and journalist. Ewen's 48-page introductory essay is followed
by 245 pages of poetry, including the long 'Germany – A Winter's Tale,' and 536
pages of prose, including 'The Rabbi of Bacharach' and other stories, essays,
newspaper articles, and letters. The volume concludes with twenty-three pages of
annotations, a brief bibliography, a chronology of the prose selections, and an
index of the German first lines of the poems (printed with the translated verse).
See also the 1,032-page volume translated and edited by Hal Draper, *The
Complete Poems of Heinrich Heine: A Modern English Version* (Boston:
Suhrkamp/Insel; London: Oxford Univ. Press, 1982). Heine's own notes and
prefaces are, in translation, in the body of the work; Draper's extensive
explanatory notes and the first lines of the poems in German are included in the
more than 200 pages of appendices at the end of the book, as are separate indexes
of titles and first lines in English, titles and first lines in German, and proper
names. For a short anthology, see, in 'Everyman's Library,' *Prose and Poetry by
Heinrich Heine*, introduction by Ernest Rhys (London: Dent, 1934), translations
by Margaret Armour and others; a few well-known short poems, such as 'The
Two Grenadiers,' are printed in German (with a prose translation).

Literature. English-language anthologies and readers

383 **A man of honor.**
Theodor Fontane. Translated, with introduction and notes by E.
M. Valk. New York: Frederick Ungar Publishing Co., 1975.
206p. bibliog.

Translation of the distinguished Berlin novelist's *Schach von Wuthenow* (1883),
with a twelve-page introductory essay, backnotes, and a brief bibliography. The
novel, characterized by Georg Lukács as 'a small historical masterpiece [which]
reveals the true and mature Fontane,' centres on the relationship of a Prussian
cavalry captain with an attractive widow and her pockmarked daughter. E. M.
Valk's translation of *A Man of Honor* can also be found, without the notes and
bibliography of the Ungar edition, in vol. 48 of 'The German Library,' Theodor
Fontane, *Short Novels and Other Writings*, edited by Peter Demetz (N.Y.:
Continuum, 1982), which also includes *Jenny Treibel*, translated by Ulf
Zimmermann, and *The Eighteenth of March*, translated by Krishna Winston.

384 **The Thomas Mann reader.**
[Thomas Mann.] Selected, arranged, edited, and with an
introduction, by Joseph Warner Angell. Translated by H. T.
Lowe-Porter. New York: Alfred A. Knopf, 1950. 754p. bibliog.

An anthology designed to illustrate 'the quality and scope and character of
Thomas Mann's art and thought,' with a concise introductory essay on the man
and his works and informative prefaces to the individual selections: two novellas,
'Tonio Kröger' and 'Death in Venice [Der Tod in Venedig]'; four short stories;
substantial excerpts from the novels *Buddenbrooks* (1901; English translation,
1924), *The Magic Mountain* ['Der Zauberberg'] (1924; translation, 1927), *Doctor
Faustus* (1947; translation, 1948), and the tetralogy *Joseph and His Brothers*
['Joseph und seine Brüder'] (1933-43; translations 1934-44, one-vol. edition,
1948); essays on Schiller, Wagner, Dostoyevsky, and Freud; a character portrait
of Goethe from the historical novel *The Beloved Returns* ['Lotte in Weimar']
(1939; translation, 1940); and four examples of Mann's political writings,
including, 'Europe Beware [Achtung, Europa!],' originally prepared as an address
to the League of Nations' Permanent Committee for the Arts and Letters in 1935,
and his famous response to the revocation in 1936 of his honorary doctorate from
Bonn University. The listing, at the end of the volume, of Mann's principal works
through 1948 cites the first editions in German and the editions in English
translation published by Alfred A. Knopf, New York.

385 **Autobiographical writings.**
Hermann Hesse. Edited, and with an introduction, by Theodore
Ziolkowski. Translated by Denver Lindley. New York: Farrar,
Straus and Giroux, 1972. 291p.

A selection, in translation, of twelve autobiographical pieces, arranged not in the
order in which they were written, but 'so that Hesse narrates his own life in
roughly chronological sequence.' The companion volume, *My Belief: Essays on
Life and Art*, edited, and with an introduction, by Theodore Ziolkowski and
translated by Denver Lindley except for two essays translated by Ralph Manheim
(N.Y.: Farrar, Straus and Giroux, 1974) includes, in addition to the four-page
title essay, 'My Belief,' over seventy selections (a number of them reviews) on a
wide range of topics.

172

386   **Seven plays.**
Bertolt Brecht. Edited and with an introduction by Eric
Bentley.   New York: Grove Press, 1961. 587p.

A thirty-nine page introductory essay by Eric Bentley, followed by seven Brecht
plays: 'In the Swamp' (1921-1923), 'A Man's a Man' (1924-1925), 'The Good
Woman of Setzuan' (1938-1940), and 'Mother Courage' (1939) are in the English
version by Bentley; 'The Caucasian Chalk Circle' (1944-1945) is in the English
version by Eric Bentley and Maja Apelman; 'Saint Joan of the Stockyards' (1929-
1930) in the English version by Frank Jones; and 'Galileo' (1938-1939) in the
English version by Charles Laughton. In the Methuen series, 'Bertolt Brecht:
Plays, Poetry and Prose,' edited by John Willett and Ralph Manheim, see the
627-page *Poems*, edited by Willett and Manheim, with the co-operation of Erich
Fried (London: Eyre Methuen, 1976), which includes a nineteen-page introduc-
tory essay, poems from 1913 to 1956 in English translation, and a list giving the
location of the German originals in vols. 8-10 of the *Gesammelte Werke*
['Collected Works'] (Frankfurt am Main: Suhrkamp, 1967). See also Brecht's
Short Stories, 1921-1946, edited by John Willett and Ralph Manheim (London:
Methuen, 1983), translated by Yvonne Kapp and others from the German
originals published in vol. 11 of the collected works (Frankfurt am Main:
Suhrkamp, 1967).

387   **Dictionary of quotations (German).**
Lilian Dalbiac.   London: Swan Sonnenschein; New York:
Macmillan, 1906. 485p.

Based in part on George Büchmann, *Geflügelte Worte*, now in its 23nd ed.,
completely rev., by Gunther Haupt and Winfried Hofmann (Berlin: Haude &
Spenersche Verlagsbuchandlung, 1972), the German counterpart to John
Bartlett's *Familiar Quotations*, edited by E. M. Beck, 15th, rev. & enl. ed.
(Boston: Little, Brown, 1980), this compendium gives an extensive collection of
German quotations together with the translation into English and the name of the
translator. There are author and subject indexes.

The Arts

General

388   Art treasures of Germany.
Edited by Bernd Lohse and Harald Busch. Introduction by Rudolf
Hagelstange. Commentaries on the ill. by Helmut Domke. Transl.
by P. Gorge.   London: B. T. Batsford, n.d.; copyright, Umschau
Verlag, Frankfurt am Main, 1958. 256p.

Twenty-three pages of text followed by good pictures (with captions in English
and German) illustrating a wide range of ancient, mediaeval, and modern works
of art, including early Germanic jewelry and Roman remains; medieval stone
sculpture, wood carving, and ecclesiastical architecture; ornately carved half-
timber houses and interior views of several baroque churches and of the
Margraves' Opera House in Bayreuth; and painting, from illuminated manuscripts
in the Middle Ages to the romantic landscape and the family portrait of the
nineteenth century. Twelve colour plates. Two other general introductions (with
good illustrations, many in colour) are *Kunstschätze in Deutschland – Art
Treasures in Germany – Trésors d'art d'Allemagne*, by H. A. Graefe (Trostberg/
Oberbayern: Dr. Heinz A. Graefe, n.d.), and *Art Treasures in Germany:
Monuments, Masterpieces, Commissions and Collections*, intro. by Stephan
Waetzoldt, general eds., Bernard S. Myers and Trewin Copplestone (N.Y.:
McGraw-Hill; London: Hamlyn, 1970).

389   The *Blaue Reiter* almanac.
Edited by Wassily Kandinsky and Franz Marc. New documentary
edition, edited and with an introduction by Klaus Lankheit. Transl.
by Henning Falkenstein.   New York: Viking Press, 1974. 296p.
bibliog. (The Documents of 20th-Century Art).

Der Blaue Reiter ['The Blue Horseman'] was conceived as a kind of yearbook for
the arts, including painting, the theatre, and music. The second (and until 1965
last) edition, published in 1914, included programmatic articles, illustrations
(particularly by the two editors), and musical compositions by Arnold Schönberg,
Alban Berg, and Anton von Webern. The German edition of 1965 was corrected
and supplemented for this English translation. For a pocket introduction, with
extracts and selected illustrations (including twenty postcard-size colour plates),
see *The Blue Rider*, by Paul Vogt, transl. by Joachim Neugroschel (Woodbury,
N.Y., & London: Barron's, 1980). There are forty-eight large colour plates in
Peter Vergo's *The Blue Rider* (Oxford: Phaidon Press, 1977). See also *The Blue
Rider. With a Catalog of the Works by Kandinsky, Klee, Macke, Marc, and Other
Blue Rider Artists in the Municipal Gallery, Munich*, by Hans K. Roethel (N.Y.:
Praeger, 1971), transl. by the author and Jean Benjamin from *Der Blaue Reiter*
(Munich: Städtische Galerie im Lenbachhaus, 1970).

390   **The Bauhaus – Weimar, Dessau, Berlin, Chicago.**
Hans M. Wingler. Transl. by Wolfgang Jabs and Basil Gilbert.
Edited by Joseph Stein.   Cambridge, Mass.: The MIT Press, 1969.
653p. bibliog.

Adapted from *Das Bauhaus* (Bramsche: Gebr. Rasch & Co.; and Cologne:
DuMont Schauberg, 1962; 2nd, rev. ed., 1968), this massive quarto volume with
twenty-four colour plates and hundreds of photographs, prints, and drawings is a
detailed account of the revolutionary school that was founded in Weimar in 1919
and moved to Dessau in 1925, where it flourished as the state-supported Institute
of Design. Committed under its founding director, the architect Walter Gropius,
to the unity of art and technology, the Bauhaus became a centre for new
directions in design – from coffee cups to cupboards to communities of workers'
houses. Always controversial, the Bauhaus was forced by the National Socialists
to leave Dessau in 1932, was reopened in Berlin by Ludwig Mies van der Rohe,
its director since 1930, and finally closed in 1933. As shown in this volume, its
tradition was continued elsewhere, particularly by the New Bauhaus (Institute of
Design) in Chicago. The extensive bibliography provides coverage not only of the
Bauhaus as an institution, but of the movement identified with it in the arts, the
crafts, and architecture. On the origins and first nine years of the Bauhaus, during
which Walter Gropius was director, see the volume prepared under his general
editorship, *Bauhaus 1919-1928*, ed. by Herbert Bayer, Walter Gropius, and Ise
Gropius (New York: Arno Press for the Museum of Modern Art, 1938, 1972;
London: Secker and Warburg, 1975). See also *Painters of the Bauhaus*, by
Eberhard Roters (N.Y.: Praeger, 1969), transl. by Anna Rose Cooper from
Maler am Bauhaus (Berlin: Rembrandt Verlag, 1965), and Gillian Naylor, *The
Bauhaus Reassessed: Sources and Design Theory* (London: Herbert, 1985).

391 Dada, art and anti-art.

Hans Richter. Postscript by Werner Haftmann. Transl. by David Britt. London: Thames & Hudson, 1966; repr., New York and Toronto: Oxford University Press, 1978. 246p. bibliog.

Translated from *Dada, Kunst und Antikunst* (Cologne: DuMont Schauberg, 1964), a lucid account, generously illustrated with sketches, black-and-white photographs, and colour plates, of an important but often ill-understood creative protest movement in the arts that began in Zurich during World War I and flowered in the early 1920s, by a noted German painter and film-maker who had been one of its leaders. See also *Dada. Eine literarische Dokumentation* ['Dada: A Literary Documentation'], ed. by Richard Huelsenbeck, with a 29-page bibliography (incl. titles in English) by Bernard Karpel (Reinbek bei Hamburg: Rowohlt, 1964).

392 Germany in the twenties: the artist as social critic – a collection of essays.

Edited by Frank D. Hirschbach et al. Minneapolis: University of Minnesota, 1980. 121p.

Published in conjunction with a festival in Minneapolis on the artist as social critic in Germany during the 1920s, this large, effectively illustrated volume includes essays on urban planning and design, the theatre, music, film, dance, and the radio culture of the working class.

393 Die bildenden Künste im Nationalsozialismus. Kulturideologie. Kulturpolitik. Kulturproduktion. (The fine arts under National Socialism: cultural ideology, cultural policy, cultural production.)

Reinhard Merker. Cologne: DuMont Buchverlag, 1983. 370p. bibliog. (DuMont-Taschenbücher, no. 132).

Competent survey of the arts under Hitler. Following a review of the ideological background, Merker traces, in the first major segment of his well-structured monograph, the development of the National Socialist cultural ideology during the formative years of the quest for power, 1920-1933. In the next segment, he relates how that ideology, once implemented as policy, led to the campaign against 'degenerate' art, persecution of artists, and often the confiscation or destruction of their works. The third segment is an assessment of what German fascism actually produced by way of art and architecture, road-building and city planning – a review of its achievements, taking into account the self-proclaimed standards of the régime. Merker concludes his study with a critical review of the literature, to which his own heavily annotated volume, with 140 well-selected black-and-white pictures and an extensive bibliography, is a useful contribution. See also the illustrated booklet edited by Gerhard Schoenberner, *Artists against Hitler: Persecution, Exile, Resistance*, transl. by Patricia Crampton (Bonn: Inter Nationes, 1984), with articles on German theatre, cabaret, cinema, painting, and literature, both in exile and in Hitler's Germany.

394 **Germany: cultural developments since 1945.**
Edited by Paul Schallück. Transl. by John Bourke et al. Munich:
Max Hueber Verlag, 1971. 216p.

Fourteen essays, including pieces on postwar German radio and television plays, concert music, opera, ballet, painting, and the cinema, translated from *Deutschland: Kulturelle Entwicklungen seit 1945* (Munich: Max Hueber Verlag, 1969).

Visual arts: painting, sculpture, architecture

395 **History of German art: painting, sculpture, architecture.**
Gottfried Lindemann. Transl. by Tessa Sayle. New York,
Washington, London: Praeger Publishers, 1971. 231p.

Translated from *Deutsche Kunst* (Brunswick, West Germany: Georg Westermann Verlag, 1971), this is a survey of German architecture, sculpture, painting, and the graphic arts from the Carolingian period to the twentieth century. The illustrations include 140 full- or half-page photographs, 64 of them in colour. See also Marcel Brion's *German Painting*, transl. by W. J. Strachan (Paris: Éditions Pierre Tisné, 1959), illustrated with 59 colour plates.

396 **German painting, XIV-XVI centuries.**
Alfred Stange. Edited by André Gloeckner. New York:
Hypérion Press, 1950. 160p. bibliog.

Based on the author's *Deutsche Malerei der Gothik* ['German Painting of the Gothic Period'], 11 vols. (Munich and Berlin: Deutscher Kunstverlag, 1934-1961; repr., Nendeln/Liechtenstein: Kraus, 1969), this large book includes an eighteen-page essay, a bibliography, and biographical notes on the forty-eight artists whose works are illustrated in 128 plates, sixteen of them in colour. See also the two beautifully produced volumes on this period in the history of German art in Albert Skira's 'Painting – Color – History' series: *German Painting: The Late Middle Ages, 1350-1500*, by Hanspeter Landolt, translated by Heinz Norden (Geneva: Skira, 1968) and *German Painting: From Dürer to Holbein*, by Otto Benesch, translated by H. S. B. Harrison (Geneva: Skira, 1966), both with bibliographies including articles as well as books.

397 **The life and art of Albrecht Dürer.**
Erwin Panofsky. Princeton, N.J.: Princeton University Press,
1955. 4th ed. 320p. plus 326 illus. bibliog.

Revised edition of the standard biography of the great Renaissance artist (1471-1528), without the handlist and concordance of the 1943 two-volume edition, but with the full text and 326 black-and-white illustrations on unnumbered pages. See also Heinrich Wölfflin's *The Art of Albrecht Dürer*, transl. by Alastair and Heide Grieve (London: Phaidon, 1971); *Essays on Dürer*, ed. by C. R. Dodwell

The Arts. Visual arts: painting, sculpture, architecture

(Manchester: Manchester Univ. Press; Toronto: Univ. of Toronto Press, 1973); and *The Writings of Albrecht Dürer*, transl. and ed. by William Martin Conway (N.Y.: Philosophical Library, 1958), with excerpts from the original German texts. For a short biography with a chronology, a select bibliography, extracts from Dürer's own writings, and many reproductions, see Franz Winzinger's *Albrecht Dürer in Selbstzeugnissen und Bilddokumenten* ['Albrecht Dürer in His Personal Testimony and Pictorial Documents'], Rowohlt's Monographs, no. 177 (Reinbek bei Hamburg: Rowohlt, 1971). On Dürer's great contemporaries, the painter Mathis Gothardt Neithardt, called Matthias Grünewald, the woodcarver and sculptor Tilman Riemenschneider, and Lucas Cranach and his sons, see *Grünewald*, by Nikolaus Pevsner and Michael Meier (London: Thames and Hudson, 1958), *Matthias Grünewald: Personality and Accomplishment*, by Arthur Burkhard (N.Y.: Hacker Art Books, 1976), and *Grünewald: The Paintings*, complete edition, with two essays by J.-K. Huysmans and a catalogue by E. Ruhmer (London: Phaidon, 1958); *Tilman Riemenschneider: His Life and Work*, by Justus Bier (Lexington: Univ. of Kentucky Press, 1982), and the 180 plates by Günther Beyer and Klaus Beyer in *Tilman Riemenschneider* (Dresden: VEB Verlag der Kunst, 1967); and Werner Schade, *Cranach: A Family of Master Painters* (N.Y.: Putnam's, 1980), transl. by Helen Sebba from *Die Malerfamilie Cranach* (Dresden: VEB Verlag der Kunst, 1974).

398 German Painting from Romanticism to Expressionism.
Ulrich Finke.   London: Thames and Hudson, 1974. 256p. bibliog.

Addressed primarily to the English-speaking reader perhaps less familiar with German than French art of the period, a well-structured account, in cultural context, of German painting from the late eighteenth to the early twentieth century. There are 163 illustrations, twelve in colour, a 'Catalogue of Artists and Illustrations' with information on the reproduced works and their painters, a bibliography in which works in English are especially noted, and an index. See also William Vaughan, *German Romantic Painting* (New Haven, Conn., and London: Yale Univ. Press, 1980), with high-quality plates incorporated into the narrative; Keith Andrews, *The Nazarenes: A Brotherhood of German Painters in Rome* (Oxford: At the Clarendon Press, 1964); the pocket-book format *Caspar David Friedrich: Life and Work*, by Jens Christian Jensen (Woodbury, N.Y., and London: Barron's Educational Series, 1981), translated by Joachim Neugroschel from *Caspar David Friedrich. Leben und Werk*, 4th, rev. ed. (Cologne: DuMont, 1977); and *German Painting of the 19th Century*, introduction and catalogue by Kermit S. Champa with Kate H. Champa (New Haven, Conn.: Yale Univ. Art Gallery; with the Cleveland Museum of Art and the Art Institute of Chicago, 1970), with a sixty-page essay, a bibliography, reproductions of the 106 paintings displayed in a travelling exhibition, 1970-71, and discussions of these works and their painters.

399 The German expressionists: a generation in revolt.
Bernard S. Myers.   New York: McGraw-Hill [1963]. Concise edition. 348p. bibliog.

Deals with the background and the origins of the Expressionist movement and the various groups identified with it – the 'independent Expressionists' (including Oskar Kokoschka, Paula Modersohn-Becker, and Ernst Barlach), the *Brücke* ['Bridge'] group and followers (including Ernst Ludwig Kirchner, Erich Heckel, and Emil Nolde), and the 'Blue Rider' artists (including Wassily Kandinsky, Franz Marc, and Paul Klee). Myers stresses the importance of the Revolution of 1918, the expectations, soon to be disappointed, with which it was welcomed, and the aftermath – from the 'new objectivity' cultivated in the Bauhaus to the grim naturalism manifested in some of the works of Max Beckmann, Otto Dix, and George Grosz. The book has twenty-four colour plates, 140 half-tone (black-and-white) plates, numerous line drawings, and a 549-entry bibliography in which significant items are marked with up to three asterisks, depending upon their usefulness or importance. See also Peter Selz, *German Expressionist Painting* (Berkeley and Los Angeles: Univ. of California Press, 1957), a large volume with 400 printed pages and 180 pages of plates, thirty-eight of them in colour. Many of the artists dealt with in the two volumes above are represented in *German Expressionism and Abstract Art: The Harvard Collections*, by Charles L. Kuhn, with an introductory essay by Jakob Rosenberg (Cambridge, Mass.: Harvard Univ. Press, 1957), with 218 black-and-white illustrations, and in *Masterpieces of German Expressionism at the Detroit Institute of Arts*, by Horst Uhr (N.Y.: Hudson Hills Press; Detroit Institute of Arts, 1982), with many colour plates.

400 **German art in the 20th century.**
Franz Roh, with additions by Juliane Roh. Transl. by Catherine Hutter. Edited by Julia Phelps. Greenwich, Conn.: New York Graphic Society, ca. 1968. 516p.

Translated from *Geschichte der Deutschen Kunst von 1900 bis zur Gegenwart* ['History of German Art from 1900 to the Present'], by Franz Roh (Munich: F. Bruckmann Verlag, 1958), with additional material on the period from 1955 to 1968 by Juliane Roh, this account of twentieth-century German art is illustrated with numerous black-and-white photographs and forty-two colour plates. More than 300 pages are devoted to painting, the remainder to sculpture and architecture. See also Gerhard Händler's *German Painting in our Time*, translated by I. Schrier (Berlin: Rembrandt-Verlag, 1956), a thirty-seven-page essay followed by 200 illustrations, including forty-four colour plates; Hans Konrad Roethel's *Modern German Painting*, translated by Desmond and Louise Clayton (N.Y.: Reynal & Co., 1957), on the first half of the twentieth century, well illustrated with colour plates; and *German Art of the Twentieth Century*, by Werner Haftmann, Alfred Hentzen, and William S. Lieberman, edited by Andrew Carnduff Ritchie (N.Y.: The Museum of Modern Art, 1957; repr., N.Y.: Arno Press for the Museum of Modern Art, 1972), with black-and-white illustrations of the first comprehensive exhibition of twentieth-century German art (excluding National Socialist art) in America since the beginning of the 1930s, in extended essays by Haftmann on painting, Hentzen on sculpture, and Lieberman on prints. The discussions are not limited to artists or works included in the exhibition; and there is an extensive bibliography and an index.

401 **Art in the Third Reich.**
Berthold Hinz. Transl. by Robert and Rita Kimber. New York: Pantheon Books, 1979. 271p. bibliog.

This account of art in Hitler's Germany, 1933-1945, where 'an exaggeratedly high social value was placed on the visual arts in all their forms' and much of modern art was rejected as 'degenerate,' is an extensively revised version of *Die Malerei*

The Arts. Visual arts: painting, sculpture, architecture

im deutschen Faschismus. Kunst und Konterrevolution ['Painting under German Fascism: Art and Counter-Revolution'] (Munich: Carl Hanser Verlag, 1974). The well-illustrated work focusses primarily on painting, but deals also with sculpture, photography, and architecture. The impact of National Socialist policy on architecture in Germany is treated by Barbara Miller Lane in *Architecture and Politics in Germany, 1918-1945* (Cambridge, Mass.: Harvard Univ. Press, 1968). The response outside Germany is illustrated by *Modern German Art*, by Peter Thoene (pseud.), translated by Charles Fullman, with an introduction by Herbert Read (Harmondsworth: Penguin Books, 1938), a 'Pelican Special' of 108 pages, with thirty-two photogravure plates, published to coincide with the notorious exhibition of 'degenerate' art held in Munich.

402 **Ernst Barlach.**
Alfred Werner. New York: McGraw-Hill, 1966. 176p. bibliog.
Concise biography of the great sculptor, graphic artist, and Expressionist writer (1870-1938), with a thirty-two page portfolio of reproductions of his stark woodcuts, lithographs, and (mostly charcoal) drawings, and photographs of some sixty of his striking sculpted works (largely in wood and bronze, but also in plaster, clay, vitrified clay, ceramic, terra cotta, and porcelain). Carl Dietrich Carls, *Ernst Barlach* (N.Y.: Praeger, 1969), a memoir-biography by an acquaintance and admirer of Barlach's (translated from the 1968 revision of a work first published in 1931 by Rembrandt-Verlag, Berlin), includes 121 pages of fine reproductions of drawings, lithographs, and woodcuts; superb photographs of sculpture; and photographs of the artist, his studio, and stage scenes from several of his plays. See also the 100 black-and-white plates, almost all of them full-page, in *Ernst Barlach. Plastik* ['Ernst Barlach: Plastic Arts'], photographs by Friedrich Hewicker, introduction by Wolf Stubbe (Munich: Piper, 1961).

403 **Käthe Kollwitz: life in art.**
Mina C. Klein and H. Arthur Klein. New York: Holt, Rinehart and Winston, 1972. 183p. bibliog.
Illustrated introduction, addressed to the nonspecialist, to an artist (1867-1945) whose moving etchings, woodcuts, and lithographs of human suffering led Romain Rolland to call her 'the voice of the silence of the sacrified.' See also the essay in German by Arnold Bauer, *Käthe Kollwitz* (Berlin: Colloquium Verlag, 1967), illustrated with eight self-portraits.

404 **Emil Nolde.**
Peter Selz. New York: Museum of Modern Art; San Francisco Museum of Art; Pasadena Art Museum, 1963. 88p. bibliog.
Annotated essay on Nolde (1867-1956) and his work, with a chronology, a select bibliography, and some seventy reproductions, a quarter of them in colour. The aquarelles and drawings in the collection at Nolde's home near the Danish border, which became a gallery after his death, are reproduced (partially in colour) in *Emil Nolde. Aquarelle und Handzeichnungen* ['Emil Nolde: Aquarelles and Drawings'], intro. by Martin Urban (Seebüll: Stiftung Seebüll Ada und Emil Nolde, n.d.). See also William S. Bradley, *Emil Nolde and German Expression-ism: A Prophet in His Own Land* (Ann Arbor, Mich.: UMI Research Press,

The Arts. Visual arts: painting, sculpture, architecture

1986), a revised dissertation, and Emil Nolde, *Mein Leben* ['My Life'], with an afterword by Martin Urban (Cologne: DuMont Buchverlag, 1976), an illustrated, 427-page one-volume abridgement of Nolde's four-volume autobiography.

405 **My life.**
Oskar Kokoschka. Transl. by David Britt. London: Thames and Hudson, 1974. 240p.

Translated from *Mein Leben* (Munich: Bruckmann, 1971), the memoirs of the Austrian-born painter and writer, active in Berlin before World War I and in Dresden after it, one of the most influential exponents of Expressionism in German-speaking Europe. See also the selection of his writings (reminiscences, stories, poetry, and plays), compiled and edited, with explanatory notes and bibliographical references, by Hans Maria Wingler, *Oskar Kokoschka. Schriften, 1907-1955* ['Oskar Kokoschka: Writings, 1907-1955'] (Munich: Albert Langen – Georg Müller, 1956).

406 **Paul Klee.**
Will Grohmann. New York: Abrams, 1985. 128p.

A concise edition of Grohmann's *Klee* (N.Y.: Abrams, 1967), with 100 illustrations, including forty plates in full colour. See also James Smith Pierce, *Paul Klee and Primitive Art*, Outstanding Dissertations in the Fine Arts Series (N.Y.: Garland, 1976).

407 **The autobiography of George Grosz: a small yes and a big no.**
[George Grosz.] Translated by Arnold J. Pomerans. London: Allison & Busby, 1982. 246p.

Translated from *Ein kleines Ja und ein grosses Nein. Sein Leben von ihm selbst erzählt* ['A Small Yes and a Big No: His Life Related by Himself'] (Reinbek bei Hamburg: Rowohlt, 1974), the illustrated autobiography of the gifted graphic artist (1893-1959) whose satirical drawings attacked the smug bourgeoisie, the profiteers, patrioteers, etc. His consciousness of being a German artist at home only in America, to which he emigrated after Hitler came to power, is discussed by John I. H. Baur in *George Grosz* (N.Y.: Macmillan for the Whitney Museum of American Art, 1954), with illustrations showing Grosz' artistic development. See also Fritz Löffler's book on Grosz' contemporary: *Otto Dix: Life and Work*, transl. by R. J. Hollingdale (N.Y. and London: Holmes and Meier, 1982), with 231 good plates, many full-page, some in colour.

408 **German Expressionist sculpture.**
Edited by Barbara Einzig et al. Introduction by Stephanie Barron. Los Angeles, Calif.: Los Angeles County Museum of Art; Chicago: University of Chicago Press, 1983. 224p. bibliog.

Beautifully produced volume, prepared in conjunction with a 1983-84 exhibition, with introductory essay, documentation, extensive (and partially annotated) bibliography, and well-written, well-illustrated essays on over thirty sculptors, including Barlach, Beckmann, Kirchner, Kolbe, Kollwitz, Lehmbruck, Marcks, and Nolde.

The Arts. Visual arts: painting, sculpture, architecture

409 **Deutsche naive Kunst.** (German naive art.)
Thomas Grochowiak. Recklinghausen: Verlag Aurel Bongers,
1976. 306p. bibliog.

Large-format, book-length, annotated monograph on the relatively neglected field of naive art in Germany, well illustrated with 378 plates, many in colour, and numerous line drawings. Includes biographical sketches (and, in many cases, photographs) of the 92 artists represented – virtually all born since the late nineteenth century, the notable exception being the north German schoolmaster Oluf Braren (1787-1839).

410 **Altes bäuerliches Holzgerät.** (Old wooden country implements.)
Gertrud Benker. Munich: Callwey, 1976. 207p. bibliog.

Some 150 different types of handmade utensils or tools for farmwork (milk pails, butter urns, beehives, whet-stone holders, yokes, etc.), eating and drinking (e.g., cutting boards, trays, spoons, bowls, and nutcrackers), and housekeeping (such as candle holders, boxes, coffee mills, birdcages, and towel racks), illustrated with 457 photographs (including several colour plates). The annotated text describes their use and discusses the carving and painting that makes many of them works of art.

411 **Topographia Germaniae.** (The topography of Germany.)
Matthäus Merian, Martin Zeiller, et al. Frankfurt am Main:
Matthäus Merian and heirs, 1642-1688. 14 vols.

The following volumes of Merian's great work, superlatively illustrated with copper engravings (many of the fold-outs) of cities, villages, and castles, reprinted in facsimile by Bärenreiter Verlag, Kassel and Basel (1960-62), edited and with afterwords (except for the volume on Westphalia) by Lucas Heinrich Wüthrich, include views of hundreds of places in West Germany as portrayed in seventeenth-century prints recognized as works of art:
Schwaben (Swabia), 1643, repr., 1960. 232p. Ninety-two views.
Westphalen (Westphalia), 1647, repr., 1961. 94p. Eighty-three views.
Braunschweig-Lüneburg (Brunswick-Lüneburg), 1654, repr., 1961. 220p. 221 views.
Niedersachsen (Lower Saxony), 1653, repr., 1962. 242p. Fifty-three views.
Franken (Franconia), 1656, repr., 1962. 118p. Forty-six views.
Bayern (Bavaria), 1657, repr., 1962. 138p. Ninety-six views.
The engravings are not included in the page count. From the *Topographia Germaniae*, Hartfrid Voss selected extracts of text on twenty cities for *Merians anmüthige Städte-Chronik* ['Merian's Charming City Chronicle'] (Ebenhausen: Wilhelm Langewiesche-Brandt, 1936), illustrated with greatly reduced, half-tone reproductions of the corresponding engravings.

412 **Illustrations of German literature.**
Munich: Heinz Moos Verlag in cooperation with Inter Nationes,
Bonn, 1973. 52p.

Annotated collection of well-reproduced illustrations, in black and white, from illuminated mediaeval manuscripts to contemporary woodcuts and photography. See also an early sixteenth-century illustrated prayer book, *The Book of Hours of*

The Arts. Visual arts: painting, sculpture, architecture

the Emperor Maximilian the First, decorated by Albrecht Dürer, Hans Baldung Grien, Hans Burgkmair the Elder, Jörg Breu, Albrecht Altdorfer, and other artists, printed in 1513 by Johannes Schoensperger at Augsburg, edited and with a detailed commentary by Walter L. Strauss (N.Y.: Abaris Books, 1974). The original illustrations and the Latin text are reprinted in facsimile, the English translation is in the margin, and an explanatory supplement, with bibliography, is appended at the end of the volume.

413   **Antique porcelain in color: Meissen.**
Hugo Morley-Fletcher.   Garden City, N.Y.: Doubleday, 1971.
119p.

Large-format introduction, by a director of Christie's specializing in European pottery and porcelain, to some of the finest German china, from the early eighteenth century through the nineteenth, illustrated with colour photographs on virtually every page. For a more comprehensive treatment – including factories in Höchst, Nymphenburg, Frankenthal, Ludwigsburg, and so forth – of the early period, see George Savage's 242-page *18th-Century German Porcelain* (London: Spring Books, 1967), with numerous black-and-white photographs, an index of marks, and a bibliography.

414   **German cathedrals.**
Introduction by Julius Baum. Photographs by Helga Schmidt-Glassner.   New York: Vanguard Press, 1956. 63p. text; 175
illustrations.

Forty-six-page, annotated text first on the Merovingian and Carolingian beginnings during the early Middle Ages, then the Romanesque and the Gothic periods, with individual segments on several cathedrals, on German Gothic architecture, and on sculpture. This essay is followed by sharp black-and-white photographs (exterior and interior views) of the great churches at Speyer, Mainz, Worms, Limburg on the Lahn, Bamberg, Naumburg, Magdeburg, Cologne, Freiburg, Regensburg, Ulm, and Munich. Hans Erich Kubach's *Deutsche Dome des Mittelalters* ['German Cathedrals of the Middle Ages'], 'Die Blauen Bücher' Series (Königstein im Taunus: Langewiesche – Köster, 1984) includes colour illustrations and three pages of clearly drawn floor plans in which the plans, eighteen to a page, are all drawn to the same scale, graphically illustrating differences in design and size. Further pictorial coverage of German ecclesiastical architecture during the Romanesque and the subsequent Gothic period is available in two large volumes, each with some 250 black-and-white photographs by a master, Harald Busch, *Germania Romanica. Die hohe Kunst der romanischen Epoche im mittleren Europe* ['Germania Romanica: The High Art of the Romanesque Epoch in Central Europe'] (Vienna: Schroll, 1963) and *Deutsche Gotik* ['German Gothic'] (Vienna: Schroll, 1969); for an abridgement of the former, see 'The Germanic Lands,' pp. 169-256, in *Romanesque Art in Europe*, ed. by Gustav Künstler (Greenwich, Conn.: N.Y. Graphic Society, [1969]). German statuary of the Gothic period, both wood and stone, is shown in 105 quality depictions in Wilhelm Pinder's *Die deutsche Plastik des fuenfzehnten Jahrhunderts* ['German Plastic Arts of the Fifteenth Century'] (Munich: Wolff, 1924), largely great works of unknown artists, but also selections from Veit Stoss, Tilman Riemenschneider, and other known artists.

The Arts. Visual arts: painting, sculpture, architecture

415 **Cathedrals and abbey churches of the Rhine.**
Ernst Gall. Transl. and adapted by Olive Cook. Photographs by H.
Schmidt-Glassner. London: Thames & Hudson; New York:
Abrams, 1963. 78p. of text plus 200p. of plates. map.

An introduction to sixty-three churches in the extended Rhineland region,
illustrated with twenty-eight figures (floor plans and line drawings), a map, and
200 black-and-white plates. The book is based on Ernst Gall's *Dome und
Klosterkirchen am Rhein* ['Cathedrals and Cloister Churches on the Rhine']
(Munich: Hirmer, 1956), which has the same plates and map, but a far longer text
with eighty-two figures and treatment of eighty-two churches (citing the relevant
literature). For more detail on the cathedral at Aachen, begun by Charlemagne
ca. 800 A.D., see Walter Maas, *Der Aachener Dom* ['The Aachen Cathedral'],
photographs by Herbert Woopen (Cologne: Greven, 1984), with an insert with
translated notes on the cathedral and captions to the plates (many in colour)
showing not only the church and its ornamentation, but priceless works of
mediaeval art in the cathedral treasury. Ninety-one peerless colour plates
(captions also in English) in *Die romanischen Kirchen in Köln* ['The Romanesque
Churches in Cologne'], by Hiltrud Kier and Ulrich Krings, photographs by Celia
Körber-Leupold (Cologne: Vista Point Verlag, 1985) capture the beauty of the
Romanesque churches in Cologne. On Cologne's Gothic cathedral, the largest in
northern Europe, see Hans Peters, *Der Dom zu Köln, 1248-1948* ['The Cathedral
at Cologne, 1248-1948'], photographs by K. H. Schmölz (Düsseldorf: Schwann,
1948). *The Horizon Book of Great Cathedrals*, ed. by Jay Jacobs et al. (N.Y.:
American Heritage, 1968) includes thirty-six pages of pictures and text on the
cathedrals at Freiburg im Breisgau, Mainz, Speyer, and Worms, as well as
Aachen and Cologne.

416 **German Renaissance architecture.**
Henry-Russell Hitchcock. Princeton, N.J.: Princeton University
Press, 1981. 379p. of text plus 262p. of plates. bibliog.

A scholarly, annotated account of architecture in Germany from the early
sixteenth century to the outbreak of the Thirty Years' War more than a century
later, discussing palaces, churches, chapels, town halls, burgher houses, etc.,
illustrated with seventy-four figures (floor plans, line drawings, etc.) and 457
black-and-white photographs.

417 **Baroque churches of Central Europe.**
John Bourke. Photographs by Thomas Finkenstaedt. London:
Faber and Faber, 1962. 2nd., rev. & enl. ed. 309p. 3 maps. bibliog.

Well-written introduction, addressed to the English-speaking layman, by an
Englishman teaching in Munich, to the seventeenth- and eighteenth-century
baroque and rococo churches that are among the greatest treasures of southern
Germany and neighbouring regions, with sixty-six black-and-white photographs,
ground plans, appendices on symbolism and technical terms, and a select
bibliography. A short guide is T. H. B. Burrough's *South German Baroque. An
Introduction Based on a Group of Ten Churches: Obermarchtal, Weingarten,
Ettal, Steinhausen, Wies, Biernau, Zwiefalten, Ottobeuren, Rott am Inn, Wiblingen*
(London: Alec Tiranti, 1956). See also the study by Karsten Harries, *The
Bavarian Rococo Church: Between Faith and Aestheticism* (New Haven, Conn.,

The Arts. Visual arts: painting, sculpture, architecture

and London: Yale Univ. Press, 1983), with 154 black-and-white illustrations and sixteen colour plates, and the regional volume in a fine series of compact German guides, *Deutsche Kunstdenkmäler. Ein Bildhandbuch. Bayern südlich der Donau* ['German Monuments of Art: A Pictorial Handbook – Bavaria South of the Danube'], ed. by Reinhardt Hootz (Munich: Deutscher Kunstverlag, 1977), a heavily illustrated, 435-page pocket-sized manual, which, as part of a larger picture, includes ecclesiastical architecture of the baroque and rococo style.

418 **Rococo architecture in southern Germany.**
Henry-Russell Hitchcock. London: Phaidon, 1968. 428p. map.
bibliog.

A study of eighteenth-century architecture primarily in the area of the present-day states of Bavaria and Baden-Württemberg, dealing with secular as well as ecclesiastical architecture. The work is extensively annotated, includes a glossary, a bibliography, and a map, and is illustrated with over forty figures (sketches and ground plans) and 218 black-and-white plates, including palaces and residences in Würzburg, in Munich, and at Kisslegg east of Ravensburg. For a detailed, illustrated account of the palace built at Brühl near Bonn in the 1730s by Prince-Elector Clemens August, Archbishop of Cologne, see Wilfried Hansmann, *Schloss Falkenlust*, photographs by Heinpeter Schreiber (Cologne: Verlag M. DuMont Schauberg, 1973).

419 **Evangelischer Kirchenbau im 19. und 20. Jahrhundert.**
Geschichte – Dokumentation – Synopse. (Protestant churchbuilding in the 19th and 20th century: history, documentation, synopsis.)
Gerhard Langmaack. Kassel: Johannes Stauda Verlag, 1971.
382p. bibliog.

Scholarly, carefully structured overview and compendium, illustrating Protestant churchbuilding from 1831 to 1969 (text, numerous black-and-white photographs, and floor plans). Relates the Protestant ecclesiastical architectural tradition to broader developments and, with documentation (largely recent, but also facsimile reproductions of treatises from 1649 and 1712), introduces the reader to the discussion of ecclesiastical architecture within the German Protestant community, particularly since 1945.

420 **Modern architecture in Germany.**
Introuction by Ulrich Conrads. Captions by Werner Marschall.
Transl. by James Palmes. London: The Architectural Press, 1962.
231p.

Postwar architecture of West Germany and West Berlin shown on 206 pages of black-and-white photographs and plans, from private homes to factories and urban renewal projects. The introductory essay and the captions are in English as well as German. See also the large, well-illustrated volume on contemporary German architecture (with title, text, and captions in English, French, Spanish, and German), *Architecture in Germany*, by Alfred Simon (Essen: Verlag Richard Bacht, 1969).

421 **Der Kirchenbau des 20. Jahrhunderts in Deutschland: Dokumentation, Darstellung, Deutung.** (Church architecture of the 20th century in Germany: documentation, presentation, interpretation.)
Hugo Schnell. Munich: Verlag Schnell & Steiner in association with Inter Nationes, Bonn – Bad Godesberg, 1973. 256p. bibliog.

Introduction to twentieth-century German ecclesiastical architecture, taking into account the cultural and religious context (e.g. the liturgical movement) and the impact of new building materials (especially reinforced concrete), with 300 black-and-white illustrations (sketches and photographs) and twenty colour photographs. In addition to bibliographies on ecclesiastical architecture at the end of each of the four segments (to 1918, 1918-1945, 1945-1960, and since 1960), there are select lists of periodicals with contributions on modern Christian art and on ecclesiastical architecture. Seventy-six pages on eighteen German churches, illustrated with black-and-white photographs supplemented by drawings, are included in G. E. Kidder Smith's *The New Churches of Europe* (N.Y.: Holt, Rinehart & Winston, 1964), with description in Spanish as well as English, bibliographical references, and an index of architects (with dates of completion of the churches).

Music

422 **History of music: a book for study and reference.**
Karl H. Wörner. Translated and supplemented by Willis Wager. New York: Free Press; London: Collier Macmillan, 1973. 712p. bibliog.

Translated from *Geschichte der Musik*, 5th ed. (Göttingen: Vandenhoeck & Ruprecht, 1972), this work presents the history of music in the Western world chronologically through the Renaissance and then treats in separate chapters the principal types of music that have developed during the past centuries, such as the opera, orchestral music, and keyboard music, with attention to individual composers and performers. There are extensive chapter bibliographies, a guide to bibliographical resources, and detailed (three-column) indexes of subjects and of names. See also Hans Joachim Moser's *Geschichte der deutschen Musik* ['History of German Music'], rev. & exp. ed., 3 vols. (Stuttgart and Berlin, 1928-1930; repr., Hildesheim: Georg Olms, 1968), with supplemental notes and an essay on the period 1928-1963 at the end of vol. 3 (pp. 527-552), and Moser's *Die Evangelische Kirchenmusik in Deutschland* ['Protestant Church Music in Germany'] (Berlin and Darmstadt: Verlag Carl Merseburger, 1954).

423   **The lives of the great composers.**
Harold C. Schonberg. New York: W. W. Norton, 1981. Rev. ed.
653p. bibliog.
Readable biographical essays varying in length from seven to twenty-five pages,
with illustrations in black and white and select bibliography of books in English.
Among the composers from German-speaking lands are Bach, Händel, Mozart,
Beethoven, Schumann, Mendelssohn, Wagner, Brahms, Wolf, Bruckner, Mahler,
Reger, and Webern. See also vol. 51 of 'The German Library,' *Writings of
German Composers*, ed. by Jost Hermand and James Steakley (New York:
Continuum, 1984), for translated selections providing insight into the lives and the
art of forty-four composers from the sixteenth century to the twentieth, including
Telemann, Gluck, Czerny, Bartholdy, Richard Strauss, Hindemith, Weill, and
Henze.

424   **German opera – then and now: reflections and investigations on the
history and present state of the German musical theatre.**
Wulf Konold. Transl. by Patricia Crampton.   Kassel: Bärenreiter,
1980. 127p. bibliog. (Commissioned by Inter Nationes).
After describing the origins and early history of the opera in Germany, and
reviewing its development – with particular attention to Bayreuth and to the
short-lived experiment of the Berlin Kroll Opera (1927-1931) – through the first
half of the twentieth century, this illustrated study gives 'a situation report' on
opera in the Federal Republic of Germany, describing the organization and
subsidization, the status of the performers and the staff, the repertory, audience
structure, and the prospects for the future. For general reference, see Gerhart
von Westerman's *Opera Guide*, ed., with an intro., by Harold Rosenthal, transl.
by Anne Ross (London: Thames and Hudson, 1964), a compact, 584-page volume
with sixty-two black-and-white illustrations. Translated from *Knaurs Opernführer*
(Munich: Droemersche Verlagsanstalt, 1952), it provides an introduction to the
history of opera and to individual operas (with plot summaries set in smaller
type). It includes individual chapters on the beginnings of opera in Germany,
Gluck, Mozart, 'The German National Opera and "Fidelio",' German romantic
opera, Wagner, Wagner's successors, Richard Strauss and his contemporaries,
and ' "New Music" and Opera,' with treatment, among others, of Arnold
Schönberg, Alban Berg, Paul Hindemith, Kurt Weill, Carl Orff, and Boris
Blacher.

425   **Music in Germany.**
K. H. Ruppel. Munich: F. Bruckmann, 1952. 79p.
A 'situation report,' illustrated with numerous black-and-white photographs, on
the revival of serious music in the Federal Republic within six years after the end
of World War II. An important factor in this revival, as Ruppel notes, was the
German tradition of regional and local support for music – a tradition that for
generations had brought fine music not just to the national capital and one or two
other great centres, but had also led to a number of smaller cities becoming
significant musical centres, some with an international reputation. During the late
nineteenth and early twentieth century, that reputation was reinforced by an
American book, Amy Fay's *Music-Study in Germany* (Chicago: McClurg, 1880;
repr., N.Y.: Dover, 1965), a collection of letters Fay sent between 1869 and 1875

The Arts. Music

from Germany to her family in the United States. She writes of Franz Liszt, with
whom she studied, of Clara Schumann, Anton Rubinstein, Joseph Joachim, and
many others. With over twenty printings in America, Macmillan's edition in
London, with a preface by Sir George Grove, and a French translation with an
introduction by Vincent d'Indy, it is considered to have been an important factor
in the decision of hundreds to study in Germany during the decades before World
War I.

426   **The German lied and its poetry.**
Elaine Brody and Robert A. Fowkes.   New York: New York
University Press, 1971. 316p. bibliog.

A professor of German and the chairman of the music department at New York
University, having jointly offered a course on the subject, collaborated on this
volume. Discussing them as poetry and as music, they focus on fifty German
songs – from a mediaeval forerunner (a minnesong by Neidhart von Reuenthal)
to a poem by Paul von Heyse set to music by Hugo Wolf in 1896 – and often offer
insight helpful in their performance. The bibliography separately lists *Lieder*
texts, scores, musical literature, and literary bibliography. There is a general
index and an index in which songs are alphabetized both by title and by first line.

427   **Deutsche Weisen: Die beliebtesten Volkslieder für Klavier mit Text.**
(German songs: the most popular folk songs arranged for piano
with text.)
Edited and arranged by Willy Schneider.   Stuttgart: Lausch &
Zweigle, 1958. 320p.

Close to 350 songs, including hymns, rounds, drinking and Christmas songs
arranged for easy playing. See also two paperback, pocket-sized collections edited
by Ernst-Lothar von Knorr (both with a single line of melody, the first with 168
songs, the second with sixty), *Deutsche Volkslieder* ['German Folksongs']
(Stuttgart: Reclam, 1972) and *Kinderlieder* ['Childrens' Songs'] (Stuttgart:
Reclam, 1959).

428   **The golden age of German music and its origins.**
Grace O'Brien.   London: Jarrolds, 1953. 222p. bibliog.

A concise narrative, addressed to the layman, with twenty-five black-and-white
illustrations. The first half of the book reviews the history of music since
Antiquity, the origins of secular song during the Middle Ages, and the
development of polyphonic music by the sixteenth century, setting the stage for
the remarkable flowering of German music during the eighteenth and nineteenth
centuries. The second half focusses on Händel (1685-1759), Bach (1685-1750), the
opera and Gluck (1714-1787), the symphony and Haydn (1732-1809), Mozart
(1756-1791), and Beethoven (1770-1827). For more detailed treatment of the
seventeenth and eighteenth centuries, see also Claude V. Palisca, *Baroque Music*,
2nd ed. (Englewood Cliffs, N.J.: Prentice-Hall, 1981), with chapters (each
followed by bibliographical notes) on 'The Sacred Concerto in Germany' (with
consideration, among others, of Praetorius and Schütz), 'Organ and Clavier
Music in Germany' (Buxtehude, Pachelbel, et al.), and Johann Sebastian Bach.

429   **Heinrich Schütz: his life and work.**
Hans Joachim Moser. Transl. by Carl F. Pfatteicher.   St. Louis:
Concordia Publishing House, 1959. 740p. bibliog.

Born a century before Bach, Heinrich Schütz (1585-1672) was the greatest German musician of the seventeenth century and, after Luther, the most important figure in the history of German Protestant church music. The Concordia edition of Moser's standard biography includes seventeen photographic plates and the numerous musical examples of the original, *Heinrich Schütz. Sein Leben und Werk*, 2nd, rev. ed. (Kassel and Basel: Bärenreiter Verlag, 1954). The first part of the book, which focusses on the life of Schütz as a man of his time, begins with an introductory chapter on the German world when he was born and ends with an epilogue on the German world when he died; the second part, which deals with his works as a composer, similarly begins with a review of the state of music at the time of his birth and concludes with an epilogue on the musical situation at the time of his death. For a brief introduction to Schütz, together with a selective discography and listing of editions of his musical works, see the biographical essay by Moser, translated and edited by Derek McCulloch, *Heinrich Schütz: A Short Account of His Life and Works* (N.Y.: St. Martin's, 1967).

430   **J. S. Bach.**
Albert Schweitzer. Preface by C. M. Widor. Transl., with a
foreword, by Ernest Newman.   Leipzig: Breitkopf and Härtel,
1911; repr., New York: Dover Publications, 1966. 2 vols.

This full-length study of Bach and his music by the celebrated Strasbourg theologian and organist was translated, with the author's additions and revisions, from the German edition of 1908 published in Leipzig by Breitkopf and Härtel. The first volume provides an historical introduction to the music of Bach's age, an account of his life, and an analysis of his instrumental works; the second is primarily concerned with the great body of Bach's choral music, employing the combined resources of choir, orchestra, and organ in setting sacred texts to music for worship. Throughout both volumes, Schweitzer offers recommendations for the performance of Bach's works. There are bibliographies at the beginning of chapters, and, in the second volume, a general index, an index to Bach's compositions, and a numerical listing of his church cantatas. A volume, in German, edited by Walter Blankenburg, *Johann Sebastian Bach* (Darmstadt: Wissenschaftliche Buchgesellschaft, 1970), contains some twenty-five articles regarding recent German scholarship on Bach's development, on his place in the history of music, and on various questions pertaining to his musical compositions and style. *The Bach Reader: A Life of Johann Sebastian Bach in Letters and Documents*, ed. by Hans T. David and Arthur Mendel, rev. ed., with a supplement (N.Y.: Norton, 1966) is comprised largely of seventeenth- and eighteenth-century documentation in translation, with illustrations from the time, annotations, and bibliographical notes.

The Arts. Music

431 Handel.
Herbert Weinstock. New York: Alfred A. Knopf, 1946. 326p.
bibliog.
Biography of the composer who was born in Halle and baptized Georg Friedrich
Händel (1685-1759). In 1710 he became conductor of the court orchestra of the
Elector of Hanover who in 1714 ascended the British throne as King George I.
Handel spent the greater part of his life in England (where he changed the
spelling of his name). The volume includes twenty-six illustrations, a general
index, and an index of Handel's works.

432 Music in the classic period.
Reinhard G. Pauly. Englewood Cliffs, N.J.: Prentice-Hall, 1973.
2nd ed. 206p. bibliog, (Prentice-Hall History of Music Series).
A survey of the classic period in the history of music, defined as the second half of
the eighteenth and the beginning of the nineteenth centuries: the age of Haydn
(1732-1809), Mozart (1756-1791), and the early Beethoven (1770-1827), whose
later works were increasingly characterised by the qualities that were to become
typical of Romanticism. For a biography of Haydn with consideration of his
compositions, see *Haydn: A Creative Life in Music*, by Karl Geiringer in collab.
with Irene Geiringer, 3rd, rev. & exp. ed. (Berkeley and Los Angeles: Univ. of
California Press, 1983).

433 Mozart.
Wolfgang Hildesheimer. Translated by Marion Faber. New
York: Farrar Straus Giroux, 1982. 408p.
A biography translated from the German (published in Frankfurt by Suhrkamp in
1977), this is a critical reexamination of the life of 'perhaps the greatest genius in
recorded human history,' based insofar as possible on primary autobiographical
sources (mostly annotated in German), consciously challenging, in many respects,
the idealized, conventional view. The volume concludes with a detailed
chronology of Mozart's life and indexes of names and of his works. See also
Alfred Einstein, *Mozart: His Character, His Work* (N.Y.: Oxford Univ. Press,
1945); *The Mozart Companion*, ed. by H. C. Robbins Landon and Donald
Mitchell (N.Y.: Oxford Univ. Press, 1956); and, for an overview of recent
German scholarship on Mozart, the 505-page volume edited by Gerhard Croll,
Wolfgang Amadeus Mozart (Darmstadt: Wissenschaftliche Buchgesellschaft,
1977).

434 Thayer's life of Beethoven.
[Alexander Wheelock Thayer.] Revised and edited by Elliot
Forbes. Princeton, N.J.: Princeton University Press, 1967. Rev.
ed. 2 vols. bibliog.
Fine English edition of the classic biography of Beethoven by Thayer, who had
drafted it in English for publication in German. The complete work appeared
only after his death, as *Ludwig van Beethovens Leben*, transl. and ed. by
Hermann Deiters [who also died before it was finished], revised and completed by
Hugo Riemann, 5 vols. (Leipzig: Breitkopf and Härtel, 1907-1917), and
subsequently in English as *The Life of Ludwig van Beethoven*, ed. by Henry

Edward Krehbiel, 3 vols. (N.Y.: The Beethoven Association, 1921; repr., with an intro. by Alan Pryce-Jones, London: Centaur Press, 1960). The Princeton edition, initially published in 1964 and reissued with corrections, revised translations, and a thoroughly revised index, is a carefully annotated, readable revision, 'using all the new research on Beethoven that Thayer would have used himself had it been available.' The 1,056-page text of the narrative is supplemented by several appendices, including Franz Grillparzer's funeral oration, and a general index as well as an index to Beethoven's compositions. See also *The Beethoven Companion*, edited by Denis Arnold and Nigel Fortune (London: Faber and Faber, 1971), published in the United States as *The Beethoven Reader* (N.Y.: Norton, 1971), a 542-page volume with fourteen authoritative essays on various aspects of Beethoven's life and work, as well as the scholarly German articles in *Ludwig van Beethoven*, ed. by Ludwig Finscher (Darmstadt: Wissenschaftliche Buchgesellschaft, 1983).

435 **Music in the Romantic era.**
Alfred Einstein.   New York: W. W. Norton, 1947. 371p.

Not just an account of composers and their works from Beethoven's death to Wagner's, but rather a history of music, in a broader cultural context, as a central element in the Romantic movement of the nineteenth century. Considerable space is given to Germany, as the author notes, in view of the extent to which that country was affected by Romanticism. Einstein begins with such questions as the place assumed by music in the arts by the nineteenth century, the increasing importance of nationalism and folk music, and the use of new forms and adaptation of old ones, as in the Romantic symphony. The body of his work is a history of music in the Romantic era from Schubert to Wagner and Verdi. In the last part of his book, Einstein deals with aesthetics, the convergence of the arts, and the rise of musicology as 'a child of the Romantic era', discussing major nineteenth-century works of musical history bearing the stamp of Romanticism, and noting the transition to 'philological or purely historical research into facts,' marked with the appearance in 1866 of vol. 1 of Thayer's life of Beethoven. Schubert, the only composer to whom Einstein devotes a full chapter in this volume, is also the subject of his full-length biography, *Schubert: A Musical Portrait* (N.Y.: Oxford Univ. Press, 1951). For a concise biography of Liszt, with a bibliography and an appendix on inaccuracies in biographies of him, see Walter Beckett's volume in 'The Master Musicians Series,' *Liszt*, rev. ed. (London: Dent, 1963). Two recent biographies of central figures in nineteenth-century German music are Nancy B. Reich, *Clara Schumann: The Artist and the Woman* (Ithaca, N.Y.: Cornell Univ. Press, 1985) and Peter Ostwald, *Schumann: The Inner Voices of a Musical Genius* (Boston: Northeastern Univ. Press, 1985). See also Robert Schumann, *On Music and Musicians*, ed. by Konrad Wolff, transl. by Paul Rosenfeld (Berkeley and Los Angeles: Univ. of California Press, 1982).

436 **Richard Wagner: his life, his work, his century.**
Martin Gregor-Dellin. Translated by J. Maxwell Brownjohn. San
Diego/New York/London: Harcourt Brace Jovanovich, 1983. 575p.
bibliog.

The recent biography by the Wagner authority who coedited the diaries of the
composer's second wife, Cosima Wagner (available in translation from the same
publisher), translated from *Richard Wagner. Sein Leben, sein Werk, sein
Jahrhundert* (Munich: Piper, 1980) with a condensed bibliography citing major
sources and works available in English, but only a few of the most important
German titles in the bibliography in the original edition. The classic study on
Wagner in English is the biography by Ernest Newman, *The Life of Richard
Wagner*, 4 vols. (N.Y.: Knopf, 1933-1946); see also the biography by Robert W.
Gutman, *Richard Wagner: The Man, His Mind, and His Music* (N.Y.: Harcourt,
Brace & World, 1968). For Wagner as a writer, see the sample of his work in
translation in *Richard Wagner: Stories and Essays*, selected, ed., and introd. by
Charles Osborne (London: Peter Owen, 1973), and the study in 'Twayne's World
Authors Series' by Robert Raphael, *Richard Wagner* (N.Y.: Twayne, 1969). Hans
Mayer's *Richard Wagner in Selbstzeugnissen und Bilddokumenten* ['Richard
Wagner in His Personal Testimony and Pictorial Documents'], Rowohlt's
Monographs, no. 29 (Reinbek bei Hamburg: Rowohlt, 1959) is a concise,
illustrated account (incorporating passages form Wagner's writings), with a
chronology and a bibliography. See also Mayer's subsequent full-length study,
Richard Wagner. Mitwelt und Nachwelt ['Richard Wagner: Contemporary World
and Posterity'] (Stuttgart: Belser, 1978); Theodor W. Adorno's essay, *In Search
of Wagner* ([London:] NLB, 1981), transl. by Rodney Livingstone from *Versuch
über Wagner* (Frankfurt am Main: Suhrkamp, 1974); L. J. Rather's *The Dream of
Self-Destruction: Wagner's 'Ring' and the Modern World* (Baton Rouge: Louisiana
State Univ. Press, 1979); and the compilation of essays, with a bibliography and
an index of Wagner's works, edited by Peter Burbidge and Richard Sutton, *The
Wagner Companion* (London: Faber and Faber, 1979).

437 **Johannes Brahms: his work and personality.**
Hans Gal. Translated by Joseph Stein. New York: Alfred A.
Knopf; London: Weidenfeld & Nicolson, 1963. 245p. bibliog.

Published in German as *Johannes Brahms. Werk und Persönlichkeit* (Frankfurt
am Main: Fischer Bücherei, 1961), this monograph, illustrated with eight black-
and-white plates, is a readable account of the life and work of Brahms (1833-
1897) by an authority who studied under Brahms' friend of many years, Eusebius
Mandyczewski, and collaborated with him in preparing the Breitkopf & Härtel
edition of the complete works. See also two earlier works: Karl Geiringer's
Brahms: His Life and Work, transl. by H. B. Weiner & Bernard Miall, 2nd ed.,
rev. and enl., with an appendix of Brahms' letters (London: Allen and Unwin,
1948); and the English pianist Florence May's carefully documented two-volume
biography, *The Life of Johannes Brahms*, 2nd rev. ed. (London: William Reeves
[1948]), with an introductory chapter of personal recollections of Brahms as
teacher, performer, and friend, based on her acquaintance with him from the
early 1870s, when Clara Schumann had arranged for her to study piano with him,
until her visits at his summer resort at Ischl in Upper Austria in the mid-1890s,
shortly before his death. For a biographical essay with a survey of books in

English, editions of music, and recordings, see Kathleen Dale's *Brahms* in 'The Concertgoer's Companions' series (London: Clive Bingley; Hamden, Conn.: Archon Books, 1970).

438 Bruckner, Mahler, Schoenberg.
Dika Newlin. New York: W. W. Norton, 1978. Rev. ed. 308p. bibliog.

The author, who studied under Schoenberg, has set out to prove that although the composer's work seems radical, it is in reality an organic step in musical development: He is not only 'the heir of Bruckner and Mahler, but also of the great Viennese classical tradition.' The first third of the volume is on Anton Bruckner (1824-1896), the second on Gustav Mahler (1860-1911). Against this background, Newlin gives a sympathetic and well-informed account of the development of Arnold Schoenberg (1874-1951) as a composer, his influence as a teacher, his systematization in the 1920s of atonality (or, as he preferred to call it, 'pantonality') in the 'twelve-tone scale,' and the work of his later years. The extensive bibliography cites articles as well as books, with coverage of editions and periodicals, on Bruckner, Mahler, Schoenberg, Berg, and Webern, and a selection of titles under the heading 'Arts, Ideas, History, Miscellaneous, Theory.' On Mahler, see also Michael Kennedy's volume in 'The Master Musicians Series,' *Mahler* (London: Dent, 1974); Bruno Walter's *Gustav Mahler*, transl. by James Galston, with a biographical essay by Ernst Křenek (N.Y.: Greystone, 1941; repr., N.Y.: Da Capo Press, 1970); and Alma Mahler's *Gustav Mahler: Memories and Letters*, enlarged edition, rev., ed., and with an intro. by Donald Mitchell (Seattle: Univ. of Washington Press, 1971), transl. by Basil Creighton from *Gustav Mahler: Erinnerungen und Briefe* (Amsterdam: Allert de Lange, 1940).

439 Twentieth century composers, vol. II: Germany and Central Europe.
H. H. Stuckenschmidt. London: Weidenfeld and Nicolson, 1970. 256p.

Biographical essays, illustrated with black-and-white photographs, on twenty-five composers, including Richard Strauss, Max Reger, Paul Hindemith, Carl Orff, Arthur Honegger, Hans Werner Henze, and Karlheinz Stockhausen. The German edition, *Die grossen Komponisten unseres Jahrhunderts. Deutschland – Mitteleuropa* ['The Great Composers of our Century: Germany – Central Europe'] (Munich: Piper, 1971), includes five additional essays, on Gottfried von Einem, Paul Dessau, Wolfgang Fortner, Rudolf Wagner-Regeny, and Giselher Klebe. See also Stuckenschmidt's volume in the 'World University Library,' *Twentieth Century Music*, transl. by Richard Deveson (N.Y.: McGraw-Hill, 1969).

The Arts. Music

440 **European music in the twentieth century.**
Edited by Howard Hartog. Harmondsworth, Middlesex:
Penguin, 1961. 360p.

Revision of a book published in 1957 by Routledge & Kegan Paul, with essays on
Schönberg's development towards the twelve-note system by Walter and
Alexander Goehr, on Alban Berg and Anton Webern by Iain Hamilton, on Paul
Hindemith by Norman Del Mar, and on contemporary music in West Germany
by the editor. On German music 1933-1945, see Joseph Wulf's *Musik im Dritten
Reich. Eine Dokumentation* ['Music in the Third Reich: A Documentation']
(Gütersloh: Sigbert Mohn Verlag, 1963). On Hindemith, see Ian Kemp's volume
in the 'Oxford Studies of Composers' series, *Hindemith* (London: Oxford Univ.
Press, 1970) and Giselher Schubert's illustrated *Paul Hindemith in Selbstzeugnissen
und Bilddokumenten* ['Paul Hindemith in His Own Testimony and in Pictorial
Documents'], Rowohlt's Monographs, no. 299 (Reinbek bei Hamburg: Rowohlt,
1981). See Hans Werner Henze, *Music and Politics: Collected Writings, 1953-81*,
transl. by Peter Labanyi (London: Faber & Faber, 1982), for a collection of
essays, letters, etc., including 'Gustav Mahler,' 'Paul Dessau,' and 'German
Music in the 1940s and 1950s.'

441 **Musical education in the Federal Republic of Germany.**
Kurt Jürgen Maass and Eckart Rohlfs. Translated by Brangwyn
Jones. Bonn: Inter Nationes, 1984. 39p. bibliog. (*Bildung und
Wissenschaft* [Education and Science], 1984, no. 1/2).

According to this report (which may be requested from Inter Nationes,
Kennedyallee 91-103, D-5300 Bonn 2), music as a subject was introduced in
German public schools around the beginning of the century, and today the
curriculum of primary and secondary schools in the Federal Republic calls for one
or two periods a week. In Baden-Württemberg and Bavaria, many academic-
preparatory schools (*Gymnasien*) offer music as a major subject through
graduation (i.e., matriculation by completion of the *Abitur*, a battery of
comprehensive examinations taken in the senior year). Some 700 music schools in
West Germany (with 3,000 full-time and 20,000 part-time teachers) give
instruction to well over half a million pupils, about half of them taking individual
vocal or instrumental lessons. In contrast to this relatively broad involvement,
only 12,200 students (48% women, over 14% foreign) were enrolled, in Winter
Semester 1982, in the sixteen state colleges of music, which generally admit only
one applicant in twenty, but whose graduates are virtually assured professional
careers in music. The report includes the addresses of these state colleges and also
lists the eight Protestant and six Catholic church music schools, as well as
numerous music institutes, centres, and seminars. It also gives the addresses of
seventy-five music-related organizations. It concludes with a bibliography on
music and music education, including *Studying Music in the Federal Republic of
Germany: Music, Music Education, Musicology*, published by the German Music
Council, ed. by Egon Kraus (Mainz: Schott, 1982).

Theatre and dance

442 **The German theatre: a symposium.**
Edited by Ronald Hayman. London: Oswald Wolff; New York:
Barnes and Noble, 1975. 287p. bibliog.

Compiled 'to put the present situation of the German theatre into the perspective
of its past,' a collection of thirteen essays on German dramatic literature from
Lessing to the present, European cross-currents, and questions of structure and
theatrical practice. See also Benjamin Bennett's interpretation of the history of
German drama from Lessing in the eighteenth century to Brecht in the twentieth,
stressing its central role in the development of modern European drama as a
whole, *Modern Drama and German Classicism: Renaissance from Lessing to
Brecht* (Ithaca, N.Y.: Cornell Univ. Press, 1979).

443 **Theatre, drama, and audience in Goethe's Germany.**
W. H. Bruford. London: Routledge & Kegan Paul, 1950. 388p.
bibliog.

A history of the German theatre from the beginning of the eighteenth century to
the beginning of the nineteenth. The theatre, writes Bruford of the situation in
1700, was dominated by travelling troupes of actors of low social standing offering
'completely low-brow entertainment.' There were neither standing theatres
devoted to drama nor a body of German dramatic literature. He describes how
this was changed by the work of Gottsched, Lessing, and the dramatists of the
'Storm and Stress' movement, particularly Schiller and Goethe, and concludes his
study with an account of the Weimar court theatre under the latter's direction,
Schiller's classical plays and Goethe's *Faust*, and an assessment of the German
theatre, drama, and public at the death of Schiller in 1805. The volume includes,
in addition to a select bibliography and general index, an index of plays and, as an
appendix, the Weimar repertoire in the opening months of 1803. See also Simon
Williams' *German Actors of the Eighteenth and Nineteenth Centuries: Idealism,
Romanticism, and Realism*, Contributions in Drama and Theatre Studies, no. 12
(Westport, Conn., and London: Greenwood Press, 1985), and Marvin Carlson,
The German Stage in the Nineteenth Century (Metuchen, N.J.: The Scarecrow
Press, 1972), both with extensive bibliographies.

444 **The Piscator experiment: the political theatre.**
Maria Ley-Piscator. New York: James H. Heineman, 1967. 336p.
bibliog.

Fascinating reminiscences of the widow of Erwin Piscator (1893-1966), the
politically engaged, liberal (if not radical) theatre director who opened the
Piscator Theatre in Berlin in 1927; founded the Dramatic Workshop at the New
School for Social Research in New York City in 1939; and returned to Germany
in 1951, directing plays with a message, including the premiere of Rolf
Hochhuth's *Der Stellvertreter* ['The Deputy'] in 1963. The volume includes a
detailed bibliography and a biographical outline of Piscator's life and career,
citing theatrical productions.

445 **Das Theater im NS-Staat. Szenarium deutscher Zeitgeschichte, 1933-1945.** (The theatre in the National Socialist state: scenario of German contemporary history, 1933-1945.)
Bogusław Drewniak.   Düsseldorf: Droste Verlag, 1983. 456p.
bibliog.

Scholarly monograph on the German theatre during the Hitler era by a Polish scholar. The first chapter, on the control apparatus, describes the organizations set up to guide cultural policy, particularly with reference to the theatre. The second chapter is on the theatre in Germany proper (focussing on Berlin, Munich, Dresden, Hamburg, and – as a representative example of regional theatre – Bochum); the third, on the theatre in Austria (annexed in spring 1938); and the fourth, on the theatre in Czechoslovakia (dismembered in stages, starting with fall 1938). The fifth describes the expansion of the theatre during the war and the sixth, the situation of the theatre community during Hitler's Third Reich. The remaining five chapters deal with various aspects of the dramatic and the musical stage; the eighth, for example, is on Gerhart Hauptmann and the eleventh includes consideration of the place of Richard Wagner. The volume concludes with a description of the impact of total war on the life of the theatre. In addition to an extensive bibliography, there is an index of names with biographical data (dates of birth and death, positions held, types of role, and the like). See also the illustrated compilation by Joseph Wulf, *Theater und Film im Dritten Reich. Eine Dokumentation* ['Theatre and Film in the Third Reich: A Documentation'] Gütersloh: Sigbert Mohn Verlag, 1964).

446 **The German theater today: a symposium.**
Edited with an introduction by Leroy R. Shaw.   Austin:
University of Texas Press, 1963. 141p.

Five essays, originally presented at a University of Texas symposium in 1961, on the contemporary German theatre: complementary essays by Francis Hodge on 'German Drama and the American Stage' and by Walther Karsch on 'American Drama and the German Stage'; a contribution by Wilhelm Schlag on theatre in Austria, culturally an integral part of the German-speaking world; A. M. Nagler's essay on 'Wagnerian Productions in Postwar Bayreuth,' reflecting the fact, noted by the editor, that, in the German way of thinking, the opera and the stage play 'are simply different species of theater occupying a place side by side on the cultural calendar'; and Eric Bentley's presentation, 'Epic Theater is Lyric Theater,' in the course of which he sang a number of Bertolt Brecht's poems that have been set to music, accompanying himself on the piano. (The editor notes Bentley having recorded a similar performance; it was issued in 1965 as a long-playing record by Folkways Records in New York under the title *Bentley on Brecht*.)

447   **John Cranko und das Stuttgarter Ballett.** (John Cranko and the
Stuttgart Ballet.)
Ninette de Valois et al. English transl. by Diana C. Williams.
Photographed by Zoë Dominic and Madeline Winkler-Betzendahl.
Pfullingen: Verlag Günther Neske, 1969. 128p.
Large picture book on the celebrated Stuttgart State Theatre Ballet, directed by
John Cranko, with photographs made 1969 in Stuttgart and, during guest
performances at the Metropolitan Opera House, in New York. The text and
captions are in English, French, and German.

Cinema

448   **The German cinema.**
Roger Manvell and Heinrich Fraenkel.   London: J. M. Dent &
Sons, 1971. 159p. bibliog.
Popular overview of German film from its origins before World War I to the late
1960s, with 163 black-and-white illustrations, an index of principal names, a select
index of films, and a bibliography. Useful for introductory orientation,
notwithstanding occasional imprecisions and inaccuracies in its sweeping coverage
of the very broad subject.

449   **German Expressionist film.**
John D. Barlow.   Boston: Twayne Publishers, 1982. 229p. bibliog.
(Twayne's Filmmakers Series).
A well-written, annotated, introductory survey of German film during the period
1913 to 1933, with a chronology, a selected bibliography, a filmography, black-
and-white illustrations, and an index. See also the controversial, still widely read
(and well-illustrated) interpretation by Siegfried Kracauer, *From Caligari to
Hitler: A Psychological History of the German Film* (Princeton, N.J.: Princeton
Univ. Press, 1947).

450   **The haunted screen: Expressionism in the German cinema and the
influence of Max Reinhardt.**
Lotte H. Eisner. Translated by Roger Greaves.   Berkeley and Los
Angeles: University of California Press, 1969. 360p. bibliog.
Translated from *L'Écran Démoniaque*, rev. ed. (Paris: Le Terrain Vague, 1965),
an illustrated study of the flowering of the German film as an art form during the
1920s, 'stimulated, . . . on the one hand, by the theatre of Max Reinhardt and, on
the other, by Expressionist art.' On Reinhardt, see J. L. Styan's concise
monograph in the 'Directors in Perspective' series, *Max Reinhardt* (Cambridge:
Cambridge Univ. Press, 1982), and his son Gottfried Reinhardt's *The Genius: A
Memoir of Max Reinhardt* (N.Y.: Knopf, 1979).

The Arts. Cinema

451   **Film in the Third Reich: art and propaganda in Nazi Germany.**
David Stewart Hull.   Berkeley: University of California Press,
1969; repr., New York: Simon and Schuster, Touchstone Books,
1973. 291p. bibliog.

An illustrated and annotated history of German cinema during the Hitler period,
1933-1945, with particular attention to the role of the government, and its
exploitation of the film for propaganda purposes. There is a detailed index. In
addition to Joseph Wulf's *Theater und Film im Dritten Reich*, cited above, see
Julian Petley's *Capital and Culture: German Cinema 1933-45* (London: British
Film Institute, 1979) and Erwin Leiser's pocket-format, illustrated *'Deutschland,
erwache! Propaganda im Film des Dritten Reiches* [' "Germany, Awaken!"
Propaganda in the Film of the Third Reich'], rev. and exp. ed. (Reinbek bei
Hamburg: Rowohlt, 1978); both have bibliographies and the second has also a
filmography.

452   **Leni Riefenstahl.**
Renata Berg-Pan.   Boston: Twayne Publishers, 1980. 222p.
bibliog. (Tawyne's Theatrical Arts Series).

Annotated study of a German artist who began her career as a dancer, was a film
star by the beginning of the 1930s, produced epoch-making documentaries of the
National Socialist Party Congress in Nuremberg in 1934 and the Olympic games in
Berlin in 1936, and resumed her film-making career after the war. Concludes with
an annotated bibliography, a filmography, and an index. On Riefenstahl's
remarkable film of the 1934 Party Congress, which provides the most effective
cinematographical projection of Hitler extant, see Richard Meran Barsam,
Filmguide to 'Triumph of the Will', Indiana Univ. Press Filmguide Series, no. 10
(Bloomington: Indiana Univ. Press, 1975).

453   **Kirche und Film. Kirchliche Filmarbeit in Deutschland von ihren
Anfängen bis 1945.** (Church and film: ecclesiastical cinematography
in Germany from its beginnings until 1945.)
Heiner Schmitt.   Boppard am Rhein: Harald Boldt Verlag, 1979.
382p. bibliog. (Schriften des Bundesarchivs, 26).

Published by the West German Federal Archives, this is a meticulously
documented monograph, by a member of its staff, on filmmaking in both the
Catholic and Protestant churches in Germany, with a very extensive bibliography
(including coverage of newspaper and journal articles) and 106 pages of
descriptive listings of films – with a film index – produced by the churches during
the period covered.

454   **The new German cinema.**
John Sandford.   London: Oswald Wolff, 1980. 180p. bibliog.

Survey of contemporary West German film, illustrated in black and white. Begins
with an historical overview: the postwar recovery, leading to the commercially
lucrative mid-1950s, was soon followed by a crisis, triggered by television (there
were a million sets in West Germany in 1957, four million by 1960, over sixteen
million by 1970); as cinemas and established studios closed, a new generation of

German filmmakers emerged, twenty-six affirming in the 'Oberhausen Manifesto' of February 1962 their commitment to 'the creation of the new German feature film.' The new cinema soon flourished, underwritten in part by state subsidization under the Film Promotion Law of 1968, supplemented by funding under the 1974 Film/Television Agreement, whereby the state-controlled television provided not only a share of film production costs, but 'no-strings-attached' grants to develop new filmscripts. Against this background, Sandford concentrates on the work of seven directors (Alexander Kluge, Jean-Marie Straub, Volker Schlöndorff, Werner Herzog, Rainer Werner Fassbinder, Wim Wenders, and Hans Jürgen Syberberg), but also notes other films, such as the one by Sohrad Shahid Saless on Turkish workers in Berlin, and a collaborative work, 'Germany in Autumn' (1978). The well-annotated volume includes a filmography of the seven directors named and an annotated bibliography. See also Hans Günther Pflaum and Hans Helmut Prinzler, *Cinema in the Federal Republic of Germany: The New German Film – Origins and Present Situation. A Handbook* (Bonn: Inter Nationes, 1983), transl. by Timothy Nevill from *Film in der Bundesrepublik Deutschland. Der neue deutsche Film. Herkunft/Gegenwärtige Situation. Ein Handbuch* (Munich: Hanser, 1979), with a directory of German organizations and institutes concerned with the cinema.

455 **New German filmmakers: from Oberhausen through the 1970s.**
Edited by Klaus Phillips. New York: Frederick Ungar, 1984.
462p. bibliog. (Ungar Film Library).

An introductory essay and seventeen original contributions written for this extensively annotated volume, addressed primarily to the American reader interested in contemporary German film, provide an informative, critical assessment, to 1980, of twenty-one filmmakers – including several whose works are less well known outside Germany, such as Hark Bohm, Peter Lilienthal, and Edgar Reitz. The selected bibliographies on the filmmakers list titles in English and German separately, and the filmographies note films of which copies are available free of charge to educational groups for nonprofit screenings from the film library of the Embassy of the Federal Republic of Germany in Washington, D.C. See also three other recent studies: James Franklin, *New German Cinema: From Oberhausen to Hamburg* (Boston: Twayne, 1983), in 'Twayne's Filmmakers Series'; Eric Rentschler, *West German Film in the Course of Time: Reflections on the Twenty Years since Oberhausen* (Bedford Hills, N.Y.: Redgrave, 1984), with a year-by-year checklist on West German film, 1962-1981, and an eighteen-page bibliography of readings in English on West German film; and the critical study focussing on Wenders, Fassbinder, Schlöndorff, Kluge, Herzog, and Syberberg by Timothy Corrigan, *New German Film: The Displaced Image* (Austin: Univ. of Texas Press, 1983).

Folklore, customs, and festivals

456 **German festivals & customs.**
Jennifer M. Russ. London: Oswald Wolff, 1982. 166p. bibliog.
Informative description of present-day customs and festivals and their background, addressed to both the serious student and the interested general reader with no knowledge of the language. Well illustrated with black-and-white photographs, includes an appendix listing legal holidays in the Federal Republic of Germany, a subject index with listings in German and English alphabetized separately, and an index of names and places. See also *A Calendar of German Customs* by Richard Thonger (Chester Springs, Pa.: Dufour Editions; London: Oswald Wolff, 1968), based on *Volksbrauch im Jahreslauf* ['Popular Customs throughout the Year'], by Hedi Lehmann (Munich: Ernst Heimeran Verlag, 1964).

457 **Das deutsche Volksschauspiel. Ein Handbuch.** (The German folk play. A handbook.)
Leopold Schmidt. Berlin: Erich Schmidt Verlag, 1962. 516p. 6 maps.
A comprehensive, systematic study of a long neglected area: German folk plays, including Christmas pageants, passion plays, puppet theatre, processions, etc. The greater part of the volume consists of a review of these traditional folk activities in each of forty-one German-speaking regions of Europe. Over a hundred pages of notes include extensive bibliographical citations. Sixteen black-and-white photographs illustrate the plays. See also Hans Moser (to whom the Schmidt handbook is dedicated) and Raimund Zoder, *Deutsches Volkstum in Volksschauspiel und Volkstanz* ['German Folk Heritage in Folk Plays and Folk Dance'] (Berlin: Walter de Gruyter, 1938), with forty-eight black-and-white photographs of masks, plays, dances, etc. On the most famous of the German folk plays, the Oberammergau Passion Play, and the controversy that led, before the 1980 production, to cuts and alterations of the text in about three dozen places (on the advice of Joseph Cardinal Ratzinger, then Archbishop of Munich-Freising), see Saul S. Friedman, *The Oberammergau Passion Play: A Lance against Civilization* (Carbondale and Edwardsville: Southern Illinois Univ. Press, 1984) and the bibliography cited there.

458 **Das Spielzeug im Leben des Kindes.** (Toys in the life of the child.)
Paul Hildebrandt. Berlin: Söhlke, 1904; repr., Düsseldorf and Cologne: Eugen Diederichs, 1979. 421p. bibliog.
Written with style and conviction, this encyclopaedic, discursive monograph is meant as a source for adults to inform themselves thoroughly on one of the most important means to delight and educate children: toys. Beyond toys as such, there is extensive coverage of all kinds of games. There are many black-and-white illustrations and passages from writers regarding toys and games of their childhood. The last two of the eleven chapters are essays on picture books, fairy tales, and stories for children, and on the celebration of family festivals and holidays throughout the year.

Food and Drink

459 Cuisine of Germany.

Edda Meyer-Berkhout. Translated by Sara Harris.   London: W.
H. Allen, 1984. 191p.

First published in Italy under the title *Cucina alla tedesca* (Milan: Mondadori,
1982), this is a representative selection of German recipes in crisp, black print on
large pages of glossy paper. The 296 recipes, mostly for four servings, are
subdivided into sixteen categories, each preceded by a short introduction. There
are two recipes to a page, in two columns. Each entry consists of a good colour
photograph, a list of ingredients (with measurements in U.S., imperial, and
metric), and easy-to-follow directions. The index lists the recipes in English,
followed by the German term in parenthesis. See also the paperback edition, set
up the same way, but with the recipes rewritten for the American market, and
two indexes, one in English, the other in German: Edda Meyer-Berkhout, *Best of
German Cooking* (Tucson, Ariz.: HPBooks, 1984).

460 The cooking of Germany.

Nika Standen Hazelton et al. Photographs by Ralph Crane and
Henry Groskinsky.   Alexandria, Va.: Time-Life Books, 1969.
Rev. 1983. 4 maps. 208p. (Foods of the World).

Informative and entertaining up-to-date introduction to German cuisine contains
seventy-four recipes embedded in discourses on the many faces of German
sausage, bread, beer, etc. Throughout, correctly spelled German terms are
correctly explained. There is a glossary, recipe indices both in English and in
German, and a general index. This coffee-table volume with many colour
illustrations is accompanied by a recipe book, cited next, for use in the kitchen.

201

Food and Drink

461 **Recipes: the cooking of Germany.**
Alexandria, Va.: Time-Life Books, Inc., 1969. Rev. 1983. 120p.
(Foods of the World.)

A handy spiral-bound collection of over a hundred recipes (including the seventy-four in the large companion volume directly above) divided into nine groups: soups, fish, meat and poultry, game, dumplings, salads, breads and cookies, and cakes and desserts. There are six sets of illustrations (showing, for example, how to make a gingerbread house) and both an English and a German index.

462 **Oetker German home cooking.**
Compiled in the testing kitchen of Dr. August Oetker,
Bielefeld. Bielefeld: Ceres-Verlag Rudolf-August Oetker KG,
1983. 11th ed. 176p.

The bible of many a German cook is a new or beat-up copy of Dr. Oetker. On the German market since 1911, and continuously updated, the first English edition appeared in 1963. The recipes in this handy-format book, with about a dozen full-page colour illustrations, are simple, practical, and economical. A number call for Oetker products, such as the fabulous pudding powders, available also outside Germany in specialty stores, or *Gustin*, a corn starch. Of the fourteen sections, comprising some 450 recipes, more than half are prefaced by useful general hints.

463 **Lüchow's German cookbook: the story and the favorite dishes of America's most famous German restaurant.**
Jan Mitchell. Introd. and illustrations by Ludwig Bemelmans.
Garden City, N.Y.: Doubleday, 1952. 224p.

Founded by August Lüchow who came to the United States in 1879, Lüchow's has been a favourite with many celebrities. In addition to the boiled beef that Caruso and Flo Ziegfeld dined on and the raw meat lucullus that Pavlova and John Barrymore enjoyed, you will be able to try out 210 more of the restaurant's recipes.

464 **The Wine and Food Society's guide to German cookery.**
Hans Karl Adam. Translated by Norah Tompkinson. Cleveland,
Ohio: The Wine and Food Society in association with World
Publishing Company, 1967. 215p.

Favourite regional recipes are grouped together in nine chapters on cookery in Berlin, North and East Germany, Hesse, Westphalia, Thuringia, Silesia, Bavaria, Swabia, and the Rhineland, with introductions mixing fact and fantasy.

465   **The home book of German cookery.**
Hanne Lambley.   London and Boston: Faber and Faber, 1979.
303p.

Written for the British market, with notes on where to shop for German provisions in England, each chapter in this paperback is prefaced with a list of the items presented. See also Robin Howe's 223-page *German Cooking* (London: André Deutsch, 1954), an unillustrated collection of recipes from all over Germany, with items in the index arranged according to eighteen categories.

466   **Das neue grosse Kiehnle Kochbuch.** (The new large Kiehnle cookbook.)
Edited by Monika Graff.   Weil der Stadt: Walter Hädecke Verlag, 1984. 607p.

Thoroughly updated and modernized version of an old classic. In addition to 2,360 tried-and-true recipes (three columns per page), there are menu suggestions for festive occasions, chapters on condiments and herbs, nutrition, wine, etc., and general, useful hints for the kitchen.

467   **Baking: easy & elegant.**
Dr. Oetker.   Bielefeld: Ceres-Verlag Rudolf-August Oetker KG, 1982. 240p.

From the famous Dr. Oetker kitchens in the country known for its baked delicacies, 388 recipes, many accompanied by colour photos. Nine main categories (cookies, creative cakes, tarts & flans, quick breads & coffee cakes, yeast baking, pastries, convenience baking, confections, and holiday & special occasion baking) are followed by basic information (equivalency chart, tips for using puff pastry, etc.) and a detailed index.

468   **Bavarian cooking.**
Assembled by Olli Leeb. Transl. by Maria M. Rerrich.   Munich: O. Leeb Kochbuch-Verlag, 1983. 2nd ed. 172p. map.

'Meant above all for English-speaking tourists who enjoyed their visit' to Bavaria, this handy-format translation of *Bayerische Leibspeisen*, richly illustrated with drawings, introduces typical Bavarian specialties (serving four) with information on the land, its people, and their customs.

469   **Heritage of cooking: a collection of recipes from East Perry County, Missouri.**
Compiled by The Saxon Lutheran Memorial. Edited by Gerhardt Kramer.   St. Louis: The Concordia Historical Institute, 1970. 3rd, rev. printing. Ca. 234p.

187 pages of recipes gathered from descendants of Saxon immigrants, etc., are interspersed with an illustrated history of Saxon Lutherans who settled in Missouri around 1840. (Published by an institute of the Lutheran Church, Missouri Synod, 801 DeMun Ave., St. Louis, Mo. 63105.)

Food and Drink

470 **German cookbook for quantity service: authentic professional recipes.**
[Harry] Caleva. New York: Ahrens Publishing Company, Inc., 1956. 312p.

The recipes are listed in sixteen categories, and the basic formulas are designed to produce twenty-five servings. There are conversion tables and instructions for increasing or decreasing the formulas.

471 **The wines of Germany.**
Frank Schoonmaker. New York: Hastings House, 1966. 156p. maps. (Frank Schoonmaker's Wine Library).

Addressed primarily to the American reader, a well-informed introduction to German wines, illustrated with photographs and maps. A non-technical explanation of wine production and labelling is followed by individual chapters on the districts where most German wines exported to America originate (Moselle, Rheingau, Hesse, the Nahe, the Palatinate, and Franconia). There is a single chapter on the other wine districts (Bodensee or Lake Constance, Baden, Württemberg, Mittel-Rhein, and the Ahr), and there are brief, individual chapters on red wines and sparkling wines; buying and storing German wines; and serving and tasting them. See also *The Great German Wine Book* by Kuno F. Pieroth (N.Y.: Sterling, 1983), translated from *Das grosse Buch der deutschen Weinkultur* ['The Large Book of German Wine Culture'] (Munich: Moderne Verlags GmbH, 1980), an oversized volume illustrated in colour, with considerable information (including coverage of the German Wine Law of 1971), and a detailed index, but no documentation or bibliography.

472 **Guide to the wines of Germany.**
Hans Siegel. New York: Simon & Schuster, Cornerstone Library, 1979. 124p. map. bibliog.

Handy paperback on German wines and wine-making. Explains the regions and types of wine, has a chapter on eating in Germany, appendices on wine-tasting and sources of further information (maps, books, and addresses), and a glossary. See also the chapters on German wines in (Harold J.) *Grossman's Guide to Wines, Spirits, and Beers*, 4th, rev. ed. (N.Y.: Charles Scribner's Sons, 1964), *Hugh Johnson's Modern Encyclopedia of Wine* (N.Y.: Simon and Schuster, 1983), and *The World Atlas of Wine: A Complete Guide to the Wines & Spirits of the World*, also by Hugh Johnson (N.Y.: Simon and Schuster, 1971).

473 **The world guide to beer.**
Michael Jackson. Englewood Cliffs, N.J.: Prentice-Hall; London: Quarto Publishing, Ltd., 1977. 255p. maps.

This large-format, copiously illustrated 'book for the beer-drinker' devotes almost fifty pages to West Germany, the country with the most breweries and the largest per capita consumption. Of the 1,600 breweries in the Federal Republic, a thousand are in Bavaria. Jackson discusses the different types of German beer, regional beer-styles, laws regarding purity and strength, the oldest surviving beer (from Roman times, and now a solidified syrup), the *Oktoberfest*, beer-gardens, etc., and shows the brewing-towns on two maps. The volume starts with general information on the art of brewing and what goes into the brew. A more recent and full-length treatment of beer in Germany, albeit in German, is the entertaining and informative 423-page *Das grosse Lexikon vom Bier* ['The Large Encyclopaedia of Beer'] (Stuttgart: Scripta Verlags-Gesellschaft, 1982) by Jochen Bernay and others. The idea that beer might be fattening is dispelled, its medicinal qualities are praised, over sixty recipes are given, and there is a profusion of colour illustrations. The volume concludes with an alphabetical listing of German breweries, noting that approximately forty of the smaller ones (located mostly in the south) have been going out of business every year. For a technical book in German about the production of beer and the analysis of the ingredients, see Wilfried Rinke, *Das Bier* ['Beer'], 'Grundlagen und Fortschritte der Lebensmittelforschung [Basic Studies and Advances in Research on Foodstuffs],' vol. 10 (Berlin and Hamburg: Paul Parey, 1967), with drawings, tables, photos, and bibliographical citations in German and English.

Sports and Recreation

474 **Sport und Industriegesellschaft.** (Sports and industrial society.)
Christian Graf von Krockow.   Munich: R. Piper Verlag, 1972.
102p. (Serie Piper, no. 25).

The noted German sociologist and political scientist begins this essay – in
uncomplicated German – on the place of sports in modern, industrial society with
consideration of the origins and principles of sports, as illustrated by the English
tradition. A discussion of the organizing and social functions of sports follows,
with special reference to Germany. The essay concludes with an evaluation of the
ideological advocacy of sports and of the critical condemnation of it, particularly
on the part of the 'New Left,' followed by Krockow's own view of the very
significant place of games and sports in the world in which we live. There are
many bibliographical citations, German and English, in the notes. In addition, see
the twenty-seven page essay by Ulfert Schröder, issued as an IN-Press release,
*Zwischen Lust und Leistung – Sport und Sportbetrieb in der Bundesrepublik
Deutschland* ['Between Enjoyment and Achievement – Sports and Sports
Management in the Federal Republic of Germany'], Sonderdienst SO 2-82
(Bonn: Inter Nationes, 1982). Schröder spells out the role of sports in West
German society, describing and discussing the various sports organizations and
the sources of their support; the public image of sports; the place of sports in the
schools (not comparable to sports at American schools, least of all those where
'collegiate athletics' commands fervent alumni and public support); sports as an
academic discipline; and the politics of sports. Appended is a list of addresses of
fifteen German sports organizations (from the National Olympic Committee for
Germany to associations concerned with everything from sailing or skiing to table
tennis). Cited under Geography (tourist manuals), golf, tennis, etc. enthusiasts
will find listings of locations in the individual sections on Germany in the Fodor
guide and on pp. 844-48 in the Michelin Red Guide, for example.

475　**Munich 72.**
Christopher Brasher.　London: Paul, 1972. 152p.

This is an illustrated British account of the 1972 Olympic Games in Munich. See also *Die Spiele [The Games]: The Official Report of the Organizing Committee for the Games of the XXth Olympiad* (Munich: Pro Sport, 1974), vols. 1 and 2 in English, vol. 3 in English, German, and French. Horst Ueberhorst, a leading German historian of sports, discusses the 1936 Olympic games and the relationship between sports and politics in National Socialist Germany in 'Spiele unterm Hakenkreuz. Die Olympischen Spiele von Garmisch-Partenkirchen und Berlin 1936 und ihre politischen Implikationen [Games under the Swastika: The Olympic Games of Garmisch-Partenkirchen and Berlin 1936 and Their Political Implications],' *Aus Politik und Zeitgeschichte*, the supplement to the Bonn weekly *Das Parlament*, B31/86 (2 August 1986), pp. 3-15, with bibliographical citations in the footnotes. The 1936 games are also the subject of Duff Hart-Davis, *Hitler's Games: The 1936 Olympics* (N.Y.: Harper & Row, 1986).

476　**Studies in the geography of tourism: papers read and submitted for the working conference of the IGU Working Group, Geography of Tourism and Recreation, Salzburg, 2-5 May 1973.**
Edited by Josef Matznetter.　Frankfurt am Main: Seminar für Wirtschaftsgeographie der Goethe-Universität Frankfurt/Main, 1974. 346p. (Frankfurter Wirtschafts- und Sozialgeographische Schriften, vol. 17).

Includes Friedrich Vetter, 'On the Structure and Dynamics of Tourism in Berlin West and East' (pp.237-258, with six figures and four tables), and a paper by Jörg Maier on tourism in the Bavarian Alps and their foreland (p. 197-210), in German, with English summary on p. 209. Regarding tourism and recreation on the northeastern Bavarian border (with East Germany and with Czechoslovakia), see J. Maier and J. Weber, 'Tourism and Leisure Behaviour Subject to the Spatial Influence of a National Frontier: The Example of North-East-Bavaria,' in *Tourism and Borders – Proceedings of the Meeting of the IGU Working Group: Geography of Tourism and Recreation, Ljubljana/Trieste 15.-19.9.1978*, ed. by R. Müller et al., Frankfurter Wirtschafts- und Sozialgeographische Schriften, vol. 31 (Institut für Wirtschafts- und Sozialgeographie, 1979), pp. 111-127, with three figures, two maps, and a select bibliography.

The Mass Media and the Book Trade

General

477 Mass media in the Federal Republic of Germany.
Georg Hellack. Bonn: Inter Nationes, 1971. 36p.

The role of newspapers, magazines, the cinema, book trade, and state-operated radio and television in West Germany and West Berlin. For more current coverage, see Georg Hellack's *Presse und Rundfunk in der Bundesrepublik Deutschland* ['Press and Radio in the Federal Republic of Germany'] Sonderdienst SO 2-85 (Bonn: Inter Nationes, 1985), a thirty-six-page 'IN-Press' release. See also Hermann Meyn's *Massenmedien in der Bundesrepublik Deutschland* ['Mass Media in the Federal Republic of Germany'], 'Zur Politik und Zeitgeschichte,' vol. 24, rev., new ed. (Berlin: Colloquium, 1985), as well as his two magazine-format texts, both thirty-two pages long: *Massenmedien 1* ['The Mass Media: (Part) 1'], mainly on the print and broadcast media; and *Massenmedien 2* ['The Mass Media: (Part) 2'], on developments in the electronic media, such as videotext and satellite and cable television. Addressed to the serious student and interested layman, in non-technical language, these two illustrated and documented texts (with bibliography) appeared as issues 208 and 209, respectively, of the bimonthly, widely disseminated public education series *Informationen zur Politischen Bildung* ['Information for Political Education'] (Bonn: Bundeszentrale für politische Bildung, 1985). Copies are available (as are copies of other issues in the extensive, well-edited series published by the Federal Centre for Political Education, a nonpartisan, independent government agency) directly from the Bundeszentrale für politische Bildung, Berliner Freiheit 7, 5300 Bonn.

478   **Public opinion.**
Otto B. Roegele, Hans Wagner, and Heinz Starkulla.   Bonn:
Press and Information Office of the Government of the Federal
Republic of Germany, 1971. 81p. bibliog.

A concise monograph by members of the staff of the Institute for Newspaper
Science of Munich University. An introduction defining the function of the media
in West German society and the legal frame of reference in which they operate is
followed by a systematic discussion of the ownership, operation, control, and
impact of the broadcast and print media. The booklet includes photographs,
tables, and a bibliography of titles largely in German. On the development of
German public opinion during the period from the end of the war to the end of
the occupation ten years later, as reflected in the surveys conducted by the U.S.
Office of Military Government (OMGUS), 1945-49, and the U.S. High
Commission for Germany (HICOG), 1949-1955, see Anna J. Merritt and Richard
L. Merritt, eds., *Public Opinion in Occupied Germany: The OMGUS Surveys,
1945-49* and *Public Opinion in Semisovereign Germany: The HICOG Surveys,
1949-1955* (Urbana: Univ. of Illinois Press, 1970 and 1980, respectively). The
constitutional guarantee of freedom of expression and the institutionalization of
freedom of the press in the Federal Republic, with consideration of questions
such as professional peer control through the German Press Council (*Deutscher
Presserat*), is dealt with by Michael Haler in an article published as an 'IN-Press'
release, *Grundgesetz garantiert Meinungsfreiheit. Zeitungen, Zeitschriften und
Agenturen in der Bundesrepublik Deutschland* ['The Basic Law Guarantees
Freedom of Expression: Newspapers, Magazines, and Agencies in the Federal
Republic of Germany'], Sonderdienst SO 1-80 (Bonn: Inter Nationes, 1980). See
also the supplement *Aus Politik und Zeitgeschichte* ['From Politics and
Contemporary History'] to the 2 March 1985 issue of the government weekly *Das
Parlament* (published by the Bundeszentrale für politische Bildung [Federal
Centre for Political Education] in Bonn), with extensively annotated articles by
Jürgen Wilke, Jürgen Büssow, Markus Schöneberger, and Otto Ulrich on
contemporary media policy.

479   **Handbuch der Publizistik.** (Handbook of communication and
publication.)
Edited by Emil Dovifat.   Berlin: Walter de Gruyter & Co., 1968,
3 vols. bibliog.

The first volume of this comprehensive, collaborative, lucid work deals with the
theory of communications, the second with oral and visual communications
(speech, moving and still pictures, television, radio, etc.), and the third with every
form of written communication from the poster to the book. The three-volume
handbook, totalling over 1,500 pp., includes dozens of contributions on different
aspects and branches of the field, such as sections on comics in Germany (vol. 2,
pp. 127-132) and on the Jewish press (vol. 3, pp. 508-513). The sections have
individual bibliographies and each volume concludes with indices of persons and
of subjects.

The broadcast media

480 **Broadcasting and democracy in West Germany.**
Arthur Williams. London: Bradford University Press in
association with Crosby Lockwood Staples, 1976. 198p. bibliog.

An introduction to the broadcasting system of the Federal Republic, with an
explanation of the organization, control, programming, and financing of the West
German radio and video broadcasting corporations (which are publicly owned and
not commercially controlled), and consideration of their cultural and political
role. For detailed treatment of radio broadcasting in Germany, see Hans Bausch,
ed., *Rundfunk in Deutschland* ['Radio in Germany'], 5 vols. (Munich: Deutscher
Taschenbuch Verlag, 1980).

481 **Your reporter in Germany: a cross-section of the Deutsche Welle
program beamed to North America.**
Preface by Hans-Otto Wesemann. Editor's note by Walter
Gong. Cologne: Deutsche Welle, 1965. 227p.

An illustrated booklet with transcripts of a selection of programmes broadcast to
America in 1964 and 1965 on topics of cultural, political, and general human
interest.

Newspapers and periodicals

482 **The German Tribune: a Weekly Review of the German Press.**
Hamburg: Friedrich Reinecke Verlag, 1962- ; weekly.

Published in an airmail edition by the Friedrich Reinecke Verlag, 23 Schöne
Aussicht, D-2000 Hamburg 76, this is a weekly selection of translated articles,
with editorial cartoons, illustrations, and advertising addressed to the English-
speaking world, from leading West German newspapers – dailies, such as the
Frankfurter Allgemeine (Frankfurt am Main), *Die Welt* (Bonn), the *Süddeutsche
Zeitung* (Munich), and the *Handelsblatt* (Düsseldorf), as well as weeklies, such as
Die Zeit (Hamburg), *Rheinischer Merkur/Christ und Welt* (Bonn), and *Das
Parlament* (Bonn). An occasional supplement, *The German Tribune Political
Affairs Review*, includes longer selections from periodicals such as *Europa-Archiv*
and *Aus Politik und Zeitgeschichte* ['From Politics and Contemporary History'],
the supplement to the weekly *Das Parlament.*

The Mass Media and the Book Trade. Newspapers and periodicals

483 **FBIS Daily Report: Western Europe.**
Springfield, Va.: National Technical Information Service (NTIS); daily.

Current news and commentary from West German news agency transmissions, newspapers, periodicals, and broadcasts are published, Monday through Friday, in English translation in vol. VII, *Western Europe*, of the Foreign Broadcast Information Service's *Daily Report*. Available by subscription on paper or microfiche from NTIS, U.S. Dept. of Commerce, 5285 Port Royal Road, Springfield, VA 22161.

484 **The Week in Germany.**
New York: German Information Center, 1970- ; weekly.

Weekly bulletin in English, published since 1970 (initially under the title *Relay from Bonn*), with six pages of political, economic, and cultural news of Germany and German-American relations, and two pages of representative editorial selections translated from the West German media. The bulletin is available on request from the German Information Center, 950 Third Avenue, New York, NY 10022. The German Information Center's *Statements and Speeches* series, with translated text of selected speeches by the federal president, the chancellor, and others, is also distributed on a complimentary basis, as is an eight-page German-language weekly newsletter, *Deuschland-Nachrichten* (or *DN*) ['News of Germany']. Its coverage is comparable to that in *The Week in Germany*, but it includes a sports page with reports on the West German soccer league. *DN* is used in a number of high schools and colleges where German is taught with an emphasis on current events and contemporary life.

485 **German Studies: a Review of German-language Research Contributions.**
Tübingen: Institute for Scientific Co-operation. Sections I-III, 1968- ; semi-annual. Section IV, 1965- ; quarterly.

Issued from D-7400 Tübingen, Landhausstr. 18, this English-language review of scholarly German publications (with select bibliography of many unreviewed titles) is published in three semiannual sections that have appeared since 1968: I. *Philosophy and History*; II. *Modern Law and Society*; and III. *Literature, Music, and Fine Arts*. Section IV, *Mundus*, covering German research publications on Asia, Africa, and Latin America in the arts and science, has appeared quarterly since 1965. The titles of the works are translated into English, as are the reviews, except those originally written in English, as, for example, the extensive contribution by Paul R. Sweet, the American biographer of Wilhelm von Humboldt, on the concluding volume of the 'Study Edition' of the Humboldt papers (*German Studies*, section I, vol. XVI [1983], pp. 108-113).

486 **German Book Review.**
Published [i.e., compiled] by Hans Winterberg. Boston, Mass.,
and Bonn: Goethe Institute, in cooperation with Inter Nationes
Book Department, 1974- ; currently semiannual.

A compilation of reviews duplicated in facsimile, largely from leading English and
American journals (though significant reviews from the Federal Republic, in
German, are also included), for complimentary distribution, on a limited basis, by
Inter Nationes, Kennedyallee 91-103 D-5300 Bonn 2.

487 **Der Spiegel.** (The mirror.)
Hamburg: Spiegel-Verlag Rudolf Augstein GmbH, 1947- ;
weekly.

The most widely circulated weekly news magazine in the Federal Republic, with
selective but intensive, at times encyclopaedic, and not infrequently controversial
coverage of political, economic, and cultural affairs in Germany and abroad –
often on the basis of sophisticated investigative reporting. For its role in the most
serious cabinet crisis of the Adenauer administration, see David Schoenbaum,
The Spiegel Affair (N.Y.: Doubleday, 1968).

The book trade

488 **Johann Gutenberg: the inventor of printing.**
Victor Scholderer. London: The Trustees of the British Museum,
1963. 32p. bibliog.

An introductory essay on the man and his work with sixteen unnumbered pages of
photographical plates, four of them in colour. For a concise, illustrated biography
of Gutenberg, with a chronology and a bibliography, see Helmut Presser's
Johannes Gutenberg in Zeugnissen und Bilddokumenten ['Johannes Gutenberg in
Testimony and Pictorial Documents'], Rowohlt's Monographs, no. 134 (Reinbek
bei Hamburg: Rowohlt, 1967). Carl Wehmer's *Deutsche Buchdrucker des
fünfzehnten Jahrhunderts* ['German Book-Printers of the Fifteenth Century']
(Wiesbaden: Harrassowitz, 1971) is a large-format volume with a hundred full-
page reproductions of samples from the work of several dozen fifteenth-century
masters, with detailed explanations (not translations) on the facing pages. For
illustrated introductions to the development of printing, particularly in Germany,
since the time of Gutenberg, see Elisabeth Geck, *Johannes Gutenberg. Vom
Bleibuchstaben zum Computer* ['Johannes Gutenberg: From Lead Letters to the
Computer'] (Bad Godesberg: Inter Nationes, 1968) and Helmut Presser,
Gutenberg-Museum der Stadt Mainz. Weltmuseum der Druckkunst ['Gutenberg
Museum of the City of Mainz: World Museum of the Art of Printing'] (Mainz:
Gutenberg-Museum, 1975).

489 **Geschichte des Buchhandels vom Altertum bis zur Gegenwart.
Teil I: Bis zur Erfindung des Buchdrucks sowie Geschichte des
deutschen Buchhandels.** (History of the book trade from Antiquity
to the present. Part I: To the invention of printing, as well as a
history of the German book trade.)
Hans Widmann. Wiesbaden: Otto Harrassowitz, 1975. 2nd, rev.
ed. 308p. bibliog.

This history of printing and publishing begins with a survey of the Western world
from Antiquity to the Reformation. Widmann focusses on twentieth-century
Germany, to which he devotes half the book, giving individual chapters to the
postwar period, to book production and distribution in East Germany, and to the
book trade in West Germany. There are unusually extensive bibliographical
references in chapter headnotes as well as in the copious annotations. (A second
volume, by Hans Furstner, deals with the Low Countries.) Charles H.
Timperley's thousand-page *Encyclopaedia of Literary and Typographical Anec-
dote*, 2nd, rev. ed. (London: Henry G. Bohn, 1842; repr., in 2 vols., with an
introduction by Terry Belanger, N.Y.: Garland, 1977), is a chronologically
structured, extensively indexed compendium on printing and publishing through
the early nineteenth century, focussed primarily on England, but with much on
Germany, too. See also Reinhard Wittmann, *Ein Verlag und seine Geschichte.
Dreihundert Jahre J. B. Metzler Stuttgart* ['A Publishing-House and Its History:
Three Hundred Years of J. B. Metzler in Stuttgart'] (Stuttgart: J. B. Metzler,
1982); Paul Raabe, ed., *Das Buch in den zwanziger Jahren* ['The Book in the
Twenties'], Wolfenbütteler Schriften für Geschichte des Buchwesens, vol. 2
(Hamburg: Hauswedell, 1978); Gary D. Stark, *Entrepreneurs of Ideology:
Neoconservative Publishers in Germany, 1890-1933* (Chapel Hill, N.C.: Univ. of
North Carolina Press, 1981); and Siegfried Unseld, *The Author and His Publisher*
(Chicago: Univ. of Chicago Press, 1980), translated by Hunter Hannum and
Hildegarde Hannum from *Der Autor und sein Verleger. Vorlesungen in Mainz
und Austin* ['The Author and His Publisher: Lectures in Mainz and Austin']
(Frankfurt am Main: Suhrkamp, 1978).

490 **A social history of the German book trade in America to the Civil
War.**
Robert E. Cazden. Columbia, S.C.: Camden House, 1984. 801p.
bibliog.

Chapter III (pp. 63-77) is a concise introduction to 'The Book Trade in Germany
after 1800,' noting its transformation by innovative publishing, the founding of a
German booksellers' association, a revolution in printing technology, and the
development of new markets. Cazden goes on to show that although there was a
market in America for books printed in Germany, it was increasingly shared by
the products of the native German-American publishing industry flourishing in
the Western Hemisphere by the eve of the Civil War. See *The German-language
Press in America*, by Carl Wittke (Lexington: Univ. of Kentucky Press, 1957), for
coverage of the German periodical and daily press in America through the mid-
1950s.

The Mass Media and the Book Trade. The book trade

491 **How to obtain German books and periodicals.**
Edited by Börsenverein des deutschen Buchhandels EV,
Aussenhandelsausschuss. Frankfurt am Main:
Buchhändler-Vereinigung, 1982. 4th ed. 104p. bibliog.

Prepared by the Foreign Trade Committee of the German Publishers and
Booksellers Association, Grosser Hirschgraben 17-21, Postfach 2404, D-6000
Frankfurt am Main, this booklet provides information on obtaining German
books and periodicals; on the organization of the German book trade; on
exhibitions (including the annual Frankfurt Book Fair); on German book and
periodical exports; on translation and publication rights; and on sources for more
detailed information. It includes a descriptive bibliography of standard references,
bibliographies, and trade publications; and it lists export wholesalers, retailers,
and publishers, indicating their areas of specialization. For a 9,123-page listing of
German books in print, see the German Publishers and Booksellers Association's
annual *Verzeichnis lieferbarer Bücher [VLB] 86/87 – German Books in Print*, 16th
ed., 5 vols. (Munich: K. G. Saur for the Verlag der Buchhändler-Vereinigung,
1986), compiled from a database containing 429,784 titles available from 6,598
publishers. In one single alphabetical sequence, full entries with bibliographical
data are carried under authors' names; titles and key-words are listed, but
generally only with cross-references to the appropriate full entries. The
VLB – German Books in Print series also includes, annually, an index to German
books listed in numerical sequence by ISBN number, as well as a multi-volume,
cross-referenced guide that lists German books in print by subject. Weekly and
cumulative semiannual listings of new German bibliography, published by the
German Booksellers Association, are cited in the final entry (*Deutsche
Bibliographie*) of the section on bibliography. The useful bimonthly, *Das
Deutsche Buch: Auswahl wichtiger Neuerscheinungen* ['The German Book:
Selection of Important New Publications'], issued in conjunction with *Deutsche
Bibliographie*, was discontinued in 1984, but the *Harrassowitz Book Digest*, cited
in the next entry, continues to provide convenient, competent coverage.

492 **Harrassowitz book digest: a selective list of recent European
publications.**
Otto Harrassowitz. Wiesbaden: Harrassowitz, since the early
1950s.

Issued for over thirty years by the major Wiesbaden library agency and publishing
house, the *Harrassowitz Book Digest* is available on request from Otto
Harrassowitz Booksellers & Subscription Agents, POB 2929, D-6200 Wiesbaden,
West Germany. Published since 1983 in a fully computerized databased format
(giving Library of Congress class, ISBN, and price, in addition to other
information), the *HBD* provides extensive coverage of recent European
publications, particularly in the German-language area: the Federal Republic, the
German Democratic Republic, Austria, and Switzerland. (It also lists English-
language titles published in continental European countries.) To facilitate its use
in the various library and academic departments to which it is primarily
addressed, the *HBD* is published in nine different subject area sections (in each of
which, depending on the volume of publishing in a given area, several catalogues
may be issued annually): Philosophy and Theology; Languages and Literatures;
Arts and Archeology; Music and Dance; History; Economics, Political Science,

214

The Mass Media and the Book Trade. The book trade

and Law; Education, Psychology, and Sociology; Sciences and Technology; and Life and Health Sciences. Musical scores are not announced in the *HBD* Music-Dance section, but in the *European Music Catalogue*. The *EMC*, which is usually issued nine times yearly, is indexed annually, and is available on request, presents a listing of the latest European musical scores, excluding popular music.

Archives, Libraries, and Museums

493 **Archives and libraries in Germany.**
Erwin K. Welsch. Pittsburgh, Pa.: Council for European Studies, 1975. 275p. bibliog.

A comprehensive guide, addressed to U.S. scholars. See also the section on archives and libraries in the Federal Republic (pp. 41-52) in Christoph M. Kimmich's guide to research and research materials listed under History, and Holger H. Herwig, 'An Introduction to Military Archives in West Germany,' in *Military Affairs*, vol. 36 (December 1972), pp. 121-24.

494 **Libraries in the Federal Republic of Germany.**
Gisela von Busse, Horst Ernestus, and Engelbert Plassmann. Translated by John S. Andrews. Wiesbaden: Otto Harrassowitz, 1983. 2nd, rev. & enl. ed. 288p. map.

A translation of *Das Bibliothekswesen der Bundesrepublik Deutschland* (Wiesbaden: Otto Harrassowitz, 1983), this volume provides a current overview of the West German library network and profession in historical context.

495 **The records of German history in German and certain other record offices with short notes on libraries and other collections/Die Archivalien zur deutschen Geschichte in deutschen und einigen anderen Archiven mit kurzen Bemerkungen über Bibliotheken und andere Sammlungen.**
Carl Haase. Boppard am Rhein: Harald Boldt Verlag, 1975. 194p.

A concise guide to German archives and libraries, primarily in the Federal Republic of Germany and the German Democratic Republic. The text is in German, but there is a glossary with the English translation of technical terms.

496 **Der deutsche Museumsführer in Farbe. Museen und Sammlungen
in der Bundesrepublik Deutschland und West-Berlin.** (The German
museum guide in colour: museums and collections in the Federal
Republic of Germany and West Berlin.)
Edited by Klemens Mörmann. Frankfurt am Main: Wolfgang
Krüger, 1983. 2nd, rev. & enl. ed. 1,066p. bibliog.

Extensive, profusely illustrated directory to West German museums and art
collections, arranged in alphabetical order by location, with information on
addresses and telephone numbers, hours and admission fees, availability of
catalogues and tours, scope and focus of collections, etc., and with two indexes.
The bibliography includes listings of regional museum guides for Baden-
Württemberg, Bavaria, Hesse, Lower Saxony and Bremen, North Rhein-
Westphalia, the Rheinland, and Schleswig-Holstein. Information on museums will
also be found in tourist guides cited in the geography section, particularly the
volume on West Germany and Berlin in the Michelin green series.

497 **Museums, sites, and collections of Germanic culture in North
America: an annotated directory of German immigrant culture in
the United States and Canada.**
Compiled by Margaret Hobbie. Westport, Conn., and London,
England: Greenwood Press, 1980. 155p. bibliog.

The first chapter of this directory consists of descriptive entries on repositories of
German-American and German-Canadian material culture (books, graphics,
artifacts, etc.), compiled on the basis of standard directories and of responses to
questionnaires mailed to some 280 potential repositories. The entries indicate the
character and scope of the collections, whether or to what extent they are
catalogued, when they may be viewed, and whether they are available for loan.
The second chapter describes sites of German-American significance listed in the
National Register of Historic Places (Washington, D.C.: U.S. Department of the
Interior, 1976). The short third chapter is a selected list of European museums
and archives. The volume concludes with a bibliography and two indexes.

Directories and Encyclopaedias

498   **Wer ist Wer? Das deutsche Who's Who. Bundesrepublik**
      Deutschland und West-Berlin. (Who Is Who? The German 'Who's
      Who': The Federal Republic of Germany and West Berlin.)
      Established by Walter Habel.   25th, rev. ed. Lübeck: Verlag
      Schmidt-Römhild, 1986. 1,566p.

Current (1986/87) edition of the leading West German biographical directory,
with over 40,000 entries, some with photos; a directory of the governments of the
Federal Republic, the constituent states, and West Berlin; and glossaries in
German, English, and French of frequent abbreviations.

499   **Lexikon der deutschen Geschichte. Personen, Ereignisse,**
      Institutionen von der Zeitwende bis zum Ausgang des 2.
      Weltkrieges. (Encyclopaedia of German history: persons, events,
      institutions from the first century to the conclusion of the Second
      World War.)
      Edited by Gerhard Taddey with collaboration of historians and
      archivists.   Stuttgart: Alfred Kröner Verlag, 1977. 1,352p.

A one-volume (two-column format) encyclopaedia of German history from the
Germanic migrations to 1945, with concise articles and bibliographical references
(Arminius has half a column and one reference, Hitler three columns and
fourteen references). Louis L. Snyder's 410-page *Encyclopedia of the Third Reich*
(N.Y.: McGraw-Hill, 1976) has topical and biographical articles of varying length,
many of them illustrated. The origins and aftermath of the National Socialist
régime are dealt with selectively. 'The Nuremberg Trial,' for example, covers the
International Military Tribunal, but not the subsequent series of war crimes trials
conducted at Nuremberg. The extensive bibliography cites books and periodical

218

literature. *Who's Who in Nazi Germany* (London: Weidenfeld and Nicolson, 1982), by Robert Wistrich, a former editor of the *Bulletin* of the Wiener Library in London, is a 359-page volume with concise biographical articles on over 300 individuals prominent or significant during the Hitler régime.

500 **Verzeichnis deutscher Institutionen.** (Directory of German Institutions.)
Baden-Baden: Nomos Verlagsgesellschaft, 1979. 3 vols.
(Schriftenreihe zum Handbuch für Internationale Zusammenarbeit, vols. 1-3).

Three-volume set of directories, uniform in format, providing coded data on German institutions engaged in international activities.

Vol. 1: *Deutsche Partner der Entwicklungsländer* ['German Partners of Developing Countries'], sel. & ed. by Margot Adameck and Ruth Schlette, 248 pp., gives a full profile of 242 institutions and five pages of addresses of consulting firms, plus a four-page bibliography of relevant periodicals published in the Federal Republic;

Vol. 2: *Deutsche Partner in der internationalen wissenschaftlichen Zusammenarbeit* ['German Partners in International Scientific and Scholarly Collaboration'], published under the auspices of the Deutscher Akademischer Austauschdienst (DAAD) [German Academic Exchange Service], sel. & ed. by Manfred Stassen and Hans Wilhelm, 158 pp., lists some 130 institutions and organizations; and

Vol. 3: *Deutsche Partner im internationalen Kulturaustausch* ['German Partners in International Cultural Exchange'], published under the auspices of the Institut für Auslandsbeziehungen (IfA) [Institute for Foreign Relations], sel. & ed. by Gertrud Kuhn and Hans Wilhelm, 168p., lists some 200 institutions (including, on pp. 80-85, the Goethe Institute, headquartered in Munich, with addresses and telephone numbers around the world).

See also the listing of major institutions and organizations in the Federal Republic in *What's What in Germany 84*, cited in the first section of this bibliography.

501 **Der grosse Brockhaus.** (The large Brockhaus.)
Wiesbaden: F. A. Brockhaus, 1977-81. 18th rev. ed. 12 vols.

Standard, comprehensive encyclopaedia, with maps, illustrations, and bibliographical references, with some 200,000 entries. Also available, for easier handling, in a 26-vol. edition, the last two volumes of which are a supplement, updating it to 1983. There is also a paperback version with over 130,000 entries, the *dtv-Brockhaus-Lexikon* ['dtv-Brockhaus-Encyclopaedia'], 20 vols. (Munich: Deutscher Taschenbuch Verlag, 1982). See also *Meyers Grosses Universallexikon* ['Meyer's Large Universal Encyclopaedia'], 15 vols. (Mannheim: Bibliographisches Institut, 1981-86), a comprehensive encyclopaedia comparable in scope and quality to the large Brockhaus; and the corresponding paperback version, with some 150,000 entries, *Meyers Grosses Taschenlexikon* ['Meyer's Large Pocket Encyclopaedia'] 24 vols. (Mannheim: Bibliographisches Institut, 1983).

Bibliographies

502 **The Federal Republic of Germany: a selected bibliography of English-language publications.**
Arnold H. Price.   Washington, D.C.: U.S. Government Printing Office for the Library of Congress, 1978. 2nd ed. 116p.
An indexed bibliography of 1,325 titles, articles as well as books, by the Central European Area Specialist of the Library of Congress, who concludes the volume with a chapter on Berlin, on which he listed basic material in German in a supplement to an earlier guide, *East Germany: A Selected Bibliography* (Washington, D.C.: U.S. Government Printing Office for the Library of Congress, 1967). As in *The Federal Republic of Germany: A Selected Bibliography of English-Language Publications with Emphasis on the Social Sciences* (Washington, D.C.: U.S. Government Printing Office for the Library of Congress, 1972) – in which Dr. Price included some earlier titles not cited in the 1978 edition – Library of Congress call numbers and National Union Catalog location symbols are provided.

503 **The German-speaking countries of Europe: a selective bibliography.**
Margrit B. Krewson.   Washington, D.C.: Library of Congress, 1985. 121p.
This recent volume has 639 entries on Austria, the Federal Republic of Germany, the German Democratic Republic, Liechtenstein, and Switzerland, but fewer titles, because some works are listed in more than one place (rather than being cross-referenced). It provides select coverage, largely from the 1980s, of publications in German and English, in seven subject areas: bibliographies and reference works; description and travel; economy; intellectual and cultural life; politics and government; religion; and society. Most references to works on the period before 1949 are included among the 312 entries on the Federal Republic of

220

Germany. When it comes to the postwar period, some titles dealing with the two German states, such as the Merritts' bibliography cited below, are listed only among the 91 entries on the German Democratic Republic. The volume includes a name index.

504 A bibliography of German studies, 1945-1971: Germany under Allied Occupation; Federal Republic of Germany; German Democratic Republic.

Gisela Hersch. Bloomington and London: Indiana University Press: 1972. 603p. (A publication of the Institute of German Studies, Indiana University).

The thousands of titles in this indexed but not annotated compendium, reflecting selected holdings at Indiana University, are grouped in seven categories: Germany under occupation, the German Question and Berlin, the Federal Republic of Germany, the German Democratic Republic, biographical material on contemporary Germans, government publications, and German newspapers and periodicals. Works in English in each category are listed under 'West European and American Publications.'

505 After Hitler: Germany, 1945-1963.

Helen Kehr. Introduction by Ilse R. Wolff. London: Vallentine, Mitchell for the Wiener Library, 1963. 261p. (The Wiener Library Catalogue Series, no. 4).

A systematic, indexed bibliography of over 2,700 entries, based on holdings of the Wiener Library, dealing with wartime plans for Germany; the occupation; Berlin; expellees and refugees and their integration; the new Germany (including a section on Hitler's Third Reich in retrospect); the Federal Republic of Germany; the German Democratic Republic; Germany between East and West; and Jews in post-war Germany. The listings, largely in German or English, include many items not (or not widely) available in trade, such as government brochures, mimeographed reports, and the like.

506 Politics, economics, and society in the two Germanies, 1945-75: a bibliography of English-language works.

Anna J. Merritt and Richard L. Merritt. Urbana, Chicago, and London: University of Illinois Press, 1978. 268p.

A facsimile of an unannotated computer printout of articles and books. An elaborate table of contents clearly describes the topically divided listing of 8,548 sequentially numbered items, followed by an alphabetical index of the 5,116 authors, with reference to their individual works by number.

Bibliographies

507 **Materialien zur Landeskunde: Basisbibliographie.** (Materials on [German] area studies: basic bibliography.)
Edited by Robert Picht, Barbara Picht, et al. Bonn: Deutscher Akademischer Austauschdienst (German Academic Exchange Service), 1979. 156p.

This two-part compilation (with a single author index) is a select bibliography of works in German (pp. 9-110) and in English (pp. 111-150) on the bibliography, history, politics, economy, society, and culture of contemporary Germany, particularly the Federal Republic. The first part, with one title per page, provides a critical evaluation of each German work, its parameters, purpose, and potential applicability, as well as references, in many cases, to related articles and books. The judicious but unannotated English listings include several useful works not published commercially, but issued by agencies and institutes such as the German Academic Exchange Service, D-5300 Bonn 2, Kennedyallee 50.

508 **Bibliographie Bundesrepublik Deutschland.**
Dietrich Thränhardt. Göttingen: Vandenhoeck & Ruprecht, 1980. 178p. (Arbeitsbücher zur modernen Geschichte, Band 9).

Concentrating on German publications, this unannotated, unindexed bibliography carries works alphabetized by author under forty-three topical headings, e.g., 'Justiz,' 'SPD,' and 'Frauen.'

509 **Bibliographie zur Politik in Theorie und Praxis.** (Bibliography on politics in theory and practice.)
Revised edition by Ulrich von Alemann et al. Düsseldorf: Droste Verlag, 1976. 576p. (Bonner Schriften zur Politik und Zeitgeschichte, 13).

The 7,901 unannotated entries of this revised and expanded edition of a standard bibliography on political science and contemporary history, include articles and books in English, as well as German and other languages, on the Federal Republic.

510 **Deutsche Bibliothek im Ausland: Bibliographie.** (German Library abroad: bibliography.)
Foreword by Carl Peter Baudisch. Bonn: Inter Nationes, 1971. 2 vols.

A 523-page standard list recommended for German cultural centres abroad. In contrast to the highly selective, descriptive evaluations of some eighty German titles in Picht's *Materialien zur Landeskunde: Basisbibliographie*, cited above, this is a carefully structured model catalogue for a collection of several thousand volumes (almost exclusively in German). Compiled at Inter Nationes, a government-supported, autonomous cultural exchange centre in Bonn (D-5300 Bonn 2, Kennedyallee 91-103), the list includes selected current and classical German fiction as well as nonfiction titles (with prices) insofar as commercially available in the original edition or as reprints in mid-1971.

511 **Schrifttum über Deutschland 1918-1963. Ausgewählte Bibliographie zur Politik und Zeitgeschichte.** (Writings on Germany 1918-1963: select bibliography on politics and contemporary history.) Foreword by Helmut Arntz. Prepared by the Forschungsinstitut der Deutschen Gesellschaft für Auswärtige Politik [Research Institute of the German Society for Foreign Policy] for Inter Nationes Bonn. Wiesbaden: Franz Steiner Verlag for Inter Nationes, 1964. 2nd, exp. ed. 292p.

A select bibliography of works on Germany from 1918 to 1963 published since the Second World War and, with some exceptions, commercially available (with list prices cited). The titles in Part I (to p. 185), published in occupied West Germany or the Federal Republic, are in German; many in Part II, published abroad, are in English. The entries, which include chapter titles (or a corresponding indication of contents) are not annotated, but critical reviews of several works are cited at length in backnotes. There is an index of names. Publications on Germany issued by the government of the Federal Republic, or published with its sponsorship (and not normally available in trade) are listed in a 198-page companion volume, *Dokumentationen über Deutschland. Auswahl amtlicher und von amtlicher Seite geförderter Publikationen* ['Documentation on Germany: A Selection of Official and Officially-Supported Publications'], foreword by Helmut Arntz, 2nd rev. ed. (Bonn: Inter Nationes, 1964); the first part (to p. 90) includes publications in German, the second part publications in foreign languages (whereby 'Englisch' and 'US-Englisch' are listed separately).

512 **German military history, 1648-1982: a critical bibliography.** Dennis E. Showalter. New York & London: Garland, 1984. 331p. (Military History Bibliographies, vol. 3; Garland Reference Library of Social Science, vol. 113).

An extensive listing, organized by periods, of books and articles in German, English, and French, with an author index. The individual entries are unannotated, but many of the works are discussed in critical bibliographical essays at the beginning of each segment.

513 **German military aviation: a guide to the literature.** Edward L. Homze. New York & London: Garland, 1984. 234p. (Military History Bibliographies, vol. 2; Garland Reference Library of Social Science, vol. 193).

Like the foregoing bibliography in the same series, an extensive listing of pertinent works with bibliographical essays on the major periods (early flight; World War I; the interwar years; World War II; and the postwar years).

Bibliographies

514 **German naval history: a guide to the literature.**
Keith W. Bird. New York & London: Garland, 1985. 1,121p.
(Military History Bibliographies, vol. 7; Garland Reference
Library of Social Science, vol. 215).

Published in the same series as the two bibliographies listed above, this
substantially longer volume is organized differently; the 4,871 titles on German
naval (and maritime) history are in a single list, alphabetized by author, in the last
third of the volume, following Bird's extensive historiographical treatment of
German naval history in the context of German history and historiography.

515 **German history and civilization, 1806–1914: a bibliography of**
scholarly periodical literature.
John C. Fout. Metuchen, N.J.: Scarecrow, 1974. 342p.

Topically arranged listing of 5,701 articles in English, German, and French from
some 150 journals, published from the 1840s to the early 1970s. Detailed table of
contents and author/editor index.

516 **The Weimar Republic: a historical bibliography.**
Santa Barbara, Calif., and Oxford, England: ABC-Clio
Information Services, 1984. 285p. (ABC-Clio Research Guides,
no. 9).

An annotated bibliography, with author and subject indices, of journal articles
published during the decade 1973-1982, from the ABC-Clio Information Services
database. The 1,035 entries are divided into nine topical chapters: the Weimar
Republic in historical context; the beginnings of the Republic; government,
politics, and the economy; Weimar culture and society; the Jews of Weimar;
Christianity in transition; the growth of German communism; the road to Nazi
hegemony; and the end of the Republic.

517 **From Weimar to Hitler Germany, 1918-1933.**
Edited by Ilse R. Wolff. London: Vallentine, Mitchell & Co. for
the Wiener Library, 1964. 2nd, rev. & enl. ed. 269p. (The Wiener
Library Catalogue Series, no. 2).

The expanded edition in the second of a series of systematically organized and
indexed shelflists, this volume gives the titles of some 3,000 individual works, plus
holdings of newspapers and periodicals.

518 **The Third Reich, 1933-1939: a historical bibliography.**
Santa Barbara, Calif., and Oxford, England: ABC-Clio
Information Services, 1984. 239p. (ABC-Clio Research Guides,
no. 10).

An annotated bibliography, with author and subject indices, of 932 journal articles published during the decade 1973-1982, from the ABC-Clio Information Services database. The entries are divided into seven chapters: Nazi Germany in historical context; domestic policies and politics; Nazi foreign policy; culture and society in Hitler's Germany; the crushing of German Jewry; Christianity in crisis; and the Left under siege.

519 **Persecution and resistance under the Nazis.**
Edited by Ilse R. Wolff. London: Vallentine, Mitchell & Co. for
the Wiener Library, 1960. 2nd rev. & enl. ed. 208p. (Wiener
Library Catalogue Series, no. 1).

The first volume of the systematically organized and indexed listing of holdings at the library in London: 1,943 enumerated entries, plus appendices covering holdings of periodicals of Germans in exile and of illegal pamphlets and periodicals.

520 **The Third Reich at war: a historical bibliography.**
Santa Barbara, Calif., and Oxford, England: ABC-Clio
Information Services, 1984. 270p. (ABC-Clio Research Guides,
no. 11).

An annotated bibliography, with author and subject indices, of journal articles published during the decade 1973-1982, from the ABC-Clio Information Services database. The 1,061 entries are divided into seven topical chapters: wartime Germany; wartime trade and diplomacy; invasion and occupation of Poland; war with Western Europe; war in East and Southeast Europe; war with Russia; and the Holocaust.

521 **Der Deutsche Widerstand im Spiegel von Fachliteratur und
Publizistik seit 1945: Bericht und Bibliographie.** (The German
resistance as reflected in professional literature and [other]
publications since 1945.)
Regine Büchel. Foreword by Jürgen Rohwer. Munich: Bernard
& Graefe, 1975. 215p. (Schriften der Bibliothek für Zeitgeschichte,
Heft 15).

A heavily annotated 68-page essay is followed by an extensive, unannotated bibliography on German opposition against Hitler's Third Reich in which works are listed according to a systematic outline. There is no author index. Most titles are in German, but there are also many in English, as well as a number in French, Russian, and other languages.

522 **Guide to Jewish history under Nazi impact.**
Jacob Robinson and Philip Friedman. Forewords by Benzion
Dinur and Salo W. Baron. New York: Marstin Press for Yad
Washem Martyrs' and Heroes' Memorial Authority, Jerusalem,
and YIVO Institute for Jewish Research, New York, 1960. 425p.
(Joint Documentary Projects for Yad Washem and YIVO:
Bibliographical Series, no. 1).

Divided into four parts dealing with (1) the Jewish catastrophe in historical
perspective, (2) reference tools, (3) research (institutions, methods, and
techniques), and (4) documentation, this encyclopaedia-format, double-columned
volume has 3,841 entries in twenty-four languages, with annotations in English
(including, in many cases, citations of critical reviews). An extensively subdivided
table of contents shows the sequence of the enumerated, cross-referenced entries.
These are indexed, in up to six separate indices, by name, corporate author, title,
list of defendants in war crimes trials, places, and subjects (with entries in
Hebrew, Russian, and Greek separately alphabetized at the end of each index).

523 **The Holocaust: the Nuremberg evidence. Part one:**
documents – digest, index, and chronological tables.
Jacob Robinson and Henry Sachs. Jerusalem: Alpha Press,
Jerusalem, for Yad Vashem Martyrs' and Heroes' Memorial
Authority, Jerusalem, and YIVO Institute for Jewish Research,
New York, 1976. 370p. (Joint Documentary Projects of Yad
Vashem and YIVO).

A companion volume to the *Guide to Jewish History under Nazi Impact* cited
above, this is a bibliographical guide to the extensive documentation published in
book form after the Nuremberg war crimes trials, as well as to the documents that
were duplicated and ultimately deposited in various archives, but not included in
the published record. The volume has three parts: a digest that indicates the
subject and location of each of over 3,000 enumerated documents; a cross-
referenced index by name, place, and subject; and a chronology giving the date of
origin of each document.

524 **Bibliographie zur Deutschlandpolitik 1941-1974.** (Bibliography on
German policy and politics 1941-1974.)
Edited by Albrecht Tyrell. Frankfurt am Main: Alfred Metzner
Verlag for the Ministry of Intra-German Affairs, 1975. 248p.
(Dokumente zur Deutschlandpolitik, Beihefte, Band 1).

A sequentially enumerated listing of some 3,220 publications on *Deutschlandpolitik*, meaning, as used here, both policy and politics pertaining to Germany.
An initial general section (through entry 493a), with bibliographies, documentation, general literature on the German Question, etc., is followed by Part II, with
coverage of the period 1941-49 (through entry 1,137) and Part III on Germany
from 1949 to December 1974. There is an alphabetical index of authors. The

listings (in several languages, predominantly German) include journal articles as well as books. To facilitate use of the volume, fundamentally important publications are emphasized with heavy type and publications that lend themselves to ready reference are identified by asterisks.

525 **Bibliographie zur Deutschlandpolitik 1975-1982.** (Bibliography on German policy and politics 1975-1982.)
Edited by Karsten Schröder. Frankfurt am Main: Alfred Metzner Verlag for the Ministry of Intra-German Affairs, 1983. 219p.
(Dokumente zur Deutschlandpolitik, Beihefte, Band 6).

Published in the same series as the similarly structured volume described in the foregoing entry, this bibliography, with some 3,030 entries, provides updated coverage of the period 1941-1974 and new coverage from 1975 through 1982 (it is *not* focussed solely on the period 1975-1982).

526 **Bibliography of German law in English and German: a selection.**
Edited by the German Association of Comparative Law.
Introduction to German law by Fritz Baur. Foreword by Ernst von Caemmerer. Translated by Courtland H. Peterson. Karlsruhe: Verlag C. F. Müller, 1964. 584p.

This selective bibliography of German law was prepared, with support from the Federal Ministries of Justice and of Scientific Research and the Thyssen Foundation, for the use of the foreign reader. With a few compelling exceptions, its listings are restricted to twentieth-century books and periodicals, thus excluding articles in periodicals, dedicatory works (*Festschriften*), etc. The volume includes a long introductory essay on German law, with the English translation and the German original on facing pages (pp. 2-161), and a detailed outline-form table of contents (through p. XLI), also with English and German on facing pages, and an extensive index.

527 **Die politischen Parteien in Deutschland nach 1945: ein bibliographisch-systematischer Versuch.** (The political parties in Germany after 1945: a bibliographical-systematical attempt.)
Hans-Gerd Schumann. Foreword by Jürgen Rohwer. Frankfurt am Main: Bernard & Graefe, 1967. 223p. (Schriften der Bibliothek für Zeitgeschichte, Heft 6).

This bibliography, the use of which is facilitated by an index of authors and editors, provides systematically organized coverage of publications (largely but not exclusively German) on the political parties and their role in postwar Germany, East as well as West, with consideration of federal and state elections through 1965, the parties' function in representative democracy at the regional and national level, and their interaction with interest groups.

528 **Bibliographie zur Sozialen Marktwirtschaft. Die Wirtschafts- und Gesellschaftsordnung der Bundesrepublik Deutschland 1945/49-1981.** (Bibliography on the social market economy: the economic and social order of the Federal Republic of Germany 1945/49-1981.)
Karl-Peter Dapper and Gerhard Hahn. Edited by the Ludwig-Erhard-Stiftung e.V., Bonn. Baden-Baden: Nomos Verlagsgesellschaft, 1983. 269p.

A systematically organized, unannotated bibliography on the political economy and social philosophy of postwar West Germany. The 4,598 enumerated listings, mostly in German, include books and articles in journals, yearbooks, and collections such as *Festschriften*, as well as relevant publications (often not available in the book trade) of political, social and economic organizations and interest groups, foundations, and major corporations. There is a detailed subject index and a separate index of names in which references to persons who are the subject of listed works are italicized, but references to authors are not.

529 **Die Berliner Mauer: Vorgeschichte, Bau, Folgen, Literaturbericht und Bibliographie zum 20. Jahrestag des 13. August 1961.** (The Berlin Wall: its historical background, construction, and consequences – a report on the literature and bibliography on the twentieth anniversary of 13 August 1961.)
Michael Haupt. Foreword by Jürgen Rohwer. Introductory note by Willy Brandt. Munich: Bernard & Graefe, 1981. 230p. map on endpapers. (Schriften der Bibliothek für Zeitgeschichte, Band 21).

Issued on the twentieth anniversary of the construction of the Berlin Wall, this volume, which has an index of authors, provides extensive coverage of monographic and periodical literature on Berlin from 1945 to 1961, of the crisis that culminated with construction of the wall, and of subsequent developments, including the watershed early in the seventies, the Four-Power Agreement on Berlin – though entries on this agreement and its implications are not listed under a separate heading, but simply included among 'developments after construction of the wall.'

530 **Bibliography of German culture in America to 1940.**
Henry A. Pochmann, compiler. Arthur R. Schultz, editor. Millwood, N.Y.: Kraus International Publications, 1982. Revised and corrected, with addenda, errata, and expanded index. 775p.

The 1953 edition of this standard bibliography of books, articles, pamphlets, and notes on manuscript sources and archives dating from the late seventeenth century to 1940 had about 13,400 entries. In the expanded edition, some 4,900 new items are separately printed as 'Addenda,' but included in the single, comprehensive index at the end of the volume, in which authors, compilers, editors, translators, principal subjects or topics, and place names (but not book or publication titles) are listed in a single alphabet. The balance and mix of the coverage of the enlarged edition is essentially the same as that of the original compilation: largely primary documentation (mostly in German), travel and descriptions, memoirs, letters, records and documents of clubs and organizations, biography, and local history, plus a relatively small number of secondary studies and monographs. The 'Addenda' include considerable additional material on emigration from Germany, on the German-American experience of World War I, and extended listings of family histories and genealogies. For publications during the four decades since 1940, see the continuation of Pochmann's bibliography, compiled by the editor of its revised edition, Arthur R. Schultz, *German-American Relations and German Culture in America: A Subject Bibliography, 1941-1980*, 2 vols. (Millwood, N.Y.: Kraus International, 1984), with well over 20,000 entries (some annotated) listing books, monographs, articles, and dissertations, and reviews thereof, as well as 'appropriate manuscript collections and various unpublished works that discuss some aspect of German-American culture and relations.'

531 **German-American history and life: a guide to information sources.**
Michael Keresztesi and Gary R. Cocozzoli. Detroit: Gale Research Co., 1980. 372p. (Ethnic Studies Information Guide Series, vol. 4).

An annotated inventory of English-language materials with over 1,300 entries, beginning with a twenty-page glossary defining perhaps unfamiliar names and terms occurring in the book titles and annotations. In addition to the topically organized bibliography comprising the bulk of the volume (entries 123-929), there are separate sections on scholarly series and on journals and periodicals, and a directory of repositories of German-American archival and literary resources. Separate author, title, and subject indexes. See also Kathleen Neils Conzen, 'The Writing of German-American History,' in *The Immigration History Newsletter*, vol. XII, no. 2 (Nov. 1980), pp. 1-14, published by the Immigration History Society (ed., Carlton C. Qualey, Minnesota Historical Society, 690 Cedar St., St. Paul, Minn. 55101), an extensive, annotated historiographical essay, citing German and English book and periodical literature, including bibliographies and dissertations, on German migration to America and on German-Americans, by the author of 'Germans' in the *Harvard Encyclopedia of American Ethnic Groups*, ed. by Stephan Thernstrom (Cambridge, Mass.: Harvard Univ. Press, 1980), p. 405-425.

532 **Research possibilities in the German-American field.**
Heinz Kloss. Edited with introduction and bibliography by La Vern J. Rippley. Hamburg: Helmut Buske Verlag, 1980. 242p. bibliog.

Originally submitted in 1937 to the Carl Schurz Memorial Foundation in Philadelphia under the title 'Report on the Possibilities for Research Work of an American-German Institute,' this is a detailed report of a survey made in 1936-37 of the status of research in German-American cultural history throughout the United States, describing printed records, archives, and museum collections on 'the German-American element,' and the German-American contribution to the building of America. There are extensive bibliographical references throughout the report, to which the editor has appended a select bibliography of German-Americana published, with some exceptions, since 1937.

Bibliographies

533 **Theses on Germany accepted for higher degrees by the universities of Great Britain and Ireland, 1900-1975: a bibliography.**
Gernot U. Gabel & Gisela R. Gabel. Hamburg: Edition Gemini, 1979. 89p.
A list of 930 theses subdivided by area, with author and subject indices.

534 **Deutsche Bibliographie. Halbjahres-Verzeichnis Juli-Dezember 1985.** (German bibliography: semiannual catalogue, July-December 1985.)
Deutsche Bibliothek. Frankfurt am Main: Buchhändler-Vereinigung, 1986. 4 vols.
A two-part catalogue of German publications of the second half of 1985, issued in four volumes by the German Booksellers Association in a series compiled by the Deutsche Bibliothek in Frankfurt am Main (the German national library) since 1947. The first part, in two volumes, is an alphabetical listing of titles; the second part, also two volumes, is a catch-word and subject index. It is based on the weekly listings of German-language publications in Germany and abroad, announced by the German Library in two of the weekly catalogues in the *Deutsche Bibliographie* ['German Bibliography'] serial series, *Reihe A (Erscheinungen des Verlagsbuchhandels)* ['Series A (Publications Available in the Book Trade)'] and *Reihe B (Erscheinungen ausserhalb des Verlagsbuchhandels* ['Series B (Publications Unavailable through the Book Trade)']. Included also in the German Library's *Deutsche Bibliographie* publication series: *Das Deutsche Buch. Auswahl wichtiger Neuerscheinungen* ['The German Book: Selection of Important New Publications'], an annotated bimonthly bibliography (to 1984 only, when it was discontinued); a quarterly cartographic catalogue, *Reihe C (Karten)* ['Series C (Maps)']; a weekly listing of forthcoming books, *Neuerscheinungen-Sofortdienst (CIP)* ['New Publications – Quick Service (CIP [Cataloguing in Publication])']; and a *Fünfjahres-Verzeichnis* ['Five-Year Catalogue'] cumulatively listing all publications, including periodicals and maps. For earlier publications, see Reinhard Oberschelp, ed., *Gesamtverzeichnis des deutschsprachigen Schrifttums 1911-1965* ['Complete Bibliography of German-Language Publications 1911-1965'], microform ed., 77,000 pp. on 400 fiches (Munich: K. G. Saur, 1984). See also the annual *Verzeichnis lieferbarer Bücher – German Books in Print*, cited above under the listings on the German mass media and the book trade.

Index

The index lists, in alphabetical sequence, authors (personal and corporate), titles, and subjects. Index entries refer both to the principal citations and to further works mentioned in the annotations. Titles of books and articles are italicized. The numbers refer to entry rather than page numbers.

233

234

235

240

development of new technologies
309, 312
seas 312
smog alarm 310
statistics (environment) 306, 308
waste disposal 309, 312
waterways 312
Conservatism
emergence (ca. 1750-1818) 96
Constance
higher education 330
Constitution 1, 126, 219-230
1871 230
1919 230
Baden-Württemberg 225
Basic Law of the Federal Republic
of Germany 122, 186, 216, 219
Bavaria 225
Berlin 225
Bremen 225
documents 212, 230
drafting of the Basic Law of the
Federal Republic (1948-49) 122, 126
freedom of expression 478
freedom of the press 239
Hamburg 225
Hesse 225
Lower Saxony 225
North Rhine-Westphalia 225
position of churches 228
Rhineland-Palatinate 225
Saarland 225
Schleswig-Holstein 225
text of Basic Law (English
translation) 219
Constitutional Court 222-224
decision on the Basic Treaty 261-262
interpretation of the Basic Law 220
landmark cases 222
Constitutional history *see* History
*A Constitutional History of Germany in
the Nineteenth and Twentieth
Centuries* 230
*Constitutionalism in Germany and the
Federal Constitutional Court* 222
*Contemporary Germany: Politics and
Culture* 8
*The Contemporary Novel in German:
A Symposium* 354
Continuing education *see* Education
(continuing)
Control Council (military occupation
1945-54)

laws and directives 119
Convents 50
Conversion tables
British to metric measures 20
Conway, John 102
Conway, William Martin 397
Conzen, Kathleen Neil 531
Cook, Olive 415
The Cooking of Germany 460
Cooney, James A. 267
Cooper, Anna Rose 390
Cooperative movement
agriculture 287
Copplestone, Trewin 388
Corbet, G. B. 74
Corporation law *see* Law
*The Correspondence between Schiller
and Goethe* 359
Corrigan, Timothy 455
The Cost of Discipleship 199
Costumes
regional (photographs) 57
Countess Mitzi or *The Family
Reunion* (play) 374
A Country Doctor (novella) 377
Court of Justice of the European
Communities 229
Courths-Mahler, Hedwig 347
Courts 224, 242
law on organization 235
United States Court for Berlin
250
Cow parsnip (hogweed) 67
Cowan, Marianne 324
Crafts and trades
Bauhaus 390
bibliography 305
map 31
statistics 305
Craig, Gordon A. 98, 267
Crampton, Patricia 393, 424
Cranach: A Family of Master Painters
397
Cranach, Lucas 397
Crane, Ralph 460
Credit 296
policy of the European Community
281
rural cooperative credit movement
287
Creighton, Basil 438
*The Crime and Punishment of I. G.
Farben* 282

253

261

263

268

269

Garland, Henry 332
Garland, Mary 332
Garten, H. F. 378
Gassner, John 378
Gastarbeiter [guest workers] 132, 300
  language and communication 158
  status in Common Market 305
  Turkish workers in Berlin (film) 454
  use of state welfare provisions 301
Gatzke, Hans W. 266
Gawronsky, Dimitry 181
Gay, Peter 109, 145, 201, 349
Gaynor, Frank 317
Gazetteer Federal Republic of
  Germany: Preliminary Edition
  Niedersachsen 26
Gazetteers 25-28
Geck, Elisabeth 488
Gedanken im Kriege 365
Die Gefahr geht von den Menschen aus
  241
Geflügelte Worte 156, 387
Gehlen, Arnold 169
Geiler, Heinz 70
Geimer, Hildegard 314
Geimer, Reinhold 314
Geiringer, I. 432
Geiringer, Karl 432, 437
Geist und Tat 365
Die geistige Situation der Zeit 183
Geld und Banken im 19. und 20.
  Jahrhundert 278
General Economic History 272
General Plan for Education (Abridged
  Version) 326
The Genesis of German Conservatism
  96
Genius: A Memoir of Max Reinhardt
  450
The Genius of the German Theater 338,
  378
Genocide *see* Gypsies, and Holocaust
Gentry, Francis G. 374
Geography 5, 15-58, 213
  Baden-Württemberg 23
  bibliography 5, 15, 17, 20, 504, 510
  climate 20
  coastal regions 20
  cultural 15
  division of Germany 19
  economic 20, 22-23, 31
  economic (map) 31
  evolution of landscape 20

gazetteers 25-28
  historical 20-22
  maps and atlases 15, 20, 29-36
  Moselle River 21
  physical 15, 20, 21-23, 31
  physical (maps) 31, 35
  place names 20, 25-28
  reference books 15, 20
  river systems 20-21
  Ruhr 22
  social 16, 22
  social (map) 31
  statistics 308
  textbooks 15-19, 24
  tourism 476
  tourist guides 37-50
Geology
  map 31
Georg Büchner 360
Georg Büchner and the Birth of the
  Modern Drama 360
Georg Büchner Prize (1960)
  address by Celan, Paul 370
Georg Wilhelm Friedrich Hegel in
  Selbstzeugnissen und
  Bilddokumenten 175
George I, King 431
George, Stefan 375
  poems 375
George Grosz 407
Gerhard, Dietrich 90
Gerlach, Richard 70
German Academic Exchange Service
  327, 507
German Actors of the Eighteenth and
  Nineteenth Centuries: Idealism,
  Romanticism, and Realism 443
German Aesthetic and Literary
  Criticism: Winckelmann, Lessing,
  Hamann, Herder, Schiller, Goethe
  341
German Agricultural Policy,
  1918-1934: The Development of a
  National Philosophy toward
  Agriculture in Postwar Germany
  286
German American Chamber of
  Commerce 296
German-American History and Life: A
  Guide to Information Sources 531
German-American Relations 267
German-American Relations and
  German Culture in America: A

273

277

283

284

History *contd.*
420-421, 439-440, 445-451,
453-454, 478, 489, 504-506, 509,
511, 513, 516-529
Agricola 86
agriculture 286-289
American-German relations
(1776-1976) 266, 271
Anglo-German naval relations
(1894-1944) 20
antiquity 80-81, 84-86, 388
architecture 87, 395, 414-421
Arminius 84, 499
art 80-81, 87, 388-412
artist as social critic (1920s) 392
arts 355, 388-458
Augsburg Confession (1530) 195
aviation
civil 295
military (bibliography) 513
banking 278
baroque churches 417
Basic Law of the Federal Republic
(drafting, 1948-49) 122
Basic Treaty (1972) 256, 260-262
Bauhaus 390
Bavaria 55
Berlin 245, 247-251, 316, 529
Bethmann Hollweg, Theobald von
95
bibliographies 83, 91, 109-110, 172,
189, 259, 272, 282, 485, 492, 499,
504, 532
Bismarck, Otto von 98-100, 133
book trade 489-490
borders of Germany in 1937 30
Caesar 85
car 293
cathedrals 414
Charles V, Emperor 133, 195
children's books (18th-20th
centuries) 351
children's books (under National
Socialism) 351
Christian churches 188
church-state relations 88, 228
church architecture (baroque and
rococo) 417-418
churchbuilding (Protestant, 1831-
1969) 419
cinema 350, 392-394, 448-450
concentration camps 107, 113-114,
370

conservatism 96
constitutional 82-83, 88, 102, 109,
122, 222, 230-232
contemporary (bibliographies) 504-
509, 511, 527-529
Crystal Night Pogrom 114
cultivated plants 289
cybernetic revolution 172
Dada movement 391
development of the modern
economic system, 232, 272
dialects 152, 155, 158
Diocletian 85
diplomatic 82, 110, 116, 120, 252-271
division of Germany 19, 259-265,
524-525
documents 114-116, 118-120, 142,
188-189, 194-195, 212, 214, 230,
246, 248, 261, 268, 323, 351, 523
dogma 196
domestic animals 289
drama 338
economic 82, 102, 120, 133, 232,
258, 269, 272-280, 528
economic (bibliography) 273
education 187, 268, 323, 325-326,
330, 351
education (religious) 187
Educational Exchange Program
between Germany and the United
States of America (1945-54) 268
encyclopaedia 499
English-language reviews of
publications 485-486
Enlightenment 173, 180, 200, 337,
358
Expressionism 338, 348, 398-399,
402, 404-405
family 206
Farben cartel 282
farmers (political) 286
Federal Centre for Political
Education 325
Federal Republic of Germany's
reparations payments to Israel 255
feminist movement 207
fiction (historical) 336, 340, 352, 384
folklore, customs and festivals 456-
457
foreign aid (1956-66) 258
foreign investment (1870-1914) 278
foreign policy (1918-45) 110, 115-
116, 259, 516-520

290

291

Inflation 276
  during the 1920s 278
*An Informal History of the German
  Language with Chapters on Dutch
  and Afrikaans, Frisian and
  Yiddish* 150
Informationen zur Politischen Bildung
  477
Infrastructure investment
  impact of population changes 129
*Der innerdeutsche Handel aus
  internationaler Sicht* 297
*Der innerdeutsche Handel – ein
  Güteraustausch im Spannungsfeld
  von Politik und Wirtschaft* 297
Insect Phylogeny 78
Insects 78
  bibliography 78
  Dipterous 78
  Hemimetabolous 78
  Hymenopterous 78
Inside the Third Reich: Memoirs 105
*Insight and Action: The Life and Work
  of Lion Feuchtwanger* 340
Institut für Angewandte Geodäsie 26
Institut für Auslandsbeziehungen (IfA)
  500
Institut für Landeskunde 31
Institut für Raumforschung 31
Institut für Sozialforschung 185
Institute for the History of German
  Jews 200
Institute of Design (Bauhaus) 390
Institute of Social Research 185
Institutes *see* the names of individual
  institutes
Institutional history *see* History
Institutions
  ecclesiastical (legal status) 228
  educational 327
  engaged in international activities
    500
  engaged in international cultural
    exchange 500
  engaged in international scientific
    and scholarly collaboration 500
  European Community 229
  institutional structure 1, 3
  music-related 441
  reference books 3, 500
  scientific 314
  see also Archives, Libraries, and
    Museums

Insurance funds
  health (Krankenkassen) 211
Insurance, National *see* Welfare
*The Intellectual Migration: Europe and
  America, 1930-1960* 145
*The Intellectual Tradition of Modern
  Germany: A Collection of Writings
  from the Eighteenth to the
  Twentieth Century* 355
Intellectuals
  migration (1930-60) 145
  Weimar Republic 349
Inter Nationes 244, 329, 331
*International Banking in the 19th and
  20th Centuries* 278
International Institute of Social
  Research (Columbia University,
  New York) 185
International Military Tribunal
  Nürnberg Trial 116, 499
*Interpreting the World: Kant's
  Philosophy of History and Politics*
  174
Intra-German relations 5-6, 10, 252-
  254, 256-257, 259-265
*Intra-German Relations: Development,
  Problems, Facts* 260
Intrigue and Love (play) 374
An Introduction to German Poetry
  375
*Introduction to Library Research in
  German Studies: Language,
  Literature, and Civilization* 334
*An Introduction to Military Archives in
  West Germany* 493
Investiture Contest 88
Investment 296
  foreign (1870-1914) 278
  foreign (developing relations) 299
Iowa
  Amanas 140
Ireland, Republic of
  accession to European Community
    298
*The Ironic German: A Study of
  Thomas Mann* 364
Ischl 437
Iserloh, Erwin, 194
Israel 189
  Federal Republic of Germany's
    agreement to provide
    compensation for material losses
    under Hitler 255

relations with the Federal Republic
of Germany 255

J

Jabs, Wolfgang 390
Jäckel, Eberhard 104
Jackson, Marian 100
Jackson, Michael 473
Jackson, Paul A. 295
Jacobs, Jay 415
Jacobs, Noah Jonathan 189
Jacobsen, Hans-Adolf 8, 115
Jahn, Gerhard 244
Japan
    United States Military Government
        (1944-52) 118
Jaspers, Karl 169-170, 179, 182-183,
    259, 355
    autobiography 183
    bibliography 183
    writings 183
Jay, Martin 185
J. B. Metzler (publishing house)
    history 489
Jean Paul 341, 357
    bibliography 357
    biography 357
Jean Paul im Urteil seiner Kritiker 341
Jenny Treibel 383
Jensen, Jens Christian 398
Jeremias, Joachim 197, 200
Jesus
    Protestant historical scholarship 197
    Roman Catholic interpretation 190
Jewelry
    Germanic 388
Jews 200-205
    Academy for the Science of Judaism
        204
    anti-Semitic riots in Poland (1938)
        113
    anti-Semitism in Europe (1918-38)
        113
    bibliography (Judaism) 200
    birthplaces of those executed in
        France for resistance 113
    communal life 130
    congregational libraries (statistics)
        308
    culture 201
    dialogue with Catholicism 203

during the Holocaust 107, 112-113
Eastern escape route for Polish Jews
    113
economic life 200
forced labour in World War II
    (attempts to gain compensation)
    238
German-Jewish symbiosis 201
German translation of the Hebrew
    scriptures 204
Hebrew Union College 202
history 107, 112-114, 189, 200-201,
    205, 522
influx of Holocaust survivors from
    Eastern Europe 130
Institute for the History of the
    German Jews 200
Jewish congregations (statistics) 308
Jewish tradition 200-205
living outside Israel and North
    America 130
modern Western Judaism 201
philosophers 169, 201
post-war period 205
post-war (bibliography) 505
rabbis (statistics) 308
relations with Christians 189
religious education (1820s to 20th c)
    187
Roman Catholic Church and the
    Jewish question 192
statistics 308
synagogues (statistics) 308
Third Reich (bibliography) 518-520,
    522-523
Weimar Republic (bibliography) 516
see also Holocaust
The Jews and Modern Capitalism 200
Joachim, Joseph 425
Joeres, Ruth-Ellen B. 207
*Johann Gutenberg: The Inventor of
    Printing* 488
Johann Sebastian Bach 430
Johann Wolfgang von Goethe 358
*Johann Wolfgang von Goethe in
    Selbstzeugnissen und
    Bilddokumenten* 358
*Johannes Brahms: His Work and
    Personality* 437
*Johannes Brahms. Werk und
    Persönlichkeit* 437
*Johannes Gutenberg in Zeugnissen und
    Bilddokumenten* 488

305

see also France, United States of
America
Military occupation of Berlin (since
1945) 245-251
bibliography 529
Quadripartite Agreement (1971)
248-249
Military tribunals (war crimes) see
Nürnberg Trials
Milk pails 410
Millar, J. 196
Millepedes 78
The Mind of Germany 358
Minder, Robert 50
Mining
map 31
Minneapolis 392
Minorities see Holocaust, Jews, and
Race and ethnic minorities
Mintzel, Alf 217
Mission on the Rhine: Reeducation and
Denazification in
American-Occupied Germany 326
Missouri
German immigrants 140
Mit Raiffeisen fing es an 287
Mitchell, Alan 63
Mitchell, Donald 433, 438
Mitchell, Edwin Knox 196
Mitchell, Hannah 340
Mitchell, Jan 463
Mitchell, Stanley 340, 364
Mitscherlich, Alexander 169
Mittel-Rhein
wine 471
Mock, Wolfgang 210
Modern Architecture in Germany 420
Modern Drama and German
Classicism: Renaissance from
Lessing to Brecht 442
Modern German Art 401
Modern German Corporation Law 236
Modern German Dialects 158
Modern German Literature: A Library
of Literary Criticism 356
Modern German Literature: The Major
Figures in Context 346
The Modern German Novel 1945-1965
354
Modern German Painting 400
Modern German Philosophy 170
Modern German Poetry 1910-1960 375
Modern Law and Society 485

Modersohn-Becker, Paula 399
Moehling, Karl A. 184
Mohn und Gedächtnis 370, 375
Mohr, Adrian 52
Mommsen, Theodor 85
Mommsen, W. J. 210
Monadology and Other Philosophical
Essays 173
Monarchy 97
Revolution of 1918-19 101
Moneta, Erich H. 293
Monetary policy 276
European Monetary System (EMS)
279
Money 163
Mönikes, Wolfgang 323
Monkhouse, F. J. 20
Montgomery, Marshall 381
Montgomery, W. 197
Moore, Harry T. 369
Moore, Richard 44
The Moral Law: Kant's 'Groundwork
of the Metaphysic of Morals' 174
Morgan, Bayard Quincy 373
Morgan, F. W. 20
Morgan, Roger 252, 257, 268
Morgenstern, Lina 357
bibliography 357
Mörike, Eduard 357
bibliography 357
biography 357
fairy tales (literary) 374
Morley-Fletcher, Hugo 413
Mörmann, Klemens 496
Morphology
dialects 158
Morriën, Adriaan 369
Morris, Walter D. 365
Morrow, Ian F. D. 101, 361
Morwitz, Ernst 375
Mosbacher, Eric 199
Moselle
wine 471
Moselle River
historical geography (58 A.D. to
1974) 21
The Moselle: River and Canal from the
Roman Empire to the European
Economic Community 21
Moser, Hans 457
Moser, Hans Joachim 422, 429
Moser, Hugo 152-153
Mosquitoes 78

National parks 60
  maps 60
National Register of Historic Places 497
National security
  institutions 5
National Socialism and the Third
    Reich 20, 82-83, 95, 98, 103-116,
    188, 190, 192, 202, 516-523
  accounts of the lives of ordinary
    German citizens (1933-45) 108
  agriculture 286
  'anti-intellectual interregnum' 352
  anti-Nazi writers in exile 350, 353
  architecture 393, 401
  art 393, 401, 407
  arts 393
  'Aryan-Nordic' dogma 20, 109
  background, development and
    impact 109
  bibliographies 83, 95, 102-103, 109-
    111, 113-116, 188, 190, 192, 350-
    353, 393, 509, 511-514, 516-525
  big business 102
  biographical studies of the National
    Socialist leadership 106, 499
  biographies (Barth, Karl and
    Bonhoeffer, Dietrich) 199
  cabaret 393
  children's literature 351
  Christianity in crisis (bibliography)
    518
  churches 188, 192, 198
  cinema 393, 445, 451-453
  Concordat 188, 192
  Confessing church 188, 198
  consolidation 102
  constitution 230
  control over publishers 351
  control over school curricula 351
  control over school libraries 351
  control over writers 351
  cultural achievements 393
  cultural ideology 393
  cultural policy 351
  culture 102, 445
  culture (bibliography) 518
  diplomacy (bibliography) 520
  domestic policies (bibliography) 518
  economy 273
  eugenic policies 192
  euthanasia 192
  Farben cartel 282
  film 393, 445, 451

film comedy 350
folk plays and folk dance 457
foreign policy (bibliography) 116,
  518
Heidegger, Martin 184
historical novel 350
ideology (use of children's literature)
  351
impact on administration 20
impact on education 20, 188
impact on government 20
impact on the law 20
impact on public health 20
ineffectively propagandized in the
  United States of America 144
inner emigration 107, 350
interpretation of Nietzsche 179
Jugendliteratur [youth literature] 350
Krupp family 282
legal theories 231
literature 350-353, 393
memoirs of Albert Speer 105
music 440
novel 352
opposition to the Bauhaus 390
organization of the National Socialist
  Party 20
painting 393, 401
Party Congress of 1934 (Riefenstahl
  film documentary) 452
persecution of artists 393, 401
photography 401
politics (bibliography) 518-521
propaganda (use of cinema) 451-453
racial dogma of the 'pure race' 20
religious education 187
repression of the Left (bibliography)
  518-519
road-building 393
scientists 318
secret police reports on the churches
  188
society (bibliography) 518-521
song 350
sport 475
theatre 393, 445
trade (bibliography) 116, 518, 520
women 207
writers 346, 350, 352-353
see also Concentration Camps,
  Holocaust, Refugees and
  expellees, Resistance, and World
  War II

310

311

Niethammer, Jochen 74
Nietzsche, Friedrich Wilhelm 176, 179,
    346, 355, 357
  bibliographies 179, 357
  writings 179
Nietzsche and Christianity 179
Nietzsche contra Wagner 179
*Nietzsche: Philosopher, Psychologist,
    Antichrist* 179
Nietzsche und das Christentum 179
*The Nightmare of Reason: A Life of
    Franz Kafka* 367
1985 Michelin Deutschland 41, 474
Ninety-five Theses or *Disputation on
    the Power and Efficacy of
    Indulgences* 194
Nisbet, H. B. 341
Noakes, Jeremy 109
Nobel Prize winners 165
Noble, C. A. M. 158
Noise control 309, 312
Nolde, Emil 399, 404, 408
  autobiography 404
  bibliography 404
  biographies 404
  reproductions (works) 404
Nord, F. E. 330
Norden, Heinz 95, 396
Nordhorn, Karlhugo 301
Nordic labour market 305
North Africa
  birds 75, 77
North Atlantic Treaty Organization
    (NATO) 253, 270
  impact of antinuclear protest
    movement 217-218
  nuclear strategy 270
  policy of Federal Republic of
    Germany 252-256
  role of the Army of the Federal
    Republic of Germany 218, 270
  role of the Federal Republic of
    Germany 254, 259
North Carolina
  German immigrants 140
North Rhine-Westphalia
  bibliography (museum guides) 496
  constitution 225
North Sea
  ports 20
  sea mammals 72
Northern Europe
  man's use of plants and animals 289

reptiles 71
Northern Germany
  physical geography 20
  regional recipes 464
  tourist guides 39-50
Northern Pacific
  sea otters 72
Northrup, Herbert R. 303
Northwestern Europe
  sea fishes 70
Norway
  relations with the European
    Community 298
  labour market agreement with other
    Scandinavian countries (1957) 305
Nossack, Hans Erich 357
  bibliography 357
*The Notebooks of Malte Laurids
    Brigge* 374
Novalis (pseudonym of Friedrich,
    Freiherr von Hardenberg)
  fairy tales (literary) 374
Novel 336, 352, 354, 371
  baroque 336
  during the period 1850-1900 343
  during the period 1939-44 352
  emigrants 352-353
  historical 340, 350
  historical (in exile after 1933) 340, 353
  history 336, 352, 354, 371
  image of the United States of
    America 372
  personal development 336
  post-1945 354, 371
  relationship between the aristocracy
    and middle classes (19th-century
    northern Germany) 343
  Romantics 336
  short (and stories) 377
  Weimar Republic 349
  see also the names of individual
    novelists
Novella 339, 343, 360, 377
  anthologies in English translation
    377
The Novels of the German Romantics
    336
*The Novels of Hermann Hesse: A
    Study in Theme and Structure* 366
Nover, Kurt 287
Nowell, John 358, 368
Nowell, Robert 191, 193
Nuclear power

opposition 311
opposition (bibliography) 311
Nuclear strategy
North Atlantic Treaty Organization
270
protest movement and NATO 218
Nürnberg
National Socialist Party Congress
(1934) 452
Nürnberg Trials 114, 116, 499
bibliography 523
documentation 114, 116
proceedings 116
Nutcrackers 410
Nuts 289
*Nutzen-Kosten-Analyse für Städtische
Verkehrsprojekte* 293
Nymphenburg
porcelain factory 413
Nyrop, Richard F. 5

O

*'O the Chimneys': Selected Poems,
Including the Verse Play 'Eli'* 375
Oberammergau Passion Play 457
*The Oberammergau Passion Play: A
Lance against Civilization* 457
'Oberhausen Manifesto' (filmmakers)
454-455
Oberhauser, F. 50, 354
Oberhauser, G. 50, 354
Obermarchtal
Church 417
Oberndörfer, Dieter 258
Oberschelp, Reinhard 534
O'Brien, Grace 428
*Observations on 'The Spiritual
Situation of the Age':
Contemporary German
Perspectives* 354
Ockenden, Ray 193
Ockenden, Rosaleen 193
O'Connor, Richard 136
O'Dell, A. C. 20
O'Donnell, Michael 55
Oellers, Norbert 341
Oetker, Dr. August (test kitchens)
462, 467
Oetker German Home Cooking 462
Offizierausbildung in der Bundeswehr
325

Oktoberfest 473
*Old Europe: A Study of Continuity,
1000-1800* 90
Old-age
pensions and health insurance 301,
305
Oldenburg 205
Olives 289
Olympic Games
Berlin (1936-Riefenstahl film
documentary) 452, 475
Munich (1972) 475
On Being a Christian 193
On Being in Exile 146
On the Essence of Truth 184
On Four Modern Humanists 346
On Jewish Learning 204
On Judaism 203
On Music and Musicians 435
On Poetry and Poets 358
*On the Structure and Dynamics of
Tourism in Berlin West and East*
476
On Translating: An Open Letter 194
On the Unity of German Literature
376
On Writing and Politics, 1967-1983 371
O'Neill, Patrick 373
*'Only a God Can Save Us': The
'Spiegel' Interview (1966)* 184
Opera *see* Music
Opera Guide 424
Opposition Poetry in Nazi Germany
353
Orchestral music *see* Music
Orff, Carl 424, 439
Organ music *see* Music
Organization for Economic
Co-operation and Development
329
Orient
use of plants and animals in ancient
times 289
*The Origin of the West German
Republic* 122
*Originalanmerkungen,
Herkunftsnachweise, Nachwort.*
Vol. 3 of *Kinder- und
Hausmärchen* 379
*The Origins of British National
Insurance and the German
Precedent 1880-1914* 210
The Origins of Modern Germany 88

313

315

316

317

Q

Quadripartite Agreement on Berlin
(1971) *see* Four-Power Agreement
(1971)
*The Quadripartite Agreement on Berlin
of September 3, 1971* 248
Qualey, Carlton C. 531
The Quest for a United Germany 259
*The Quest of the Historical Jesus: A
Critical Study of Its Progress from
Reimarus to Wrede* 197
The Question of German Guilt 183
Quinn, Edward 193
Quotations
dictionaries 387

R

Raabe, Paul 334, 489
Raabe, Wilhelm 357
bibliography 357
The Rabbi of Bacharach (story) 382
Rabbits 289
Rabinbach, Anson 130
Race and ethnic minorities 130-132,
205
'Ayran-Nordic' dogma 20
ethnic composition of the Germans
20
Gastarbeiter 132
German Jewry 130, 200-205
Gypsies 131
Holocaust 112-114
National Socialist racial ideology 109
transfer of German minorities (1939-
41) 20
Radio broadcasting 477, 479-481
control 480
corporations 480
cultural role 480
culture of the working class (1920s)
392
finance 480
plays (post-1945) 369, 376, 394
political role 480
programming 480
reference book on broadcast
journalism 479
Radvanyi, Miklos K. 241
Rahner, Karl 186, 191
philosophical theology 191

writings 191
A Rahner Handbook 191
A Rahner Reader 191
Rahy, Philip 377
Raiffeisen, Friedrich Wilhelm 287
Railways 20, 280, 291, 294
bibliography 294
development projects abroad
involving German consultants 294
Federal Railways 280, 294
history 294
maps 29, 33
one-day excursions (tour guide) 46
photographs 294
steam train excursions 39
Trans-Siberian Railway (escape of
Jews during World War II) 113
Rainer Maria Rilke 362
*Rainer Maria Rilkes Deutung des
Daseins. Eine Interpretation der
Duineser Elegien* 362
Rainer Maria Rilke: The Poetic Instinct
362
RAND Corporation 218
Raphael, Robert 436
Rapp, Georg 101
Rather, L. J. 436
Ratzinger, Joseph 193, 457
*The Ratzinger Report: An Exclusive
Interview on the State of the
Church* 193
Rautenstrauch, Rudolf 39
Read, Herbert 401
Reade, Winwood 73
Reams, Joanne Reppert 9
*Reason and Revolution: Hegel and the
Rise of Social Theory* 175
*Reason in History: A General
Introduction to the Philosophy of
History* 175
Rebhausen
school (case study) 328
*Rechtfertigung. Die Lehre Karl Barths
und eine katholische Besinnung*
193
*Die Rechtslage Deutschlands nach dem
Grundlagenvertrag vom 21.
Dezember 1972* 262
*Der Rechtsstatus des Landes Berlin.
Eine Untersuchung nach dem
Viermächte-Abkommen vom 3.
September 1971* 249
Recipes *see* Cuisine

323

Reitz, Edgar 455
Relay from Bonn now *The Week in Germany* 484
Religion 13, 20, 186-205, 355
  baroque churches (Central Europe) 417
  bibliographies 171, 186-188, 198, 417, 492, 503, 516
  cathedrals 414
  cathedrals and churches (illustrated) 51-58
  Catholic music schools 441
  Christianity 189, 191, 193, 196-197, 199, 202, 518
  Christianity (Weimar Republic – bibliography) 516
  Christians' relations with Jews 189, 201
  church affairs (statistics) 308
  church architecture 318, 414-419, 421
  church-state relations 88, 186, 188
  churches (baroque) 388
  churches and politics 186
  churches under Hitler 188
  dogmatic theology 191
  ecclesiastical architecture 414
  ecclesiastical cinematography 453
  ecclesiastical organization (maps) 186
  education 187, 323
  institutions 3, 186-188, 500
  Jaspers, Karl 183
  Jesus 190, 197
  Jewish tradition 130, 200-205
  Judaism 182, 189, 200-205
  legal position of churches 228
  liturgical movement 421
  Lutheranism 92, 189, 194-195
  Nietzsche and Christianity 179
  Pauline research 197
  philosophy 171, 182-183, 190, 201
  Protestant Church music 422
  Protestant music schools 441
  Protestant tradition 194-199
  relations between Jews and Christians 189, 201
  religious affiliation (maps) 31, 186
  rococo churches 417
  Romanticism (intellectual origins) 345
  Saxon Lutherans (Missouri) 469
  science 320

  secularization 186
  taxation and the churches 228
  see also Jews, Luther, National Socialism and the Third Reich, Reformation, and the names of individual churches and theologians etc.
Religion der Vernunft aus den Quellen des Judentums 201
Religion of Reason out of the Sources of Judaism 201
Religious Education in German Schools: An Historical Approach 187
Religious history *see* History
Remarque, Erich Maria 347
The Reminiscences of Carl Schurz: vol. 1, *1829-1852;* vol. 2, *1852-1863;* vol. 3, *1863-1869* 142
Remnant, Peter 173
Renaissance
  architecture 416
  architecture (photographs) 416
  impact on ideas and institutions of the Middle Ages 90
  philosophy 168
Renier, Fernand G. 316
Rentschler, Eric 455
Reparations
  termination 278
  to Israel 255
Replies to My Critics [Buber, Martin] 182
Report of the Federal Government on Education, 1970: The Federal Government's Concept for Educational Policy 326
Report on the Possibilities for Research Work of an American-German Institute 532
Reptiles
  bibliography 71
  Central Europe 71
  Northern Europe 71
  photographs 71
The Reptiles of Northern and Central Europe 71
Republic to Reich: The Making of the Nazi Revolution 102
Rerrich, Maria M. 468
Research
  education 328
  environmental protection 309, 312

Roman Catholic Church *contd.*
music schools 441
organization 308
political ideology 192
post-war period 188
Rahner, Karl 186, 191
relations with the National Socialists
188, 192
resistance movement 192
stastics on membership 308
support of Catholics for Hitler's wars
192
taxation 308
Vatican conflict with Hans Küng 193
see also Cathedrals
*Roman Germany: A Guide to Sites and
Museums* 37
Romanesque Art in Europe 414
Die romanischen Kirchen in Köln 415
Romans 37, 83-86
advance from the Rhine to the Elbe
84
archaeology and archaeological sites
37, 81, 84-85, 388
art 37, 81
Augustus 84
Caesar 85
clash with Germanic tribes 81, 83-85
Diocletian 85
legal system 231-232
museum collections of artefacts 37,
497
project to canalize Moselle River 21
Tacitus 86
use of plants and animals 289
*Romans on the Rhine: Archaeology in
Germany* 81
Romantic Religion 189
Romanticism 231, 398, 432, 435
literature 345
music 432, 435
painting 398
rise of musicology 435
see also the names of individual
composers, poets, etc.
Romoser, George K. 213
Rome
Nazarenes (painters) 398
Treaty (1957) 281, 305
Römische Geschichte, vol. 5: *Die
Provinzen von Caesar bis
Diocletian* 85
La Ronde (play) 374

Röntgen, Wilhelm Conrad 355
*Roots in the Rhineland: America's
German Heritage in Three
Hundred Years of Immigration,
1683-1983* 138
Rosenberg, Arthur 101
Rosenberg, Jakob 399
Rosencranz, Armin 313
Rosenfeld, Paul 435
Rosenthal, Harold 424
Rosenzweig, Franz 201
bibliography 204
biography 204
writings 204
Roses 289
Roskamp, Karl W. 280
Ross, Anne 424
Roters, Eberhard 390
Rothe, Wolfgang 349
Rothenberg, Jerome 375
Rothfels, Hans 111
Rott am Inn
Church 417
Royal Institute of International Affairs
(London) 119
Rubel, Maximilien 178
Rubinstein, Anton 425
Rudel, Detlev 311
Rüdenberg, Werner 162
*Rudolf Virchow: Doctor, Statesman,
Anthropologist* 316
Rueschemeyer, Dietrich 243
*Der Ruf der neuen Welt: Deutsche
bauen Amerika* 134
Ruhm von Oppen, Beate 119, 123
Ruhmer, E. 397
Ruhr
historical and economic geography
22
smog alarm system 310
*The Ruhr: A Study in Historical and
Economic Geography* 22
Rump, Gerhard Charles 331
The Runagate Courage 380
Rundfunk in Deutschland 480
Rupp, E. G. 92
Ruppel, K. H. 425
Rural areas
school case study (Rebhausen) 328
Rush, Kenneth 249
Russ, Jennifer M. 456
Russia
education 323

334

335

338

Turkey
  railway projects involving German
    consultants 294
Turner, George 330
Turner, Henry Ashby, Jr. 102, 104
Tusken, Lewis W. 169
Twain, Mark 50
Twelve Articles of Peasantry 374
Twelve German Novellas 377
Twelve Literary Essays [vols. 1-3, and
    5 of the *German Men of Letters*
    series] 357
Twentieth Century Composers, vol. II:
    Germany and Central Europe 439
Twentieth Century Music 439
The Twilight of the Idols 179
Two Germanys in One World 263
The Two Grenadiers (poem) 382
*Two Types of Faith: A Study of the
    Interpretation of Judaism and
    Christianity* 189, 203
*The Tyranny of Greece over Germany:
    A Study of the Influence Exercised
    by Greek Art and Poetry over the
    Great German Writers of the
    Eighteenth, Nineteenth and
    Twentieth Centuries* 344
Tyreil, Albrecht 524
Tyrker 139

U

Ubbelodhe, Otto 379
Ueberhorst, Horst 475
Uhr, Horst 399
Ulich, Robert 323
Ulm
  Cathedral 414
  Cathedral (photographs) 414
  higher education 330
Ulrich, Otto 478
Ulrich, Paul S. 249
*Umweltschutz in der Bundesrepublik
    Deutschland* 309
*The Uncompleted Past: Postwar
    German Novels and the Third
    Reich* 354
Underwood, J. A. 99
Unemployment insurance *see* Welfare
Unfehlbar? Eine Anfrage 193
The Unfortunate Lord Henry 374
Ungar, Frederick 375

Unification of Germany (19th century)
    98, 189, 259
Union of Soviet Socialist Republics 18
  Berlin Blockade 245, 247
  Final Quadripartite Protocol (1972)
    248-249
  Four-Power Agreement on Berlin
    (1971) 245, 248-249
  government recruitment of German
    scientists in postwar period 147
  photographs of works of art 54
  relations with the Federal Republic
    of Germany 254
  relations with the United States of
    America 247
  treaties with German Federal
    Republic 261
  World War II (bibliography) 520
  see also Ostpolitik
United Church *see* Evangelical Church
United Kingdom *see* Britain
United Nations
  admittance of the German
    Democratic Republic 256
  admittance of the German Federal
    Republic 256
  Conference on the Standardization
    of Geographical Names, Third 26
  Monetary and Financial Conference
    (Bretton Woods, 1944) 279
United States of America
  American drama on German stage
    446
  American educational reform efforts
    in Germany (post-1945) 362
  American-German private law
    relations cases (1945-55) 238
  archives (American holdings on
    postwar occupation of Germany)
    118
  archives (repositories of
    German-American material
    culture) 497
  as reflected in contemporary
    German literature 372
  Berlin occupation (since 1945) 245-
    251, 259, 262
  bibliographical essay on
    German-American relations 266
  book trade (social history prior to
    the Civil War) 490
  conflict with USSR over Berlin 245-
    247

343

345

Map of West Germany

This map shows the federal capital, the state capitals, and Berlin.

NORTH SEA

BALTIC SEA

Bremerhaven
(State of Bremen)

Kiel

SCHLESWIG-
HOLSTEIN

GERMAN
DEMOCRATIC REPUBLIC
(EAST GERMANY)

HAMBURG

BREMEN

LOWER SAXONY

Hanover

Elbe R.

POLAND

West

East

BERLIN

Oder R.

Oder R.

NETHERLANDS

Ems R.

Weser R.

NORTH RHINE -
WESTPHALIA

Düsseldorf

BELGIUM

Bonn

HESSE

RHINELAND-
PALATINATE

Wiesbaden

Mainz

Main R.

Nesse R.

Elbe R.

LUXEM-
BOURG

SAARLAND

Saarbrücken

Rhine R.

CZECHOSLOVAKIA

FRANCE

BADEN-
WÜRTTEMBERG

Stuttgart

BAVARIA

Danube R.

Munich

SWITZERLAND

AUSTRIA

0   100   200 km